To Laura

The Lover of Elephants

and

Big Dogs ~

Thanks for all that
you do ~

Dugan's Love
Other Mama

ELEPHANTS

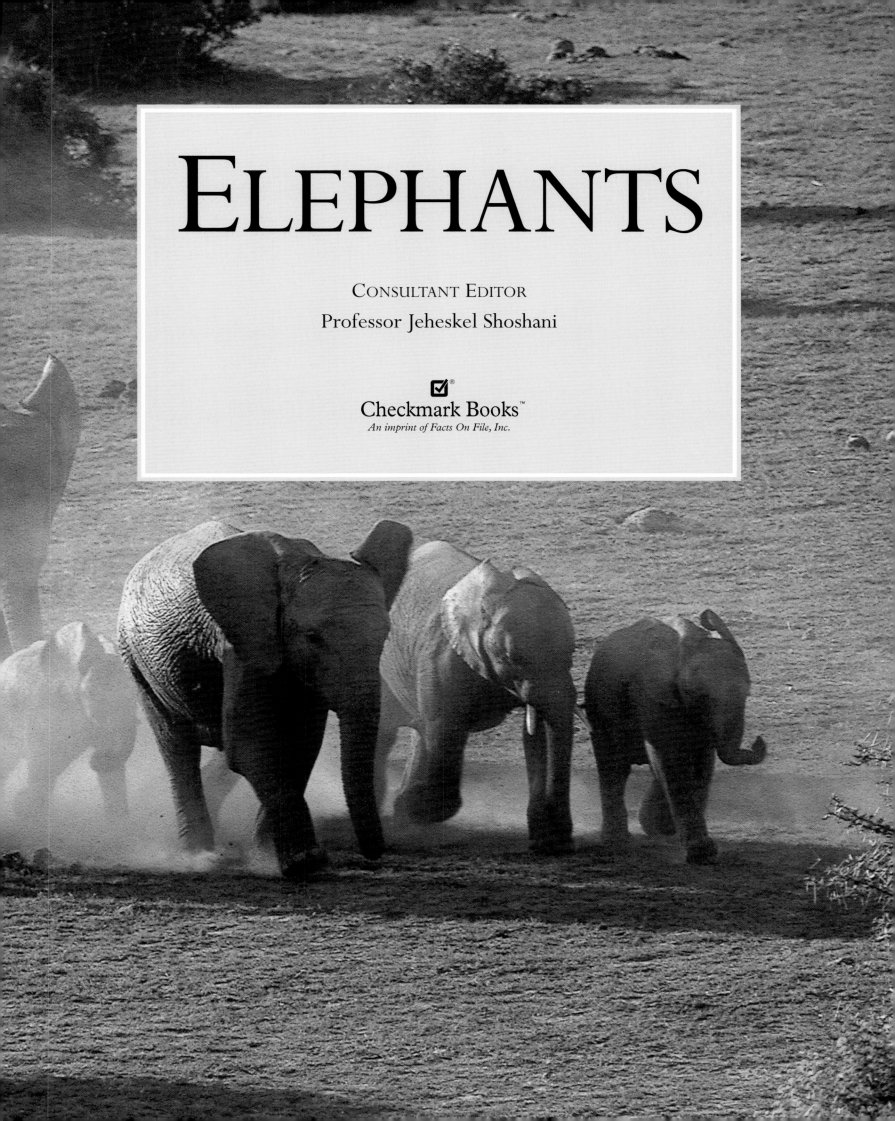

ELEPHANTS

CONSULTANT EDITOR

Professor Jeheskel Shoshani

Checkmark Books™

An imprint of Facts On File, Inc.

Published in the United States by
Checkmark Books
An imprint of Facts On File, Inc.
11 Penn Plaza, New York, NY 10001

Conceived and produced by Weldon Owen Pty Limited
59 Victoria Street, McMahons Point, NSW 2060, Australia
A member of the Weldon Owen Group of Companies
Sydney • San Francisco

Chief Execuitve Officer: John Owen
President: Terry Newell
Publisher: Sheena Coupe
Project Editor: Lu Sierra
Project Coordinator: Sarah Anderson
Picture Editor: Jenny Mills
Design: Andi Cole
Series Design: Sue Burk
Production Manager: Helen Creeke
Production Assistant: Kylie Lawson
Vice President International Sales: Stuart Laurence

Checkmark Books
An imprint of Facts On File, Inc.
11 Penn Plaza
New York, NY 10001

ISBN 0-8160-4294-2

Library of Congress Cataloging-in-Publication Data

Elephants: majestic creatures of the wild/ consulting editor, Jeheskel Shoshani;
illustrations, Frank Knight
p. cm—(Mighty creature series)
Includes bibliographical references (p.).
ISBN 0-8160-4294-2
1. Elephants. I. Shoshani, Jeheskel. II. Knight, Frank, 1941– III. Title. IV. Series.
QL737.P98 E445 2000
599.67—dc21
99-059491

Checkmark Books are available at special discounts when purchased in bulk quantities for
businesses, associations, institutions or sales promotions. Please call our Special Sales
Department in New York at (212) 967-8800 or (800) 322-8755.

You can find Facts On File on the World Wide Web at http.//www.factsonfile.com

Printed by Kyodo Printing Co. (Singapore) Pte Ltd
Printed in Singapore

10 9 8 7 6 5 4 3 2 1

A WELDON OWEN PRODUCTION

Updating of most of the factual details in this edition, such as the number of species of the
African elephants, was done by the consulting editor Professor Jeheskel Shoshani.

FRONT COVER: African elephants on the move, led by the matriarch.
Photo by Jen and Des Bartlett/Survival Anglia

PAGE 1: An African elephant drinking.
Photo by Corel Corporation

PAGES 2–3: A family of elephants in Addo Elephant Park, South Africa.
Photo by J. Bracegirdle/Planet Earth Pictures

PAGES 4–5: An Asian elephant feeds on aquatic vegetation in Assam, India.

PAGE 7: Elephants are very "tactile" animals—young elephants, especially, constantly
crave physical closeness. Samburu, Kenya.
Photo by Michael Denis-Huot/Jacana/Auscape

PAGES 10–11: A herd of African elephants fords a river at Samburu, Kenya.

BACK COVER: Indian elephants lying down bathing.
Photo by Corel Corporation

Anup Shah/Animals Animals/Stock Photos

CONTENTS

ELEPHANTS AND HUMANS

CONSERVATION AND MANAGEMENT

Elephants are magnificent and awe-inspiring by virtue of their size, mobile trunk, huge tusks and a longevity approaching ours. But when I began research on elephants about twenty-five years ago, knowledge of them was largely anecdotal and anatomical. The period since the 1960s has seen an enormous development in the understanding of elephant biology. At the same time their populations have been increasingly put at risk by the expanding human population and the growth of the illegal ivory trade.

It is now known that elephants have a complex social behavior and a life history similar to humans. Their societies are based on the family unit, typically containing an old female, her youngest mature daughter and their surviving immature offspring. These family units combine and recombine to form larger units such as extended families (tens) and larger still clans (a few hundreds) and populations (a few thousands).

The elephant life history in some ways is very similar to that of humans. The calf is born after a lengthy gestation period of twenty-two months and remains close to its mother until sexual maturity, usually at an age of ten to fourteen years. Like humans, this allows a long learning period for the transfer of experience. The bulls are driven out of the family unit at sexual maturity to spend the rest of their lives mainly alone but forming temporary associations with family units when cows come into estrus. Females cease to breed in their fifties, rather like our own species, but remain an important element in elephant society.

Earlier studies have been succeeded by long-term research programs in which individual elephants, recognized by natural markings, have been followed over decades so that the complexities of elephant society have become better understood. Recent research has shown that African elephant bulls as well as Asians enter musth seasonally and that it appears to be a key factor in their sexual behavior. More recently still, it has been shown that elephants communicate over long distances by infrasound. There is no doubt that there are further significant discoveries to be made.

Like humans, elephants occupy a wide range of habitats, from desert to tropical rainforests, from coastal beaches to mountain uplands. Elephants need 100–400 kilograms (200–880 pounds) of food and 100–200 liters (26–52 gallons) of water per day. Their diet encompasses a wide diversity of food plants and, by virtue of their flexible trunks, they can feed on plants from ground level up to woodland canopy and dig for water in dry river beds.

Their ubiquity brings them into conflict with human societies and their preferred habitats, characterized by higher rainfall, are similar to those preferred by people. As human populations continue to increase, elephants are compressed into smaller and smaller areas. As this happens they reach high densities locally and may then destroy the woody vegetation which enables them to survive the dry season.

Anup & Manoj Shah/Planet Earth Pictures

In the 1960s, the introduction of management culling (systematic, controlled killing) was attempted in parts of East Africa in order to stabilize densities at lower levels in balance with vegetation. This was controversial, but not tested, because circumstances changed—there was a complete breakdown of law and order in Uganda leading to excessive poaching, and opposition to wildlife management in Kenya. Subsequently, in Kenya, some ten thousand elephants died of starvation because there were insufficient trees and bushes to carry the population through the dry season. One consequence was the destruction of the complex social organization of these herds. It also marked an increase in the illegal ivory trade because the resulting carcasses meant that ivory from them was to be had for the taking. Later, the open grassland habitats that had succeeded dense bush made elephants easy to find and the availability of automatic weapons meant that they were easy to kill. Existing ranger forces were inadequate to protect the elephants.

A ban on international trade in ivory, now in force, is intended to bring poaching under control. Elephant populations, however, have the potential to increase naturally at 6 percent a year and so if poaching and human competition for land can be controlled, management will again be necessary, as is the case now in some southern African reserves and national parks. Furthermore, in political terms, economic justification is needed for setting land aside for wildlife. Research has shown that the cost of successfully protecting such areas in Africa is about US$200 per square kilometer (approximately $500 per square mile) per year; for a large national park, such as Tsavo, this represents an annual cost of over $4 million! If local communities can be persuaded that the parks or reserves are of value to them they have a vested interest in their protection, but this requires that they receive direct benefits from tourism, sport hunting, culling, or other forms of management. The alternative is to decide what level of protection can be afforded and to reduce the size of protected areas accordingly. The best strategy for most wildlife areas may be somewhere in between. This complex situation creates a serious dilemma for conservationists, but in my view it must be squarely faced if the survival of elephants is to be secured for posterity.

This book brings together a roster of internationally known scientists and professionals who have shared with us invaluable up-to-date information, written and edited in a lucid and easy-to-follow style. The text and illustrations contain the historical, anatomical, and evolutionary data which will be handy references for many years.

Richard M. Laws

▲ A group of thirsty, mud-caked elephants taking a refreshing drink at a waterhole in Namibia.

EVOLUTION

AND BIOLOGY

WHAT IS AN ELEPHANT?

JEHESKEL SHOSHANI AND SANDRA LEE SHOSHANI

Most people develop an idea of an elephant at an early age, whether there are living elephants in their daily lives or not. Yet it is not so simple to define an elephant, in the broadest sense of the term, in a scientific manner.

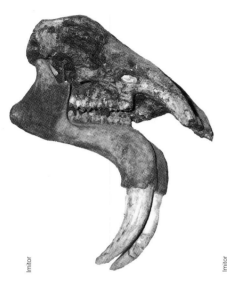

▲ The fossil skull of a *Deinotherium*, showing two of the features suggesting its relationship with modern elephants: powerful grinding molars, and a general skull architecture indicating that it may have supported a heavy, muscular, flexible trunk.

▲ (Right) A museum reconstruction of a *Deinotherium*, a long-extinct relative of the elephant. Derived from two words of ancient Greek, its name means "terrible beast".

Common names can often help one define what an animal or plant is, and so also can scientific names. Many people who have been around elephants all their lives have at least two or three names for this animal. Also there are specific tribal or regional names adopted over time. Take, for example, Kenya. In Swahili (officially it is spelled Kiswahili), the language spoken in many East African countries, an elephant is called "Ndovu" (usually in literature) or "Tembo" (also meaning beer). Hunters and tourists may refer to it as "Jumbo", and the local tribes of Mount Elgon (for example, the Elkony tribe) refer to the elephant as "Benionclet". In India, people who write Sanskrit call the elephant "Hastin", that is, literally, the animal "having a hand". The English word "elephant" means "huge arch" (*ele*, from Greek for arch; and *phant*, from Latin for huge, by way of the word phantasia). People the world over use similar words to describe and name elephants, generally emphasizing their special features.

Elephants are the living members of a larger group or order called "Proboscidea" (named after the most distinguishing organ—the proboscis, or trunk). Dissecting the word "Proboscidea" into its components, we learn that *pro* means "before" (from Greek), *boscis* translates into "mouth" (also from Greek), and *-idea* and *-oidea* mean "appearance" or "kind" and are suffixes usually employed for orders or other ranks in mammalian taxonomy (see the section, "Classification"). "Proboscidea" was coined by the naturalist Carl D. Illiger at the beginning of the nineteenth

century. Direct evidence indicating the presence of a proboscis as a soft anatomy organ has been known in both the living elephants and woolly mammoths, family Elephantidae, for many years.

The living elephants (African, *Loxodonta africana* and L. *cyclotis*, and Asian, *Elephas maximus*) are the sole survivors of an extensive radiation of ungulate-related mammals which began their differentiation at the end of the Paleocene epoch some 58 million years ago.

Indirect evidence for the presence of the proboscis in extinct species comes from our knowledge of the skull. The upper portion of the skull (the cranium) contains an opening that is the beginning of the nostrils and where the trunk begins in the living species. In the usual mammalian type, this opening, or external naris, is situated at the front of the cranium. In elephantid species the naris is elevated, that is, it is located higher and farther back. Thus, any deviation from the general mammalian pattern in the hard anatomy found in elephants and mammoths is interpreted as evidence for the possible presence of a trunk-like structure in the extinct species. It is of interest that this single narial opening serves as an important hint of the affinity (biological similarity indicating derivation from a common source) of a group of animals. Fossil evidence indicates that the earliest proboscideans (for example, *Moeritherium*) did not possess trunks, not even in primordial forms. If this is true, then what are the characters we use to define members of this order?

It is beyond the scope of this book to go into the details of the characters with which scientists define the boundaries of the order Proboscidea. Suffice it to say that these features must satisfy the criteria for all members of this order, extinct and extant, but for no member outside this order. Anatomical details, such as tooth structure, type and number of teeth, and bone architecture, are important considerations. These boundaries are not engraved in stone because newly discovered material may bring with it new characters that may alter previous interpretations. One must bear in mind that diagnostic features which were present in earlier members of this group could have changed and be absent in living species.

Before the defining features were established, it was really confusing to try to classify an animal. As an example of the fluctuating status of a fossil mammal, let us look at a strange animal called

Deinotherium. When partial fossil skulls were first discovered, some of the naturalists of the early nineteenth century believed this mammal to be a herbivorous sea monster looking like a manatee or dugong (sirenians) with large tusks, while others saw it as a carnivorous beast that climbed trees, because of a pair of formidable downcurved "canines". It is not surprising then that Kaup, in 1829, named it "a terrible beast" (*deino* plus *therium*). Kaup himself did not at first consider it to be a proboscidean but rather a hippopotamus. Later he related it to mastodons and sloths, and even further on in his studies to a cetacean (a whale). Not only was it unclear whether this mammal was a land or sea creature but whether it was a herbivore or carnivore was not established until a partial skeleton was unearthed in a landslide on the Prague–Brunn railroad line in 1853, and the proboscidean connections became clear when hind limbs were uncovered at this time.

Close examination of the characters of Deinotheriidae (*Prodeinotherium* and *Deinotherium*) shows that most of them are more primitive than those of Elephantidae (see the section on "Evolution of the Proboscidea" for more details). The bizarre appearance of deinotheres and the presence of some primitive characters have caused researchers to group them with rhinos, tapirs, mammoths, mastodons and sloths. Nonetheless, the fact that the postcranial skeleton of a deinothere is graviportally adapted (suited for supporting heavy weight), like most other elephantoids, influenced scientists to place the deinotheres in the order Proboscidea, rather than relating them to cetaceans or sirenians. Today, based on osteological (bone architecture) characters, scientists accept them as undisputed members of the order Proboscidea.

What were the features of *Deinotherium* that on several occasions caused researchers (after Kaup) to remove it from the order and then reclassify it as a proboscidean? Opponents of the hypothesis that *Deinotherium* was a proboscidean claimed that in a mammal as large as this (some individuals reached about 4 meters, 13 feet, in height), one is bound to find features which made it adaptable to conditions similar to those where proboscideans were found, and all the similarities are due to convergence rather than common ancestry— meaning that similar structures developed for adaptation to similar conditions.

Conversely, proponents of the idea that *Deinotherium* was a proboscidean note that the number of skeletal (including dental) similarities is so great that these similarities cannot be considered to be a result of convergence. In addition, deinotheres had elevated external nares like modern elephants. The combination and association of all these characters make it highly improbable that *Prodeinotherium* and *Deinotherium* were not proboscideans.

Clem Haagner/Ardea London Ltd

A recent discovery of a species accepted as a bona fide proboscidean, *Numidotherium*, from Algeria, in sediments older than those in which *Deinotherium* is found helps us better understand the placement of *Deinotherium* within the Proboscidea. The following proboscidean characters were found in numidotheres: unique tooth structure, elevated external nares, pneumatized bones (bones with air compartments) in the cranium, radius fixed in pronation position (the foreleg is turned in such a way that the sole of the foot is facing backwards or downwards), and a well-developed medial process on the calcaneum (a bone in the ankle). As a result character analysis today places *Numidotherium* before *Deinotherium* on the evolutionary tree of the Proboscidea.

In summary, how do we define a proboscidean in order to make such judgements? Generally, the characters viewed as common to the order Proboscidea and almost exclusive to its members are: particular skull features (for example, loss of condyloid foramen, a small hole at the back of the basicranium); teeth with unique cusps and the addition of transverse ridges at the back of the teeth; specific scapular (shoulder blade) characters; the radius partially or completely fixed in the pronation position; a hind foot with an astragalus (an ankle bone named "talus" in humans) which has a prominent process on the medial side; and a wrist with serial bone arrangement. (Anatomical features are explained in detail in the sections, "Elephants and their relatives" and "Anatomy and physiology".) These characters, in conjunction with the geological time when a particular animal lived in a given locality, are useful criteria for those who evaluate the "status" of a species.

▲ Portrait of an African elephant, Botswana. Modern elephants are unmistakable because of their enormous size (the largest of all living land animals) and their unique trunk, which is highly mobile and extraordinarily sensitive. Whether these features serve to characterize all of the elephant's extinct relatives is less easy to establish.

THE ELEPHANT'S RELATIVES

JEHESKEL SHOSHANI

It is not definitely known which species are most closely related to elephants. The earliest members of the orders Proboscidea and Sirenia belong to a group named the Tethytheria ("beasts of the Tethys") by evolutionary paleontologist Malcolm C. McKenna. The name refers to the ancient Tethys Sea, of which the present-day Mediterranean is said to be a remnant.

▼ A cladogram (evolutionary tree without time reference) depicting relationships among representatives of the mammalian orders Proboscidea (elephants), Sirenia (manatees and dugongs), and Hyracoidea (hyraxes). Also shown is a zebra, as a representative of other taxa, not sharing the characteristics of the Uranotheria. Note that the living elephants and most extinct proboscideans have had a trunk. Also note that Proboscidea and Sirenia are grouped under a higher taxonomic category called Tethytheria and that all the tethytherians have double-apexed hearts, as opposed to the single-apex shape of a typical mammalian heart. Uranotheria, yet a higher taxonomic category, embraces the orders Proboscidea, Sirenia, and Hyracoidea—all of which have their wrist bones arranged one row directly above the other.

▶ Left forefoot of representatives of six mammalian orders: (A) domestic pig, *Sus scrofa*, Artiodactyla; (B) aardvark, *Orycteropus afer*, Tublidentata; (C) Asian elephant, *Elephas maximus*, Proboscidea; (D) tree hyrax, *Dendrohyrax dorsalis*, Hyracoidea; (E) Malayan tapir, *Tapirus indicus*, Perissodactyla; and (F) North American manatee, *Trichechus manatus*, Sirenia. The arrangement of the bones in the wrists of C, D, and F are unique and therefore scientists grouped these mammals into a category called Uranotheria (see diagram below).

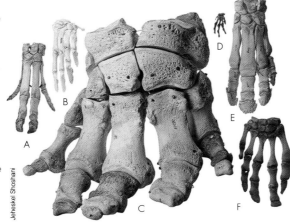

Jeheskel Shoshani

The closest living mammals to Tethytheria are, according to one hypothesis, the hyraxes (order Hyracoidea) which resemble overgrown guinea pigs. Superficially, there would be no reason to suspect that an elephant, a hyrax, and a manatee would have something in common, except of course that all are mammals. From an evolutionary perspective, however, they and some extinct mammals belong together as a particular evolutionary group within the infraclass Eutheria.

These groups of mammals have sharply contrasting external appearances and live in vastly different habitats. Elephants (*Loxodonta africana* and *Elephas maximus*) are the largest living terrestrial mammals and are classified in the order Proboscidea. Manatees and dugongs or sea cows (for example, *Trichechus manatus*, and *Dugong dugon*), belong to the order Sirenia, are the size of small dolphins, and are strictly aquatic. Hyraxes (for example, *Procavia capensis*) are rabbit-sized and dwell among the rocks.

These mammals seem so different from each other that eighteenth and nineteenth century investigators classified elephants with other pachyderms such as rhinoceroses and hippopotami; hyraxes with rodents; and manatees with seals and sea lions. Recent fossil, anatomical, and molecular data, however, provide evidence for close association among these seemingly unrelated orders of mammals.

Hyraxes have been of interest throughout recorded history. Their saga begins with a mention in the Holy Scriptures ("... the rocks are a refuge for the conies ..."—Psalms, 104:18). Among the pastoral Maasai tribe of East Africa, there is a legend which dubbed the hyrax as "little brother of the elephant". The earliest fossil hyracoids date to the early Eocene epoch, about 50 million years ago; some reached the size of a tapir, for example, *Titanohyrax* from northern Africa.

Hyraxes, extinct and extant, were adapted to a variety of ecological herbivorous niches, though today they are restricted to tropical and subtropical habitats, at altitudes ranging from 400 meters (1,300 feet) below sea level at the shores of the Dead Sea to mountains 3,500 meters (11,500 feet) above sea level in East Africa.

If it seems strange that a hyrax is a "little brother" to the elephant, then consider how unusual the "sister" relationship of a manatee is. Not only are manatees and dugongs "seagoers" but the sirenians have lost the external portion of the hind limbs. In the past, sailors regarded seacows as "mermaids", and song and legend depict them as luring ships onto rocks.

The list of characters which unite the Proboscidea, Sirenia, and Hyracoidea is too detailed for discussion here, but the example of the wrist (carpal) bones is one specialized morphological character that can be easily explained.

Most mammals have their carpal bones arranged in a staggered fashion, like bricks in a

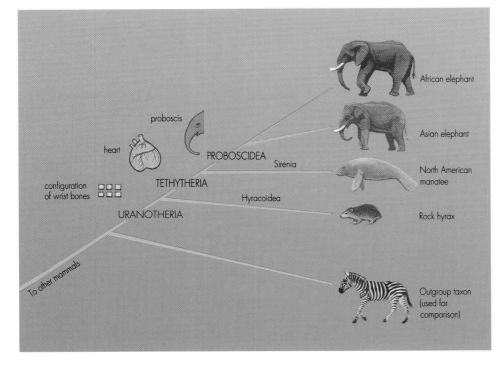

Jeff Foott/Bruce Coleman Limited

wall, with one half of a brick in contact with the ones on the left in the upper and lower rows, and the other half in contact with the ones on the right in the upper and lower rows.

This is the primitive or generalized mammalian condition, and any major deviation constitutes a specialized or derived condition. Zoologists consider these specializations important and they group animals that show similar characters in a category by themselves.

Proboscideans, sirenians, hyracoideans, and some related extinct mammals have their carpal bones arranged serially; that is, one bone is in contact mostly or only with one other carpal bone above and below (see illustration on page 16). Also all the results from bio-chemical experiments (immunology and amino acid sequencing of proteins) unequivocally show that the closest living relatives of elephants are sirenians, hyraxes, and aardvarks.

If the scenario of evolutionary relationships depicted here withstands scientific scrutiny, then size and habit should not be used as criteria. The ancestors of elephants, hyraxes, and manatees may

Jeheskel Shoshani

have been the size of a small dog and through adaptive radiation they took different courses of evolution, resulting in size and habitat differences. The current evidence, both morphological and molecular, shows that Hyracoidea shared a common ancestor with Tethytheria (Proboscidea and Sirenia) some 65 to 60 million years ago, and all three orders are therefore classified in a higher category called Uranotheria.

▲ A manatee, *Trichechus manatus*, at Crystal River, Florida. Manatees, and their relatives the dugongs, occur in large rivers and shallow seas in tropical areas around the world, feeding mainly on aquatic vegetation. They are believed to have shared a common ancestor with the elephants, branching off at the beginning of the Eocene epoch some 55 million years ago, or earlier.

◄ Present-day hyraxes are gregarious herbivores that, like the elephants, represent only the remnants of a group that was once much more diverse. About the size of a rabbit, and found in Africa and the Middle East, they are the elephant's nearest relatives on land, despite their very different appearance.

EVOLUTION OF THE PROBOSCIDEA

JEHESKEL SHOSHANI

"One of the most spectacular stories in mammalian evolution is that of the order Proboscidea—the mastodons, elephants, and related types," wrote the famous paleontologist Alfred S. Romer in his book *Vertebrate Paleontology*, published in 1966. The Proboscidea contains examples of parallel and convergent evolution, giants, dwarfs, and bizarre forms.

This vast array of species was "molded" through the natural selection and adaptive radiations during the geological times of the Cenozoic era, a spread of about 58 million years from the end of the Paleocene through the Holocene epochs. The fossil record indicates that proboscideans inhabited parts of Africa, Asia, Europe, North America, and South America. Their geographical distribution ranged from austral to boreal latitudes and from below sea level to high mountain habitats. Within this geographical distribution, they expanded from the semi-aquatic habitat of the moeritheres (*Moeritherium lyonsi*) to swamps, rivers, shallow lake edges, savannahs, forests, tundras, as well as to the other extreme—the desert habitat (for example, the extinct *Mammuthus africanavus* of desolate North Africa, *Platybelodon grangeri* of the Gobi Desert, and some populations of present-day *Loxodonta africana* in the Namib Desert).

Throughout their evolution, the proboscideans developed some very specialized characters as well as some generalized or primitive ones. The specialized characters are manifested by the presence of the trunk (the proboscis) and by the very large and peculiar dentition, whereas the generalized features are represented by parts of the circulatory system, some of the skeletal features (for example, the large number of ribs), and locomotion. Because the specialized features appear to overshadow the primitive ones, the proboscideans are considered to be among the most specialized mammals, but this may not necessarily be true.

EVOLUTIONARY TRENDS OF PROBOSCIDEANS

It appears as though the most significant trend of proboscidean species has been the progressive increase in size. Concomitant with the increase in size came the enlargement of the tusks and elongation of the trunk. The extraordinarily varied groups of proboscideans were also marked by certain other dominant trends. The summary which follows is modified after the work of the paleontologist Edwin H. Colbert who worked with the late Henry Fairfield Osborn during the last few years of Osborn's life (the list of trends is not necessarily in the order written).

- Increase in size—except for the earliest forms, most proboscideans became giants.
- Lengthening of limb bones and development of short, broad feet.
- Growth of the skull, including teeth, to extraordinary size—this was particularly noticed in the cranium, where air cells (diploe) developed.
- Co-evolution of infrasonic communication and the ability to store water in the pharynx.
- Shortening of the neck—since the skull and its associated structures (tusks and trunk) became large and heavy, the neck was reduced in length to shorten the lever between the body and the head.
- Elongation of the lower jaw—in many of the later proboscideans there was a *secondary* shortening of the lower jaw, but lengthening of the jaw was an early, primary trend. The secondary shortening co-evolved with the shift of the center of gravity of the skull posteriorly.
- Development of a proboscis—the elongation of the upper lip and the nostril appears to have co-evolved with the shortening of the lower jaw. As the animal became taller, the nostril was further elongated to form a very mobile trunk.

▼ The woolly mammoth, which is the best known of the mammoths, was not the only species of mammoth; there were several others, like the Columbian mammoth (*Mammuthus columbi*) of North America, shown in this reconstruction by the famous paleontological artist Charles R. Knight.

▲ Cranium of *Moeritherium* (as seen from below). One of the earliest members of the order Proboscidea, *Moeritherium* was a pig-sized animal that lived in Africa about 50–35 million years ago. It had no trunk but its skull and teeth were specialized.

▲ The cranium (upper) and mandible (lower) of *Barytherium*, from Libya. This African proto-elephant was roughly contemporaneous with *Moeritherium*, and is a member of the group that appears to represent the first of the radiation events in the ancestry of the elephants.

* Forward/horizontal displacement of cheek teeth (premolars and molars).
* Reduction in number of teeth from the full placental mammal dentition (this trend started with *Moeritherium*)—throughout the history of the Proboscidea there was a decrease in the numbers of premolars, canines, and especially incisors.
* Excessive growth of the second incisors to form tusks—some of these were straight, curved down, or upwards; they have functioned in food-gathering, defense, offense, and display.
* Enlargement and specialization of the cheek teeth—by increasing the number of cross-ridges (or lamellae), together with thinning of enamel, thereby molarifying the deciduous premolars.
* Rate of evolution in the head, particularly the molars and premolars, is faster than the rate of evolution of other organ systems in the body.

DENTAL FEATURES

Our knowledge of the evolution of Proboscidea is based mostly on dentition because teeth are the most durable biologically produced structures, thus they are the most common skeletal remains found in fossil sites. As noted earlier, an important evolutionary trend among the Proboscidea has been their increase in size. Compare, for example, the *Moeritherium* of 125 kilograms (275 pounds) to the *Mammuthus* of more than 5,000 kilograms (more than 11,000 pounds). Increase in body size resulted in increase of tooth size, along with increase of complexity of the chewing surfaces.

A natural development which resulted from the elongation of the cheek teeth was the evolution of horizontal tooth displacement. This process is believed to have begun at about the Oligocene–Miocene boundary. If so, the genetic make-up for such a mechanism was manifested in members of the family Mammutidae, or possibly earlier. Once the teeth of proboscideans became longer and taller there was a need for an alternative mechanism to replace the worn ones. Two possibilities existed: either the skull could elongate to accommodate the teeth at one time, or the tooth succession could be accomplished in a "conveyor belt" system, with one behind replacing one in front. Mammutids, gomphotheriids, stegodontids, and elephantids evolved this horizontal (as opposed to vertical) tooth displacement. In these advanced proboscideans the skulls were greatly deepened, and the teeth were formed in the alveoli within the jawbone, then came into the occlusal, or chewing, surface one at a time. It is possible that there was more than one tooth in the jaws at one time, especially when these were smaller premolars rather than molars. Those teeth which were in the front of the mouth eventually reached the edge, fragmented, and pieces of teeth then either fell out or were swallowed, as happens in modern elephants; tooth fragments have been retrieved from the feces of African and Asian elephants.

MAJOR PHYLETIC LINES OF THE PROBOSCIDEA

The accumulated knowledge of this mammalian order reveals that during the past 55–50 million years of evolution, proboscideans appear to have been subjected to three major radiation events, possibly due to the availability of new niches in their evolutionary history. Some scientists refer to these radiating (or "sprouting") events as "punctuated" evolution (as opposed to gradual evolution).

In brief, these radiating events were: first, at the end of the Paleocene and through the Oligocene (about 58–25 million years ago); second, at the beginning and during most of the Miocene (about 24–10 million years ago); and third, during the latest part of the Miocene, and during the Pliocene to the Pleistocene (about 10–0 million years ago.) The first and least defined assemblage included earlier proboscideans (moritheres, numidotheres, barytheres, deinotheres, palaeomastodons, and mammutids), the second involved the gomphotheres and stegodontids, and the last major adaptive radiation encompassed members of the family Elephantidae.

Given below are brief descriptions of the extinct and living proboscideans as they appear on the evolutionary tree (see pages 26–27) beginning at the bottom of the chart (the oldest forms).

THE FIRST RADIATION—THE EARLIEST PROBOSCIDEANS
Moeritheres, e.g., *Moeritherium lyonsi* (family Moeritheriidae)

The *Moeritherium*, named after the ancient Lake Moeris in Egypt where it was first discovered, was a primitive proboscidean that lived in the Eocene epoch and into the Oligocene epoch, about 50–33 million years ago, in the Fayum Basin of Egypt, some 60 kilometers (37 miles) southwest of Cairo, in what is now the valley of the Nile River. Later, moritheres were recovered from localities on the fringes of the Sahara from Libya to Mali and Senegal.

Moritheres were small, pig-sized animals, with long, heavy bodies, moderately short tails, and stout legs. Their limbs already were of distinctly elephantine type. They did not possess a trunk or proboscis, although *Moeritherium lyonsi* may have had a thick upper lip.

Numidotheres, e.g., *Phosphatherium escuilliei* (family Numidotheriidae)

Like many discoveries, the finding of *Phosphatherium escuilliei*—the earliest known proboscidean—was accidental. Its genus is derived from the Phosphates Basin of Ouled Abdoun in Morocco, and its species is in honor of Mr. F. Escuillié who noted the fossil skull fragments there in 1994–1995, while excavating for commercial minerals, including phosphate. Based on the material found, *P. escuilliei* is estimated to have weighed 10–15 kilograms (22–33 pounds), apparently the smallest non-dwarf extinct proboscidean found to date. It is dated to the late Paleocene, about 58 million years ago.

Numidotheres, e.g., *Numidotherium koholense* (family Numidotheriidae)

Named after Numidia, an ancient kingdom and Roman province in northeastern Africa, and the El Kohol locality where its remains were discovered in 1983 in Algeria. *N. koholense* stood about 1–1.5 meters (about 3 feet 5 inches–5 feet) at the shoulder and, based on the position of the external naris, it may have had a short proboscis, perhaps like that of a tapir. Based on the skeletal features and its stratigraphic position within the African geology, this animal is thought to have lived in the middle Eocene epoch (about 45–40 million years ago).

Barytheres, e.g., *Barytherium grave* (family Barytheriidae)

Much of our understanding of the evolutionary history of Barytheriidae is based on material collected in the Fayum, Egypt, by Charles W. Andrews in the early 1900s, and in Dor el-Talha, Libya, by Robert J. G. Savage during the 1960s. The two localities are about 1,500 kilometers (930 miles) apart and are interpreted as having been part of a semi-aquatic environment, in what is today northern Africa. R. Savage believed that he could identify two barythere species from Libya: one *Barytherium grave* (the same species as was found in Egypt) which was about the size of the modern Asian elephant, and the other was probably smaller than a bovine. It is entirely plausible that these two species also lived in Egypt, since the geographical distance between the two localities can be traveled in about 60–90 days.

The significance of basic knowledge of barytheres stems from their taxonomic position as one of the earliest offshoots of the Proboscidea. Thus, understanding the Barytheriidae automatically allows for better understanding of the relationships among more advanced proboscideans.

Deinotheres, e.g., *Deinotherium giganteum* (family Deinotheriidae)

The first deinotheres discovered, found in the Miocene sediments of East Africa, exhibited both primitive and highly specialized characters. Other discoveries were made in Asia and Europe (none was found in the New World); these were of early–late Miocene, Pliocene, and Pleistocene ages.

Prodeinotherium and *Deinotherium* (Deinotheriidae) shared a number of characters. A deinothere had a flat cranium on its dorsum and there were no tusks in the upper jaw (most advanced proboscideans have had high, domed crania). The external naris was elevated; a character which may be interpreted as the presence of a well-developed trunk. There were long, down-

The Bettmann Archive

recurved tusks in the mandible (no other proboscidean had such a unique character). Deinotheres had primitive dental characters: only two or three ridges, with simple cusps (whereas those of the *Loxodonta africana* and *Elephas maximus* have up to 29 ridges, with complex patterns); enamel on teeth of deinotheres was much thicker than on those of elephantids (about 5–8 millimeters, 0.2–0.3 inches, compared to 1–5 millimeters, 0.04–0.2 inches); and cheek teeth were replaced in a vertical rather than horizontal fashion as in elephantids. Deinotheres shared some primitive skeletal features with moeritheres which were not shared with members of the Elephantidae. The dental features in particular may indicate an animal adapted to browsing more than grazing.

Based on fossil evidence, deinotheres may have had rapid initial evolutionary development which was followed by a long period of evolutionary stability at a high level of specialization. All remains of deinotheres discovered thus far indicate animals of large proportions comparable to those of present-day elephants. *Deinotherium bavaricum*, however, was about the size of a small female Asian elephant. *D. giganteum* (based on long bones) was, as its name implies, a giant, towering over even the modern *Loxodonta africana* species; this deinothere stood as tall as 4 meters (13 feet) at the shoulder. (Additional information on deinotheres is found in the section "What is an elephant?" by J. and S. Shoshani.)

Palaeomastodontids, e.g., *Palaeomastodon beadnelli* (family Palaeomastodontidae)

One of the first proboscideans to be described from the Fayum Basin, Egypt, was properly given the name "Palaeomastodon", the ancient mastodon,

Imitor

▲ (Top) Taken in 1928, a contemporary news photograph shows Professor Elmer S. Riggs and Robert C. Thorne, part of a team from the Field Museum of Natural History, Chicago, unearthing a *Cuvieronius* skeleton on the banks of the Rio Quequen, Argentina. *Cuvieronius* was one of a few proboscideans to reach Central and South America, and showed a number of links with modern elephants, including very large size, tusks, and air-cells in the cranium.

▲ (Above) This "terrible beast", as its name *Deinotherium* implies, was once classified as a carnivore, a marsupial, and as a cetacean. Today, deinotheres are accepted as undisputed members of the mammalian order Proboscidea. The splitting time of the family Deinotheriidae from the main proboscidean stock may be at the end of the Eocene some 40 million years ago, although the first deinotheres were discovered in the Miocene sediments of East Africa, and later in Asia and Europe (none were found in the New World).

CLASSIFYING ELEPHANTS

JEHESKEL SHOSHANI AND PASCAL TASSY

To classify an animal or a plant means to give it a first and last name (genus and species) and put it in a file (a family or a higher category). This process is no different from naming an object in a store or at home and placing it in a labeled box so that everybody can find it easily.

People around the world speak different languages; so if animals and plants had only common names, it would create confusion among people from one country who wish to study the wildlife of another country whose language they do not know.

To avoid this possible lack of communication, scientists have developed a universal language with certain simple, and not so simple, rules to follow (published in the International Code of Zoological Nomenclature). In using these rules, the name of a species must be of at least two parts (hence the term "binomial" classification); the first is the genus and the second is the species. In an organizational sense, the genus name is the broader grouping and is analogous to a family name because each member of the group (genus) has the same family name plus its own individual name like a forename (or species).

All genera and species names must be Latinized, although their origin may be Latin, Greek, or another language. The first letter of the genus is capitalized and all subsequent letters of the genus and species are lower-case (even if the species is named after a locality or a person). For example, the scientific name of the Asian elephant is *Elephas maximus* and that of the American mastodon is *Mammut americanum* (note that the names are italicized). When there is sufficient anatomical evidence to divide a species into two or more subspecies, then we use three names (hence the term "trinomial"). For example, the scientific name of the Sri Lankan Asian elephant is *Elephas maximus maximus*, and the mainland Asian elephant is *Elephas maximus indicus*.

After naming an organism on the genus and species level, the next step is to decide to which higher category it belongs. In the Linnaean system of classification, the primary categories, from higher to lower, are: kingdom, phylum, class, order, family, genus, and species. There are subdivisions of these primary categories—as can be seen in the example of the African elephant given above, scientists determined that, based on anatomical characters it shares with Asian elephants (*Elephas maximus*) and woolly mammoths (*Mammuthus primigenius*), all belong in the family Elephantidae. Since the skeleton of *Mammut americanum* possesses very different sets of characters, it was decided to classify it in another family, the Mammutidae. Elephantidae, Mammutidae, and other families that share similar characters due to common ancestry were then grouped under the umbrella of a higher category called order, in this case, the order Proboscidea. Similar orders are classified together in one class, classes are grouped in a phylum, and phyla in a kingdom. An example of a simplified classification of the Proboscidea within Animalia, and detailed proboscidean classifications are given here.

One of the most important rules in nomenclature (the practice of giving names to animals and plants) and classification is the "principle of priority". It states that if two different names have been given to the same animal or plant by two different researchers, the one that was published first is valid. To give a concrete example, in 1806, the famous French anatomist G. Cuvier coined the name

"Mastodonte" for an animal which was found in Big-Bone Lick site, not far from the Ohio River, Kentucky, USA. In 1814, Rafinesque coined the scientific name *Mastodon* for the same animal, endorsed by Cuvier in 1817. In 1799, however, J. F. Blumenbach, a German naturalist, had named the same animal *Mammut* (as the generic name for the American mastodon), and thus, the older name has prevailed.

A PARTIAL CLASSIFICATION OF PROBOSCIDEA
(Elephants and relatives)

Category	Taxon
Kingdom	Animalia
Phylum	Chordata
Subphylum	Vertebrata
Class	Mammalia
Order	Proboscidea
Family	Mammutidae
Genus	*Mammut*
Genus and species	*Mammut americanum*[1]
Family	Elephantidae
Genus	*Loxodonta*[2]
Genus and species	*Loxodonta cyclotis*[3]
	Loxodonta africana[4]
Genus	*Elephas*[2]
Genus and species	*Elephas maximus*[5]
Subspecies	*Elephas maximus sumatranus*[6]
	Elephas maximus indicus[7]
	Elephas maximus maximus[8]
Genus	*Mammuthus*
Genus and species	*Mammuthus columbi/imperator*[9]
	Mammuthus primigenius[10]

1. The American mastodon, now extinct (remains found in North America).
2. Includes living and extinct species.
3. The forest African elephant species, living.
4. The bush or savanna African elephant species, living.
5. The Asian elephant, living.
6. The Sumatran Asian elephant subspecies, living (found on the island of Sumatra).
7. The mainland Asian elephant subspecies, living (found in India and Indochina).
8. The Sri Lankan Asian elephant subspecies, living (found on the island of Sri Lanka, formerly Ceylon).
9. The imperial mammoth, now extinct (remains found in North America).
10. The woolly mammoth, now extinct (remains and intact carcasses found frozen in the Arctic).

The content of the family Gomphotheriidae (given on the following page) within the superfamily Gomphotherioidea is only a small sample of extremely varied (heterogeneous) gomphotheres, the taxonomy of which has been under investigation for many years. There are more disagreements about content of Gomphotheriidae than about the content of any other proboscidean group.

Until additional evidence comes to light, members of the family Anthracobunidae (*Anthracobune, Ishatherium, Jozaria, Lammidhania* and *Pilgrimella*) may be removed from Proboscidea and placed in Tethytheria *incertae sedis* (of uncertain position; Tethytheria includes the orders Proboscidea, Sirenia and Desmostylia). McKenna, Bell et al. (1997) classified the Anthracobunidae in Proboscidea *incertae sedis*.

A SIMPLIFIED CLASSIFICATION OF THE PROBOSCIDEA

(This table contains only taxa mentioned in this book; modified after Shoshani *et al.*, 1998, and McKenna, Bell, *et al.*, 1997)

Class Mammalia Linnaeus, 1758
  Subclass Theria Parker and Haswell, 1897
   Supercohort Placentalia Owen, 1837 (=Eutheria Gill, 1872)
   Cohort Epitheria McKenna, 1975
    Superorder Ungulata Linnaeus, 1766
    Grandorder Uranotheria McKenna, Bell, et al., 1997 (=Paenungulata
      Simpson, 1945, in part)
     Mirorder Tethytheria McKenna, 1975
      Order Proboscidea Illiger, 1811
       Family Moeritheriidae Andrews, 1906 †
        Genus *Moeritherium* Andrews, 1901 †
       Family Numidotheriidae Shoshani and Tassy, 1992 †
        Genus *Phosphatherium* Gheerbrant et al., 1996 †
        Genus *Numidotherium* Mahboubi et al., 1986 †
       Family Barytheriidae Andrews, 1906 †
        Genus *Barytherium* Andrews, 1901 †
       Family Deinotheriidae Bonaparte, 1841 †
        Genus *Prodeinotherium* Ehik, 1930 †
        Genus *Deinotherium* Kaup, 1829 †
      Suborder Elephantiformes Tassy, 1988
       Family Palaeomastodontidae Andrews, 1906 †
        Genus *Palaeomastodon* Andrews, 1901 †
       Family Phiomiidae Kalandadze and Rautian, 1992 †
        Genus *Phiomia* Andrews and Beadnell, 1902 †
       Infraorder Elephantimorpha Tassy and Shoshani, 1997 in
        Shoshani et al., 1998
       Parvorder Mammutida Tassy and Shoshani, 1997 in
        Shoshani et al., 1998†
        Superfamily Mammutoidea Hay, 1922 †
         Family Mammutidae Hay, 1922 †
          Genus *Eozygodon* Tassy and Pickford, 1983 †

          Genus *Zygolophodon* Vacek, 1877 †
          Genus *Mammut* Blumenbach, 1799 †
       Parvorder Elephantida Tassy and Shoshani, 1997 in Shoshani et al., 1998
        Superfamily Gomphotherioidea Hay, 1922 †
         Family Gomphotheriidae Hay, 1922 (trilophodont gomphotheres)
          Genus *Gomphotherium* Burmeister, 1837 †
          Genus *Amebelodon* Barbour, 1927 †
          Genus *Platybelodon* Borissiak, 1928 †
          Genus *Archaeobelodon* Tassy, 1984 †
          Genus *Rhynchotherium* Falconer, 1868 †
          Genus *Cuvieronius* Osborn, 1923 †
       Superfamily Elephantoidea Gray, 1821
        Family incertae sedis Genus Tetralophodon Falconer, 1857
         (tetralophodont gomphothere) †
        Family incertae sedis Genus Anancus Aymard, 1855
         (tetralophodont gomphothere) †
        Family Stegodontidae Osborn, 1918 †
         Genus *Stegolophodon* Schlesinger, 1917 †
         Genus *Stegodon* Falconer, 1857 †
       Family Elephantidae Gray, 1821
        Subfamily Stegotetrabelodontinae Aguirre, 1969 †
         Genus *Stegotetrabelodon* Petrocchi, 1941 †
         Genus *Stegodibelodon* Coppens, 1972 †
        Subfamily Elephantinae Gray, 1821
         Genus *Primelephas* Maglio, 1970 †
         Tribe Loxodontini Osborn 1918
          Genus *Loxodonta* Anonymous, 1827
         Tribe Elephantini Gray, 1821
          Genus *Elephas* Linnaeus, 1758
          Genus *Mammuthus* Brookes, 1828 †
† = Extinct taxon (species, genus, family, order).

Note: In each rank or category, the name of a taxon (plural, taxa) is followed by the name of the author who named that taxon and the year of publication; for example, the genus *Mammuthus* was first named by Brookes in 1828.

Note that arrangements of genera, families, or higher categories in this classification (from top to bottom) follow the general sequence of the branching pattern in the evolutionary tree (from bottom to top, on pages 26–27). Ideally, classification schemes and evolutionary trees, or cladograms, should corroborate one another (that is, the branching patterns should be exactly as listed in the classification), but ideal conditions are seldom encountered, and the evolutionary history of the Proboscidea is no exception. (See also boxed note on the previous page, on Gomphotheriidae and Anthracobunidae.)

Cynthia Moss

▲ The bush African elephant is one of three surviving species; they are the only remnants of a once much richer and more varied assemblage of magnificent animals.

Jeheskel Shoshani

▲ The emergence of *Gomphotherium* marks the onset of the second major radiation event in the history of the proboscideans. Widespread in Africa, Asia, Europe, and North America during the Miocene epoch, *Gomphotherium* was about the size of an Asian elephant, and had tusks in both the upper and lower jaws. It is believed to have had a trunk, and its pattern of tooth replacement may have had a horizontal component, like that of modern elephants. The skeleton shown, originally identified as *Gomphotherium*, subsequently was reclassified by P. Tassy as *Archaeobelodon*.

because it was thought to be related to a mastodon. Named after the British explorer Hugh J. L. Beadnell, *Palaeomastodon beadnelli* lived during the Oligocene epoch (34–30 million years ago). It is believed to have been about 2 meters (about 6 feet 6 inches) at the shoulder and may have had a less developed trunk-like structure.

The molars of *Palaeomastodon* were essentially of bilophodont type with a tendency to develop a cusp (central conule) in the middle of each ridge. These dental features are consistent with the forest and open woodland habitats where *Palaeomastodon* may have lived.

Mammutids, e.g., *Mammut americanum* (family Mammutidae)

American mastodons were prehistoric elephant-like mammals that were separate from the family Elephantidae, including the two living elephants and the extinct mammoth. A mastodon was as different from a mammoth as a dog is from a cat; the mastodon is classified in the family Mammutidae, and the mammoth in the family Elephantidae and neither was a direct ancestor of the modern elephants; they are placed at different branches of the evolutionary tree.

The name mastodon is derived from the Greek, meaning "nipple-tooth", which the cusps of the teeth resemble. On the other hand, the name *Mammut*, and also *Mammuthus*, originated from a Tartar word *Mamut* which means "a gigantic burrowing rat".

The American mastodon is believed to have inhabited a variety of environments but browsed on conifers and other trees. Radiocarbon dates indicate that *M. americanum* became extinct about

10,000 years ago. The map on page 29 depicts the locations of fossil proboscidean remains discovered in the New World. As of 1990 the minimum estimate of *M. americanum* fossils found in the New World was 1,473 animals (an increase of about 187 percent since the first survey was made 70 years earlier). Some of the specimens of the American mastodon and mammoth were collected from the continental shelf of the Atlantic Ocean, off the coast of the northeast and southeast United States where fishermen found them in their nets. (Additional information on the American mastodon is found in the sections "Classifying elephants" by J. Shoshani and P. Tassy, and "Comparing mammoths and mastodons" by J. Shoshani.)

THE SECOND RADIATION—GOMPHOTHERES AND THEIR ALLIES

Miocene proboscidean genera and species which were considered a generalized stock from which later taxa evolved were classified in a group called "gomphotheres". They were widespread throughout most of the geographic distribution of the Proboscidea, that is, on all the continents except Australia and Antarctica. Some of these gomphotheres were placed in a family named Gomphotheriidae.

During the last thirty years, many proboscidean taxa of uncertain taxonomic position which showed resemblance to the general plan of gomphothere were classified in the Gomphotheriidae—thus, this family became the "wastebasket" of the Proboscidea, much like the function the order "Insectivora" served for the class Mammalia, or "Condylarthra" for ungulate-related taxa. Pascal Tassy, a French proboscideanologist, has been using the common name "gomphothere" without giving an inclusive scientific name of a higher category to harbor these genera. More recently, J. Shoshani and P. Tassy have conducted a detailed analysis of gomphothere characters to elucidate and perhaps to resolve these phylogenetic problems. Given below is a brief summary of some of the better known gomphothere taxa, arranged in approximate sequence as they appear on the evolutionary tree; they are *Gomphotherium*, *Amebelodon*, *Platybelodon*, *Rhynchotherium*, *Cuvieronius*, and *Anancus*.

Gomphotheres, e.g., *Gomphotherium angustidens* (family Gomphotheriidae)

Gomphotherium is the type genus of the family Gomphotheriidae. It is a well-known and widespread member of this group, whose remains were discovered in Miocene deposits in Africa (for example, Egypt and Kenya), Asia (for example, Israel and Pakistan), Europe (for example, France), and North America (for example, United States of America). Based on skeletal remains, it is estimated

American Museum of Natural History

that *Gomphotherium* was nearly as large as an Asian elephant, with two pairs of tusks; one in the upper jaw (with a band of enamel) and the other in the lower jaw. Speculation that *Gomphotherium* had a well-developed trunk is based on the position of the external nasal (naris) opening, the short neck, and long limbs.

Dental characters of gomphotheres were of the generalized elephantid type; that is, all teeth of subsequent elephant genera and species included features already found in gomphotherids. A close examination of gomphothere cheek teeth reveals that the first two molars had three pairs of transverse, conical cusps; when worn, these cusps display clearly defined narrow closed loops of thick enamel, bordering within them typical dentine found in all proboscideans. Enamel and dentine are distinctly contrasted by their color and durability; the former is more durable, shiny, and lighter in color, whereas the latter is dull brown. The third molar of many gomphotheres was elongated by the development of a "heel" behind the last 3 paired cusps: each third molar had 3–4 complete ridges.

Each successive tooth was larger than previous ones, and tooth displacement is believed to have occurred in a horizontal as well as vertical fashion. Horizontal tooth displacement, as opposed

to vertical, can be used as a shared derived character (synapomorphy) to group genera belonging to these taxa: Elephantidae, Stegodontidae, "gomphotheres", and Mammutidae. These four taxa were grouped under the name Elephantoidea. The evolution chart (pages 26–27) and the section on classification (pages 22–23) depict these relationships.

Amebelodontids, e.g., *Amebelodon floridanus* (family Gomphotheriidae)

A. floridanus is one of a few amebelodontid species; it lived in Florida and other areas in the United States from about 10–5 million years ago. It stood about 2 meters (about 6 feet 6 inches) tall; other species may have been taller. The skull, particularly the mandible, was elongated and was equipped with upper tusks of varying length which were round to oval in cross-section. The lower incisors developed into a flattened scoop-like ladle. To the untrained observer, the cheek teeth of amebelodontids were similar to those of gomphotheres with additional subsidiary cusps. Amebelodons are believed to have fed on vegetation found in savannahs and around margins of wetlands, such as swamps or floodplains.

▲ The American mastodons (*Mammut americanum*) were contemporaneous with mammoths, but were restricted to North America. This is the Warren mastodon, painted by Charles R. Knight, 1908.

▶ (Following pages) This "family tree" shows the direct line of ancestry of *Elephas* (the animal at center, top of this figure) as passing through *Primelephas*, *Gomphotherium*, *Palaeomastodon*, and "ancestral proboscideans". All other proboscideans depicted are "side branches". Examine this figure with the classification table on page 23 and the migratory map on page 29, and observe the following points.
1. There are three major radiation events: (a) all pre-Miocene proboscideans; (b) all gomphotheres and stegodontids; and (c) all members of the Elephantidae.
2. Members of the family Mammutidae are distinctly separated from the Elephantidae—in particular, *Mammut americanum*; even though it was contemporary with *Mammuthus*, it was a very different animal.
3. Members of the family Stegodontidae were not ancestors of the family Elephantidae as was once thought; each family constitutes a different branch on the evolutionary tree.
4. Moving from the Eocene to the Holocene, these changes occurred: increase in the size of the animals, their tusks and teeth, and an increase in trunk length. This is shown in the left-hand column.

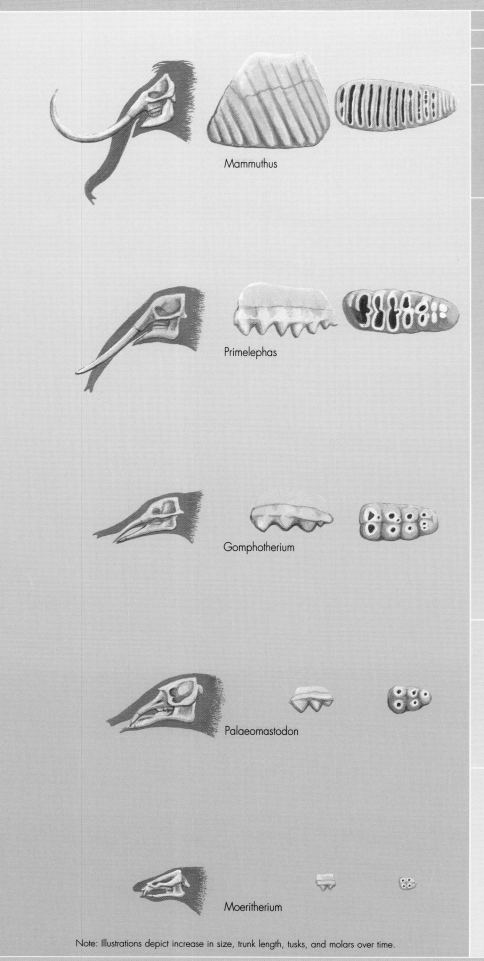

Mammuthus

Primelephas

Gomphotherium

Palaeomastodon

Moeritherium

Note: Illustrations depict increase in size, trunk length, tusks, and molars over time.

Mammut

Cuvieronius

Zygolophodon

Rhynchotherium

Ancestral Mammutids
eg. Eozygodon

Moeritherium

Note: white hatchings on branches denote lack of evidence for precise origin

A SIMPLIFIED EVOLUTIONARY TREE OF THE PROBOSCIDEA

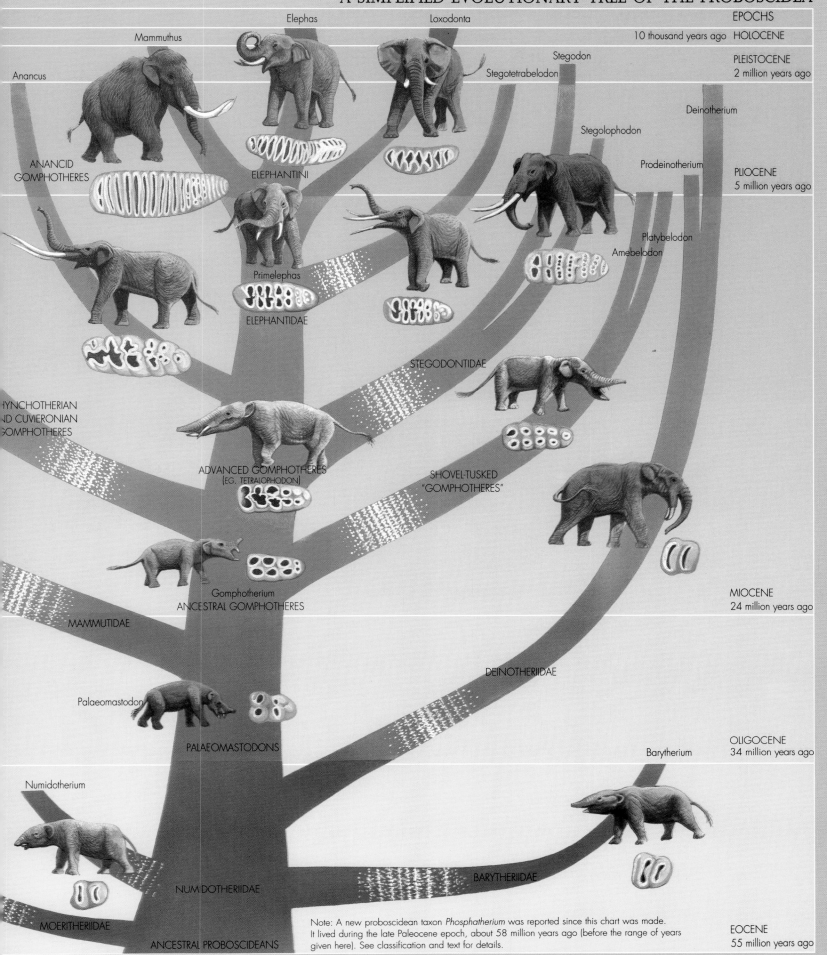

EPOCHS

10 thousand years ago — HOLOCENE

PLEISTOCENE
2 million years ago

PLIOCENE
5 million years ago

MIOCENE
24 million years ago

OLIGOCENE
34 million years ago

EOCENE
55 million years ago

Elephas

Loxodonta

Mammuthus

Stegodon

Anancus

Stegotetrabelodon

Deinotherium

Stegolophodon

Prodeinotherium

ANANCID
GOMPHOTHERES

ELEPHANTINI

Platybelodon
Amebelodon

Primelephas

ELEPHANTIDAE

STEGODONTIDAE

HYNCHOTHERIAN
ND CUVIERONIAN
GOMPHOTHERES

ADVANCED GOMPHOTHERES
(EG. TETRALOPHODON)

SHOVEL-TUSKED
"GOMPHOTHERES"

Gomphotherium
ANCESTRAL GOMPHOTHERES

MAMMUTIDAE

DEINOTHERIIDAE

Palaeomastodon

Barytherium

PALAEOMASTODONS

Numidotherium

BARYTHERIIDAE

NUMDOTHERIIDAE

Note: A new proboscidean taxon *Phosphatherium* was reported since this chart was made.
It lived during the late Paleocene epoch, about 58 million years ago (before the range of years
given here). See classification and text for details.

MOERITHERIIDAE

ANCESTRAL PROBOSCIDEANS

27

▲ About 12,000 years ago, the glaciers which covered the area known today as Michigan, in the United States, were melting and the front of the ice was receding; plants took root soon after the ice melted, and plant-eaters followed. The Shelton Mastodon Site, shown here, contained two of about 250 mastodon remains found in Michigan up to 1992.

▶ This half jawbone belongs to a mastodon (*Mammut americanum*) found at the Shelton Mastodon Site, shown above. Based on a tusk found at the site and on the cheek teeth and their state of wear, Daniel Fisher and Jeheskel Shoshani proposed that this individual was between 13 and 17 years old when it died about 12,000 years ago.

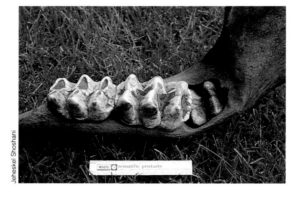

Platybelodontids, e.g., *Platybelodon grangeri* (family Gomphotheriidae)

One of the best known gomphotheres, *Platybelodon* became a celebrity in the scientific and popular literature when it was discovered in the 1920s because of the similarity of its lower tusks to a shovel. Uncovered in the Miocene of Asia, *Platybelodon* was about 2 meters (about 6 feet 6 inches) tall at the shoulder and had small upper tusks but its lower tusks were flattened and grew in juxtaposition to form a shovel. This "shovel" is believed to have been used to uproot marshy vegetation within a similar niche to that of *Amebelodon* but in widely separated habitats.

Rhynchotheres, e.g., *Rhynchotherium falconeri* (family Gomphotheriidae)

As its name implies, this "beaked beast" (*rhynchos* means snout or beak, from Greek) was essentially a specialized gomphothere, and lived, apparently,

only in North and Central America from about 12–3 million years ago. It stood over 2 meters (6 feet 6 inches) tall, and in most aspects it resembled a *Gomphotherium*, except that its lower jaw was curved downwards in front, and it had two pairs of tusks of unusual shape. The upper pair, over 1 meter (3 feet 3 inches) long each, were slightly spiraled, and in the mandible, the tusks were about one-third of the length of the uppers and possessed a longitudinal band of enamel; the two pairs did not touch each other. The cheek teeth were not much different from those of *Gomphotherium*.

Cuvieronians, e.g., *Cuvieronius humboldtii* (family Gomphotheriidae)

Here is an example of a scientific name where the genus (*Cuvieronius*) and the species (*humboldtii*) were named after two persons—Georges Leopold Chretien Frederic Dagobert Cuvier (to give his full name), the most famous French anatomist and paleontologist of his day (1769–1832), and the distinguished voyager Baron Friedrich Heinrich Alexander von Humboldt (1769–1859).

Cuvieronius was one of a handful of proboscidean genera which reached South America; its distribution included southern North America and Central America. *Cuvieronius* was an advanced gomphothere in the sense that it was of elephantine proportions, and its cranium contained air-cells—chambers also found in *Mammut*, *Loxodonta*, *Elephas*, and *Mammuthus*. *Cuvieronius* had cheek teeth with 4–5 ridges of complex trefoil patterns and the upper tusks were long (over 1 meter, 3 feet 3 inches), slightly twisted, and with reduced or no enamel band. Like all gomphotheres, the displacement of cheek teeth included a horizontal component.

It is believed that, from the Pliocene until the end of the Pleistocene (5–1 million years ago), *Cuvieronius* inhabited wooded plains and was probably a grazer as well as a browser.

Anancids, e.g., *Anancus arvernensis* (superfamily Elephantoidea, family uncertain)

Anancine proboscideans are one of the experimental side branches of the main evolutionary trunk. There are ten species of *Anancus* listed in the monograph *Proboscidea* of the late H. F. Osborn, and at least three new species have been described since then. One of these, *A. osiris*, was unearthed in Egypt and was named after Osiris, the Egyptian god of the underworld. In these Miocene, Pliocene, and Pleistocene taxa, the lower jaws became shorter and devoid of tusks; the upper tusks became longer. *A. arvernensis*, a Pliocene European species, had long straight tusks which reached 3 meters (almost 10 feet) in length. Analysis of material

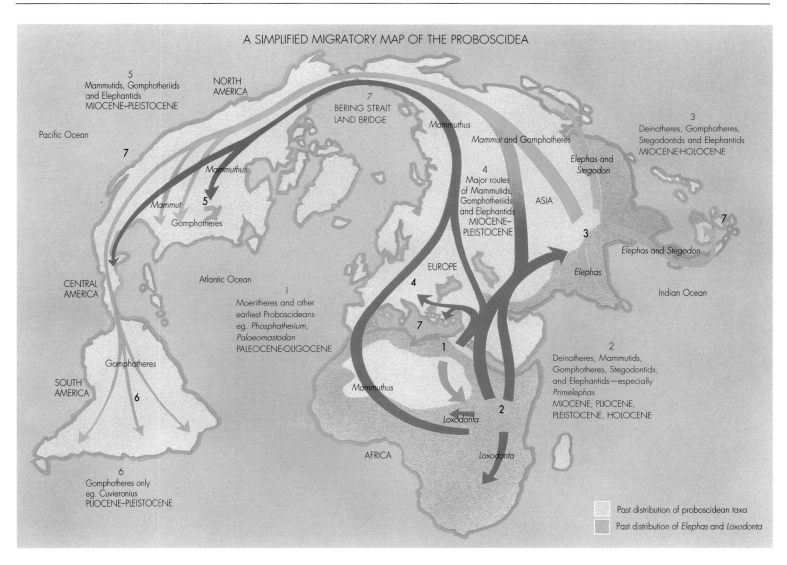

A SIMPLIFIED MIGRATORY MAP OF THE PROBOSCIDEA

5
Mammutids, Gomphotheriids
and Elephantids
MIOCENE–PLEISTOCENE

NORTH
AMERICA

7
BERING STRAIT
LAND BRIDGE

Mammuthus

Mammut and Gomphotheres

3
Deinotheres, Gomphotheres,
Stegodontids and Elephantids
MIOCENE–HOLOCENE

Pacific Ocean

7

Mammuthus

Elephas and
Stegodon

Mammut

5

Gomphotheres

4
Major routes
of Mammutids,
Gomphotheriids
and Elephantids
MIOCENE–
PLEISTOCENE

ASIA

3

7

Elephas and Stegodon

CENTRAL
AMERICA

Atlantic Ocean

1
Moeritheres and other
earliest Proboscideans
eg. Phosphatherium,
Palaeomastodon
PALEOCENE–OLIGOCENE

EUROPE

4

Elephas

Indian Ocean

Gomphotheres

SOUTH
AMERICA

6

7

1

2
Deinotheres, Mammutids,
Gomphotheres, Stegodontids,
and Elephantids—especially
Primelephas
MIOCENE, PLIOCENE,
PLEISTOCENE, HOLOCENE

Mammuthus

Loxodonta

2

6
Gomphotheres only
eg. Cuvieronius
PLIOCENE–PLEISTOCENE

AFRICA

Loxodonta

Past distribution of proboscidean taxa

Past distribution of Elephas and Loxodonta

from the Awash Valley, in Afar region, Ethiopia, by Jon Kalb and his colleagues, reveals progressive evolutionary trends among anancid species.

Stegodontids, e.g., *Stegodon ganesa* (family Stegodontidae)

All the available evidence suggests that, contrary to earlier beliefs, Stegodontidae were not ancestral to Elephantidae; rather, both families evolved in parallel from a gomphothere-like ancestor during the late Miocene and early Pliocene epochs. Stegodons and true elephants were found in Africa and Asia. Skeletal anatomies, skull architecture, grinding teeth morphology are a few examples of similarity.

Unspecialized stegodons (for example, *Stegolophodon*) could easily be placed as intermediate forms between certain gomphotheres (for example, *Tetralophodon*) and the least advanced elephantids. The cheek teeth were composed of transverse ridges, or lamellae, and each of these was in turn made up of tiny cusps, or small cones (conelets). Correlated with dental changes came the lengthening of the cheek teeth and the increase in number of ridges or plates

per tooth. For example, the third molar of *Gomphotherium* had up to 5–7 ridges, that of *Stegodon* had 12–13, and *Mammuthus* may have had over 30 plates. Stegodons, like elephantids, displaced their cheek teeth horizontally. As noted earlier, this trend may have begun to manifest itself during the Oligocene.

Many stegodon specimens were collected in Myanmar (formerly Burma) along the valley of the Irrawaddy River, named after the Hindu god Airavata (see also "Elephants in folklore, religion and art" by J. A. McNeely). One of the best known stegodons is *Stegodon ganesa* which was named after the Hindu god Ganesa (sometimes spelled Ganes or Ganesh), the famous elephant-deity, the god of wisdom and good fortune. The generic name may be broken down into *steg* (meaning "roof" from Greek) and *odon* ("of tooth", also from Greek), referring probably to the arched occlusal surface of the lower molars.

S. ganesa grew to a height of about 3.5 meters (11 feet 6 inches); its height, however, was not its most attractive feature. The upper tusks were formidable in size and architecture; they nearly reached the ground and were curved sideways and

▲ The early travels of the proboscideans. The routes on this map were constructed based on fossil material discovered at different localities of different geological times. Like the classification and the evolutionary tree, this map is subject to constant changes with the discovery of new fossils and/or different interpretations of old material. In this reconstruction, it has been hypothesized that during the course of evolution of the Proboscidea, there were three major centers of radiation: northeast Africa, eastern Africa, and Southeast Asia. Numbers 1 and 2 correspond roughly to the first major radiation of the Proboscidea; 2, 3, 4, 5, and 6 correspond to the second radiation and are all part of the extremely varied gomphothere assemblage; and 2, 3, 4, and 5 correspond to the third radiation; and 7 refers to islands in the Mediterranean, off the coast of California, USA, Wrangel Island in the Siberian Arctic, and Southeast Asia, where remains of dwarf proboscideans (extinct elephants, mammoths and stegodons) were found.

FRANCE
ITALY
PORTUGAL
SPAIN
Mediterranean Sea
TURKEY
SYRIA
IRAN
MOROCCO
ALGERIA
IRAQ
KUWAIT
WESTERN
SAHARA
(MOROCCO)
LIBYA
EGYPT
SAUDI
ARABIA
MAURITANIA
MALI
NIGER
CHAD

The forest African elephant
Loxodonta cyclotis

Red Sea
YEMEN
SENEGAL
SUDAN
ERITREA
GAMBIA
DJIBOUTI
GUINEA-
BISSAU
BURKINA
FASO
GUINEA
BENIN
NIGERIA
SOMALIA
SIERRA
LEONE
IVORY
COAST
CENTRAL
AFRICAN
REPUBLIC
ETHIOPIA
Atlantic Ocean
LIBERIA
GHANA
TOGO
CAMEROON
EQUATORIAL
GUINEA
CONGO
UGANDA
GABON
KENYA
DEMOCRATIC REPUBLIC
OF THE CONGO
RWANDA
BURUNDI
TANZANIA
ANGOLA
MALAWI
ZAMBIA
MADAGASCAR
MOZAMBIQUE
NAMIBIA
ZIMBABWE
BOTSWANA
SOUTH
AFRICA

The bush African elephant
Loxodonta africana

30

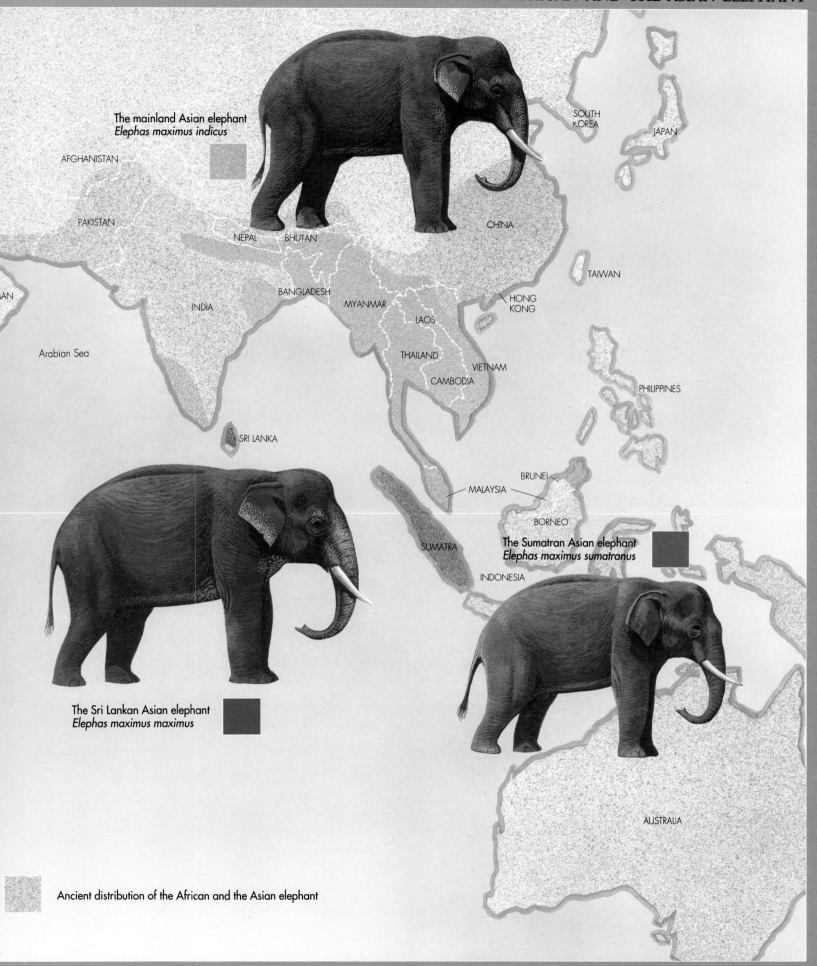

The mainland Asian elephant
Elephas maximus indicus

AFGHANISTAN

PAKISTAN

NEPAL BHUTAN

CHINA

SOUTH
KOREA

JAPAN

TAIWAN

HONG
KONG

BANGLADESH

MYANMAR

INDIA

LAOS

Arabian Sea

THAILAND

VIETNAM

CAMBODIA

PHILIPPINES

SRI LANKA

BRUNEI

MALAYSIA

BORNEO

The Sumatran Asian elephant
Elephas maximus sumatranus

SUMATRA

INDONESIA

The Sri Lankan Asian elephant
Elephas maximus maximus

AUSTRALIA

Ancient distribution of the African and the Asian elephant

31

▲ The second major proboscidean radiation saw the emergence of several animal groups that strongly resemble modern elephants in general appearance. *Stegodon* arose in Asia and had roots in a gomphothere-like ancestor. Like modern elephants, these animals showed a horizontal pattern of tooth replacement. Some reached 3–5 meters tall (9 feet, 10 inches–16 feet 5 inches) and had a formidable pair of tusks. They may have inhabited forests where their diet included bamboo shoots, leaves, and fruit.

◄ (Previous pages) A map showing the past and present distribution of the African and the Asian elephant. In ancient times, a resident in the valley of the Euphrates and Tigris Rivers or in the floodplain of the Nile River may have encountered a pastoral scene with hundreds of indigenous elephants foraging on the lush vegetation. Elephants and humans, as well as many other animals, have competed for the same fertile lands. As a result, today, only a fraction of elephants' past distribution has remained; habitat fragmentation due to agricultural use and human settlements is the main cause. Poaching has been a major contributor to their sharp decline, but poaching itself is one of the results of an overpopulated planet.

upwards. Stegodons are believed to have inhabited forested areas close to water sources, and their diet may have consisted of bamboo shoots and leaves.

THE THIRD RADIATION—ELEPHANTS
The elephants (family Elephantidae)
Most of the osteological characters which indicate that a particular proboscidean is an elephant are found in the skull. Among the list of Elephantidae characters are: high elevation of the basicranium; the wing of the alisphenoid bone is oriented vertically; the glenoid surface (that hinge point between the mandible and the cranium) is rounded; presence of a deep postglenoid depression; loss of enamel band on the upper tusks; molars with at least five ridges or laminae, each of these laminae forms separately and consists of a "shell" of enamel filled with dentine, and valleys between ridges are V- or U-shaped. The plates are held together by a substance called "cement". It is a requisite that *all* members of the family Elephantidae, extinct and extant, possess a well-developed proboscis. This assumption is based on the elevated position of the external naris (this feature is discussed in detail in the section, "Anatomy and physiology", and earlier in this chapter). The presence of the trunk was particularly important in those species whose lower jaws were extremely shortened. With the trunk, elephantids could reach foliage high above their heads, as well as grasses low to the ground.

As of the end of 1990, fossil specimens of Elephantidae were collected from sites in Africa, Europe, Asia, North America, and Central America; no authentic/indigenous material was reported from South America or from Australia. All six genera discussed briefly below—not necessarily the same species—were found in Africa, which is believed to be the cradle of Elephantidae evolution.

The family name Elephantidae was established by J. E. Gray in 1821. At that time only three elephant species were known: the African elephant, the Asian elephant, and the mammoth. According to most recent workers, this family includes six genera and twenty-seven elephant species. The African elephant (*Loxodonta africana*) and the Asian elephant (*Elephas maximus*) are the only living representatives; members of the other four genera are extinct. The mammoth *(Mammuthus)*, whose numerous fossil remains have been unearthed in Africa, Eurasia, and North America, is the next best known genus. The other three genera, *Stegodibelodon, Stegotetrabelodon,* and *Primelephas,* are more primitive forms of the Miocene–Pliocene epochs.

Family Elephantidae, subfamily Stegotetrabelodontinae
Stegotetrabelodon and Stegodibelodon
Both genera were restricted to Africa and both are known from fragmentary material. Nevertheless, they are important taxa since they are the earliest members of the Elephantidae and provide us with a database for comparison with later forms. They occur in the latest Miocene and early Pliocene in sediments which may be interpreted as patchy environments, that is, forests mixed with savannahs. All the elephantid characters previously mentioned apply to these genera. There were two species assigned to *Stegotetrabelodon* and one to *Stegodibelodon*. The first part of each name is "Stego" because early investigators incorrectly considered these taxa to be related to stegodons.

The important differences between stegodons and true elephants include the following: the architecture of the crown of the molars, including the spacing between the ridges (in stegodons the ridges are narrowly spaced); the V-shaped valleys between the ridges (stegodons have Y-shaped ones); and the presence of incisors in the lower jaws of early elephantids.

Family Elephantidae, subfamily Elephantinae
Primelephas gomphotheroides
The generic name of this taxon is a clear indication of the familial or subfamilial association. In 1965 Yves Coppens described a specimen from Chad and named it *Stegodon korotorensis*. Five years later, Vincent J. Maglio re-examined the same specimen and other material and concluded that this species should be reclassified as elephantid, not stegodontid, and named it *Primelephas gompho-theroides*, to indicate that it was a primitive type of elephant related to the gomphothere stock.

P. gomphotheroides stood about as tall as a female African elephant. It had two pairs of tusks protruding forward, the uppers over 1 meter (3 feet 3 inches) long and the lowers much shorter, no more than 20 centimeters (just under 8 inches). Remains of *Primelephas* date to the latest Miocene epoch of East Africa, dating to circa 7–6 million years ago. The environment in which this species was found is interpreted to have been an open wooded savannah. In reconstructing the phylogenetic history of the Elephantinae, Maglio depicted *Primelephas* as having given rise to all later taxa, including *Loxodonta* (with three species), *Elephas* (with eleven species), and *Mammuthus* (with seven species).

Loxodonta africana and *Elephas maximus*

Living elephantid species *(Loxodonta africana and Elephas maximus)* are the results of over 50 million years of evolution and they carry with them the genetic makeup of their ancestors, including the ability to grow to be very bulky. The African elephant is the largest land mammal living today. The largest terrestrial mammal, *Indricotherium* (formerly *Baluchitherium*), that ever existed was related to rhinoceroses. Size, up to a point, is a definite advantage against predators, but more importantly, large animals lose less heat per unit of their surface area than small animals. Heat loss requires increased search for food and subsequent exposure to hazards.

The African elephant *(Loxodonta africana)* is believed to have migrated in prehistoric times throughout the African continent but not beyond. Conversely, fossil evidence indicates that ancestors of the Asian elephant (*Elephas maximus*) evolved in Africa and later migrated to Eurasia. Differences between the African and the Asian elephants are summarized in the table on page 39.

Etymologically, *Loxodonta* refers to the lozenge shape of the enamel loops on the chewing surfaces of the teeth, and *africana* is self-explanatory. *Elephas* may be dissected into *ele* (meaning "arch" from Greek) and *phant* ("huge" as in phantasia, also from Greek)—thus a huge arch. The species name *maximus*, of course, means large or very large (from the Latin *maxima*).

Mammuthus primigenius

One of the best known mammoths was the extinct woolly mammoth, *Mammuthus primigenius*, which lived until the very end of the Ice Age, mostly above the Arctic Circle. Pictographs of this mammoth have been found on walls and ceilings of caves in Europe.

Drawings were only one reminder that man and mammoths were contemporaneous; bones and, more significantly, frozen well-preserved carcasses of the woolly mammoth found in Siberia and Alaska are other reminders. These carcasses also provide direct evidence of the external and internal anatomy of these proboscideans. The dense coat of hair may explain how they survived in the Arctic climate.

The Berezovka mammoth was, until 1977, the most famous frozen carcass ever found. It took a year, from about 1900 to 1901, after it was discovered for scientists to reach the desolate area and recover that huge male, and bring it to Petrograd (later Leningrad, recently renamed St Petersburg), where it is now exhibited in the Zoological Museum.

An almost complete frozen mammoth carcass, named Dima, was discovered in the Soviet Union in 1977. It was found in one piece in the permafrost of the Magadan region. Radiocarbon dating indicated conflicting ages, one of which was 40,000 years old. I was one of those fortunate individuals who studied the soft tissues (see also the section "Cloning elephants", by V. Mikhelson). Morris Goodman, the late Marion Barnhart, and I examined some muscles macro- and microscopically. To our suprise, under the microscope we found red blood cells, and in the immunological experiments we observed precipitin lines produced by ancient proteins (or their fragments).

The most recent discovery of a mammoth carcass—named Jarkov—was in Siberia in 1997, excavated in 1999.

▼ Woolly mammoths *(Mammuthus primigenius)* together with reindeer, portrayed on the River Somme, France, during the fourth glacial period. The best known of the extinct elephantids, this animal is characteristic of the third and final phase of proboscidean radiation. It lived in Arctic regions of Europe, Asia and western North America during the Ice Age. Contemporaneous with humans, it is portrayed in cave paintings and its remains are found in middens at several prehistoric sites.

American Museum of Natural History

MY EXPERIENCES WITH THE LATE HENRY FAIRFIELD OSBORN

EDWIN H. COLBERT

The two genera encompassing three species of living elephants represent a sadly diminished remnant of a once varied and abundant class of mammals, which were widely distributed throughout the earth during some fifty million years of geological time. For a proper understanding of the elephants now living in Africa and Asia it is necessary to view them against their long evolutionary history. And in the elucidation of this history Henry Fairfield Osborn looms large among paleontological scholars.

It was my destiny to have worked in close association with Osborn as his research assistant during the last five years of his life. Thus I became well acquainted with him during those years. As one of the few people now living who knew Osborn, I will attempt in this brief sketch to present a vignette of the man, especially as he appeared to me during those final years when he was devoting much of his time and energy to the completion of his vast publication on the Proboscidea, which was such an important part of his life.

First it may be helpful to look at Osborn as a person. He was a large and dignified man who stood high in the scientific world, and who in those final years of his life had a rather overwhelming appreciation of his own scientific reputation. For this reason his personality grated on the sensibilities of many scientists of the day, who considered him as almost insufferably conceited and even arrogant. Yet he must be viewed in the context of his times. He was a child of wealth and used to having his own way, yet he was a hard-working, dedicated scholar with large and visionary ideas.

Early in his career he foresaw for himself the writing and the publication of several large monographs on fossil vertebrates, one of them to be concerned with the proboscideans.

The initiation of this particular project may be dated back to 1900, when Osborn published a paper on the angulation of the limbs in the elephants and certain other large mammals. Beginning with that paper and up to the appearance of the first volume of the Proboscidea monograph, he published altogether some fifty-seven papers dealing with the subject of the evolution and distribution of this particular order of mammals through time.

When I joined Osborn on the Proboscidea project in 1930 he was, of course, well along with his studies. He had completed work on the first volume of the monograph, devoted to the moeritheres, deinotheres, and mastodons (although this work was not published until 1936, the year after his death) and was busily engaged with the second volume, on the stegodons and the elephants, fossil and recent. The problem of the moment had to do with the length of enamel in the third upper and lower molars of various elephants, and the significance of this enamel length, not only as related to the

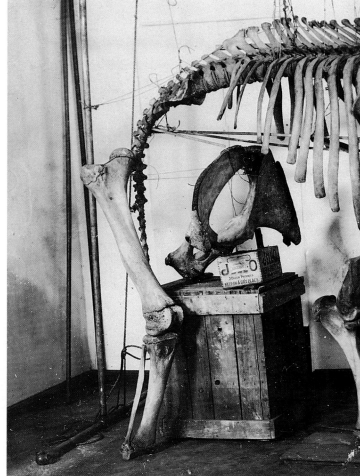

Photographs courtesy Edwin H. Colbert

evolutionary development of the elephants through Pleistocene time, but also as to the subdivision of the Pleistocene epoch.

Since the elephants of early Pleistocene time had smaller molars with fewer dental laminae and therefore shorter cumulative enamel lengths than the late Pleistocene forms, Osborn thought that here was a measure of elephant evolution and of Pleistocene time as well. So in my first years with Osborn I spent many hours measuring elephant third molar enamel lengths, often utilizing teeth that had been longitudinally sectioned with a specially designed rock saw. The measurements obtained, and frequently supplemented by numerous extrapolations, eventually revealed that in many of the advanced elephants the cumulative enamel lengths amounted to as much as 9 meters (about 30 feet) per third molar.

All of this pleased Osborn, and he decided to present the results at a meeting of the American Philosophical Society in Philadelphia. Lantern slides would not suffice. He had to have full-scale, colored bar diagrams, on strips of heavy paper 9 meters (about 30 feet) long. These I displayed at the meeting, holding one end of each long strip while Professor William Sinclair of Princeton University, who had been dragooned for the purpose by Osborn, held the other end. Sinclair did not particularly agree with Osborn on this enamel length technique, so while Osborn lectured, Sinclair held up his end of the chart and grumbled away, providing a discordant obligato accompaniment to Osborn's words. Subsequently, at a meeting of the British Association for the Advancement of Science in London, the performance was repeated, without Sinclair's dissensions.

I wasn't entirely in agreement with Osborn either, and on numerous occasions I made my objections to elephant enamel and other Osbornian concepts known to him. He did not like to be opposed, yet I felt that it was my duty to tell him how I saw things. In the end I think he respected me for my divergent views, even though he did not always accept them.

For five years such was my role. I studied fossil proboscideans for Osborn at the American Museum and at various other museums in the United States and Europe. I presented him with written reports and tables of measurements, the results of this research, many of which he incorporated into his own text for the Proboscidea monograph. And in particular I worked on the problem of stratigraphic and geographic relationships of the proboscideans.

Henry Fairfield Osborn died quietly, and without warning, in late 1935, with the second volume of the monograph still unfinished. It was up to those of us who remained to complete the work, which we did. The massive work appeared in 1942.

▼ (Left) Osborn takes a genial pause from his studies. This snapshot was taken on a clear, sunny day in the early 1930s when he was about 75 years old. The dress is typical of Osborn in the field: smart attire with necktie, showing little evidence of having performed messy work with a pick and shovel.
(Center) Colbert working on the skeleton of a small African elephant that he mounted at the University of Nebraska State Museum in 1929. He was a graduate student assistant in the Museum at the time.
(Right) The 29-year-old Colbert on a Sunday walk in upper Manhattan, New York City, in 1934. Amongst other things, he was then serving as Osborn's research assistant, working on the second volume of the massive Proboscidea monograph.

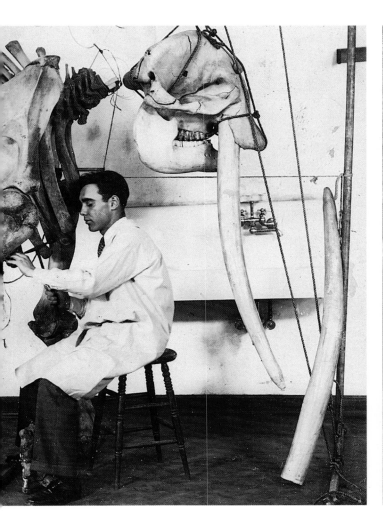

COMPARING THE LIVING ELEPHANTS

JEHESKEL SHOSHANI

▼ An Asian elephant feeds on grass in Yala National Park, Sri Lanka. One of the fundamental differences between Asian and African elephants is that the former are essentially grazers, while African elephants are mostly browsers, feeding mainly on tree foliage, bark, and fruit.

For those of us who study mammalian or proboscidean evolution, comparing two species is meaningless if the aim is to reconstruct their evolutionary history because two species will always be close to each other. Thus, we must have at least one more species, preferably the entire "cast of characters" within the Proboscidea, in order to better understand the similarities and differences between living species.

POSITION OF THE LIVING ELEPHANTS ON THE "FAMILY TREE"

Conducting a comprehensive approach provides us with a database for determining which of the two living genera is more primitive (generalist) or derived (specialist) than the other. The determination of relatively generalist versus specialist between the African and the Asian elephants is the fundamental foundation for our understanding of the differences in their anatomy, behavior, and ecology.

Based on the available evidence, scientists believe that at the base of the "elephant family tree" are pig-sized mammals which lived some 60–50 million years ago. They made up the basic stock from which other elephant-like creatures, collectively known as proboscideans, evolved. The earliest proboscideans did not have trunks, and their tusks were small. In fact they did not resemble the living elephants as we know them today. Those which bear closest resemblance to the living elephants are mammoths and American mastodons whose remains are often unearthed in the northern hemisphere, especially in the Arctic Circle. Superficially, bones of mammoths and mastodons, and those of the African and the Asian

▼ A magnificent African elephant strides slowly across a waterhole in Botswana taking up a trunkful of water as it goes. Unlike many mammals, the elephant's testes are located deep within the body. In both sexes the genitalia are more or less concealed in folds of baggy skin, and there are few other external clues to sex. In the African elephant both sexes have tusks, but in the Asian elephant tusks are largely confined to the male.

▲ An African elephant of the forest species *Loxodonta cyclotis*, Garamba, Democratic Republic of the Congo. This species differs from other populations of the African elephant in being substantially smaller, and in having slenderer, straighter tusks, which are often parallel in front view.

▶ The trunk of the African elephant looks more wrinkled and more flexible than that of the Asian elephant, and has two "fingers" at the tip rather than only one.

from the evolutionary tree that mammoths (genus *Mammuthus*) and the living Asian elephants (genus *Elephas*) were more closely related to each other than either of them is to the living African elephants (genus *Loxodonta*). It is generally accepted that among the four proboscidean taxa mentioned above, *Mammut* is the most primitive, followed successively by *Loxodonta*, *Elephas*, and *Mammuthus*; the last being the most specialized. Pertinent to our species comparison, then, *Loxodonta* exhibits more primitive characters than *Elephas*. Further, it is believed that between the species of the African elephant, the forest-dweller (*L. cyclotis*) is more primitive that the bush-dweller (*L. africana*) for the following reason. Except for island populations, the trend in mammalian evolution is to become bigger. The original population probably lived in forested areas and contained smaller individuals—subsequent generations grew bigger and taller and inhabited more open gallery forests and savannahs.

SPECIES COMPARISON

Here we start with zero assumptions and stress the similarities between the living elephants and then proceed with the differences. The most obvious shared similarity is the possession of a proboscis, or a trunk as it is commonly known. This feature was used by early naturalists to group them in the order Proboscidea. Other shared external features include the large size with an overall arch-shaped body from tip of trunk to tip of tail, relatively large ears, long tusks, lack of hair on most body parts, columnar legs, and the inguinal (between the hind legs) position of the genitalia of both males and females. Internal anatomical similarities include thick skin (hence the name "pachydermous"), lungs attached to the diaphragm, heart with double apices (instead of the typical one-point mammalian heart), two anterior vena cavae, lack of a gall bladder, testes located inside the abdomen near the kidneys, and brain well protected in the cranium— the walls of which are composed of thick yet light bones (due to diploe, or "honeycomb" structure). This list is by no means complete, nor is it intended to imply that all are specialized characters; rather, it gives a starting point for this discussion.

The contrast between the living elephant species becomes clearer when we take a closer look at the features that make them so unlike. These characters are summarized in the table. It is well known that the most obvious superficial difference between the African and the Asian elephant is the size of their ears—those of the African are larger. An important anatomical difference is found in the structures of the chewing surfaces of their teeth— that of the African elephant is composed of lozenge-shaped plates (hence the name "Lox" meaning lozenge, and "odon" referring to a tooth), whereas the plates on a tooth of an Asian elephant are closed compressed loops. There are,

elephants resemble each other. Note however that basic differences become evident once these bones are examined carefully.

Early naturalists believed that the American mastodons were the predecessors of mammoths or other members of the family Elephantidae. We know today that this is unlikely. A glance at the evolutionary tree of the Proboscidea on pages 26–27 reveals that the branch of the American mastodon *(Mammut americanum)* terminates.

Anatomical differences between the living species provide the basis for zoological classifications. In the partial classification of the Proboscidea on page 22, note that elephants and American mastodons are placed in different families to stress how different they are. It is also evident however, many other differences, some (only the highlights) of which are listed in the table.

African elephants are generally heavier and taller; a bull African may weigh 7,000 kilograms (about 15,430 pounds) and measure as much as 4 meters (over 13 feet) tall. The African has a concave back, as compared with the Asian which is convex. Tusks are usually present in the African elephant of either sex; in the Asians mostly in the males. The trunk of the African has more folds of skin in the form of "rings" or annulations, and its tip possesses two instead of one finger-like process. The trunk of the African species appears to be "floppy", while that of the Asian seems slightly more rigid (this can best be seen when they raise their trunks towards their forehead; that of *Loxodonta* flattens, while that of *Elephas* does not). Anatomical differences are usually manifested in corresponding observable behavior. One scientist demonstrated how captive African elephants pick up objects with their trunks using the "pinch" method (the two "fingers" are used to hold an object and bring it to the mouth), while the Asians rely mostly on the "grasp" method (the end of the trunk is curled around an object which is "squeezed" and brought to the mouth) but sometimes they would use the "pinch" method.

SPECIES COMPARISON
The African elephant (*Loxodonta africana*)
The subspecies of the living elephants which are compared in the accompanying table are based mostly on external characters. The two species for the African and the three subspecies for the Asian elephant are a synthesis of the many more subspecies assigned in the past. Differences between the bush African elephant (*Loxodonta africana*) and the forest African elephant (*Loxodonta cyclotis*) include these features: *L. cyclotis* is not as tall as *L. africana*; the ears of *L. cyclotis* are more rounded; and *L. cyclotis* has straighter and more slender tusks than those of *L. africana*.

Other less obvious and apparently inconsistent differences have been noted. *L. cyclotis* has a darker skin; has more hair, especially on the trunk and around the mouth; and has 4 instead of 3 "toe-nails" in the forefoot and 5 instead of 3 in the rear foot of adults. The habitat of the bush elephant (*L. africana*) species is different from that of the forest (*L. cyclotis*) species; as their names imply, the latter occupies areas with greater canopy forest than that of the former. Adaptations to such vastly differing environments undoubtedly accounted for the overall anatomy and natural history of these species. The so-called "pygmy" elephants attracted much attention for centuries. It appears that all the "pygmy" and/or "water" elephants have been varieties of the forest and/or the bush African elephant species. The two African elephants, hitherto considered subspecies, have been elevated to species level; the accumulating

MAJOR DIFFERENCES BETWEEN THE AFRICAN AND THE ASIAN ELEPHANT

	AFRICAN (*Loxodonta africana*)	ASIAN (*Elephas maximus*)

Weight	4,000–7,000 kilograms (8,820–15,430 pounds)	3,000–5,000 kilograms (6,615–11,020 pounds)
Height at shoulder	3–4 meters (10–13 feet)	2–3.5 meters (6 feet 7 inches–11 feet 6 inches)
Skin	More wrinkled	Smoother
Number of ribs	Up to 21 pairs	Up to 20 pairs
Highest point	At top of shoulder	At top of head
Size of ears (pinnae)	Larger, do exceed height of neck	Smaller, do not exceed height of neck
In mature individuals dorsal of pinnae	Fold medially	Fold laterally
Shape of back	Concave	Convex or level
Shape of belly	Slopes diagonally downwards from front to back	Either almost horizontal or "sagging" in the middle
Shape of head	No compression; no bulges, no dish 	Compressed antero-posteriorly; has dorsal bulges, dished forehead
Teeth	Lozenge-shaped loops	Narrow compressed loops
Food	Mostly browser	Mostly grazer
Tusks	Both sexes possess tusks; larger in males	Males usually carry tusks; in females tusks are vestigial or absent
Trunk	Has more rings (annulated) Less rigid	Appears to have less annulation More rigid
Tip of trunk	Two "fingers" 	One "finger"
Number of nail-like structures (toes)	Forefeet 4 or 5 Hind feet 3, 4 or 5	Forefeet 5 Hind feet 4 or 5

MAJOR DIFFERENCES AMONG SPECIES AND SUBSPECIES OF ELEPHANTS

WITHIN THE AFRICAN ELEPHANTS, LOXODONTA SP.*

	Bush species (L. africana)	Forest species (L. cyclotis)
Weight	4,000–7,000 kilograms (8,820–15,430 pounds)	2,000–4,500 kilograms (4,410–10,000 pounds)
Height at shoulder	3–4 meters (10–13 feet)	2–3 meters (6 feet 7 inches–10 feet)
Skin	On average lighter	On average darker
Shape and size of ears	Triangular, extend below line of neck	Rounder, do not extend below line of neck
Skull, cranium	Much pneumatized	Less pneumatized
Skull, mandible	Shorter	Longer
Tusks	Curved out and forward, thicker	Straighter, downpointing, slender
Number of nail-like structures ("toes") in adults	Forefeet 4 or 5 Hind feet 3, 4 or 5	Forefeet 5 Hind feet 4 or 5

WITHIN THE ASIAN ELEPHANTS, ELEPHAS MAXIMUS**

	Sri Lankan subspecies (E. m. maximus)	Mainland subspecies (E. m. indicus)	Sumatran subspecies (E. m. sumatranus)
Weight	2,000–5,500 kilograms (4,410–12,125 pounds)	2,000–5,000 kilograms (4,410–11,020 pounds)	2,000–4,000 kilograms (4,410–8,820 pounds)
Shoulder height	2–3.5 meters (6 feet 7 inches– 11 feet 6 inches)	2–3.5 meters (6 feet 7 inches– 11 feet 6 inches)	2–3.2 meters (6 feet 7 inches– 10 feet 6 inches)
Skin color	Darkest, with large and distinct patches of depigmentation on ears, face, trunk, and belly	Color and de-pigmenation in between the other two subspecies	Lightest, with least depigmentation
Size of ears	Most have large ears	Vary in size	Apear large compared to body size
Tusks incidence	Lowest	Intermediate	Possibly the highest
Number of ribs	19 pairs	19 pairs	20 pairs

*Loxodonta cyclotis is more primitive than L. africana for these reasons: forest dweller, smaller, slender and downpointing tusks, and other skull characters discussed by Grubb et al. (2000).**Elephas maximus sumatranus is possibly the most primitive Asian subspecies for these reasons: forest dweller, smallest, has largest number of ribs, possibly has highest incidence of tusks, has least depigmented skin and other characters discussed by Deraniyagala (1955).

Jana Schneider/The Image Bank

evidence compelled us to re-evaluate their systematic positions.

The Asian elephant *(Elephas maximus)*

Subspecies differences of the Asian elephant are not as distinct as those of the African elephant. According to some authors, the three subspecies of the Asian elephant are *Elephas maximus maximus*, the Sri Lankan Asian elephant (found on the island of Sri Lanka, formerly Ceylon); *E. m. indicus*, the mainland Asian elephant (found in India and Indochina); and *E. m. sumatranus*, the Sumatran

Asian elephant (found on the island of Sumatra). The distinguishing characters among these three forms could be a part of evolutionary trends or a matter of degree of change of a character from one extreme to another—beginning at Sri Lanka and ending with Sumatra at the east. (The elephants on the island of Borneo are believed to be descendants of elephants from the mainland.) A generalized change in the characters among the elephants across their range from the east to the west is as follows. Elephants from Sumatra are the smallest, the lightest in color, and the least

depigmented. Those elephants from Sri Lanka (the other extreme) are the largest and the darkest in color and possess the largest ears. They have distinct patches of depigmentation on their ears, faces, trunks and bellies. The elephants from Indochina, Myanmar (formerly Burma), Thailand, Laos, Vietnam, Cambodia and China—an area between the two extremes—exhibit a mixture of characters; their size, color, and depigmenation are between the other two forms.

Alain Compost/Bruce Coleman Limited

▲ Perhaps the most immediately obvious single difference in appearance between Asian and African elephants is that an Asian elephant's back (as seen here) is humped or rounded, while the back of an African elephant sags noticeably between the shoulders and hips.

◄ A young Sumatran elephant at Nay Kambas National Park, Indonesia. This easternmost population of the Asian elephant is distinguished from mainland populations by its smaller size and weight, and paler skin.

FAMILY ELEPHANTIDAE
Loxodonta africana
The bush African elephant

APPEARANCE This is the largest living land mammal. In front the elephant has a prehensile appendage, the trunk, which can reach the ground, and at the rear it has a relatively long tail with hair reaching the heel. From tip of trunk to tip of tail, the total length may be 7–8.8 meters (23–29 feet). The profile of the back is concave. The long and flexible trunk with two "fingers" at its tip can weigh 150–200 kilograms (330–440 pounds). The ears are enormous and may reach about half of the height of an individual. In contrast, the eyes are small and are protected with long eyelashes. Hair can be seen at the tip of the tail, on the chin, and in the elbow and knee regions. The skin color is light gray, but it can vary in appearance to reddish brown depending on the color of the soil and mud where the elephants may have bathed and dusted. A close examination of the head reveals that in profile that of the male is round whereas that of the female is angular. Males usually carry longer and heavier tusks.

SIZE An adult bush African elephant may reach 4 meters (about 13 feet) in height and weigh 7,000 kilograms (about 15,430 pounds). Males are larger than females of comparable ages.

HABITAT AND DISTRIBUTION The species occupies a variety of habitats from open grasslands to forested regions, including open arid savannas or deserts, and the contrasting wet areas of marshes and lake shores, from sea level to mountainous regions above the snowlines. Its distribution spans most of the African continent below the Sahara.

REPRODUCTION Elephants mate in the usual quadruped position. The young are born after a gestation period of 18–22 months, the longest pregnancy of any known living mammal. Elephants usually give birth to a single offspring, rarely twins. Newborns weigh about 75–115 kilograms (165–255 pounds) and measure approximately 100 centimeters (3 feet 3 inches) tall at the shoulder. Elephants reach sexual maturity between the ages of 8 and 13 years. Adult male African elephants exhibit a period of heightened sexual activity known as musth. The external reproductive organs are not easily distinguishable except during sexual activity. The vulval opening is located between the female's hind legs, not under the tail as in some other animals such as bovids and equines. This unusual position of the female genitalia can be confusing and has sometimes led to some males being identified as females. A female elephant can give birth every 4–6 years, and has the potential of giving birth to about 7 offspring in her lifetime, which may be 60–70 years.

DIET About three-quarters of the elephant's life is devoted to feeding or moving toward a food or water source. The diet is strictly herbivorous. Most elephants consume 75–150 kilograms (165–330 pounds) of food and 80–160 liters (20–40 gallons) of water per day, but very large males may eat twice this amount. The African elephant is adapted to be a browser rather than a grazer. Leaves of acacia trees are among the favorite delicacies; other foliage and fruits are consumed as well as grass species.

FAMILY ELEPHANTIDAE
Loxodonta cyclotis
The forest African elephant

APPEARANCE To the untrained observer, this species (*L. cyclotis*) is similar, if not identical, to the bush African elephant (*L. africana*). Indeed, unless they are compared next to each other (rarely in nature, but sometimes in captivity) they are not easily distinguishable. The most important observable differences are noticed in the ears and the tusks. In *L. cyclotis* the ears are smaller and rounder, and the tusks are more slender and straighter than in *L. africana*. Other differences are noted in the table on page 40.

SIZE Small individuals and females may weigh less than 2,000 kilograms (4,410 pounds) and adult males can weigh 4,500 kilograms (10,000 pounds). An adult male forest African elephant may reach 3 meters (about 10 feet) in height at the shoulder. Males are larger than females of comparable ages.

HABITAT AND DISTRIBUTION This species occurs in equatorial forested regions of central and western Africa, and its distribution may overlap with that of the bush African elephant, *L africana*. *L. cyclotis* also ventures into gallery forests and into areas which are intermediate between forests and grasslands.

REPRODUCTION Less is known about the reproduction of this species than of its closest relative, the bush African elephant species. Nevertheless, it is believed that all aspects of reproduction of the two African elephant species are very similar. This includes the length of the gestation period, which lasts 18–22 months. Single offspring is the rule, although twinning may occur. Newborns weigh about 50–100 kilograms (110–220 pounds) or more, and measure approximately 80–100 centimeters (2 feet 8 inches–3 feet 3 inches) tall at the shoulder. Sexual maturity is attained between the ages of 8 and 13 years. The external reproductive organs are not easily distinguishable except during sexual activity. A female elephant can give birth every 4–6 years, and has the potential of giving birth to about 7 offspring in her lifetime, which may be 60–70 years.

DIET About three-quarters of the elephant's life is devoted to feeding or moving toward a food or water source. The diet is strictly herbivorous. Most elephants may consume 60–120 kilograms (130–265 pounds) of food and 60–120 liters (16–32 gallons) of water per day. This species is adapted to a browsing diet more than any other living elephant. Leaves and fruits constitute the main food items, but they are not the only items on its menu; certain grasses and roots may be favored at different times.

FAMILY ELEPHANTIDAE
Elephas maximus maximus
The Sri Lankan Asian elephant

APPEARANCE The profile of the back, unlike that of the African elephant, is convex or level instead of concave. Thus, in a side view from the tip of the trunk to the tip of the tail, this elephant appears like one huge arch; the total length may be 6.7–8 meters (22–26 feet). Another obvious difference between the African and the Asian elephant is the size of the ears; those of the Asian are smaller and do not exceed the height of the neck. Other differences appear in the table on page 39. The long and flexible trunk with one "finger" at its tip can weigh 125–200 kilograms (275–440 pounds). Generally, the Asian elephant has more hair on its body than the African elephant; it is seen on top of their heads and backs, and it is especially conspicuous on the newborn and young. The body color is dark gray of different shades, depending on the color of the soil and mud where the elephants have bathed and dusted. Often there are areas where the skin is depigmented, with white blotches on the ears, face, trunk and belly. The head of the male has large and pronounced bulges; those of the female are smaller. In addition, males may carry tusks (in some cases even longer and heavier than those of the African species). While the occurrence of tusks in females is not common, it is more frequent than generally believed.
SIZE An adult Asian elephant from Sri Lanka may reach 3.5 meters (11 feet 6 inches) in shoulder height and weigh 5,500 kilograms (12,125 pounds). Males are larger than females of comparable ages.
HABITAT AND DISTRIBUTION This subspecies is confined to the island of Sri Lanka (65,605 square kilometers, 25,332 square miles)

off the southern coast of India. It occupies a variety of habitats from open grasslands to forested regions, including open savannas, wet areas of marshes and lake shores, from sea level to mountainous regions. *E. m. maximus* is often found in transitional habitats (ecotones) between forests and grasslands where a greater variety of food types is available.
REPRODUCTION Like the African elephant, the Asian elephant secretes fluid from the musth gland during musth (a period of heightened sexual activity and aggressive behavior) although the chemical content and consistency of this fluid may be different. The young are born after a gestation period of 18–22 months. Elephants usually give birth to a single offspring, rarely twins, and more rarely triplets. Newborns weigh about 75–115 kilograms (165–255 pounds) and measure approximately 100 centimeters (3 feet 3 inches) tall at the shoulder. Elephants reach sexual maturity between the ages of 8 and 13 years. A female elephant can give birth every 4–6 years, and has the potential of giving birth to about 7 offspring in her lifetime, which may be 60–70 years.
DIET About three-quarters of the elephant's life is devoted to feeding or moving toward a food or water source. The diet is strictly herbivorous. Most elephants consume 75–150 kilograms (165–330 pounds) of food and 80–160 liters (20–40 gallons) of water per day, but very large males may eat twice that. The Asian elephant is adapted to be a grazer rather than a browser. A variety of grass species is consumed, as well as juicy leaves and fruits.

FAMILY ELEPHANTIDAE
Elephas maximus indicus
The mainland Asian elephant

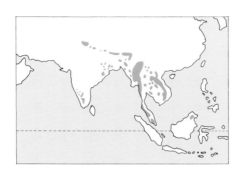

APPEARANCE Variations in body size, shape and color of
E. m. indicus correspond to its varied distribution in many Asian
countries. It resembles the Sri Lankan elephant, although it may be
lighter gray in color, and the depigmented areas are reduced to the
ears and trunk. Both sexes may have tusks. They occur more
frequently and are larger in males than in females.

SIZE Ranging in size between the Sri Lankan *(E. m. maximus)* and
the Sumatran *(E. m. sumatranus)* elephant, an adult mainland Asian
elephant *(E. m. indicus)* may reach 3.5 meters (11 feet 6 inches) in
height and weigh 5,000 kilograms (11,020 pounds). As in other
subspecies, males are larger than females of comparable ages.

HABITAT AND DISTRIBUTION This subspecies is found in 12
Asian countries on the mainland of Asia: from India in the west
to Indonesia in the east (the elephants of northern Borneo are said
to be descendants of domesticated stock from the mainland).
E. m. indicus occupies a variety of habitats but it appears to prefer
forested areas (often those with galleries) and transitional zones
(ecotones) between forests and grasslands where a greater variety

of food types is available. Its habitats range from sea level to
mountainous regions at about 2,000 meters (6,500 feet) above sea
level or even higher.

REPRODUCTION In the mainland Asian elephant reproduction is
the same as for the other Asian elephant subspecies. The young are
born after a gestation period of 18–22 months. Elephants usually
give birth to a single offspring, rarely twins, and more rarely triplets.
Newborns weigh about 75–115 kilograms (165–255 pounds) and
measure approximately 100 centimeters (3 feet 3 inches) tall at the
shoulder. Elephants reach sexual maturity between the ages of 8 and
13 years. A female elephant can give birth every 4–6 years, and has
the potential of giving birth to about 7 offspring in her lifetime,
which may be 60–70 years.

DIET About three-quarters of the elephant's life is devoted to
feeding or moving toward a food or water source. Elephants
consume 75–150 kilograms (165–330 pounds) or more of food and
80–160 liters (20–40 gallons) of water per day. A variety of grass
species is consumed, as well as tender twigs, barks, leaves, and fruits.

FAMILY ELEPHANTIDAE
Elephas maximus sumatranus
The Sumatran Asian elephant

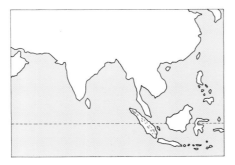

APPEARANCE Of the three subspecies of the Asian elephant, *E. m. sumatranus* is the smallest, the shortest, the lightest in color and the least depigmented; depigmentation is confined to the ears. The ears of some individuals appear to be larger than those of either of the other two subspecies, but this difference may be due to the small body size of the Sumatran elephants observed. All other features are similar to those of *E. m. maximus* and *E. m. indicus*.

SIZE The smallest of the three Asian subspecies, an adult Sumatran elephant may reach 3.2 meters (10 feet 6 inches) in shoulder height and weigh over 4,000 kilograms (8,820 pounds). As in other subspecies, males are larger than females of comparable ages.

HABITAT AND DISTRIBUTION This subspecies is found mostly in forested regions and in patchy habitats. It is confined to the island of Sumatra (414,000 square kilometers, 160,000 square miles).

REPRODUCTION   Reproduction in the Sumatran subspecies is the same as for the other Asian elephant subspecies. Young are born after a gestation period of 18–22 months. Elephants usually give birth to a single offspring, rarely twins, and more rarely triplets. Newborns weigh about 75–115 kilograms (165–255 pounds) and measure approximately 100 centimeters (3 feet 3 inches) tall at the shoulder. Elephants reach sexual maturity between the ages of 8 and 13 years. A female elephant can give birth every 4–6 years, and has the potential of giving birth to about 7 offspring in her lifetime, which may be 60–70 years.

DIET   About three-quarters of the elephant's life is devoted to feeding or moving toward a food or water source. The diet is strictly herbivorous. Most elephants consume 75–150 kilograms (165–330 pounds) of food and 80–160 liters (20–40 gallons) of water per day. A variety of plant species is eaten, as well as tender twigs, fruits, and leaves.

PROBING PREHISTORIC PROTEINS

JEROLD M. LOWENSTEIN

Istarted out trying to track ancient apes and humans but found myself on the trail of mammoths and mastodons instead. It happened like this. I'm a physician who specializes in nuclear medicine. Years ago my interest in the evolution of the thyroid gland drew me to the Galapagos Islands, where I studied the thyroid function of marine iguanas and lava lizards. Later I met and married Adrienne Zihlman, a professor of anthropology at the University of California, Santa Cruz, who does research on human origins.

In 1976 Adrienne went to an anthropology conference in Cambridge, England, and I came along. I was fascinated by the emotional debates between competing schools of anthropologists. Some thought that a fourteen-million-year-old fossil hominoid called *Ramapithecus* was the earliest human ancestor. But a group of molecular anthropologists said that *Ramapithecus* couldn't be human, because the human lineage is not much more than five million years old. They found that human, gorilla and chimpanzee proteins were 99 percent identical and, from known rates of protein evolution, that meant these three "African hominoids" had a common ancestor—presumably an ape—about five million years ago.

From the arguments for and against *Ramapithecus*' hominid status, it seemed that it might be possible to clarify evolutionary questions like this by studying the proteins in the fossils themselves. I knew the amounts of protein left in fossils would be very small, if there were any at all, but in my medical research I had used a technique called radioimmunoassay (RIA) which is capable of detecting very low concentrations of various proteins in blood and tissues. I decided to see if this technique would work on fossils.

After several months of trying different techniques, I settled on a method called solid phase double antibody RIA. First, the protein to be tested, or a solution extracted from fossils, is placed in a little plastic cup, where some of the protein sticks to the plastic (that's why it's called a solid phase). Second, antisera made by injecting proteins into rabbits are added to the cup, and some of these antibodies bind to the plastic-bound protein. Next, a second antibody, made by injecting rabbit antibody into goats, is added to the cup, and these antibodies have a radioactive label. The amount of radioactivity in the cup tells how much protein there is, and the antibodies are highly specific for particular animals.

I was now ready to test my RIA on a fossil. Someone had given me a bone of an Egyptian mummy which was three thousand years old. Extracts from this bone tested positive for human collagen (the main structural protein of bone) and human albumin (the main serum protein)!

At this point I applied to the National Science Foundation for research support. My proposal was rejected. The expert reviewers wrote that everyone knows there are no proteins left in fossil bones; the proteins, they said, are completely replaced by minerals. It didn't matter that my test on the mummy showed otherwise.

One day I visited Vince Sarich at Berkeley. He is the molecular anthropologist who first questioned the establishment view of *Ramapithecus* as a human ancestor. I showed him my RIA results, and he suggested I join the hunt for mammoth proteins going on in Allan Wilson's lab, where Vince works. Wilson had managed to get a piece of muscle from Dima, a frozen baby mammoth.

▼ (Below) The famous Dima, an eight-month-old mammoth, being examined at a laboratory in Saint Petersburg in 1977. Its body was found frozen in an excavation site in north-eastern Siberia on June 23, 1977; radio-carbon dating indicates it died about 40,000 years ago.

▼ (Bottom) Investigating protein by radioimmunoassay (RIA) requires these steps: first, a sample of protein extract, an "antigen", is placed in a microcup and some of the proteins bind to the plastic; second, antibodies against proteins of various species produced in rabbits are added to the well; third, radioactive antibodies produced in goats against rabbit antibodies are finally added to the cup.

UPI/The Bettmann Archive

A Protein solution in microtiter cup

B Rabbit antibody binds to protein

C Radioactive goat antibody binds to rabbit antibody

Dima had been unearthed from the Siberian permafrost in 1977 after being preserved there for forty thousand years. The Berkeley lab had made antisera to the albumins of the two living species of elephants, African and Asian, but the amount of albumin in Dima's muscle was too low to detect by the standard immunological method of complement fixation.

RIA is a thousand times more sensitive than complement fixation. When I tested extracts of Dima's muscle for elephant albumin, the levels were so high that I had to dilute the solution to bring it down into measurable range.

Not only was there plenty of albumin in the samples (actually, it was about 1 percent, as much as would be found in a living elephant's muscle), but it was more than 99 percent identical immunologically to the albumins of the Asian and African elephants, which are more than 99 percent identical with each other. This means that these three proboscideans, like the human–chimpanzee–gorilla trio, had a common ancestor within the past five million years.

Now, for the first time, it was demonstrably possible to study the molecular evolution of extinct as well as extant species. Based on similarities of the teeth, it had been thought that the mammoth was more closely related to the Asian than to the African elephant, but RIA showed a three-way split with no pair closer than any other.

Jeheskel Shoshani and Morris Goodman at Wayne State University were also working on mammoth proteins, and I collaborated with them in comparing the concentrations of albumin and collagen in three Siberian mammoths of different ages. Naturally, the older fossils had less protein, and we could show with RIA precisely how much these proteins decreased with time.

It's perhaps not too surprising that deep-frozen mammoth proteins survived for thousands of years. But what about bones buried at normal temperatures? A fossil mastodon called Elmer, discovered while excavating for a Michigan housing project, helped to answer that question. Shoshani made extracts of Elmer's bones and injected these extracts into rabbits to make antisera.

RIA demonstrated the presence of elephant-like albumin and collagen, making it possible for the first time on the molecular level to show the evolutionary relationship between the extinct mastodon and mammoth and the two extant species of elephant.

Paleontologists have come up with many different hypotheses about the relationships of the dozens of kinds of proboscideans found in the fossil record of the past fifty million years. The protein probe provides us with molecular evidence, which is independent of the standard comparisons of bones and teeth, as another tool for tracing elephantine evolution.

▼ The family tree of the mammoth and its living and extinct uranothere relatives: elephants, mastodons, Steller's sea cows, and hyraxes. It is assumed from geological evidence that this group diverged from other mammals about 65 million years ago. Traditional results based on tooth and skull similarities, and findings from recent molecular studies, show that mammoths are closer to Asian than to African elephants. Immunological results shown in this chart suggest that the mammoth is equidistant from the African and Asian elephants rather than closer to the latter. The different results obtained by traditional versus molecular methods may be due to the degradation of the 40,000-year-old protein of the mammoth.

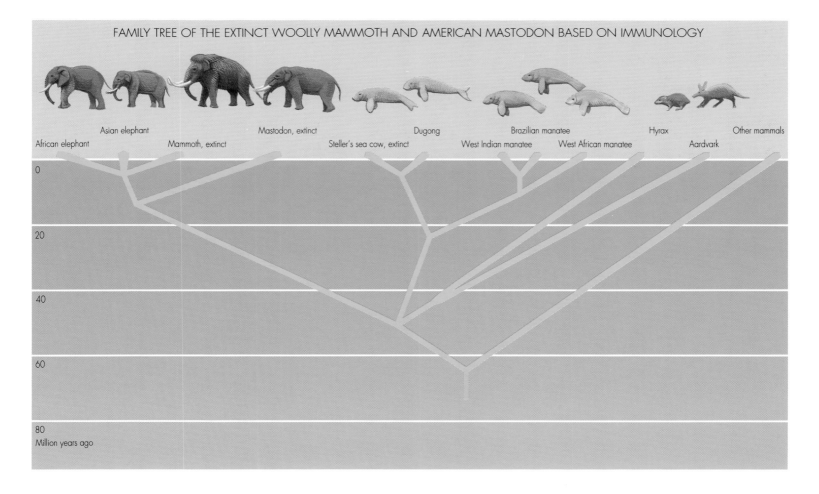

FAMILY TREE OF THE EXTINCT WOOLLY MAMMOTH AND AMERICAN MASTODON BASED ON IMMUNOLOGY

African elephant | Asian elephant | Mammoth, extinct | Mastodon, extinct | Steller's sea cow, extinct | Dugong | West Indian manatee | Brazilian manatee | West African manatee | Hyrax | Aardvark | Other mammals

0

20

40

60

80
Million years ago

THE MAMMOTH SITE OF HOT SPRINGS, SOUTH DAKOTA, USA

LARRY D. AGENBROAD

In June 1974, an extraordinary collection of mammoth remains was unearthed by accident on a construction site in Hot Springs, South Dakota, USA. The site is now considered the primary exhibit for the study of the mammoth in the western hemisphere.

Initial inventory of the bones found in the excavations revealed as many as six to eight mammoths. By 1976, paleontologists estimated that more than one hundred mammoths might be found but what seemed to be an optimistic prediction at the time is in fact more conservative today. By the close of the 1990 field season, the number uncovered had already reached 44 mammoths with approximately 70 percent of the site still unexplored.

Most of the animals have been identified as the Columbian mammoth *(Mammuthus columbi)*, but also three woolly mammoths *(Mammuthus primigenius)* have been discovered.

The site in which the ancient mammoths lie consists of tan to gray Pleistocene sand and silt, surrounded by a Permian–Triassic red shale. (The Pleistocene epoch covers the time from 1.7 million years ago to 11,000 years ago; the Permian–Triassic boundary occurred approximately 220 million years ago.)

As it stands today, the site is actually the reverse of its original topographic expression. While the bones were found near the top of a small hill in the local topography, this hill was actually once the floor of a large sinkhole (karst depression) in which the mammoths were entrapped. The sinkhole was caused by a collapse in subterranean limestone caverns that lay 100 meters (330 feet) below the surface. Situated at the southern end of an anticlinal (domal) uplift known as the Black Hills of South Dakota, the limestone carried abundant ground water under artesian pressure. This artesian water fed upward through the collapsed caverns, creating a warm, spring-fed pond in the bottom of the sinkhole. Three drill holes indicate the deposit is spoon-shaped. The depth of fill in the deepest area tested is more than 20 meters (66 feet).

Paleontologists believe it was either the warm water or the bankside vegetation—even in a late Pleistocene winter—that may have enticed young mammoths on a one-way trip, into the sinkhole.

To date, the most gentle slope paleontologists have exhumed for the sinkhole edge is 60 degrees, while the slope near the conduit varies from 60 degrees to overhanging. The hypothesis is that an animal with the body size and foot configuration of a mammoth became trapped in the pond if submoistening of the red shale above the pond occurred. The unfortunate victim could only await death by starvation or drowning. That scenario was repeated multiple times over a period estimated to range from as little as 300 years to as long as 1,000 years. Several radiocarbon dates place the time of active entrapment of the mammoth at approximately 26,000 years ago. As the bone collagen has been leached from the bone, these dates are primarily derived from bone apatite (chemical component of bone) and should be considered a minimal age.

▲ A view from the northeastern edge of the sinkhole. The excavation tiers shown here represent different seasonal increments between 1976 and 1979. There are more than eight mammoths partially exposed in this portion of the site. The skull of "Beauty", as it was named by the excavation crew, is one of many deposited in the sediments near the "eye" of the artesian spring.

The processes experienced by the skeletal remains (or taphonomy) provide several interesting conclusions. In the early sessions of excavation it became clear that certain skeletal elements were more abundant than others. For example paleontologists found there were relatively more flat, angular, or curved bones (scapulae, pelves, tusks) unearthed than there were long bones (humeri, femora, radii, ulnae). A working hypothesis is that by nature of their shape, flat, angular and curved bones rotated in the soil in a sideways and downwards path, remained high in the sedimentary fill, and were naturally the first to be discovered, while bones that were more cylindrical in shape rolled down the steep, subaqueous slopes of the pond floor. Because these would be at a greater depth in the excavation they would take longer to be found.

The skeletal structures of at least three whole mammoths were found relatively intact, while the skeletal remains of most of the victims indicate that they were possibly trampled by later victims or moved by a subaqueous down-slope movement.

Paleontologists also found complete articulated feet which indicate a low level of decomposition during deposition. In some specimens delicate bones such as hyoids (tongue support bones) had been preserved in their original anatomical position. A three-dimensional computer model is being developed to test some of the hypotheses for the taphonomic distributions.

By comparison with other studies, analysis of the age of the mammoths has provided an unexpected find, with 82 percent falling into the juvenile and young-adult categories. Paleontologists believe the population is most probably juvenile and young-adult males. This hypothesis is supported by a pelvic measurement ratio recently developed by Adrian Lister of Cambridge, England. It revealed that all pelves that could be measured for the appropriate criteria are male.

In addition to the mammoth, other animals were trapped in the site. Notable finds include the cranium, half the mandible, several vertebrae and ribs, plus some long bones, of the giant short-faced bear (Arctodus simus). Teeth of the gray wolf (Canis lupus), possibly of the coyote (Canis latrans), camel (Camelops sp.) and an undetermined variety of shrub ox have also been recovered. The bear was unquestionably part of the entrapped assemblage, whereas the remains of lesser animals may have been washed into the sinkhole from surrounding uplands. A variety of mammalian microfaunal remains have been recovered, plus fish and invertebrates. Pollen recovery has been sparse, but what has been found is indicative of a cold steppe–grassland environment.

The land containing the deposit and the area immediately surrounding it were sold by the owner/contractor Phil Anderson at cost to a newly developed non-profit organization—The Mammoth Site of Hot Springs, South Dakota, Incorporated. The initial idea was to develop the excavation in a manner that would keep the majority of specimens in situ, just as they were deposited.

In 1976, Mr Anderson donated materials and labor for a small temporary structure over a portion of the site. In 1984–85 a large building, covering the entire sinkhole, was erected. The Mammoth Site now has a facility of more than 2,100 square meters (about 23,000 square feet) to house the remains as they are exposed, and to provide an interpretive exhibit area.

The Site has also developed an outreach program for regional schools, training for in-service teachers in summer workshops and for Earthwatch volunteers and has hosted an international symposium related to the Quaternary of that geographic region. It is open to the public, for guided tours, twelve months a year.

THE MAMMOTH "DEATH TRAP"

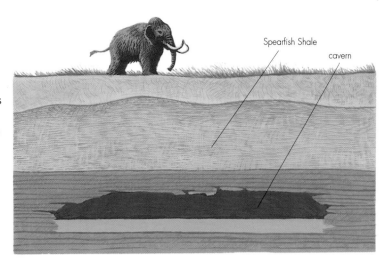

▲ Before about 26,000 years ago the area was stable, over an underground solution cavern in limestone, and posed no threat to the local mammoth population. When a portion of the cavern collapsed, a section of the overlying Spearfish Shale fell into the cavern void, creating a funnel-like shaft (a sinkhole).

▲ The caved-in column of rock (breccia pipe) provided a chimney through which water trapped beneath could escape. Mammoths, seeking to drink or feed on the edge of the spring-fed pond thus formed, slipped down the steep, muddy walls of Spearfish Shale to inescapable death.

▲ Over time, the weak shale encircling the sinkhole weathered away; however, the mammoth remains in the sinkhole, protected by a shroud of hardened sediments, were more resistant to erosion. What was originally sinkhole fill eventually became a hill above the modern ground level.

COMPARING MAMMOTHS AND MASTODONS

JEHESKEL SHOSHANI

Why is it so important to differentiate between mammoths and mastodons? It is important because, to the uninformed reader, they appear similar in terms of size and overall anatomical characters, and thus in the past, and to some extent at present, they are often considered as similar and belonging to the same "family".

DIFFERENCES BETWEEN EXTINCT MASTODONS AND MAMMOTHS

	American mastodon *Mammut americanum*	Mammoths For example, *Mammuthus primigenius*
BODY COVERING	1. Unknown. The possibility exists that body covering included underfur and long hair	1. Long hair, dense underwool; skin thickness similar to that of living elephants; subcutaneous fat up to 9.0 cm ($3^1/_2$ in) thick
SKELETON	1. On the whole, stockier, with heavier frame 2. Head and shoulders are slightly above hindquarters 3. More thoracic vertebrae (20–21 pairs)	1. More delicately built 2. Head and shoulders are much above hindquarters 3. Fewer thoracic vertebrae (18–20 pairs)
CRANIUM	1. Flattened on top and bottom (low-domed) 2. Borders of eye socket are rounder 3. Tusks project slightly below horizontal, curve outward and then inward	1. Flattened on front and back (high-domed) 2. Borders of eye socket are squarer 3. Tusks project much below horizontal, curve outward and then much more inward
MANDIBLE	1. Elongated 2. Sometimes possess a pair of incisors (tusks) at front	1. Shortened (brevirostry) 2. No incisors (see under dentition)
DENTITION	1. Nipple-like chewing surface (bunodont, adapted for browsing) 2. Low-crowned (brachyodont) 3. Crown without or with very little bonding material (cement) 4. Thicker enamel 5. Fewer ridges per a given length (low Laminary Index) 6. Dental formula is: $\dfrac{1\ 0\ 3\ 3}{0\ 0\ 3\ 3}$ or $\dfrac{1\ 0\ 3\ 3}{1\ 0\ 3\ 3}$, a total of 26–28 teeth	1. Flat chewing surface with ridges (lophodont, adapted for grazing) 2. High-crowned (hypsodont) 3. Crown with much cement 4. Thinner enamel 5. High Laminary Index 6. Dental formula is: $\dfrac{1\ 0\ 3\ 3}{0\ 0\ 3\ 3}$, a total of 26 teeth
FEEDING HABITS	1. Fed on a variety of plant material, twigs and leaves being most commonly eaten (mostly browser) 2. Jaws used in a crushing action mostly in side-to-side motion	1. Fed on a variety of plants, grasses being the most commonly eaten (mostly grazer) 2. Jaws used in grinding action in a forward-backward motion

Added to this confusion is the fact that they were contemporaries, that is, mammoths and mastodons lived during the same time interval. In North America their skeletal remains are sometimes found in the same excavation site (perhaps this might be compared to two unrelated persons being buried under an avalanche and being discovered a few generations later, and their discoverers assuming that they were husband and wife).

It is true that on a larger scale mastodons and mammoths are similar, in that they share some common features, just as do a dog and cat, or a chimpanzee and human. To help us better understand the similarities and differences between a mammoth and a mastodon, let us go back in time and study the entire "elephant family tree", not just two of its twigs.

At the base of this tree, some 60 to 50 million years ago, as scientists believe, pig-sized mammals made up the basic stock from which other elephant-like creatures, collectively known as proboscideans, evolved. Following the pathways of mammutids (family Mammutidae) and elephantids (family Elephantidae) as shown on the evolutionary tree on pages 26–27, we note that mammoths (genus *Mammuthus*, family Elephantidae) and mastodons (genus *Mammut*, family Mammutidae) were contemporaneous for a period spanning about 4 million years during the Pliocene and Pleistocene epochs. In North America their distribution overlapped, especially during the Pleistocene epoch, and particularly in the eastern part of the continent. Based on the available evidence, there were at least seven species of mammoths, and their geographic distributions ranged from sites in East Africa, Eurasia and North America. On the other hand, there were at least two species belonging to the genus *Mammut*, and its remains were found in Eurasia and North America (note, however, that both families are believed to have originated in East Africa).

A close examination of the evolutionary tree shows that the branch of the family Mammutidae does not rejoin the branch of the mammoths (family Elephantidae) but terminates. Mammutids, thus, were not the forefathers of mammoths or other members of the family Elephantidae, to which mammoths and living elephants belong. Another important observation on this evolutionary tree is the time of separation of mastodons and mammoths from the main trunk. Mammutids were the first to split and thus, in evolutionary terms, they possessed more generalized or more primitive characters than mammoths. Not only did mastodons diverge earlier (by about 20 million years) than the branch of mammoths but their skeletal anatomy did not change much during the last 25 million years of their history. Mammoths, on the other hand, have been part of a more specialized group (family Elephantidae) and changed significantly.

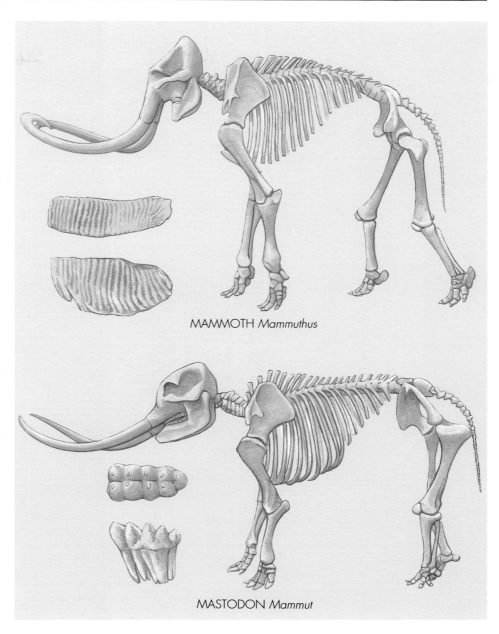

MAMMOTH *Mammuthus*

MASTODON *Mammut*

SKELETAL SIMILARITIES AND DIFFERENCES

The contrast between mastodons and mammoths becomes clearer when we take a closer look at the features that made them so unlike. These characters are summarized in the table and accompanying illustrations. Once these anatomical differences are understood, it should also become clearer how students use such data as a basis for zoological classifications, one of which is given in the table in the section, "Classification", see pages 22–23. In the evolutionary tree and the partial classification of the Proboscidea, note that not only are mammoths and mastodons not grouped together in the same family, but also they are placed in a different hierarchy between a family and an order to stress how different they are. It is also evident from the tree on pages 26–27 that the living Asian elephant (genus *Elephas*) is more closely related to mammoths (genus *Mammuthus*) than to the living African elephant (genus *Loxodonta*).

▲ Skeletons of a mammoth (top) and an American mastodon (bottom), and their respective teeth. At first glance the skeletons look very similar; on a closer look, however, that of the mammoth is more slender, and its skull is taller than that of the mastodon. The structure of their teeth also differed: that of the mastodon had rounded cusps, and it is believed to have been a browser more than a grazer, whereas the mammoth is said to have preferred grasses to branches, twigs, and leaves. Both mammals lived in North America and became extinct at the end of the Ice Age, about 10,000 years ago.

CLONING MAMMOTHS

VIKTOR M. MIKHELSON

In the upper north of Siberia there is an enormous area that is covered by what is known as "permafrost". In this area the ground, except for the surface soil, has temperatures below −5°C (23°F) even in summer; and it hasn't thawed for thousands of years. The bones and tusks of mammoths can be found here and sometimes whole mammoths' carcasses which have been preserved by ice entombment are found. No more than ten such discoveries have been recorded since the beginning of the eighteenth century, when Russian explorers came to Siberia for the first time.

► Viktor Mikhelson with the tusk of a mammoth found in permafrost on the banks of the River Semijariskiai, Siberia, in July, 1978.

Viktor Mikhelson

The soft tissue of these carcasses often looks remarkably well preserved and it has been recorded that draft dogs will willingly eat the meat of such mammoth remains. This has given rise to the hope that these carcasses might contain living cells, from which scientists may be able to clone living mammoths and so restore this extinct species.

In 1977 a group of gold diggers was working not far from the town of Magadan, in the upper reaches of the Kolyma River. In the ice lens at a depth of 2.5 meters (around 8 feet) they discovered the intact body of a baby mammoth which was dubbed "Dima". At the time of death it was approximately eight months of age. Radiocarbon dating indicated that the carcass was about 40,000 years old.

Samples from Dima were taken at the site, before the soft tissues thawed. Later, in the laboratory, we attempted, using a variety of culture techniques, to culture samples of psoas muscle (found in the lumbar region, close to the vertebral column), subcutaneous tissue, blood vessel wall, liver, kidney, and other tissues in the hope of finding live fibroblasts (cells found in fibrous connective tissue). None of these cultures was

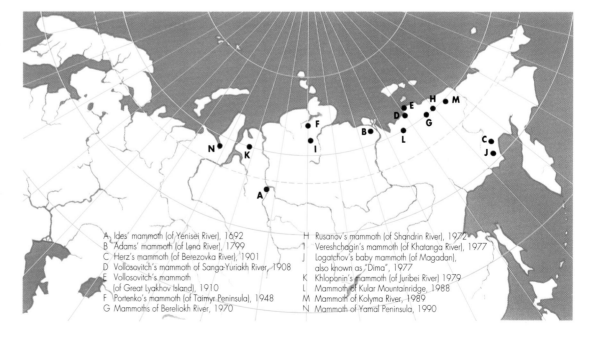

► A generalized map showing main localities where partial or complete carcasses of mammoths have been found. Note that the vast majority of these specimens were collected inside the Arctic circle (dashed line), Siberia, Russia. Not shown on this map are two locations in Alaska (USA) where mammoth tissue remains have also been found, and the discovery of Jarkov mammoth in 1997.

A Ides' mammoth (of Yenisei River), 1692
B Adams' mammoth (of Lena River), 1799
C Herz's mammoth (of Berezovka River), 1901
D Vollosovitch's mammoth of Sanga-Yuriakh River, 1908
E Vollosovitch's mammoth (of Great Lyakhov Island), 1910
F Portenko's mammoth (of Taimyr Peninsula), 1948
G Mammoths of Bereliokh River, 1970

H Rusanov's mammoth (of Shandrin River), 1972
I Vereshchagin's mammoth (of Khatanga River), 1977
J Logatchov's baby mammoth (of Magadan), also known as "Dima", 1977
K Khloponin's mammoth (of Juribei River) 1979
L Mammoth of Kular Mountainridge, 1988
M Mammoth of Kolyma River, 1989
N Mammoth of Yamal Peninsula, 1990

successful. Later, when these tissues were studied under an electron microscope, some cells were found: liver and kidney cells, erythrocytes (red blood cells), and neutrophils (a type of white blood cell). However, they were all dead.

Whether or not we have a chance of finding live cells in the mammoth tissues excavated from such sites, thousands of years after the animals' deaths, is a matter of controversy. Even if the probability of success does exist, it is extremely low. Cells are known to die when stored for even short periods above -70°C (-94°F). On the other hand, there are reports of an amphibian found alive after being frozen for several years, and recent expeditions to Antarctica have discovered viable bacteria which have been preserved in ice for 10,000–15,000 years.

Let us assume that live mammoth cells *can* be found. Remembering that they are most likely to be somatic (body) cells rather than sex cells, what is the possibility of producing a full-bodied organism from one such cell?

Every somatic cell contains complete genetic information; so cloning a full-bodied individual from such a cell is a theoretical possibility. In the 1960s, J. B. Gurdon at the University of Cambridge was able to produce normal little frogs from the skin cells of *Xenops laevis*. A breakthrough in mammalian embryology occurred in 1997 when a team led by Ian Wilmut from Scotland's Roslin Institute announced the birth of Dolly, a lamb cloned from an udder cell of an adult ewe.

Nevertheless, if we do manage to find a live mammoth cell, the plan is as follows. A mature infertile egg cell will be obtained from an Asian elephant cow by hormonal techniques. The nucleus of this egg will be killed using a narrow beam of ionizing radiation. Under special conditions a fusing of the elephant's nucleus-deprived egg and a somatic mammoth cell will be carried out. An artificial "zygote" will be created containing a nucleus with all the mammoth chromosomes. This zygote will be implanted in the uterus of an elephant cow and, if the pregnancy is successful, a baby mammoth will be born. It must be stressed that the baby born will be a pure mammoth, not a hybrid, as the elephant nucleus was killed by irradiation. The technique of implanting a zygote of one species into another has been used in captive animals to preserve endangered species.

It is not only the carcasses of mammoths that are found in the permafrost. Frozen extinct animals may be found in the permanent snow on high mountains in other countries in addition to the upper north of Siberia. Perhaps a frozen moa bird will be found in the mountains of New Zealand, where, particularly in the South Island, there are ridges up to 4,000 meters (about 13,000 feet), which are covered by permanent snow. As it has only been extinct for two hundred years there is every reason to expect to find moa bodies in a good state of preservation.

The possibilities of reviving extinct species from frozen carcasses are exciting!

▲ A hypothetical scheme for cloning a mammoth. To clone a mammoth calf, if and when it becomes possible, scientists will have to: (1) obtain a live cell from a mammoth; (2) obtain an ovum from a female Asian elephant; (3) destroy the nucleus in the ovum of the Asian elephant; (4) transfer the nucleus of the mammoth cell into the ovum of the Asian elephant; (5) implant the artificial "zygote" in the uterus of the Asian elephant; and (6) if all goes well, and if the 22-month pregnancy is successful, then a baby mammoth may be born.

DWARF ELEPHANTS OF THE PAST

LUCIA CALOI AND MARIA RITA PALOMBO

Modern elephants are large pachyderms, with columnar stout limbs, big cumbersome tusks and enormous skulls with pneumatized bones (containing air cavities to reduce weight). It surprises many people to learn that they are very competent and quite fast swimmers; in fact, they are among the best swimmers of all land animals.

Various people have reported elephants swimming across rivers, lakes, and oceans (to and from the islands of Kenya; among the Andaman Islands; off the coast of Sri Lanka; and captive elephants off the coast of South Carolina, USA)—single elephants, mothers and calves, and groups (as many as 79

lands. Nevertheless, elephants were among the most common colonizers of the Mediterranean islands. They also reached Indonesia and the Californian islands. Today, of course, these elephants are extinct, and what we know of them comes only from fossil records.

▶ An 1894 engraving of an elephant swimming across a river accurately shows the use of the trunk as a snorkel.
Mary Evans Picture Library

Frans Lanting/Minden Pictures

individuals in one report!). Elephants have been reported at different times as swimming for as long as six hours at a time without touching the bottom, going as far as 48 kilometers (30 miles) at a stretch, and swimming as fast as 2.1 kilometers per hour (1.3 miles per hour). It seems that swimming comes instinctively to calves.

This swimming ability appears to have been shared by extinct Pleistocene forms, allowing them to colonize various island districts during the Pleistocene epoch (about 1,700,000 to 10,000 years ago). During this period the combination of tectonic (crustal movements of the earth's surface) and glacioeustatic (movements due to alternating glaciation and deglaciation) factors meant that the sea level dropped at times, reducing the distance between mainland and islands. This made it more feasible for elephants, venturing on arid and desolate emerged continental shelf strips, to cross sea barriers to reach sometimes uninhabited islands.

Selection would probably have dictated that only the strongest and best swimmers survived, such that possibly only a few arrived on the new

The environment in the new lands strongly affected the way founding populations evolved. The pioneers underwent a rapid evolutionary process due to a number of factors: reduced gene pool; endogamy (mating within the tribal group); varying selection pressures which changed relationships both with other species and between members of the same species; change of growth, reproduction, and extinction rates; and the presence or absence of particular ecological niches. The most notable result was a size reduction; others were very important modifications to the skull, to the teeth, and, especially, to the limb structure.

The limb structure of these dwarf elephants had to bear less load tension and had a consequent reduction in weight-bearing structure. The morphological and functional modifications (including limbs set closer to the center of the body, and increased front and back movements in the joints) allow both more secure movements on hard, uneven terrain and a more agile gait. Molars of the dwarf elephants also often show a reduction in the number of laminae and a relative increase in the enamel thickness compared to tooth size, most probably an adaptation to improve their chewing efficiency, enabling coarser vegetation to be eaten.

Some authors view these apparent simplifications as degenerative processes. Actually, they are due to the appearance of new specialized characters. On each island, or group of islands, the evolutionary process was independent, even when starting from similar founders. In some cases the process was repeated many times, following each new invasion, such that the number of endemic species was relatively high.

▼ African elephants swimming in Botswana. Elephants of both species love bathing, and show no hesitation in entering water well out of their depth. One Asian elephant is reported to have gone on a grand tour of islands in the Bay of Bengal, covering passages of several kilometers, taking 12 years and covering a total of some 300 kilometers (185 miles) in its marine wanderings.

Lucia Caloi and Maria Rita Palombo

▲ Their classification in a state of flux as research continues, remains of dwarf elephants of several species have been found on many islands in the Mediterranean, especially Sardinia, Sicily, Crete, Cyprus, and Malta. This family group of reconstructed skeletons, including a male, female and two young males, came from Spinagallo Cave in Sicily. The male stood about 90 centimeters (35.4 inches) high at the shoulder.

THE MEDITERRANEAN SEA

Known to science since the early part of the nineteenth century, the fossils of most dwarf elephants found on Mediterranean islands belong to the paleoloxodontine line (extinct elephants of the subgenus *Palaeoloxodon* that appeared in Africa about 4 million years ago and migrated to Eurasia about 2 million years ago). *Palaeoloxodon* is a subgenus of *Elephas*. These elephants were mostly adapted to a forest environment and seem to have preferred mild temperatures.

The Sardinian elephant, on the contrary, belongs to the mammoth line. (Extinct elephants of the genus *Mammuthus* were present in Africa about 3,500,000 years ago. The Eurasian forms are attributed to the two subgenera *Archidiskodon* and *Mammuthus*.) Some doubts exist on the phyletic relationships of the smallest elephant of Sicily. It is not clear if the ancestor belongs to the paleoloxodontine or the mammoth line.

Elephants of the Sicily–Malta area are among the most studied endemic forms.

Three species, which for decades were considered a result of a progressive size reduction process of one species, were originally described, based on remains collected in Malta: *Elephas mnaidriensis*, about 2 meters (6 feet 7 inches) at the shoulders; *E. melitensis*, about 1.4 meters (4 feet 7 inches); and *E. falconeri*, less than 90 centimeters (about 3 feet). Unfortunately, the stratigraphic setting of the Maltese deposits is unclear, so relationships are difficult to establish.

These species have been reported in Sicily also, where *E. namadicus* (syn. *E. antiquus*) *leonardii* (slightly reduced in size and generally considered the ancestor of Sicilian–Maltese elephants) was also present. New biostratigraphic data allows us to assert that, at least in Sicily, elephants of *E. falconeri* size remains are older than those of *E. mnaidriensis* size. It is not possible to

infer where the medium-sized forms fit, since they may refer to more than one species. Hypotheses regarding the origin and evolution of Sicilian elephants are questionable—a re-examination of the Sicilian–Maltese remains is necessary.

We believe that elephants arrived in Sicily in at least two waves. The first, at the early-middle Pleistocene boundary (about 800,000 years before present), was when the ancestors of some medium-sized forms and of Spinagallo dwarf elephant (generally reported as *E. falconeri* but their conspecificity with *E. falconeri* of Malta must be confirmed) colonized Sicily. Later, during the late-middle Pleistocene, *E. namadicus* arrived in Sicily and gave rise to *E. n. leonardii*, the medium-sized species of Puntali, and, perhaps, a slightly smaller elephant recently found in Favignan (Egadi Islands). Relationships of these species with the Sicilian–Maltese forms are still unclear.

The ancestor of *Mammuthus lamarmorae* of Sardinia, slightly smaller than *E. mnaidrienis*, may have been an advanced form of the Villafranchian *Mammuthus (Archidiskodon) meridionalis*; however, it cannot be excluded that the ancestor may have been *Mammuthus (Mammuthus) armeniacus*. This species could have migrated into Italy in the middle Pleistocene, around 800,000 years ago. The migration from Italy to Sardinia seems to have taken place early in the middle Pleistocene, across strips of a partially emerged continental shelf of Liguria and Tuscany.

In Crete, in the Aegean area, two elephantine invasions are believed to have taken place. The first was in the late-early Pleistocene, when a paleoloxodontine form arrived from Peloponnesus, across a very discontinuous and unstable land bridge. This "invader" may have been the ancestor of *E. creticus*, a species which was the size of *E. melitensis*, reported only from Cape Maleka. The second invasion of *E. namadicus* gave rise to the medium-sized *E. creutzburgi*. This widely distributed species disappeared before the arrival of Neolithic man.

In the Cyclades, few remains of paleo-loxodontine elephants are reported and their sizes seem to be varied. It is entirely possible that there were more than one species present.

In the Dodecannesus, in the late Pleistocene on Rhodes, a paleoloxodontine form around the same size as *E. mnaidriensis* was reported. On Tilos, a population of the size of *E. falconeri*, derived from a paleoloxodontine form, survived until about 7,000 years ago. This form showed a marked sexual dimorphism and modifications of their limb bones are similar to those of Spinagallo elephants.

In Cyprus, the remains of *E. cypriotes* (a species as small as *E. falconeri*) have been found in middle and late Pleistocene deposits. The primitive molars show a paleoloxodontine morphology, but the relationship with *E. namadicus* or any other form is unclear. A few remains of a larger form are also reported. If they arrived by sea these elephants would have had to swim at least 32 kilometers (20 miles) to reach Cyprus.

INDONESIA

The small "*Mastodon*" *bumiajuensis* from Satir in Java (from about 1.5 million years before present and probably derived from Pliocene–Pleistocene proboscideans from Myanmar) lived in an area covered partially with mangrove forests. This species probably became extinct around 1.2 million years before present, coinciding with the arrival of a new fauna from Ci Saat when Java became connected with the mainland of Asia.

In Sulawesi, "*Elephas*" *celebensis*, which has functional incisors present in the mandible and hypsodont (high-crowned) molars, has been classed by recent taxonomical review as a gomphothere.

The dwarf stegodons in the Pleistocene of Sumba, *Stegodon florensis* of Flores, *Stegodon timorensis* of Timor, and *Stegodon sompoensis* of Sulawesi, show a tendency toward hypsodonty (having high-crowned teeth), probably as an adaptation for chewing coarse vegetation. In Flores, the extinction of dwarf stegodons seems to have been caused by the arrival of *Homo erectus* and accompanying fauna.

The small stegodons of Luzon (for example, *Stegodon luzonensis*) and Mindanao (*Stegodon mindanensis*) seem to have been smaller than those of Sulawesi, Flores, and Timor.

CALIFORNIA

In the northern Channel Islands off the west coast of California, USA, dwarf mammoths, derived from mainland *Mammuthus columbi* (or *M. imperator*), may have arisen for the first time in the middle Pleistocene. In the late Pleistocene, a second invasion may have led to the contemporaneous presence of more than one species in the islands. Repeated fragmentation of the "super" island, Santarosae, into the four northern Channel Islands, followed by regroupings, would have complicated this scheme, with possible interbreeding among dwarf forms and among *M. columbi*.

The Santa Rosa Island elephants (*M. exilis*), most of which had shoulder heights between 105 and 215 centimeters (3 feet 5 inches–7 feet), survived until 11,800 years ago. Many remains of dwarf mammoths occur also on San Miguel Island, while on Santa Cruz Island only a few specimens of great size seem to be present.

WRANGEL ISLAND, SIBERIAN ARCTIC

The mammoths of Wrangel Island are classified as a new subspecies of *Mammuthus primigenius*, namely, *M. p. vrangeliensis*. Estimates of its shoulder height of about 180 centimeters (72 inches) and a weight of around 2,000 kilograms (4,400 pounds), are based mostly on dental material. This isolated historical population of mammoth survived until about 3,700 years ago, close to the time when the pyramids were built in Egypt.

◄ People once thought that pygmy elephants could still be found in parts of Africa, but it was later discovered that these smaller elephants in fact belonged to the forest African elephant species, *Loxodonta cyclotis* which is smaller than the bush African elephant, *Loxodonta africana*. Reaching only the height of a person's chest, these individuals at Surrey Zoological Gardens, Surrey, England, are supposedly mature.

Mary Evans Picture Library

PEARSON. Sc.

H. Weir.

EXTINCTION OF THE ELEPHANT'S "ANCESTORS"

JEHESKEL SHOSHANI AND DANIEL C. FISHER

The literature on extinction is voluminous; all the cardinal questions (what, where, when, why, and how) have been asked but they have been only partly answered. Perhaps the most difficult (and the most common) of all questions is *why* organisms have become extinct. Since three species of proboscideans, the Asian and the African elephants, are still living, discussion here refers to other species and higher orders which became extinct, some as recently as 10,000 years ago.

▶ Mammoths are often portrayed in Paleolithic (Magdalenian) cave paintings, like this one illustrating both mammoths and ibexes in a cave at Rouffignac in the Dordogne region of France. Their selection as subjects for portrayal suggests that the artists were familiar with these extinct proboscideans and that some element of importance was attached to them, but the exact nature of this relationship is uncertain.

C. M. Dixon

When discussing extinction of large vertebrates, some people automatically think of the extinction of dinosaurs. Yet proboscideans (mammals) are not dinosaurs (non-mammals); these groups were not even contemporaneous. Dinosaurs lived during the Mesozoic era, from about 225 to 65 million years ago, and proboscideans have been living during most of the Cenozoic era, from about 58 million years ago to the present. Further, there is no evidence that comet or asteroid impact, thought by some to be a cause of dinosaur extinction, had anything to do with proboscidean extinction.

Extinction is the result of complex changes and interactions between organisms and their environment. Since such interactions may or may not be identical for different species, the extinction of each species, genus, or lineage of proboscidean should ideally be studied independently. Even if two genera were contemporaneous, one should not "lump" them together. For example, American mastodons, *Mammut americanum,* and mammoths, *Mammuthus* sp., lived at the same time, but their demise may have resulted from different causes since they are believed to have derived from two different stocks separated by about 20 million years, and their skeletal anatomies

are distinctly different. Thus, it may be possible that some of their physiological adaptations (for example, degree of tolerance to changes in environmental temperatures) may have been different. Similarly, the two living elephants, the African and the Asian, although contemporaneous, are subjected to different environmental factors but both are being subjected to shrinking habitats due to encroachment by humans and are under mounting pressure from this factor.

The fossil record provides only limited evidence as to which factors contributed most to extinctions of proboscideans during the Cenozoic. Two principal explanations are climate change, including any of its many consequences (such as effects on available food, moisture, temperature extremes, or length of growing season), and competition with other species. As an example of extinction due to climatic change, *Platybelodon grangeri* of Asia is believed to have been specialized for feeding on swampy vegetation and may have become extinct towards the end of the Miocene (some 8 to 5 million years ago) due to desertification. It is difficult to attribute any one proboscidean extinction to any single instance of competition, but members of the mammalian orders Perissodactyla (including horses and rhinos) and Artiodactyla (including bison and camels) utilize some of the same food resources as proboscideans, and this could have been a factor contributing to ecological stress.

The extinctions that occurred at the end of the last Ice Age (10,000 years ago) are perhaps most impressive, for they resulted in the worldwide loss of mammoths, as well as regionally significant losses of some elephantids (for example, some species of *Elephas* in Asia), gomphotheres (for example, *Cuvieronius* in South America), and the American mastodon. Climate change (and/or one of its consequences) is often cited as a probable factor in these extinctions, but one additional factor may have been overhunting by early humans. Changes in climate at this time are undeniable and may well have stressed proboscideans, possibly through changes in the plant communities on which they fed. Yet mammoth dung from dry caves in southwestern North America preserves

◄ A fanciful early impression of an Ice Age mammoth hunt. The causes of mammoth extinction remain mysterious; mammoths may have been hunted, or even exterminated, by prehistoric humans, but there is little unequivocal evidence of this. Early humans certainly used the skins, bones and other parts from mammoths, but these may have been obtained by scavenging rather than hunting.

remains of plants that are abundant nearby today. For a long time, the only evidence of American mastodon diet was reports of masses of vegetation, usually identified as coniferous needles, bark, and branches, in conjunction with some skeletal remains. Since spruce forests suffered a substantial northward restriction after the last Ice Age, dependence on spruce has been suggested as a factor in American mastodon extinction. A mass of intestinal contents (confirmed as such by discovery of enteric bacteria) was recently discovered in association with American mastodon bones at a site in Ohio, USA. This material included a wide range of plant types from low-lying wetland areas, with no conifer material at all. Although more evidence would be useful for characterizing regional and seasonal variation in diet, it seems likely that American mastodons ate a wide variety of plants, many of which are still thriving.

There is a wide range of evidence for human association with Pleistocene proboscideans, but the nature of this interaction is usually not self-evident. In Europe, mammoths are featured in cave paintings that may depict hunting, and, at several sites in the Ukraine, archeologists have found dwellings constructed partly from mammoth bones and tusks, often assumed to represent the victims of successful hunts. Likewise, in North America, there are many sites where mammoth skeletons are found along with a characteristic assemblage of tools. South America has yielded some similar finds involving gomphotheres. Proboscidean hunting is often portrayed as an important part of the subsistence of some humans from the late Pleistocene epoch (about 25,000–10,000 years

ago). Even when proboscidean bones and human artifacts are found in immediate association, it may be difficult to determine whether the proboscideans were actually hunted, or instead were dead or dying from some other cause and were simply scavenged by humans making opportunistic use of their meat, hides, or bones.

A slightly different problem is presented by occurrences of the American mastodon. These have only rarely been found with human artifacts but, in a number of cases, their bones show marks apparently produced during butchery of the carcass by humans. It is likely that many cases of human/proboscidean association represent hunting, but alternative interpretations should be considered as well. At present, it is difficult to quantify the relative importance of hunting and scavenging or to assess the impact of human hunters on late Pleistocene proboscidean populations.

Whether climate change or hunting by humans was the critical stress on late Pleistocene proboscideans, it is probable that their susceptibility to this stress was greater because of their large body size and their resultant long generation time and small population size (relative to smaller-bodied animals). In addition, overspecialization may have been a factor in this process. Mammals that are highly specialized for a particular habitat and diet are likely to be affected more by changes than less specialized mammals would be. Whatever the cause or causes of proboscidean extinction, it is critical for our understanding of these magnificent animals that we join forces so that the fate of the remaining three species, the Asian and the African elephants, will not be that of their cousins.

ANATOMY AND PHYSIOLOGY

JEHESKEL SHOSHANI

An understanding of anatomy ("cut up" from Latin and Greek) and physiology ("study of nature" from Greek) is a prerequisite to our understanding elephants' behavior and ecology, which in turn are fundamental to our understanding of elephants' interactions with animals and plants in their ecosystems, the units we must save. For, after all, conserving elephants is our ultimate goal.

▶ Elephants often bathe, then use their trunks to spray clouds of dust over themselves, resulting in a sort of armor-plating of caked mud that protects the skin from insect bites, sunburn, and perhaps moisture loss.

▼ The wrinkled skin of an elephant's trunk conceals an organ of extraordinary complexity. Made up of at least 150,000 individual muscle units, it is powerful enough to tear limbs from trees, and so dextrous that it can easily pick up from the ground objects as small as a coin.

In addition, a basic knowledge of the anatomy and physiology of the living species is the key to comparative anatomy which helps us to better evaluate skeletal characters of extinct species (and possible interpretations of them) and the positions of these species on the evolutionary tree. This chapter contains only brief guidelines for these subjects, beginning with the external covering (the skin) and ending with complex topics like musth.

THE SKIN

"Pachydermata", the old name of the order Proboscidea, refers to their thick skin. Thicknesses vary, however. The skin is paper thin on the inside of the ears, around the mouth, and the anus, and as thick as 2.5 centimeters (1 inch) or more around the back and in some places on the head. Despite its thickness, it is a sensitive organ system as it has a rich nerve supply.

The skins of *Loxodonta* and *Elephas* are usually gray in color. African elephants often appear brown or reddish from wallowing in mudholes of colored soil which becomes plastered on their bodies. In Asia wallowing usually results in darker or lighter gray colors than the original body color. Wallowing is an important behavior in elephant societies; the mud seemingly protects against ultraviolet radiation, insect bites, and moisture loss. Scratching against trees and bathing seem to be important behaviors related to skin care. Soon after bathing, elephants cover themselves with dust and the cycle repeats itself.

Elephants in Asia sometimes lack color on certain parts of their skin, especially on and around the ears and forehead. This depigmentation is believed to be controlled by genetics, nutrition, and habitat. Elephants from Sri Lanka, for example, exhibit more depigmentation than those from India, Indochina, and Malaysia. These differences have been used as subspecies characters (see table on page 40). Rarely, an elephant is depigmented on most or all of its body, in which case it is called an albino and may be perceived as sacred.

Brownish to reddish hair covers the bodies of young elephants, especially the back and head. Hair grows in specialized areas called hair tracts which are easily seen on fetuses. The amount of hair reduces with age; its color also darkens. On adult elephants sparse hair and bristles are distributed unevenly on their bodies. Hair concentrations are most noticeable around the eyes, ear openings, chin, genitalia, and the end of the tail. It is of interest to scientists who specialize in classifying animals that the African elephant is less hairy than the Asian. This is especially true of juveniles. It is

Karl Ammann

SIMPLIFIED SECTION OF ELEPHANT SKIN AND ASSOCIATED STRUCTURES

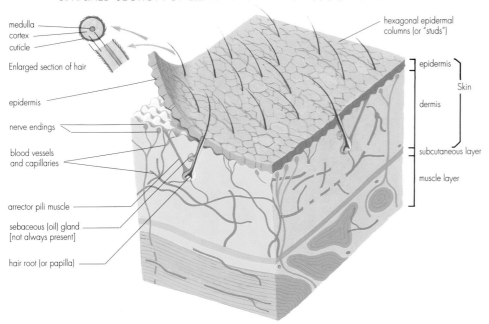

medulla
cortex
cuticle
Enlarged section of hair

epidermis

nerve endings

blood vessels
and capillaries

arrector pili muscle

sebaceous (oil) gland
[not always present]

hair root (or papilla)

hexagonal epidermal
columns (or "studs")

epidermis

Skin

dermis

subcutaneous layer

muscle layer

Masahiro Iijima/ARDEA

▲ Elephants are surprisingly hairy at birth, especially on the head and back, but hairiness gradually decreases with age, until as adults they are clad only very sparsely in hair and bristles, largely restricted to the vicinity of the eyes, ears, chin, genitalia, and the tip of the tail.

the Asian elephant which is more closely related to the woolly mammoth.

"Keeping cool" is the primary objective of an elephant, and its anatomy and physiology are geared to cope with the high temperature of the environment. Understanding this very important concept is paramount to understanding elephant anatomy and physiology.

Consider a small elephant weighing about 2,000 kilograms (about 4,410 pounds) with a surface area of 112,000 square centimeters (about 17,500 square inches) and a small mammal, a rat, of 300 grams (about 10 ounces) weight with a surface area of 300 square centimeters (about 47 square inches). In proportion to its body weight, the surface area of an elephant is $1/18$ of the rat's. In other words, small mammals have more skin area per unit of weight (or volume) from which heat can be lost; thus, they have to eat a lot of energy-rich food to keep themselves warm.

In contrast, the elephant has a small surface area compared to its body weight, and therefore it cannot dissipate heat energy as readily. To solve this problem, they are anatomically adapted with ears which function as heat radiators. Behavioral modifications, such as exposing the soles of their feet to the air, have also been observed.

THE EARS
Differences in the sizes of ears among *Loxodonta africana*, *Elephas maximus*, and *Mammuthus primigenius* can be explained based on their geographical distribution. *Loxodonta*, having originated closest to the equator in Africa and having remained within the continent, has the largest ears, and *Mammuthus*, having adapted to cooler northern climates, had the smallest. This example illustrates an ecological principle that those

species which live close to the equator have, on average, bigger ears and tails than related species of about the same body sizes which live closer to the poles. The ears of elephants function as cooling devices; numerous blood vessels on the medial sides of the ears where the skin is approximately 1–2 millimeters (up to $1/12$ inch) thick allow dissipation of heat by means of ear flapping on warm days when there is little or no wind. Large ears also trap more sound waves than smaller ones.

It has been suggested by Joyce Poole that wild bull African elephants which are in musth (a condition of heightened sexual activity and aggression) use their ears to spread the odor released from their temporal glands to inform other males and possibly females of their presence.

THE SKELETON
All mammals have skeletons with these four major divisions: the skull, vertebral column, appendages, and ribs and sternum. The cranium, with the upper jaw and teeth, and the mandible, or lower jaw and teeth, comprise the skull. The vertebral column is composed of five basic sections. They are cervical or neck vertebrae, thoracic or chest, lumbar or lower back, sacral or pelvic, and caudal or tail vertebrae. Each of these sections may vary in number according to the elephant species. The total number of bones in an elephant's body may be between 326 and 351.

Unlike other mammals, for example, a dog, where the legs are in an angular position, the elephant's legs are in an almost vertical position under the body (similar to legs of a table). This arrangement provides a strong support for the vertebral column, thoracic and abdominal contents, and the great weight of the animal. The detailed anatomy of their long bones provides additional strength to carry the elephant's massive weight. In the vast majority of mammals, a cross-section of these bones reveals a marrow cavity. In elephants, this cavity is lacking. Instead the space is occupied by a network of dense cancelous (perforated) bone through which vital hematopoiesis (manufacturing of blood cells) is possible. This actually makes the bones stronger and able to withstand more pressure than if they contained marrow cavities.

The skeleton, although built to support an elephant's weight, is also well suited to amazing mobility. Anyone who has seen wild elephants standing on their hind feet, feeding from tender acacia leaves or fruits, or has seen their footprints or skid-marks on a steep slope, knows that an elephant must have the physical structures and coordinated muscular and neurological systems to accomplish these feats.

An elephant can walk forward and backward, run, and swim, sometimes as fast as humans. It cannot, however, trot, canter, gallop, or jump like a horse. An elephant has two gaits, the walk and the amble. A walk can be slow or fast. The amble

SKELETON OF AN ELEPHANT

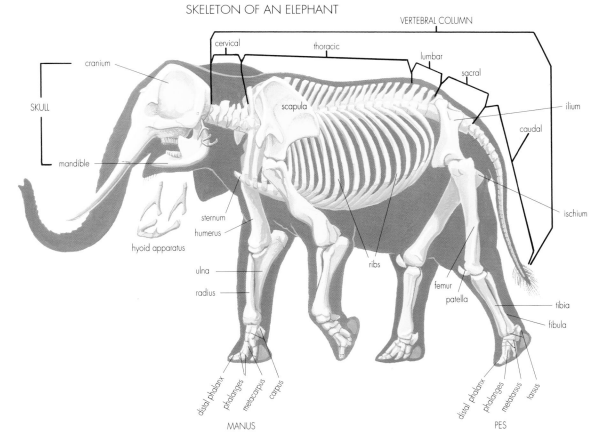

VERTEBRAL COLUMN

cervical

thoracic

lumbar

sacral

cranium

SKULL

scapula

ilium

mandible

caudal

ischium

sternum

hyoid apparatus

humerus

ulna

radius

ribs

femur

patella

tibia

fibula

distal phalanx

phalanges

metacarpus

carpus

MANUS

distal phalanx

phalanges

metatarsus

tarsus

PES

▲ Sheer size, weight, and bone structure prevent an elephant from jumping or galloping, but it can walk or amble at a very brisk pace, almost silently, and always with at least one foot on the ground.

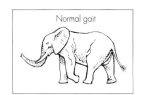

Normal gait

Karl Ammann

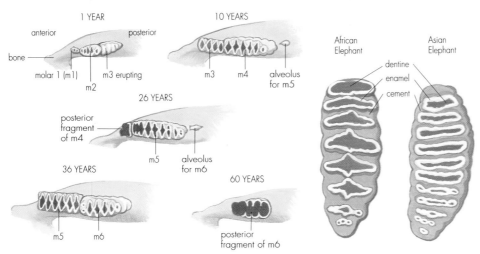

Jeheskel Shoshani

▲ (Top) The cranium and lower jaw of an African elephant. Together with its tusks and trunk, the elephant's head weighs more than 300 kilograms (660 pounds), so the cranium must be large and broad to provide secure points of attachment for the massive supporting muscle systems, but it is honeycombed with diploe (cavities) which reduce its weight. The bones of the lower jaw, however, are heavy and solid.

▲ (Above) Sequence of tooth eruption in the mandible of an elephant at various ages (after Laws, 1966). Throughout its lifetime, an elephant will use up to 24 molars, but generally only two on each jaw are in use at any one time. The process of tooth replacement is not unlike the way a conveyor belt works: as a tooth wears, it moves forward in the jaw, then fragments and eventually drops out. In the meantime, another tooth is growing forward from the back of the jaw to replace it.

► Open wide! An Asian elephant at Chester Zoo, England, presents its teeth for inspection, revealing the distinctive compressed loop shape of the plates on their chewing surfaces.

involves lifting two feet on one side together. Regardless of the gait employed, there is at least one foot on the ground at all times. The long bones (ulna and radius, see illustration of the skeleton on page 69) in the foreleg are fixed in one position (called pronation). Thus the elephant cannot rotate its "hand" (see "The muscular system" in this section). Despite these limitations, an elephant can negotiate very rough terrain.

Because the limb bones are placed almost vertically, one on top of another, and situated slightly under the body and almost "locked" in place, an elephant can remain standing for long periods without expending much energy. Sometimes, their eyes are partly closed, and they appear to doze. It is said that they are sleeping while standing; this is unlikely, unless there are other alert elephants nearby so that they feel protected. Elephants are known to sleep lying down, usually for 2–4 hours in early morning.

The skull

Much of the bulk of the cranium consists of "inflation", that is, the bones are compartmentalized with many air cells (diploe). Such a design makes the skull lighter, yet it provides the strength needed. In addition, the greater surface area on the cranium yields more room for muscle attachment towards the back; this support is needed when we consider that the head of an adult male African elephant may weigh upward of 300 kilograms (about 660 pounds). The mandible is solid, and relatively very heavy.

The teeth

Dental characters of elephants have changed dramatically during the past 58 million years due to increase in body size and type of food consumed. Canines were lost and the incisors were reduced in number. Over the lifetime of an individual, the number of teeth for both living elephant species is 26; it includes 2 upper incisors (tusks), 12 deciduous premolars, and 12 molars. One jaw quadrant of an elephant cannot accommodate all 6 cheek teeth at one time; a tooth can weigh over 5 kilograms (more than 11 pounds).

Elephants do not replace teeth in a vertical manner (a new tooth replacing the old one from above or below) as most mammals do, but rather in a horizontal progression. A newborn elephant has 2 or 3 small cheek teeth in a jaw quadrant, and as it ages, new, bigger teeth develop from behind and slowly move forward to displace old ones, as in a conveyor belt. This occurs 5 times during its lifetime, over a period of about 50 to 70 years. Worn teeth move forward, fragment, and fall out of the mouth or are swallowed.

Timing and rate of tooth development is, for all practical purposes, equal for both African and Asian species: tooth I is displaced (that is, tooth II is fully in) at the age of 2–3 years, tooth II is

Frans Lanting/Minden Pictures

displaced at 4-6 years old, tooth III at 9–15 years, tooth IV at 18–28, tooth V at 40–50, and tooth VI, or part of it, usually remains in the mouth until the animal dies at 60–70 years.

Elephants' teeth, like those of all mammals, are made up of crowns and roots. Each root includes pulp cavity which houses blood vessels, nerves, and other tissues. The tooth is composed of individual plates which are held together by a "glue" called cementum. Towards the crown the plates are divided into small "finger-like" projections. The core of each plate is dentine, and the outer cover is enamel. As a tooth is erupting through the gum, the enamel-covered plate comes into the chewing surface, and only after the hard enamel is worn is the dentine revealed as an "island" of off-white color surrounded by a shiny border of yet lighter material, in the form of a loop. The shape of the loops mentioned above differs between *Loxodonta* and *Elephas*. In the former, the loops are lozenge-shaped—hence the generic name *Loxodonta*.

Incisors, tusks, and ivory

In cross-section, a tusk exhibits a pattern of lines that crisscross each other to form small diamond-shaped areas visible to the naked eye. This pattern has been called "engine turning" and is unique to

Proboscidea. The tusks of pigs, hippopotami, and walruses are canine teeth; those of narwhals are incisors. Since none of the tusks of these mammals exhibits "engine turning", the term ivory should be strictly applied to proboscideans' tusks only. In elephants today, milk (deciduous) incisors or tusks are replaced by permanent second incisors within 6–12 months of birth. These then grow continuously at the rate of approximately 17 centimeters (nearly 7 inches) per year and are composed mostly of dentine.

The newly developing tusk bears a conical cap of smooth enamel which wears off at a later stage. Elephant incisors, as with all mammalian teeth, have pulp cavities containing highly vascularized tissues innervated by fine nerve branches; tusks are thus sensitive to external pressure. Generally about two-thirds of a tusk is visible externally. The rest is embedded in the socket or alveolus within the cranium. Although elephants usually have one pair of tusks, supernumerary tusks have been observed. As many as three to seven tusks may result from abnormal branching of the developing tusks (due to a bullet, a spear, or even a splinter) in calfhood.

Tusks are indispensable, multipurpose instruments. Elephants use their tusks to dig for water, salt, and roots; to debark trees; as levers for

▲ African elephants with impalas at a waterhole in Botswana. The elephant's pillar-like limbs must support its enormous size and weight.

Paolo Curto/The Image Bank

Michel Denis-Huot/Jacana/Auscape

▲ Despite their smaller average body size, Asian elephant bulls may grow magnificent tusks almost rivalling those of the African elephant in length, though usually somewhat slimmer and lighter in weight.

▶ (Top right) Two young sparring tuskers test their strength, disturbing their retinue of cattle egrets. Male elephants usually gather in bachelor groups, where such contests serve to establish dominance hierarchies and to determine which will have first chance to mate when the cows are in heat.

▶ (Right) Elephants rely on their tusks for a range of uses apart from sparring. Here they aid an African elephant in stripping bark from a tree for a quick snack. As humans tend to be either right- or left-handed, so elephants tend to favor one tusk over the other, so one is usually shorter, blunter, and more heavily cracked and scarred than the other.

maneuvering felled trees and branches; for work (in domestic animals); for display; for marking trees; as weapons of defense and offense; as trunk-rests; and as protection for the trunk (comparable to a bumper on a car). They may also be akin to "status symbols". Just as humans are left or right handed, so too are elephants left or right tusked; the dominant tusk, called the master tusk, is generally shorter and more rounded at the tip because of wear, and usually has grooves near the tip where the constant action of grass wears a transverse furrow in the ivory.

Being a biological product, a tusk, which is composed solely of ivory in a living adult elephant, is relatively soft, equal in hardness to calcite mineral (number 3 on the Moh's field scale of hardness used by mineralogists). Hardness and therefore carvability of ivory differs according to origin, habitat, and sexual dimorphism. For example, the ivory from western and central Africa (where the forest species, *Loxodonta cyclotis*, is more prevalent) is said to be the best ivory because it is harder than all other ivories. Yet it is also elastic, and therefore more suitable for carving

than those from eastern and southern Africa (where the bush or savannah species, *Loxodonta africana*, is more prevalent) and those from Asia (where the Asian elephant, *Elephas maximus*, prevails). Some carvers also claim that a cow's ivory is superior to that of a bull as it has a closer grain.

Ivory's composition is similar to that of bone. It is made up mostly of calcium and phosphate, but it also contains certain minerals which can be traced to the locality where a particular elephant population has been feeding and drinking. Techniques for detecting trace elements have been employed in an attempt to pinpoint the source of ivory in an effort to reduce or stop illegal ivory trade. (See also the section by N. Georgiadis.)

Once ivory is removed from an elephant body, it soon dries and begins to split along concentric lines unless it is kept cool and moist. Conversely, if it is kept in conditions which are too hot and moist, it will deteriorate.

In the African elephant, both sexes may have tusks of equal length. In the Asian species, the males usually carry tusks; in females, tusks are

vestigial or absent. A bull Asian which is tuskless is called a "Mukna" (sometimes spelled "Muckna" or "Mukhna"). Tusks of the Asian species are generally smaller than those of the African species. The longest recorded tusks for an African elephant measured 3.264 meters (10 feet 8 1/2 inches), and the heaviest weighed 102.7 kilograms (226 pounds 7 ounces). Comparable figures for Asian elephants are 3.02 meters (almost 10 feet) for the longest and 39 kilograms (86 pounds) for the heaviest. Data collected during the last few decades indicate that the average tusk weight for African elephants has decreased at an alarming rate— 0.5–1.0 kilograms (about 1 pound 2 ounces– 2 pounds 3 ounces) per year, with the weight of a tusk averaging 12 kilograms (26 pounds 7 ounces) in 1970 and 3 kilograms (6 pounds 10 ounces) in 1990.

In light of the demand for ivory and the continuing slaughter of elephants, many people have asked, is it possible to de-tusk elephants and thus avoid their slaughter? A tusk, like other teeth, has a pulp cavity containing nerve tissues. This cavity usually extends to about one-third of the

Mitch Reardon

▼ With a few exceptions, muscles of elephants, as in other mammals, are bilaterally symmetrical; they are paired, one on each side of the body. Depicted in this drawing are most of the superficial ones, and only some of the approximate total 394 muscles are labeled. Responsible for body movement, the voluntary muscles attach mostly on the skeleton and are employed at will. The trunk, for example, is raised by the maxillo-labialis muscles (also known as levator proboscidis) and is lowered by the pars rimana of buccinator (also known as depressor proboscidis). Similarly, the digastricus opens the mouth, and the temporalis closes it. An elephant flaps its ears with the aid of the auriculo-occipitalis and others. The forearms are flexed by the contraction of the biceps brachii and brachialis muscles, and are extended by the contraction of the antagonistic triceps, whereas the hind legs are moved with the help of the rectus femoris (flexion) and biceps femoris (extension). Delivery of a calf elephant may be aided by the contraction of the obliquus externeus muscles as these can compress the abdomen from both sides.

length of the tusk and possibly beyond the lip, especially in males. In some individuals, however, nerve endings may continue farther towards the tip. Thus, cutting part of the tusk may involve severing nerve tissues, and causing pain. Removal of the tusk would mean severing an even larger mass of nerve tissue.

These procedures may be further complicated by the intricacies of immobilization, recovery, and possible infection. This costly operation requires highly skilled veterinarians. Also, each animal responds differently to drugs and surgery and some may die in the process. On the other hand, the removal of the horn of a rhinoceros causes little or no pain since it involves cutting material made from keratin (the material in fingernails), not severing nerve tissues.

THE MUSCULAR SYSTEM
Like all mammals, elephants have a bilaterally symmetrical muscle system. With a few exceptions, muscles found on one side of the body are also found on the other. An elephant's muscular system is relatively easy to understand, mostly because the structures are large.

The muscles are divided into two main types: voluntary and involuntary. The former attach mostly onto the skeleton and are employed at will, and the latter are within the body and act either at regular intervals (for example, cardiac muscles) or when needed (for example, muscles associated with the digestive system). An elephant's body contains approximately 394 skeletal muscles. Blood vessels nourish muscles, and nerve endings receive or send stimuli.

Unlike humans and many other mammals, the elephant cannot rotate its "forearms"; the "hand" stays in a fixed pronation position, with the "palm of the hand" facing backward. This condition possibly co-evolved with the reduction or absence of two muscles deep in the forearm—the pronator quadratus and pronator radii teres. This character of fixed pronation has been important to students of the evolution of Proboscidea, and scientists use it as one of the features to define and classify extinct and extant proboscideans.

THE TRUNK
The trunk, or the proboscis (from Greek meaning "before the mouth"), was described by some early

THE SUPERFICIAL MUSCLES OF AN ELEPHANT

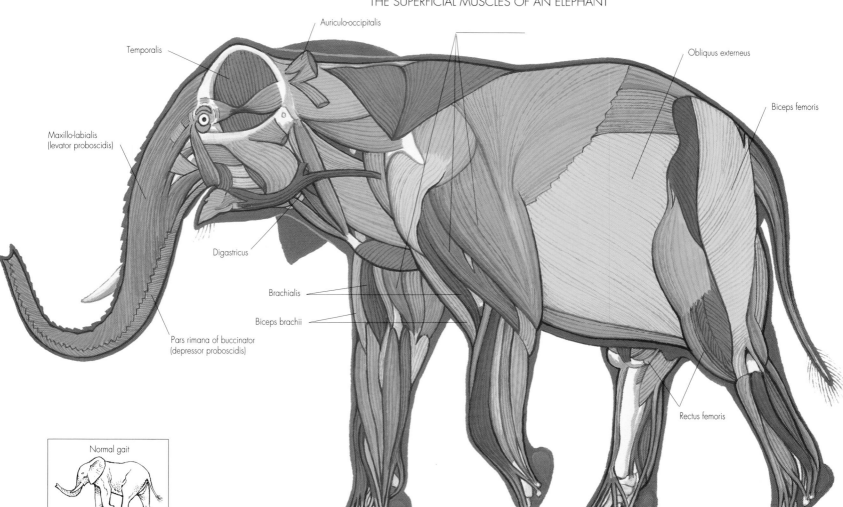

Auriculo-occipitalis

Temporalis

Obliquus externeus

Biceps femoris

Maxillo-labialis (levator proboscidis)

Digastricus

Brachialis

Biceps brachii

Pars rimana of buccinator (depressor proboscidis)

Rectus femoris

Normal gait

naturalists as the "elephant's hand". It is the character after which the mammalian order of elephants, the Proboscidea, was named. Its dexterity in performing various functions has contributed to our fascination with elephants.

Georges Cuvier, the famous French anatomist, and his colleagues examined the trunk of an elephant and estimated the number of muscles in it at about 40,000. Others have noted that some people have made an effort to count them but it is "totally useless".

The degree of flexibility and maneuverability of the trunk is extraordinary, a fact which corroborates the underlying complex anatomical and physiological basis which enables elephants to manipulate this organ through such a variety of functions. Interviews with elephant mahouts and trainers, and personal observations, show that elephants are capable of picking up objects as small as a coin and as thin as a needle.

Anatomy of the trunk

The trunk is a fusion of the nose and upper lip. It has no bones or cartilage; it is composed of muscles, blood and lymph vessels, nerves, little fat, connective tissues, skin, hair, and bristles. Cartilage is found at the base of the trunk which helps to divide the nostrils close to the single external bone opening on the cranium.

The two openings at the tip of the trunk are the nostrils, passageways which begin at the base of the trunk as separate tubes, each with a membranous lining. The dividing tissue between these passages (septum) is made up of tiny muscle

▼ The trunk is to the elephant what the hand is to the human. It has amazing strength, delicacy and versatility. In principle, the trunk is a long cone, operated by two major sets of muscles, with a pair of long, wide nasal tubes running down the middle.

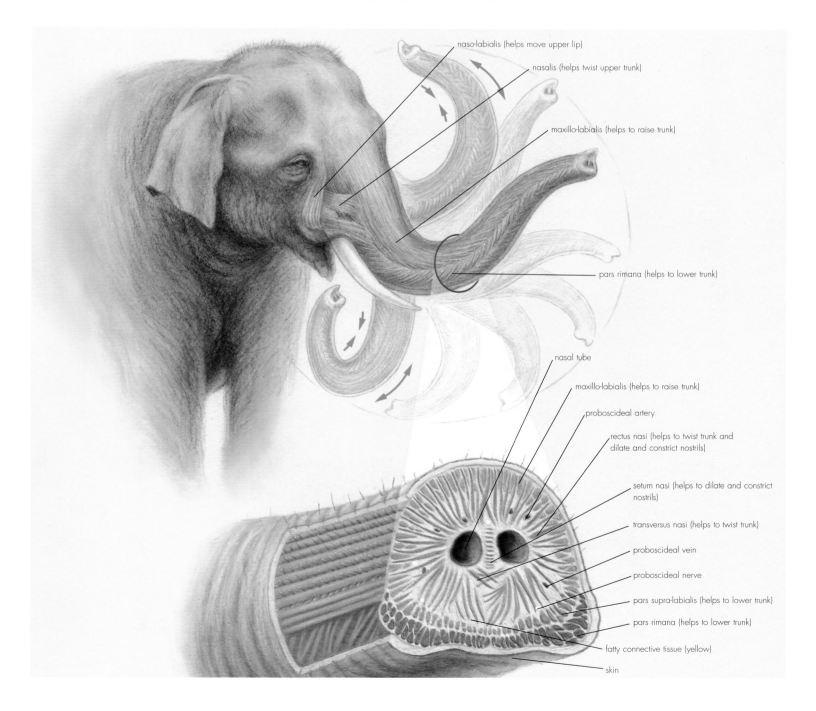

naso-labialis (helps move upper lip)

nasalis (helps twist upper trunk)

maxillo-labialis (helps to raise trunk)

pars rimana (helps to lower trunk)

nasal tube

maxillo-labialis (helps to raise trunk)

proboscideal artery

rectus nasi (helps to twist trunk and dilate and constrict nostrils)

setum nasi (helps to dilate and constrict nostrils)

transversus nasi (helps to twist trunk)

proboscideal vein

proboscideal nerve

pars supra-labialis (helps to lower trunk)

pars rimana (helps to lower trunk)

fatty connective tissue (yellow)

skin

Karl Ammann

Richard Coomber/Planet Earth Pictures

▲ Much of the African elephant's diet consists of the leaves and bark of trees, and its flexible trunk affords it extraordinary precision in reaching for sprays of foliage. Elephants frequently rear on their hind legs to reach even higher leaves.

units horizontally stretched between the nostrils. On the whole, the proboscis is a highly sensitive organ and appears to have a more complex internal structure than previously thought.

Muscles in the trunk are paired. Two major groups (superficial and internal) are generally described. The superficial are further subdivided as dorsals, ventrals, and laterals. The deeper internal muscles are referred to in groups as radiating and transverse. Results of investigations of several trunks (by C. Gans, F. Hensen-Smith, G. W. Overbeck, J. Shoshani, K. G. Watson, and C. S. Zajac) show that the myriad units of the so-called "muscles" in the proboscis are (based on histological examinations) probably parts of muscles (muscle fascicles). The proboscis of the elephant, Iki, was studied in detail. Based on extrapolation from an extensive count, the number of units or muscle

fascicles in that trunk was approximately 150,000, not quite four times more than Cuvier's estimate of the number of muscles.

Trunk capacity and functions

An adult Asian elephant's trunk can hold 8.5 liters (2¼ gallons) of water, and a thirsty adult bull can drink 212 liters (56 gallons) of water in 4 minutes 36 seconds. Using the trunk, an elephant can perform functions such as feeding, watering,

dusting, smelling, touching, sound production/communication, lifting, and defense and offense. It is indeed indispensable.

Differences in trunk anatomy between the African and Asian species are probably the bases for some observed behavioral differences. The more advanced/specialized of the living species, the Asian, has a higher degree of muscle coordination and therefore is able to perform more complicated tasks than the African.

Although the trunk of an elephant is almost indispensable in everyday living, on rare occasions elephants can function with abbreviated trunks. Both Sylvia Sikes and Julian Huxley have described seeing elephants which have lost their trunks. Huxley, in *The Conservation of Wild Life and Natural Habitats in Central and East Africa*, tells of a park warden having seen an elephant feeding by kneeling on its forelegs, raising its hind legs, and cropping grass with its lips.

▲ Functioning not unlike a garden hose, the elephant's trunk can be used to spray water, dust or mud with equal facility, reaching almost any part of the animal's body. It can hold more than 8 liters (just over 2 gallons) at a time.

INTERNAL ORGANS

The internal organs of an elephant are not proportionately larger than those of other mammals. In many cases, they are relatively small. For example, the brain of an adult elephant weighs 4.5–5.5 kilograms (10–12 pounds), and that of a human is about 1.6 kilograms (about 3 pounds 8 ounces). Thus, although the brain of an elephant is approximately three times the size of that of a human, it is proportionally one-tenth the size of a human's because the elephant's brain is one-five-hundredth of its body weight, whereas in humans the brain is about one-fiftieth. The brain of a newly born elephant weighs about 30–40 percent of adult brain weight. Not only is the elephant brain large, but it has highly convoluted areas of

cerebrum and cerebellum. The temporal lobes of the cerebrum are very large and bulge out from the sides of the brain.

The heart of an elephant is, in absolute terms, huge; it may weigh 12–21 kilograms (26 pounds 7 ounces–46 pounds 5 ounces), depending on the size and age of the elephant. In relative terms, however, it weighs approximately 0.5 percent of total body weight. In humans, the heart weight is 0.4 percent of body weight. The shape of the heart is unique; it has a bifid (double-pointed) apex instead of having the typically single-pointed heart-shape. According to Francis G. Benedict, the heartbeat is about 28 beats per minute when standing and 35 beats per minute when lying (both slower than in humans). In one female Asian elephant, a

INTERNAL ORGANS OF A FEMALE AFRICAN ELEPHANT

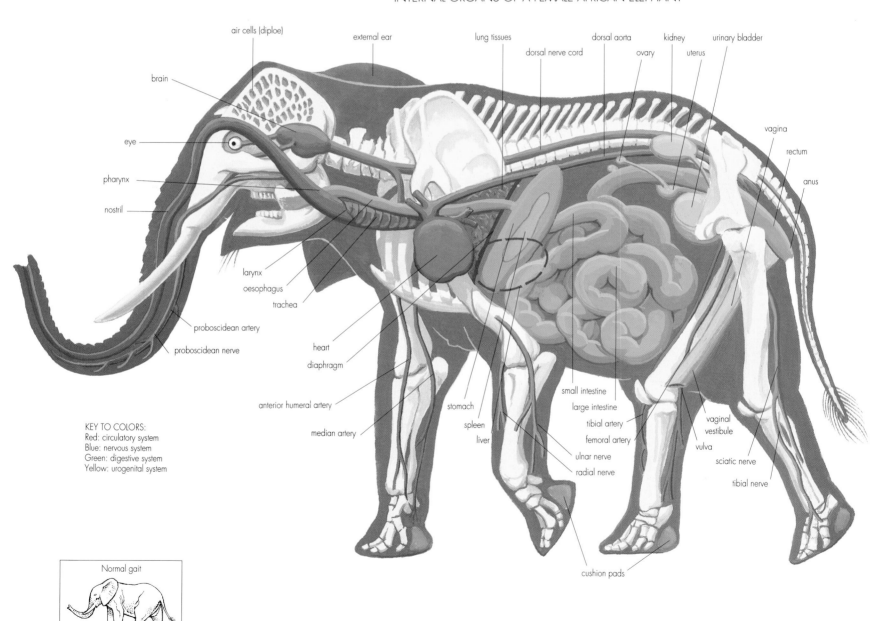

KEY TO COLORS:
Red: circulatory system
Blue: nervous system
Green: digestive system
Yellow: urogenital system

Normal gait

minimum of 113 liters (about 30 gallons) of blood was measured. It is estimated that blood, water, and other body fluids constitute about 10 percent of body weight of an elephant which approximates the value of that of humans.

The lungs adhere to the diaphragm (a muscular partition between the abdominal and the chest cavities), and breathing is performed with the aid of the diaphragm more than with the expansion of the rib cage. About 70 percent of the air is inhaled through the trunk and the rest through the mouth. Respiration rate is about 5 breaths per minute in lying or calm individuals and twice as much in standing and active ones, according to Benedict.

The digestive system is of a simple type among mammals. The combined length of the small and large intestines may reach 35 meters (about 115 feet). It takes about twenty-four hours to digest a meal. Elephant species are hind-gut fermenters (bacterial symbiosis in the cecum portion of the intestine). Most of their intake is undigested and eliminated; elephants digest only about 44 percent of what they eat, compared with 50–70 percent in cattle, sheep, and horses.

The average body temperature of an elephant is close to ours, 35.9° C (96.6° F). Unlike many mammals (the camel is another exception), the elephant's physiological mechanism apparently is capable of altering its body temperature by a few degrees on either side of the average. By doing so, it can withstand extreme environmental conditions without losing much energy. The ability to tolerate changes in habitat has been an extremely important feature in the evolution of this order and in the survival of the modern species.

REPRODUCTIVE ORGANS

The male and female reproductive systems consist of typical parts found in other mammals. The testes in males are permanently located inside the body, near the kidneys, a primitive condition among mammals. The penis, in a fully grown male, is long, muscular and controlled by a voluntary muscle, the levator penis; it can reach 100 centimeters (3 feet 3 inches) long and has a diameter of 16 centimeters (about 6 inches) at its base. The orifice or opening has a Y-shape. When fully erect, the penis has an S-shape.

In females, the cervix may not be a distinct structure in a non-pregnant individual, as found in most mammals. The clitoris is a well-developed organ; it can reach 40 centimeters (about 16 inches) long and it is manipulated by the levator clitoris muscle. Unlike bovids and equines where the vulval opening is located under the tail, in elephants it is located between the female's hind legs. The urogenital canal is very long, about 70–90 centimeters (2 feet 4 inches–2 feet 11 inches). This unusual position of the female genitalia, which is similar to the male's position,

Karl Ammann

has confused people who study or work with elephants. Because the abdominal cavity of an elephant is so large, it can easily "conceal" a pregnancy, as the fetus can occupy the space between the digestive organs and the pelvis. The mammary glands are located between the forelegs, which enables the mother to be in touch with her calf while it nurses.

Non-pregnant or non-nursing females have shrunken breasts and shriveled nipples which point downwards. In late pregnancy, the glands swell and the nipples, which may have 10–12 lactiferous ducts, distend diagonally downwards, enabling the newborn calf to reach them easily.

▲ Curling its trunk up out of the way, an elephant calf suckles from its mother's nipple. In elephants the breasts are located well forward between the forelimbs, allowing the mother to reach her calf with her trunk. Weaning is a gradual and extended process that begins late in the first year, and may not be entirely complete until the seventh or even the tenth year.

▶ Reaching about 1 meter (3 foot 3 inches), and having a diameter of about 16 centimeters (6¼ inches) when erect, the penis is small relative to the size of the elephant (a stallion's penis can reach 75 centimeters or 2 feet 6 inches). It is, however, equipped with the levator penis muscle which enables the elephant to direct this "S"-shaped organ independent of pelvic movements.

Cynthia Moss

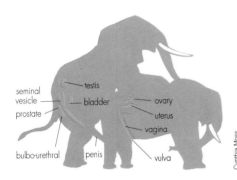

seminal vesicle — testis
prostate — bladder — ovary
— uterus
— vagina
bulbo-urethral — penis — vulva

▲ A successful mating requires a strong male which can hold its weight on the hind legs; it must have a long, strong, and mobile penis which is capable of penetrating as deeply as possible in the female's vagina so that the sperm travels the least distance.

▶ (Opposite) A magnificent tusker ambles across the grasslands of Amboseli, Kenya. As the biggest of all land animals, the African elephant is to local farmers at best a very uncomfortable neighbor. But to thousands of Westerners, this is the quintessential image of Africa, and the ecotourism industry is now one of the biggest earners of foreign currency for several African nations.

▶ A composite drawing showing the location of the temporal gland in the temporal area on the side of an elephant's head, and an enlarged section for detail. From the outside toward the inside of the head, we observe the skin, glandular tissue in lobes, arteries, veins, and muscles. The musth fluid is secreted through an orifice and stains the side of the face. The gland is present in elephants of both sexes (though much larger in males than in females) but in no other animal. Temporal glands are unique to living elephants, mammoths and possibly other extinct proboscideans. Observations of captive and wild elephants indicate that this gland functions in chemical communication and may be related to reproduction and/or social hierarchy among bulls.

THE ANATOMY OF MUSTH

Based on available evidence, the temporal gland (musth gland) may be associated with sexual activity, communication, and social hierarchy. *Musth* is Hindi for intoxicated. It is associated with swelling, secretion from the temporal gland, and dribbling of urine. Elephants which are in musth exhibit unpredictable behavior, are usually extremely difficult to control, and have even killed their own mahouts and oozies. Musth has been known to occur in the Asian elephant for centuries.

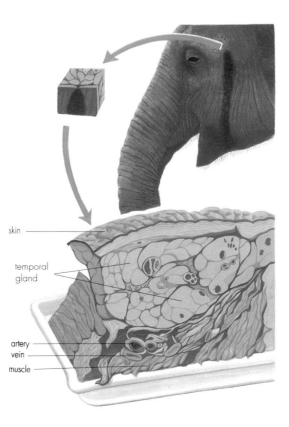

skin

temporal gland

artery
vein
muscle

In the African elephant, behavior associated with musth was known for many years but was not called "musth" until 1981. Joyce Poole and Cynthia Moss have described musth in *Loxodonta africana*. For further information on musth, see sections by Poole, Lahiri-Choudhury, Easa, Schmidt and Sikes.

The temporal gland is located midway between the eye and the ear on each side of the head. The skin here is about 2 centimeters (less than 1 inch) thick. A web of blood vessels is present between the gland and the deep muscles of the head.

In conjuction with the temporal gland, there is another organ which is just as important for elephant reproduction: the Jacobson's organ (vomero-nasal organ). This organ is located on the roof of the mouth close to the front. It has two small openings about 10 millimeters (less than ½ inch) apart which merge and lead to the brain. It functions to process chemical cues and transfer the information to the brain. When a female is in estrus (in "heat"), a bull elephant may approach her and smell the vaginal area or discharge of urine. It will then bring its trunk, with this load of information, to the Jacobson's organ to process the chemicals just smelled. Receptive females have low levels of progesterone and may have high levels of estrogen in their urine, not present in non-receptive females; these can be detected by the bull.

CAN AFRICAN AND ASIAN ELEPHANTS INTERBREED?

There is only one known case of interbreeding between African and Asian elephants. The resultant hybrid, Motty, died ten days after birth. (See the section, "Famous elephants", by S. Shoshani.)

MUSTH IN INDIAN ELEPHANT LORE

DHRITI K. LAHIRI-CHOUDHURY

In the languages of northern India, musth (from a word of Persian origin) translates as "a state of intoxication". It is used to describe abnormal or drunken behavior in either humans or elephants.

▲ An elephant in musth as a symbol of overpowering strength and virility is a frequent image in classic Sanskrit literature, and such elephants were pitted against each other in battle, as depicted in this old Bundi mural.

Various Sanskrit words for this state are derivatives of the word *mada,* which can mean "hilarity", "rapture", "excitement", "inspiration", "sexual enjoyment", "wantonness", "lust", "ruttishness", "rut" (especially that of an elephant), "pride", "arrogance", "presumption", "soma" (as in the *Rig-Veda,* the most ancient of Indian scriptures), "wine", "spirituous liquor", "the secretion of the temporal gland of an elephant" (also called *madajala,* meaning rut fluid), "honey" and so on.

Sanskrit compound words formed with *mada* give to the compound a sense of excited or agitated behavior generally (including drunkenness) or ruttish behavior. For instance, the compound words *mattahastin* and *mattavarana* (*matta,* a derivative of *mada* meaning "mad", "furious" or "in rut", "excited"; *hastin* or *varana,* "elephant") could either mean "a furiously mad elephant" or "an excited elephant in rut".

Rig-Veda Samhita (*Samhita* is the oldest part of the *Rig-Veda*) describes the phenomenon of the peculiarly strong, musty smell of the temporal gland discharge. In it we read:

> While having (thy) person in the proximity
>   of the sun,
> Thy form becomes redolent of ambrosia,
> And thou art like the cervine elephant.

Elsewhere in the *Rig-Veda* we read:

> As a wild elephant emitting the dews of
>   passion,
> He manifests the exhilaration in many places:
> No one checks thee (Indra), come to the
>   libation;
> Thou are mighty, and goest (everywhere)
>   through thy strength.
>
>   (Translated by Wilson)

Here the simile of a male elephant in musth has been used to describe the indomitable, somewhat wilful strength of Indra, the king/general of the gods. Admiration and awe for a tusker in musth must have inspired the composer.

The *Jataka* stories of Buddha's former lives (written before 200 BC) deal extensively with the theme of the elephant: Buddha (or Bodhisattva) was incarnated more than once as a white king-elephant; and before his final appearance on earth as Gautama Buddha, his mother Mayadevi had dreamt of a white elephant descending towards her womb.

Elephants in musth also figure in these stories. One of the most famous is in *Asitinipata-Jataka,* where Devadatta set the king's fierce and savage elephant Nalagiri, made "more intoxicated" with a double dose of arrack, to kill Gautama Buddha. The savage elephant, maddened with liquor, rushed at Buddha but, on seeing him and hearing his words, forgot his savageness, overcame his drunkenness and fell at Buddha's feet.

Accounts of musth elephants are more detailed in two great Indian epics, the *Ramayana* (compiled c. third century BC) and the *Mahabharata* (final form c. fourth century BC). In *Yuddhakanda* of the *Ramayana* Vibhishana tells his brother Ravana that after his abduction of Sita, the wife of Rama, Ravana's capital Lanka has become plagued by omens of impending disaster, such as the best elephants not secreting musth fluid.

Elephants with temporal glands in full flow have always been considered objects of beauty in the Sanskrit poetic *(Kavya)* tradition. This carries over to the present day. In current management practice in India the suppression of the musth phase by the application of sedative and narcotic drugs is frowned upon and considered injurious to the animal's health—a healthy animal should come into musth regularly.

Explorer

The *Mahabharata* offers some pithy similes based on the phenomenon of elephants in musth. Bhima and the professional wrestler Jimuta are locked in combat as "two great elephants in musth" (a common formula). Elephants play a major role in the *Bhishmaparva* of the *Mahabharata*, particularly in the description of the fourth day's battle. War elephants are regularly described as *matta*. But a distinction is sometimes made between *matta* ("mad", "furious") and *madasrabi* ("emitting musth fluid"). Elephants at war are classified as *madamatta* (maddened [*matta*] by fury/musth) and described with cheeks flowing with musth fluid and "smelling like lotus". At one stage elephants on the Kaurava side could not tolerate the strong smell of the musth fluid of the elephants of the opposing Pandavas—an accurate observation of elephant behavior.

It seems odd that elephants in musth, when they are known to be particularly unmanageable, would be employed in war. On the first day of the *Mahabharata* war, Duryodhana, the Kaurava chief, rides on an elephant whose cheeks are covered with musth fluid. King Bhagadatta, a hero in the *Mahabharata*, rides a great elephant, always flowing with musth. Ghatotkacha's elephants opposing Bhagadatta are also described as secreting musth fluid. Distinctions are made between several classes

of such elephants, with words for elephants emitting musth fluid; elephants smelling of musth fluid; well-trained elephants emitting musth fluid; very large elephants; *matta* elephants; and elephants which are blind with fury/drunkenness *(madandha)*. The latter could possibly have been rendered that way by alcoholic liquor. In fact, a daily ration of liquor seems to have been a part of the prescribed diet for a war elephant.

However, Abu'l Fazl Allami (1551–1602), the famous court historian of Emperor Akbar, in his *A'in-i-Akbari* gives us an insight into why war elephants always seem to be in musth. He notes that Akbar's famous war elephant Gajmukta "gets brisk as soon as he hears the imperial drum, and gets the above-mentioned discharge of musth". He notes further: "Elephant drivers have a drug which causes an artificial heat [this was probably used in combat to make the elephants come into musth and be more reckless]; but it often endangers the life of the beast. The noise of battle makes some superior elephants just as furious as at the rutting season." This could explain the musth-emitting elephants in the *Mahabharata* war as well as in the medieval battles fought in India. Apparently, some of it was due to the natural excitement of the "superior" animals at war, and some of it was drug induced. (Excitement- or stress-induced musth

▲ This old Rajasthan miniature dramatically portrays a group of armed mahouts attempting to restrain a musth bull that has snapped its holding chains and run amok.

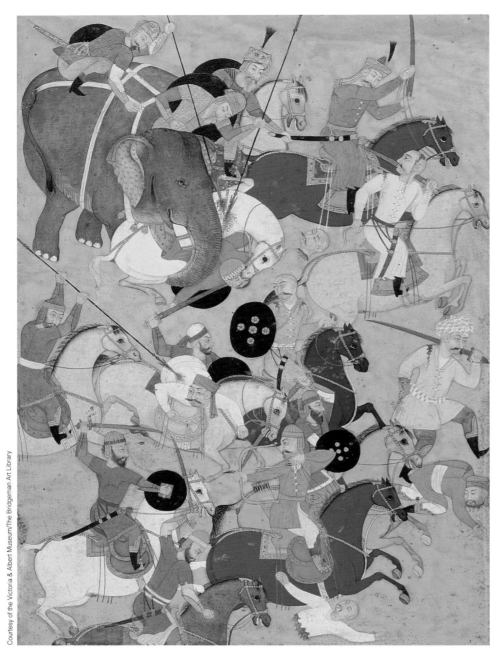

Courtesy of the Victoria & Albert Museum/The Bridgeman Art Library

▲ The discharge from the temporal gland in this rampaging war elephant suggests that it is portrayed in musth, but the difficulty in using such formidable beasts in battle is that elephants in such a state are virtually uncontrollable, liable to trample friend as well as foe.

poet Kalidasa (c. AD 400). These seven points included the two temporal orifices and the penis.

Abu'l Fazl Allami notes in his *A'in-i-Akbari* the aberrant behavior of elephants in musth and that they tend to lose interest in food, which modern observations confirm. It is also known that musth elephants rapidly lose condition. Perhaps because of this, but contrary to modern management practice, elephants in the Mughal imperial stables were allowed a larger ration of concentrated food. It might also have been given to encourage the secretion of musth fluid, the stoppage of which was supposed to lead to aggressive behavior.

In contrast, Kautilya's *Arthasatra* (written between 300 BC and AD 300), the world's first treatise on public administration, prescribes marginally smaller quantities of food for elephants in rut. Nevertheless, both authors recognize that special management is needed for musth elephants.

Bana's *Harsacharita* describes the royal elephant Darpasata in musth as drowsy, with cheeks flowing with fluid, the keepers force-feeding him and the animal scratching his temples with broken sugarcane sticks. Abu'l Fazl Allami notes that some of the imperial elephants continued in the state of musth for five years and that it was *mostly* the male elephants that came into musth. The "mostly" here is significant. Unlike their African counterparts, the female Asian elephants do not *usually* secrete from the temples; but sometimes they do, though never copiously or for more than two or three days. This writer is not aware of any research into the biochemical or behavioral aspects of this unusual phenomenon. One such modern example is Matangini, a mature female elephant belonging to the West Bengal Forest Directorate, which has been known to secrete fluid from one temple only, and only very slightly, just for two or three days during the eleventh and twelfth month of pregnancy.

An elephant in musth in Sanskrit literature is an object of grandeur and beauty. Usually the standard description includes the strong smell and bees buzzing around the temples (although it is more likely to be ordinary flies in real life). The great classical Sanskrit poet Kalidasa in his *Raghuvamsam* (c. AD 400), Canto IV, has some fine descriptions of elephants in musth, with special mention of the strong smell of the fluid and bees leaving flowers to settle on the temples of the elephants. Bana's *Harsacharita*, Canto I, describes them in a similar way.

Just as Kalidasa and Bana, modern humans continue to be moved by the sight of great elephants in musth—the embodiment of sheer overpowering virile strength. A large tusker in musth is the grandest, most awe-inspiring spectacle that India's forests can offer.

May Lord Siva, in his role of Pasupati (Lord Protector of all animals) protect and save them for future generations—of elephants and humans.

secretion has been observed in African elephants of both sexes and even in one-year-old calves, but not in the Asian species. Modern scientific observers, however, have not had an opportunity to observe Asian war elephants in field combat.)

The phenomenon of male African elephants in musth dripping urine was first reported by Cynthia Moss and subsequently in greater detail by Moss and Joyce Poole. (See sections by these two authors elsewhere in this book.) In Asian elephants this phenomenon was described nearly two thousand years ago. *Bhishmaparva* of the *Mahabharata* notes that the great war elephants of Ghatotkacha were secreting fluid from *three* points of the body, presumably the two temporal orifices and the penis. In another place the secretion is described as coming out of *seven* points of the body, an obvious epic exaggeration, also used by the great Sanskrit

MUSTH IN ASIAN ELEPHANTS

P. S. EASA

The temporal gland is an organ uniquely possessed by living elephants and extinct mammoths. When the gland becomes active it is for a varied period, and the characteristic behavior that results is known as musth. The gland is located on both sides of the head, just over the temporal arch, between the ear and the eye, while its external orifice is a slit located in the temporal depression. The active phase of the gland is marked by swelling of the surrounding skin and an overflowing of a fluid which stains the skin black and smells like phenol. Intermittent uncontrolled urine dribbling is also observed during this peak period.

The glands are found in both sexes, but they are more active in male than in female and young elephants. Female Asian elephants in particular rarely exude any temporal gland secretion. Musth is generally found in all age groups, with the exception of very young calves, and young elephants found in Sri Lanka. In India, studies have shown that musth does not appear in elephants under ten years of age and appears sporadically for the fourteen to twenty age group.

The musth period is generally shorter in old bulls than it is in young ones, with the exception of some younger bulls who were observed experiencing one or two short periods lasting only a couple of days. In the wild, normally one male in an area is observed to be in musth at a time; however, there could be overlapping due to long musth periods in a particular elephant.

The occurrence of musth is usually periodic, either annual or biannual. In Kerala State in India, for example, musth occurs mostly in winter, but it is also common in elephants in the wild during the rainy season. The duration of musth may range from one day to eleven months in captive elephants, while in wild Asian bull elephants, it lasts from one to thirty-four days. Another study shows that no seasonal difference in musth is observed in captive Asian elephants in Sri Lanka.

▼ An old Thai painting portraying white elephants in the paradise of the Pacceka Buddhas. White elephants are regarded as sacred in the Buddhist world, and, even today in Thailand, ownership of such elephants is automatically vested in the king. The prominent temporal glands on several of these animals suggest that they are portrayed in musth. Musth is the condition long associated in Asia with the breeding cycle, but recent research indicates that this is not necessarily the case.

Luca Invernizzi Tettoni

▶ An Asian elephant in musth can be extremely irritable and violent. For this reason a musth bull may be chained by his mahout for the duration of the condition, which can last up to eleven months.

Dieter and Mary Plage/Survival Anglia Ltd

Observations of both wild and captive Asian elephants have also shown that elephants are far more aggressive while in musth. Some bulls may become lethargic and indifferent to their surroundings, while unpredictability and dominance display are also observed. A captive elephant in musth shows a diminished response to commands and is considered difficult to control. It is often tied with chains and sometimes branded as rogue. Veterinary experts at Kerala State in India, which holds about 500 elephants, had to tranquilize 178 elephants over a 15-year period to control aggressive musth behavior. Over the last 10 years, these elephants have killed a total of 25 people. In one case, attendants were forced to kill one particular elephant which had killed 12 people.

However, individual variations do occur and at least a few elephants are calm and quiet during musth. One study shows that it was possible to collect temporal gland secretion from a 63-year-old musth bull elephant in captivity without chaining him. Wild musth elephants have also been reported to be tolerant of other individuals. A musth elephant covers a wide range and joins different herds within a short span of time.

Though the temporal gland was reported as early as 1734, its function is still controversial. The ancients believed in the existence of pearls in elephant skulls because the oozing fluid can have a crystalline appearance. It was also considered to be an antidote for poison, an aphrodisiac, an antiseptic, and a tonic for hair growth.

Blood plasma testosterone hormone levels are found to be high in musth elephants. In experiments conducted at Oregon Zoo, the ratio of testosterone to dihydrotestosterone was also high (the dihydrotestosterone level was low). Analyses of temporal gland secretion also showed a four- to tenfold greater concentration of the hormone androgen than in the serum (the liquid in blood after coagulation). This suggests an active concentration of steroids in the temporal glands. Instances of wild musth bulls entering elephant camps near forest areas and mating the captive cows are also reported. Possibly, these findings remotely suggest a plausible similarity between

musth and the rutting period of deer and antelope. It was shown, however, that the estrous cycle of female Asian elephants is not seasonal and so is not synchronized with musth, and therefore musth and rut may be dissimilar after all.

A strong belief among elephant workers is that musth is related to a heightened sexual activity. It is now known that the occurrence of musth can be independent of the presence of an estrous female. On the other hand, it has also been observed that a bull elephant may initiate breeding activity in the absence of temporal gland activity. The presence of musth in five males, one to two months after mating, has been reported and, moreover, a decline in the quality of sperm late in musth was noted.

Experiments with captive Asian elephants in musth have also shown increased flehmen activity to their own urine. Flehmen looks like a grimace. Elephants do this when a sample of the chemical component present in an object is brought in touch with the vomeronasal organ (a chemo-sensory organ located in the palate) via the trunk. Another animal's physiological state can be ascertained by flehmen. There are telltale chemicals in its urine. The musth secretion of one bull also evokes flehmen in another.

Scientists who have isolated the chemical components in the secretion found that it had constituents which were similar to some compounds used by insects for chemical com-munication. Elephants in the wild have been observed rubbing their cheeks on trees and other objects in the forests, which suggests a more specific communicative function of the temporal gland secretion. The secretions may mark important points, like waterholes, and contribute to the spacing of the male population.

There are indications that if animals are allowed to roam freely in the wild, the musth period becomes trouble-free. In the forest elephant camps of south India, elephants of both sexes and varying age classes are kept in a similar state to the herd concept of wild ones. During the night, they are let free to roam the surrounding forest for grazing. They have a long chain attached to them that leaves a drag mark on the ground to aid in locating them the following day. The bulls in musth in these camps are seldom aggressive and do not pose problems like those in close captivity in the private sector. The social life of the animals in this wild state could be a contributing factor to the trouble-free musth period they experience.

Although much work has to be done on musth in wild Asian elephants, experiments on captive Asian bulls and field observations have already contributed much. Similarly, the description of musth in the African elephant by Joyce Poole and Cynthia Moss has helped us to better understand the biology of these species. At present, the secret of the exact function of musth remains obscure and has led to a variety of hypotheses.

MUSTH IN AFRICAN ELEPHANTS

JOYCE H. POOLE

Jessica rushed forward, flapped her large ears, and gave out an almost deafening rumble. Fluid streamed down the sides of her face. Turning to Aristotle, she stretched her trunk towards his genitals and again ear flapped and rumbled. Then she spun around and backed into him, her head and ears high. Seconds after the pair mated, the rest of Jessica's family charged over from where they had been feeding 50 meters (about 165 feet) away. Jezebel, the matriarch of the family, led the way, followed closely by her sister Joyce. Their faces, too, were streaked by secretions from the temporal glands located behind their eyes. They, too, rapidly flapped their ears and rumbled. Jill, Joan, Jezebel's pubertal daughter, Jolene, and all of the family's calves joined in, trumpeting, roaring, and spinning around while urinating and defecating. Mating over, Aristotle stood resting with his head down and his ears flopped forward, seemingly oblivious to the females' continuing commotion.

It was April, 1985, the month of highest reproductive activity among the long-studied population of 680 elephants living in Kenya's Amboseli National Park, and Jessica was in estrus. The Amboseli Elephant Project, started by Cynthia Moss, was in its thirteenth year. I had been studying the elephants' reproductive behavior and vocal and olfactory communication since 1976.

Jessica continued her loud, modulated calls, repeatedly inspecting Aristotle and the spot where she had been mated. Aristotle now guarded Jessica closely, aggressively keeping away the younger, smaller males. Jessica made his task easier. Over the years, she had learned that by keeping close to the highest-ranking male she could avoid the harassment of young males.

Jessica stayed near for an additional reason. Aristotle, an old male in his late forties, was in musth, a period of heightened sexual and aggressive activity experienced once a year by male African elephants over thirty in peak condition. During musth, males call frequently, secrete from swollen temporal glands, and leave a continuous trail of strong-smelling urine. The duration of musth is age-related; males in their early thirties may only stay in musth for a week, while males in their late forties may be in musth from three to four months or even longer. Once in musth, a male's rank and attractiveness to females increase dramatically. He dominates all non-musth males, and his matings are more successful.

Each male comes into musth during a specific time of the year, which varies from male to male. For example, Bad Bull—one of Amboseli's three highest-ranking males—has come into musth during June, July, and August for as long as I have known him. The park's other two dominant males—Iain and Dionysus—have also entered musth at predictable times for the last eleven years. Taken together, the musth periods of these three elephants cover the eight months of the year when the majority of females conceive.

On this particular day, Bad Bull was not in musth, and Aristotle was outranked only by Dionysus and Iain. By selecting Aristotle, Jessica had chosen a large, healthy male who had survived to an old age. Perhaps her calf would also have a good chance of surviving to an old age and, in turn, producing many offspring.

I looked up from my note-taking and scanned the horizon. Over the years I had noticed that elephants have an uncanny ability to locate other, distant groups of elephants: a behavior that hunters and game wardens have often attributed to extra-sensory perception. I had frequently observed males stop, their ears extended and their eyes cast down, as if listening, and then make a beeline for a group of elephants that was kilometers away.

To the east, a single elephant strode across the open plain toward our group at a steady pace. He was about half a kilometer away, but I knew by his walk, by the set of his tusks, who he was: Dionysus. My heart quickened. I was about to see one of the rare encounters between two musth males that make all the hours of heat and dust and bumping around bearable.

▼ Estrous females can make their whereabouts known to male elephants a few kilometers away by giving out a series of loud, very low frequency calls that are not audible to the human ear. Sexually receptive females tend to show a preference for large musth bulls in their prime; this cow, having been approached by an ideal suitor, shows her interest by inviting him to sniff her urine and genitals for confirmation of her fertile condition.

Cynthia Moss

Even at a distance, I could tell—by his extended ears, by the rhythmic swinging of his head, and by the way he frantically searched the ground with his trunk for information—that Dionysus was in musth. From daily monitoring, I knew eight males were in musth. In order of descending rank they were: Iain, Dionysus, Aristotle, Kioko, Alfred, David, Harmon, and Beachball. I did not need my binoculars to distinguish Dionysus's beautiful, long, wide-set tusks and an ear that had been damaged in a fight in 1982 and not flopped backward. Although I estimated Aristotle and Dionysus to be the same age (approximately forty-eight) and weight, Dionysus was slightly taller than Aristotle and had much bigger tusks. Normally the combination of two musth males close in size would have meant a battle. But in recent years Aristotle had gone into a decline; his musth periods were becoming shorter and more sporadic and he had lost several fights to younger, smaller males. I suspected that when he detected Dionysus, Aristotle would probably flee.

The wind was blowing from the east; Aristotle would soon pick up the strong odor of the fast-approaching musth male. But how had Dionysus—upwind of our group—located us? Had he heard Jessica's series of postcopulatory calls from about 1.6 kilometers (about a mile) away?

The gap closed to about 50 meters (about 165 feet) before Aristotle started and jerked his head and trunk up to face the other male. He smelled the air briefly, then turned and ran. Dionysus passed Jessica in pursuit of the fleeing male, but then he suddenly spun around and strode back to her. The younger, non-musth males, which had taken advantage of the confusion to chase Jessica, lowered their heads and moved out of his·way. As Dionysus walked toward Jessica, he waved and folded his ears and gave a barely audible, pulsated rumble, which was answered with loud throaty rumbles from all the females. He reached Jessica, stretched his trunk out to smell her genitals, and she backed into him, urinated, and again rumbled loudly, her mouth wide open.

Dionysus now began to guard Jessica. Forty minutes later I again scanned the horizon. To the west I spotted another musth male moving steadily toward us. Although only his head and shoulders were visible above the tall grass, my immediate guess was that it was Iain.

In the thirteen years of elephant study, Iain and Dionysus had been seen together only once although their musth periods overlapped (Dionysus's from late January to mid-April; Iain's from early March to mid-June) and each had been observed well over a hundred times. On that one occasion, Cynthia Moss had watched Dionysus chase Iain over 1.6 kilometers (a mile) across Olonginya Swamp. If I had been given only one chance to see an interaction between musth males, I would have chosen these two elephants.

Joyce Poole

While in musth, males have extremely high levels of testosterone and are highly aggressive toward other males. Musth males of equal rank will fight if they meet, but fights are extremely rare, the males seeming to avoid one another. During all the years of the elephant study only thirty dangerous conflicts have been witnessed; twenty of them were between males in musth. Fighting males are often badly injured or killed.

I lifted my binoculars to my eyes. A huge bull with heavy tusks, it was Iain, Amboseli's oldest and highest-ranking male. Only in Amboseli, and in a few other isolated populations, are elephants protected well enough to allow what was about to happen. Elsewhere in Africa males with tusks that size would have been killed long ago by hunters or, more likely, by poachers. Ivory figurines to decorate the homes of the wealthy and ivory

bracelets to adorn the ladies of the world have meant that few males now live long enough to come into musth, let alone live as long as Iain and Dionysus. Most of the remaining elephants in Africa are males under thirty years old and females under thirty-five, living in fragmented families, with shattered bonds and many, many orphans.

Iain was approximately five years older than Dionysus, slightly taller, and a bit heavier. In addition, Iain had been in musth for less than a month, while Dionysus was nearing the end of his musth period and had lost condition. Still, I knew they would fight. Iain was downwind of us. He would know that Dionysus was here and guarding an estrous female. Dionysus, meanwhile, was facing east, unaware of Iain's approach. The gap between them narrowed, each step bringing Iain about a meter (more than three feet) closer: thirty

meters, twenty-five, twenty, and then Dionysus whirled around, his head and tusks high.

There were no preliminaries, no sizing-up of each other, even though the two males had spent almost no time together. They appeared to know each other's fighting abilities well, perhaps from their repeated calling and from the urine trails that each left during their constant searching for estrous females. For a moment, each tried to maneuver into a better position. Suddenly they rushed at each other, their trunks outstretched to reduce the blow, stopping only centimeters before their tusks made contact. Dust billowed up, standing out sharply against the steel blue storm clouds gathered over Kilimanjaro. Jessica, long since forgotten, was being pursued in circles by several young, non-musth males. The two musth males backed off, ear waved, rumbled the deep pulsating sound made

▲ A fight between two bulls in musth for the right to mate with an estrous female is one of the most spectacular sights in nature. This fierce contest ended a minute later when the younger bull, at left, withdrew conceding defeat.

only by males in musth, and then rushed at each other again. The loud clank of ivory against ivory rang out. They separated, danced around each other, and charged a third time. Although they matched blows, Dionysus began to back up, coming closer and closer to my car. Suddenly he spun around and fled with Iain in pursuit.

Iain pursued Dionysus for a distance of about 5 kilometers (about 3 miles) before abandoning the chase and returning to Jessica.

After the excitement, I stopped to reflect on the series of events. At 12:53 p.m., Jessica was mated by a musth male, Aristotle. She gave a series of loud, postcopulatory rumbles. Her family joined in rumbling, trumpeting, and screaming in what we have called a mating pandemonium. At 1:12, Dionysus was spotted upwind making a beeline for Jessica and Aristotle. At 1:20, Dionysus rumbled and was answered by the females with a chorus of rumbles and trumpets, a typical response to the arrival of a musth male. Forty minutes later Iain was spotted approaching fast from the west. Two minutes later Amboseli's highest-ranking males fought. The arrival of these males was not a coincidence, and the evidence pointed strongly to some form of long-distance communication.

The low-pitched vocalizations of musth males were, to my ears, barely audible. I often wondered why such large, aggressive animals made such quiet sounds. Or were they? Were the sounds made by these large males actually loud but too low in frequency for human ears to detect? Were they using these low-pitched musth rumbles to monitor one another's movements?

In 1984, during a visit to the Washington Park (now Oregon) Zoo in Portland, Katherine Payne (of the Cornell Laboratory of Ornithology) became aware of a throbbing sensation in the air as she sat quietly watching the elephants and guessed that they were making sounds below the range of human hearing. Together with her colleagues, William Langbauer and Elizabeth Thomas, Payne returned to the zoo with sensitive recording equipment. Soon afterward I received an excited phone call from her: the rumbles made by Asian elephants were full of infrasonic components. I invited her to join me and to record sounds from free-ranging African elephants. Two months later we were bouncing around Amboseli in a Land-Rover.

Over the years of the study, Cynthia Moss, biologist Phyllis Lee, and I had identified twenty-five different calls made by African elephants. Fifteen of these vocalizations were in the low-frequency group termed rumbles. Katy Payne and I concentrated on recording these low-frequency calls. We found that some of these sounds, such as the musth rumble, the estrous females' post-copulatory rumble, and the chorus of rumbles given by females to a musth male, contained infrasonic fundamental frequencies with upper harmonics that were audible to us. When analyzing

Cynthia Moss

our tapes, however, we found that we had recorded many other calls that we had been unaware of at the time.

While the discovery that free-ranging African elephants use infrasound was exciting, we were more impressed by the power of these seemingly soft calls. For example, we found that some of the musth rumbles had sound pressure levels of up to 90 decibels; the chorus of rumbles made by females in response to a musth male had sound-pressure levels of up to 99 decibels; the postcopulatory rumble was recorded with sound-pressure levels of up to 106 decibels. Very low-frequency sounds are subject to much less environmental attenuation than are high-frequency sounds of the same intensity. Therefore, some of the elephants' calls may be audible to other elephants several kilometers away.

The discovery that elephants use loud, very low-frequency sounds to communicate may explain some of the remarkable flexibility of elephant social

dynamics. Females and their calves live in a complex society of family units, bond groups, and clans. Family units are composed of several related females and their offspring. Strong, lifelong ties exist between related families. These families, known as bond groups, associate closely and greet one another with loud rumbles, trumpets, and screams after periods of separation. However, the physical proximity of family and bond group members may change dramatically from day to day, and they may be separated by long distances. The occurrence of intense infrasonic calls may help explain the uncanny ability of cows and calves to coordinate their movements while kilometers apart.

Elephants probably also use loud, very low-frequency calls as they search for mates. Adult males move through the entire population in search of receptive females. At any particular time only one female in the population may be in estrus, and she is always guarded by a musth male during her peak two days of estrus. Musth males probably locate receptive females by listening for their loud, very low-frequency estrous calls.

Equally remarkable is the ability of the aggressive musth males to avoid other bulls in the same condition as they search for estrous females. In addition to tracking the urine trails made by other males, they most likely monitor the intense, very low-frequency rumbles to determine the movements of other musth males.

Elephants are highly intelligent, with rich and complex social lives. Each year, as we learn more about their behavior, Africa's elephants decline by another 10 percent through demand for their tusks. As fifty-year-old bonds are shattered, families fragmented, and orphans left to mill helplessly around, the time has come to view elephants as something other than so many pounds of ivory.

From "Elephants in musth, lust", Joyce Poole, *Natural History*, No. 11, 1987. Reproduced with permission.

▲ In the wild, adult elephants live mainly in all-female and all-male groups or herds which tend to mingle during the breeding season. No pair bond is formed but, as each cow comes on heat, male and female may spend a day or two in affectionate company. Copulation takes thirty seconds to a minute, and may be repeated several times. The male then usually rejoins the bachelor herd within a few days, although, very occasionally, the two may remain in each other's company for several weeks.

THE ELEPHANT BENEATH THE MASK

MICHAEL J. SCHMIDT

For most people, the elephant is hidden behind a mask—a stereotyped image that few can see beyond. This view of the elephant was created in the days of antiquity and makes them seem simpler and more alike than they are in reality. To the onlooker today, the elephant may be a cartoonish Dumbo, a deadly monster, or a pleasant beast of burden. It is fascinating to chip away at that ancient mask and find out what the elephants are really like.

After eighteen years as a staff veterinarian at the Washington Park (now Oregon) Zoo, in Portland, USA, inevitably you learn to deal with all the elephantine health and reproductive problems and try to analyze the factors behind the triumphs of the world's most successful breeding herd of captive elephants. It's a process that requires work every day but gradually you get a peek at the real beast behind the mask. It is an amazing adventure.

Jeheskel Shoshani

▲ This is a rare photograph in which three generations of captive elephants are shown. On the right is Rosy, the mother of Me Tu on the left, which is in turn the mother of the baby Khun-Chorn, sired by Packy. Khun-Chorn in Thai means Mr. Elephant.

That the smallish Washington Park Zoo in the northwest corner of the United States should have become the prominent zoo in the world for breeding elephants is an unlikely story in itself. That success was—and is—due to a serendipitous combination of the best of the four basic elements of breeding elephants: (1) the elephants; (2) the people; (3) the facility; and (4) the philosophy.

THE ELEPHANTS

If you want to begin an elephant-breeding program, it helps if your elephants are young, healthy, and fertile. In 1960, Portland's zoo had acquired just such a group of elephants; beginning with Rosy (first and oldest at age eleven), Tuy Hoa (age six),

Pet (age six), Belle (age eight), and the young bull Thonglaw (age thirteen). These elephants were young and healthy, and their fertility was about to be proven in a dramatic fashion.

THE PEOPLE

The people were there, as the essential "glue" which brought elephants, philosophy, and facility together. Foremost among them all was the late Morgan Berry. Berry had been the leading importer of baby elephants into the United States for a number of years, and had developed a keen desire to see elephants breeding in captivity again in the Americas—something that hadn't happened for over forty years. He owned Belle, Pet, and Thonglaw, and when they began to breed in 1960 he decided to "board" them at the Portland Zoo, because it was closest to his farm 64 kilometers (40 miles) north in the state of Washington.

The other people who helped bring the elephant-breeding program together were Jack Marks, Zoo Director, Dr Matthew Maberry, Zoo Veterinarian, and Al Tucker, Head Elephant Keeper. These men built a facility and helped form a philosophy about elephant handling and breeding, which were twenty-five years ahead of their time.

THE FACILITY

The facility was an elephant barn of advanced design, incorporating the principles of strong concrete building construction and strong remote-controlled, hydraulically operated concrete doors. Built in 1959, that original facility (which has been improved subsequently) is still functionally superior to many brand-new elephant facilities being constructed today. Apart from its good, strong, functional design, it is superior because it has also been designed for the safe remote handling of the very dangerous bull elephants. This meant that the zoo could keep a breeding bull elephant, and thus produce baby elephants. To this day, thirty-one years later, most zoos in the world still cannot safely house a bull elephant. Fortunately, efforts are now being made to end that sad state of affairs, which is good news for elephants, as more and more zoos are able to breed these endangered animals.

THE PHILOSOPHY

With the elephants brought into a superb facility by people who were years ahead of their time in their thoughts and actions, a philosophy of keeping and breeding elephants could be created which was bound to succeed, and succeed it did. In Portland, elephants are allowed to be elephants. Since they live in secure quarters, they need not be chained at night. Since they can be handled remotely, if necessary, the bull can be moved anywhere in the facility, and is not exiled to a fortified "bull room". Consequently, the elephants were free to breed naturally when they were ready, and they were ready at a surprisingly early age. Both Pet and Tuy Hoa got pregnant at age six and calved at age eight—at the time the youngest elephant pregnancies on record.

When Belle gave birth to Packy in April 1962, followed that year by Rosy giving birth to Me Tu and Tuy Hoa giving birth to Hanako, elephant-breeding history was made. The children of Portland bought Belle and Packy from Morgan Berry, by collecting the $30,000 in a fund-raising drive, and Berry donated Thonglow and Pet. The Portland Zoo—now called the Oregon Zoo—has continued the tradition of the elephant-breeding excellence by producing twenty-five calves (number twenty-five was born in October 1991 but died from birth defects), producing the first second-generation elephants born in captivity. The research conducted at the zoo has led to the discovery of the elephant estrous cycle. The staff have also illuminated other facets of elephant reproduction on the way to developing a practical method of artificial insemination for elephants.

To illustrate what Oregon Zoo's elephant program is doing, let's take creation of an elephant pregnancy: how is it managed?

First, the breeding cycle of the cow elephant is monitored. This is done in two ways. One method is via a daily "sniff-test" wherein the bull gets to smell each cow to tell him (and the staff) where she is in her estrous cycle. Since 1974, zoo staff have recorded over 28,000 of these individual sniff-tests, and have found this a very reliable way to monitor the cow elephant estrous cycles. Since the bull elephants are maintained as solitary animals—as some would be in the wild—the daily sniff-test is the bull's one chance to check each cow during the day. The bulls look forward to this.

The other method used to monitor cow elephant breeding cycles is by means of weekly blood samples obtained from each cow. The level of the female hormone progesterone in blood samples is measured and a chart is made for each cow elephant. These charts show that each cow elephant may be mated about every four months, which is the length of their estrous cycle. This is the longest—and one of the most unusual—estrous cycles determined for any living mammal. It was Oregon Zoo workers who made this discovery. They were the first to publish a scientific article about this unique elephant trait in 1983.

When it is known that a particular cow elephant is likely to be ready to breed—by means of the sniff-test and/or blood progesterone—it is arranged for the cow and the selected bull to be together once per day in one or two of the elephant rooms in the elephant barn complex. If the calculations are correct, the cow will stand steadily for the bull, who will promptly mount her (after a bit of affectionate pushing and maneuvering), and a mating will be completed. The bull is only on the cow for thirty seconds to a minute; the animals are separated after mating. The next day, and on subsequent days, the two elephants are put together once per day. This is called "timed mating" because the time is chosen by the staff. Timed mating is also providing data which will be useful in determining the best procedure for artificial insemination. The zoo's last timed mating was as good as you can get: the cow Pet was put in with the bull Hugo, and they mated

▼ Elephants may be very big, long-lived, and wise, but they are not always dignified. This pair of young elephants playing displays just one aspect of the elephant's multi-faceted personality.

Cynthia Moss

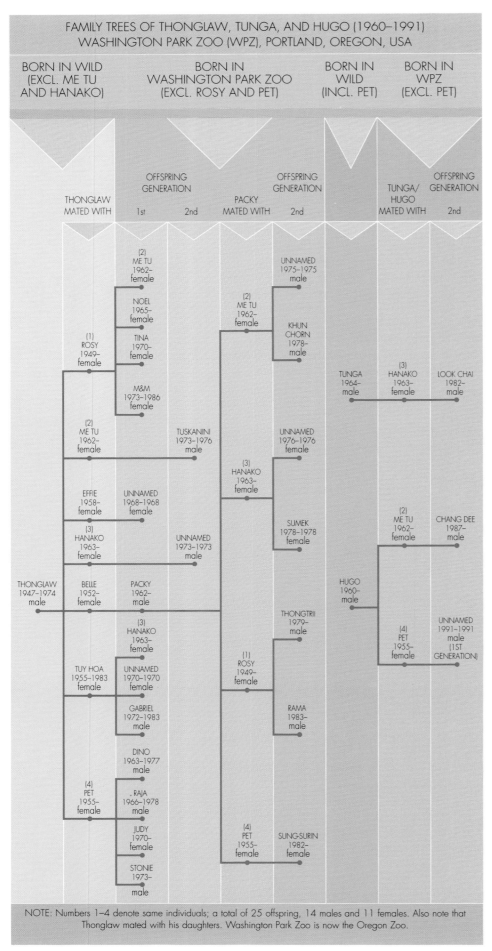

FAMILY TREES OF THONGLAW, TUNGA, AND HUGO (1960–1991)
WASHINGTON PARK ZOO (WPZ), PORTLAND, OREGON, USA

NOTE: Numbers 1–4 denote same individuals; a total of 25 offspring, 14 males and 11 females. Also note that Thonglaw mated with his daughters. Washington Park Zoo is now the Oregon Zoo.

once. The next day, Hugo made a couple of half-hearted mounting attempts, but seemed to have lost interest. Pet became pregnant by that one timed mating. Usually, the elephants will mate for three to five days.

Pregnancy is determined by means of the weekly progesterone chart. Twelve weeks after mating, the progesterone should be low in a cycling non-pregnant cow, but if the elephant is pregnant the hormone level will be high.

Elephant motherhood has long been a source of interest, primarily because of the "aunty" elephant phenomenon. When a cow elephant is close to giving birth, she develops a strong rapport with another cow who will become the aunty to the new calf. The aunty takes her role very seriously, and will protect and nurture the little elephant as vigorously as the mother.

But there is always something new to be learnt, as staff found out when the cow elephant Hanako was expecting her fourth calf. What the staff learned was most unexpected.

Hanako had always been a problem elephant. She was highly strung and unpredictable and she was bigger than the average cow elephant, weighing in at 4,080 kilograms (9,000 pounds). On top of that, her first three calves had been born with serious defects and had died before she could learn how to become a good mother.

To try to solve the birth defect problem, a new bull with unrelated genes was selected to mate with Hanako. It was hoped that Hanako could now have a stong normal baby.

To help Hanako, two aunties were selected: her own mother, Tuy Hoa, and the zoo's most dominant and successful mother elephant, Rosy. Between them, they had raised seven calves.

Finally, after the twenty-two month gestation period—the longest in the animal kingdom—Hanako gave birth to a bouncing 90 kilogram (200 pound) baby male calf, christened Look Chai. The calf was normal and was on his feet within twenty minutes, looking for the colostral milk which would protect him from infection.

Newborn elephant calves dwell in a world of giant leathery gray vertical pillars—mother's and aunty's legs; they seek these pillars out as guideposts to the milk which flows from their mother's nipples, located between her front legs. The calf finds a warm gray pillar, follows it up to the belly or chest, and hunts for the nipple.

Elation at this successful new birth was quashed when Hanako refused to let her offspring feed. The calf frantically searched for the leg to follow to a nipple, while Hanako kept up a nervous pacing, back and forth across the room.

The calf was in danger. To survive it needed the colostral milk, with its protective antibodies, within twelve hours, otherwise it would begin to digest these vital proteins it needed instead of absorbing them into its immune system.

Difficult choices of how to overcome the problem lay ahead. Should Hanako be sedated and put into a giant elephant restraint chute, while the calf fed from a ramp?

But nature took over. Rosy, one of the aunty elephants, swerved around and, pushing with her massive forehead, slammed Hanako hard in her midsection and forced her against one of the concrete walls of the front viewing room.

Hanako, who had been hit with a tremendous impact, stood stunned and quivering after this violent act. Look Chai saw his opportunity and began to search for milk from his now stationary mother. He fed successfully until twenty minutes later when his difficult mother began to recover from her shock and resumed her pacing.

Without warning both aunties this time turned and charged at the "neglectful" mother. They caught Hanako broadside and in doing so lifted her up and slammed her again onto the wall. This time, Hanako let Look Chai feed off and on for several hours. This behavior had never been witnessed before by zoo attendants.

Over the next few days, Hanako had to be reminded every time she slid back into her pacing, with the aid of aunty body slams, that a mother elephant must take proper care of her calf.

Zoo staff were very impressed with this amazing lesson in elephant behavior. It demonstrated that elephants have rules of behavior, and that they monitor behavior and administer corrective punishment for unacceptable behavior. Comparisons with human behavior are inescapable. Here were two experienced mother elephants watching a subordinate cow do a poor job of mothering. They correctly assessed the problem and took effective action, to force the mother to change her behavior and take proper care of her baby. Up until this time zoo staff thought that only humans would be capable of that sort of complex behavior.

How do humans and elephants relate? Why are elephants one of a very few species of wild animals (dolphins and whales are others) which have been captured as wild adults, tamed, and trained to work willingly for humans? It has not been done with gorillas, zebras, or lions.

While there is no complete answer to that question, at least part of the mask has been peeled away to reveal some information.

It was the dominant cow Rosy who revealed how she—and probably all other cow elephants—sees her relationship with humans.

This time it was Rosy's daughter Me Tu who'd given birth to a fine bull calf. Staff were keen to assign young teenage elephant Tamba to watch Me Tu and Rosy to see how they took proper care of a calf. Tamba would in time become a mother herself and it was hoped that by watching she would learn to be a good one. Although Tamba was a boisterous teenage elephant cow, staff at the

zoo weren't worried about the safety of the calf—not with those two large and proficient guardians. Again, there was something else to be learnt.

Tamba was taken into the nursing room and received the standard greetings and adjustments to an elephant entering a new social group. And then without warning Tamba began to pick on the calf, pushing it and pummeling it around the room. The calf squalled in outrage at this unacceptable treatment. Watching zoo staff expected that mother and aunty would immediately retaliate.

Normally, when a calf squalls, all hell breaks loose. Every cow in the barn roars and tries to run to the calf to protect it. This has created more than a few gray hairs on the heads of elephant keepers, because the calves soon figure out just the right kind of bellow that will create all sorts of action and fun. Having to scramble out of the way of a group of concerned mother and aunt elephants thundering around to find a squalling elephant calf is far from amusing. Once the calf reaches six months of age, the cows become wise to the fact that the calf is bellowing for the fun of it and they ignore it, allowing zoo staff to relax a bit.

It was surprising then that Tamba was not reprimanded for her actions by the calf's mother and aunty. Me Tu and Rosy just stood there while Tamba continued to push the calf around.

After a while it became clear that Rosy had deferred the decision of punishment for this behavior to zoo staff. It was as if they were saying that if this behavior is fine with the zoo, then neither Rosy nor Me Tu would take any action. Although Tamba was not actually hurting the calf, her behavior was wrong and she wasn't learning anything. Zoo staff left the room in the hope that Rosy would now take charge of the punishment. Immediately, Rosy charged Tamba and pushed her away from the calf and Me Tu frantically grabbed her baby and held it safely to her side.

▲ An architect's sketch of the elephant sand yard at Washington Park (now Oregon) Zoo, Portland, home of the world's most successful captive breeding herd of Asian elephants. The wall is tall enough to prevent a calf from falling into the moat. The shaded building on the far left provides shelter from the sun and rain. Elephants go into the indoor facility by entering this building and passing through the crush, illustrated on page 96; thus, the elephants lose their fear of being in the crush when it becomes necessary to hold them for treatment.

▶ Special facilities are needed to safely handle bull elephants, especially when in musth. This crush, for example, is designed to permit safe remote handling of the elephant, restricting its movements while allowing the keepers to direct it forward or backward.

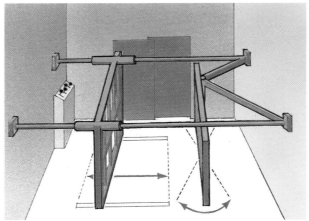

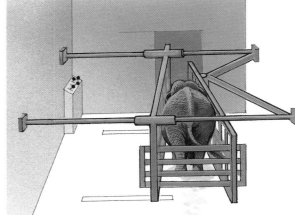

It became clear that the zoo staff's relationship with these mighty beasts was very complicated. The elephants had somehow either fitted zoo staff into their own social structure or had fitted themselves into the zoo's social structure, or perhaps a combination of the two. It would be hard to find a more dramatic example of this than deferring protection of calves to the staff—a responsibility that was happily returned to the real "herd-mates". This may be a reason why it is possible to tame adult wild elephants to work within human social structures and why humans can fit into theirs.

There is also a darker side to the elephant mask (particularly the bull elephant mask) which warrants mention: the phenomenon of musth.

Bull elephants are very large, formidable animals. A large bull Asian elephant can weigh over 6,000 kilograms (over 13,200 pounds) which is as much as a dozen large horses. Apart from his great size, a bull elephant is a highly intelligent creature and it is surprising how very quickly he can move when he wants to.

What musth does is to take this huge, intelligent, quiet animal and make him violently aggressive, to the point of madness. The term "rogue elephant" was undoubtedly, for the most part, used to describe bull elephants in musth. The prospect of dealing with musth has caused most zoos to abandon the idea of breeding elephants.

What is musth? The outward manifestations of it are obvious and unforgettable: violent irrational aggression, continual dribbling of urine down the hind legs, and a characteristic swelling and drainage from the twin temporal ("musth") glands on the sides of the bull elephant's head between the eye and the ear. Some bulls groan and act as if they are in a stupor when in the very depths of musth; all bulls lose their appetite, some not eating for weeks. In zoos and circuses, injury to, or death of, people who regularly care for a bull elephant is usually caused by musth.

The explanation for why bull elephants go through a musth every year is not yet clear. Some have reasoned that musth is a rut—like that observed in deer and antelope—but that would imply that the bull elephant does all of his breeding when in musth, and that is not the case for elephants. At the Washington Park (now Oregon) Zoo it was observed that bull Asian elephants breed best when not in musth. In fact, it was discovered that at times bull elephants are incapable of breeding when in the very depths of musth. This musth then is hardly a rut.

Experts have come to believe that, in captivity at least, musth is a means for bull elephants to determine their dominance hierarchy, so that when a cow elephant comes into heat, they will have determined which is the fittest to mate with her.

In a zoo setting, a bull in musth will challenge other bulls and dominant humans, focusing on the most dominant target he can find. When one of the bull elephants is in musth, zoo staff at Washington try hard to prevent him from harming other elephants, people, or himself, by relying primarily on a massive concrete barn and a remote-controlled concrete door.

The mental change in a bull in musth has to be seen to be believed. Here's an example of the sort of thing that can happen. One of the keepers at the zoo, who wasn't a regular elephant keeper, had made friends with the original bull, Thonglaw. Many evenings this kindly man would take the trouble to bring special treats and extra hay to this massive tusker, and they formed a happy ritual of walking together on either side of the front bars of the viewing room to the far corner, where Thonglaw would calmly accept his extra food.

This was potentially dangerous, and the keeper was warned about this, as the front bars were separated from the viewing glass by only 2.5 meters (8 feet) of space. Walking to the end placed this man almost too close to the gigantic bull elephant. To his colleagues, the keeper would always reply, "Oh me and Thonglaw, we're old friends, and I don't need to worry"—until the day that Thonglaw came into musth.

That evening, the keeper entered the barn, called to his old friend as usual, and started his customary walk along the line of heavy vertical

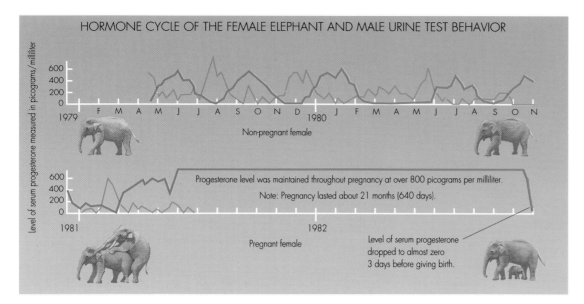

HORMONE CYCLE OF THE FEMALE ELEPHANT AND MALE URINE TEST BEHAVIOR

Level of serum progesterone measured in picograms/milliliter

600
400
200
0
1979 F M A M J J A S O N D 1980 J F M A M J J A S O N

Non-pregnant female

600
400
200
0
1981 1982

Progesterone level was maintained throughout pregnancy at over 800 picograms per milliliter.

Note: Pregnancy lasted about 21 months (640 days).

Pregnant female

Level of serum progesterone dropped to almost zero 3 days before giving birth.

◄ A chart showing relationships between levels of the female hormone progesterone and receptivity of a female. The red line shows the serum progesterone level; the blue line indicates the intensity of male sniff-testing behavior.
Top: A regular ovarian (estrous) cycle over a 24-month period, depicting about a four-month interval between estrous periods in a non-pregnant female.
Bottom: The male sniff-testing at the time of the lowest level of progesterone is capable of detecting the receptivity of the female, that is, the time at which she is most likely to conceive. Should conception occur, the progesterone level increases to a maximum and remains high during pregnancy, dropping to almost zero three days before parturition.

bars with some hay in his arms. Suddenly, without warning, he caught a terrifying vision out of the corner of his eye: Thonglaw was charging him, and as the huge bull elephant neared the bars, he lunged to his knees and slid across the concrete floor at the man, with his trunk extended to its full length of 2.5 meters (8 feet) to grab him.

Anyone can only imagine what it would be like to have a gigantic tusked monster sliding at them with the intention of squeezing them with a long, powerful muscular tube. The man ran for his life as 5,500 kilograms (12,000 pounds) of elephant slammed into the bars. He escaped the initial diving effort to grab him, but he was now trapped at the end of the line of bars in a dead-end. Thonglaw lunged to his feet, and strode to the end of the line of bars, violently lashing out with his trunk. Petrified, the keeper stood with his back pressed against the glass, feeling the hot breath of the maddened bull on his sweating face.

It was after closing time, and there was no one to come to the keeper's aid. Slowly, he began to sidle along the glass, back toward the only escape, where he had come in. The musth bull watched this for several moments, frustrated in his attempt to kill this kindly man. Then, the bull made a decision and whirled away. Striding relentlessly down the bars, the bull stopped and waited at the far side of the water trough. At first, this must have puzzled the keeper, but soon he realized what the bull was doing, and this must have chilled the very marrow in his bones. The bull was waiting for him at the point where a water tap projected outward in front of a pillar between two panes of glass; the only place along the entire line of bars where the man would have to come nearer, in order to edge around the 20 centimeter (8 inch) projection. Even in the madness of musth, the bull elephant knew where he would have the best chance of grasping the man, and then trampling him to a pulp.

Jeheskel Shoshani

The keeper had a difficult time edging sideways up to this projection and forcing himself around it, with the hot breath from the musth bull's trunk on his face. Luckily, despite the help from the water tap, the bull could not quite reach the man; which says something about carefully designing exhibit spaces for bull elephants.

Sadly, the keeper never again visited his old friend but he cannot be blamed; neither can the bull elephant. Thonglaw, or any other bull Asian elephant, could not control himself when he was in musth. For all practical purposes, a bull in musth is insane. This is the most dangerous aspect of trying to breed elephants in captivity.

Working with elephants is a fascinating business, and there is still much to learn about our large friends. The mask will never be completely off, but there is a hope that it can be peeled back just enough to make sure that the elephants will be around for a long time to come.

▲ During mating, first, the bull lays his trunk on the cow's back. He then places his forefeet on either side of her spine while most of his weight is supported by his own hind legs, as shown in this picture taken at San Diego Wild Animal Park in California. His S-shaped penis then finds and penetrates her vagina. Instead of vigorous pelvic thrusts, the transfer of genetic material is aided by muscles activated inside the penis. Coitus usually takes less than a minute.

POPULATION GENETICS OF AFRICAN ELEPHANTS

NICHOLAS GEORGIADIS

Current attempts to apply genetic technology to the conservation of African elephants is revealing much about their genetics, social behavior, and evolution.

Genetics is perhaps the least known aspect of elephant biology. Until recently, only the very basic facts for elephants were known—that both Asian and African elephants have the same number of chromosomes (the diploid number is fifty-six) and that Barr bodies (sex chromatin) were present in female but not in male elephants (a characteristic known for most mammals). However, the following genetic information may be applied to elephants with possible beneficial results.

Generally, individuals of any species differ subtly in their genetic makeup. Populations of the same species in different areas may also be genetically distinct from each other.

This geographic variation is called population genetic structure and it is affected by patterns of dispersal, mating, and other numerous evolutionary forces.

If genetic variants are unique to each area, scientists can use this information to determine the geographic origin of traded tusks. In this way, legal and illegal ivory may be distinguished. Elephant populations in many parts of Africa have been so threatened by excessive poaching for tusks that ivory-exporting countries agreed to temporarily ban the trade in 1989. The ban may be lifted in 1992 if an effective method of regulating the trade can be found. Such a method is suggested here.

Ivory offtake rates from each region need to be limited to sustainable levels. In the past a quota system limiting offtake for each population was abused by unscrupulous dealers who registered poached tusks with a false geographic origin. Through detection of genetic variants these quotas could be enforced.

However, there were three technical details to overcome.

First, DNA (deoxyribonucleic acid) must be recoverable from tusks themselves, even if they have been in storage for months or years. Minute tissue samples scraped from the base of stored tusks have yielded DNA of varying degrees of degradation and the vast majority are sufficiently intact for analysis. However, DNA is apparently not extractable from pure ivory.

Second, the elephant populations in different regions must be genetically distinct. The search for population genetic markers is focused on mitochondrial DNA (mtDNA) because it is inherited solely through maternal lineages—males do not contribute mtDNA to their offspring. Since more female elephants tend to remain in their natal population, genetic mutations unique to each population are more likely to accumulate in mtDNA.

Third, a dependable analytical method was required to reveal these genetic distinctions, even in the most degraded samples. The polymerase chain reaction (PCR), a revolutionary technique that allows specific fragments of DNA to be copied millions of times in a few hours *in vitro*, is well suited to the tusk samples.

Results show that, although there are variations within elephant populations, in some regions they *are* genetically distinct: populations in Kenya and Zimbabwe display very different mtDNA frequencies. Ivory consignments from eastern and southern Africa can therefore be distinguished, and the same will probably be true for ivory from other regions.

The genetic results that may be useful for regulating the ivory trade also reveal much about elephant movement patterns. Elephant mtDNA results confirm that female migration between populations is limited, even on an evolutionary time scale. This is remarkable considering that elephants can move vast distances, and live in almost all habitats. In addition, information about a species' evolutionary history is embedded in sequences of its DNA. This ability to reconstruct the evolutionary past from DNA sequences is a bit like being able to deduce the plot of a movie from clues in the final frame. For example, the exceptional degree of divergence between mtDNA types found within elephant populations suggests that the species is ancient and has persisted in relatively large populations for millennia.

However, these results reveal nothing about long-term patterns of male migration. Analysis of genes in the nucleus, which are inherited through both sexes, will probably show that long-distance migration by males has occurred over evolutionary time. This genetic mixing by male migration between populations may explain the low rate of African elephant speciation over the last 5 million years. At present, only two species of African elephants are described: the savannah or bush form (*Loxodonta africana*), largely confined to eastern and southern Africa, and the forest form (*L. cyclotis*) which is found in central and western Africa. Genetic analyses may reveal the degree of distinction between these species, when they shared a common ancestor, and whether or not hybridization is occurring where both are found together.

Recently, other techniques for identifying sources of elephant tusks include studying the ratios of isotopes of carbon, nitrogen, and strontium in ivory.

By documenting patterns of genetic variation within and between elephant populations, it may be possible to reconstruct evolutionary processes that have been operating for thousands or millions of years. By understanding these, we may be able to design conservation strategies to assure their continuity.

▼ A herd approaches Detema Dam in Hwange National Park, Zimbabwe, for a drink and bath. It has been shown that elephant populations in this country are probably genetically distinct from those in Kenya.

Gerald Cubitt/Bruce Coleman Ltd

LONGEVITY AND MORTALITY

S. KEITH ELTRINGHAM

Determining the age of an elephant is not an easy task, so experts have developed a variety of ways of obtaining this information: each of these has its own limitations and advantages in specific circumstances.

Measuring the height of an elephant at the shoulder is a useful technique for ascertaining the age of young animals; they show a considerable growth rate each year. This gauge, however, is less helpful with African elephants over about thirty years of age or Asian elephants over twenty, in which the increment from year to year is imperceptible to the casual observer.

In field studies, the most reliable way to estimate the shoulder height is to photograph the animal and take another picture of a graduated stick set down in the spot where the elephant was before it moved. This is not a practical method with large numbers of elephants, so an approximation of height can be obtained by comparing an animal with the largest elephant in the group. Presumably the largest elephant would be a fully grown female, whose height can be assumed to be within certain limits.

Another way of rapidly estimating the ages of large numbers of elephants has been worked out after careful observation—all one has to have is an airplane fitted with a vertical camera. It so happens that the straight line distance along an elephant's back from midway between the ears to the base of the tail is equal to the shoulder height. Hence, by photographing groups of elephants from the air and measuring the lengths of their backs from the prints (after determining the scale), the age of each individual can be estimated. As with ground estimates of shoulder height, the largest female in the photograph is taken as the scale. This is a very useful technique for scientists who wish to determine the age structure of a population.

There is a further fortunate coincidence that makes it easy to record the shoulder height, and therefore the age, of an elephant without the animal necessarily being present. Experts have found that twice the circumference of the forefoot is equal to about the shoulder height for elephants of all ages. Hence the height of an elephant can be estimated from its footprint.

▼ Fierce combat can ensue between bull elephants asserting their dominance in the herd hierarchy, or when competing for the same estrous female. Serious and even fatal injury can be the outcome.

Jen and Des Bartlett/Bruce Coleman Ltd

The weight of an elephant is also correlated to age but weight is hardly a convenient measure to capture in the field. Tusk weight is another parameter that corresponds to age, but again, it is not a field technique. It can, however, be a useful method for estimating the age structure of a population from a collection of ivory. A more practical measurement is the circumference of the tusk at the level of the lip, which shows a progressive increase with age. Some of these age relationships have been worked out in studies with captive Asian elephants whose ages were known.

Other more traditional ways of estimating the age of mammals have been used on elephants. One is weighing the eye lens, which increases in weight with age. Analysts have found that there is considerable variation in lens weight among adult elephants of the same age, so the method has been limited to distinguishing young animals from old. This is also not a very convenient technique as the lens has to be dissected from a freshly killed animal and treated carefully in preparation for weighing. More accurate estimations would be possible by measuring the concentration of a protein, tyrosine, which accumulates in the eye; but this technique has not yet been used with elephants.

The most commonly used method of age estimation in mammals is by observing tooth eruption and the degree of tooth wear. The order in which teeth erupt from the gum to replace milk teeth bears a close relationship to age and appears not to be affected by other factors such as

nutrition. The actual degree of wear on the teeth also varies with age. In elephants, each of the six teeth in a half jaw can be recognized from its size so that its presence and the degree of wear on the tooth allows the elephant to be assigned to a particular age class, but again this method cannot be used as an actual measure of age unless a sample of known age elephants is available. The correlation of known aged individuals with a particular set of teeth has been observed for both the African and Asian elephants.

Age classes are not necessarily equivalent to years but with a short-lived animal, there are few problems in finding the relationship. One merely needs to observe the eruption and wear of teeth throughout life. As elephants live about as long as people, assigning an actual age to a particular class is more problematical. Even with Asian elephants few mahouts have recorded the dental development of their animals. In practice, one assumes that the animals in the oldest age class are sixty-five or seventy years old; age estimates work backwards from there. There are many sources of error in this approach; for example, the age classes may not be of equal duration so that a simple straight line relation of age class with age is unlikely.

A number of other physical changes that occur with age help to place elephants into age classes if not to assign actual ages to them. One is the degree of turnover of the ear. As elephants age, the top of the ear tends to turn over, away from the body in the Asian elephant (as in human ears) and towards the body in the African species.

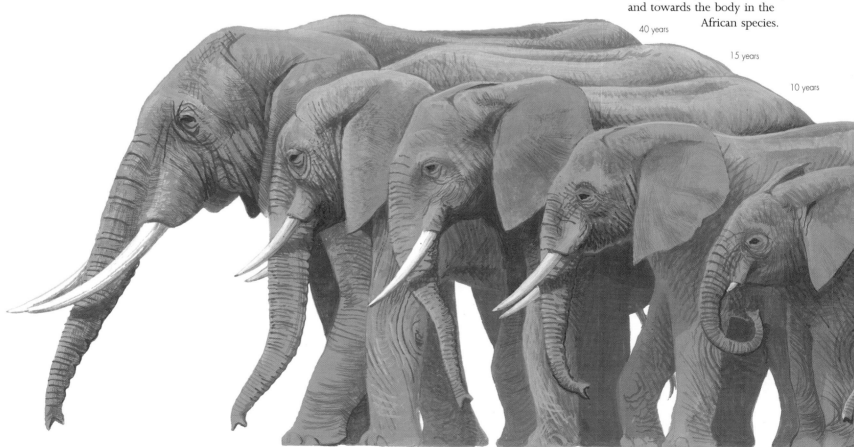

40 years

15 years

10 years

This curling of the ear may begin at any age between twenty and forty so it serves only to distinguish adults from juvenile elephants. The ears of an elephant also become torn at the edges through contact with thorns or through fighting so that an elephant with noticeably shredded edges to its ears is likely to be an old one. Such tears, incidentally, are useful in the individual identification of elephants. "Lop ear", in which the ear hangs loosely and cannot be flapped, is a different phenomenon and does not indicate age. The condition is pathological and, as it seems to run in families, is probably genetic.

Another clue to age is the sunken appearance of the face. There is always some variation in the depressions in the cheeks or temples due to nutritional factors but in addition these hollows increase with age; a really old elephant is easily recognizable from its gaunt appearance. Elephants

of intermediate ages can be roughly assigned to age classes based on the depth of these depressions. Unpigmented or pinkish patches also appear on the ears and trunks of Asian elephants and may be indicative of age. Such patches have not been documented in the African species.

The longevity of elephants is a topic of great interest to the layperson and various myths have grown up about it. The conviction of many people is that most old elephants are centenarians. In fact, very few, if any, elephants have ever lived to that age. The only ages known with certainty are those of domesticated elephants born in captivity or captured as calves, or those in closely monitored populations such as the elephants in Amboseli National Park, Kenya.

There are two documented cases of the world's "oldest elephants". One is Jessie, a female Asian elephant which lived in Taronga Zoological Park, Sydney, Australia, until the late 1930s. At the time of her death her age was estimated at between sixty-six and seventy-seven years. The second case is that of Raja, a male Asian elephant which for fifty years led an annual ceremonial procession in the city of Kandy, Sri Lanka, and was reported to be eighty-two years old when he died in 1988.

Accurate records of age have rarely been kept by elephant keepers. All the evidence seems to suggest that elephants have much the same life span as humans; that is, about seventy years. Although there are obviously less data on the African elephant, it seems to be similar to the Asian elephant in this respect, as in so many others. Most working elephants grow up with their mahout,

▲ An orphaned calf trapped in a mudhole. Without the protection and guidance afforded by a family unit, a lone, young individual is vulnerable to all manner of life-threatening peril in the wild, in addition to starvation, desiccation, and predation.

6 years

3 years

1 year

Less than 1 year

◄ This composite drawing (after Laws, 1966) represents the comparative sizes for African elephants at various ages (from left to right): 40 years, 2.5–3.5 meters (8 feet 2 inches–11 feet 6 inches); 15 years, 2.0–2.5 meters (6 feet 6 inches–8 feet 2 inches); 10 years, about 2.0 meters (6 feet 6 inches); 6 years, about 1.7 meters (5 feet 7 inches); 3 years, 1.25 meters (4 feet 1 inch); 1 year, about 1.0 meter (3 feet 3 inches); less than 1 year, up to 1.0 meter (3 feet 3 inches).

with one predeceasing the other by only a few years. Of course, not all elephants live to a ripe old age in the wild; they are open to many means of death, as the following statistics show.

Calf mortality in the African elephant was found to be about 10 percent during the first year of life in Lake Manyara National Park in Tanzania. The figure from birth to five years of age was 4–5 percent per annum for females and 8–9 percent for males. Female mortality then fell to about 2–3 percent annually up to the age of forty. Higher rates were recorded in Tsavo National Park in Kenya, with 36 percent mortality during the first year of a calf's life and 10 percent annually from one to five years of age.

Similar mortality rates have been found in the Asian elephant with, for females, about 5 percent per annum up to the age of five and 2–3 percent from five to fifteen years. There was an increase to over 6 percent per annum from fifteen to twenty years, probably due to complications during pregnancy and birth, and then to over 7 percent per annum overall. The annual mortality rate between twenty and forty years of age was much lower at around 3 percent.

The causes of death in elephants are numerous. A few calves are killed by predators. Disease may take its toll although there is little firm evidence of its significance. Many diseases are not lethal and, unlike smaller animals, elephants weakened by illness are not readily taken by predators. Because of their relative immunity to predation, elephants tend to suffer from diseases of old age, just as we do. Cardiovascular disease has been reported from many regions of Africa as well as in working Asian elephants. Affected animals may suddenly drop dead from a heart attack, and they are also liable to strokes. Postmortem examinations reveal arteries blocked by calcareous accretions of fatty deposits, and arterial walls thickened and calcified or weakened by aneurysms. The elephants so affected are invariably elderly and, those examined, more usually female than male.

The number of infectious diseases that elephants can contract makes a formidable list. Blood diseases, such as septicemia, are common in domestic elephants and probably also in wild animals. Puerperal septicemia is probably responsible for the increased mortality in young female elephants; while hemorrhagic septicemia, (pasteurellosis), is a rapidly fatal disease similar to anthrax, and is a common cause of death in Asian elephant camps. Anthrax itself has been recorded in both the Asian and the African elephant. Other diseases that have been reported include arthritis, tuberculosis, foot and mouth disease, elephant pox, rabies, tetanus, pneumonia, and dysentery. Many of these are life threatening and may account for many natural deaths in the wild.

Some elephants also die from drought or are killed accidentally. For example, they may slip on a

Peter Johnson/NHPA

steep slope or be crushed by a tree that they have succeeded in pushing over. Bulls in musth fight very fiercely and may be killed by a tusk thrust through the brain or some other vital organ. This is probably one of the reasons why, age for age, mortality in bulls is much higher than in cows. More usually, violent death is from the hands of humans, again with bulls suffering more. In southern India, one survey revealed that from two-thirds to three-quarters of male elephants died as a

result of human depredation. While sometimes they were killed in defense of crops, more often they died as a result of poaching. Females, who usually lack developed tusks, are far less prone to such mortality with under 20 percent affected. Those killed are almost always crop raiders.

Elephants can live only as long as their teeth can support them. As each tooth is worn down, it passes to the front of the mouth and falls out to be replaced by the next in line. When the last tooth is approaching the end of its useful life, the elephant is unable to chew its food properly and consequently tends to seek out the softer vegetation growing in swamps. Eventually the old animal succumbs and falls at the water's edge. The tendency for old elephants of a herd to die in the same general region has given rise to the myth of the elephants' graveyard but, unfortunately for hopeful ivory hunters, elephants do not seek out special places in which to die.

▲ An elephant herd passing by a baobab tree. Aerial shots such as this can help experts estimate quickly the age structure of any one population: the length of an individual's back, from the ears to the base of the tail, is roughly equal to its shoulder height, upon which the age of the animal is commonly determined.

▲ A seemingly "chocolate-coated" baby elephant splashes about in the mud in Amboseli National Park, Kenya.

BEHAVIOR AND

ENVIRONMENT

ELEPHANT CALVES: THE STORY OF TWO SEXES

CYNTHIA MOSS

The elephant has one of the longest lifespans of any mammal; a healthy, well-nourished individual can live well into its sixties. The elephant is also the largest land mammal. Given these two characteristics, it is not surprising that it takes an elephant a long time to grow to maturity.

A newborn African elephant calf weighs about 120 kilograms (265 pounds). By the age of ten it will weigh somewhere in the region of 900–1,360 kilograms (2,000–3,000 pounds). At birth it stands 85 centimeters (2 feet 9 inches) high at the shoulder. At ten years it will stand around 2 meters (6 feet 7 inches). But growth does not stop there. Unlike other mammals, elephants grow throughout their lives; females' growth slows down considerably after they are

twenty-five, but male growth continues at a fairly steady rate. A female will eventually weigh a maximum of about 2,700 kilograms (about 6,000 pounds), but a male might well weigh over 5,450 kilograms (12,000 pounds) by the time he is fifty years old.

However, there is more to growing up than body size. Elephants have a very long "childhood" and they have a great deal to learn during that period. Scientists sometimes argue about which

▼ When an elephant is born it immediately becomes a member of a very tightly knit family unit that is, in turn, a part of a highly social community. Under the care and guidance of its experienced elders, the young calf will absorb immense knowledge of the complex world to which it belongs.

aspects of an animal's behavior are innate and which are learned or acquired—the old "nature versus nurture" debate. No doubt elephants are born with some instinctual behavior patterns, but by and large it would appear that a great deal of what elephants eventually do as adults has to be learned.

The long childhood of an elephant and the social environment in which it is raised provide the time and teachers for an extended period of learning. Elephants live in family units consisting of adult females and their juvenile offspring ranging from newborn calves to adolescent males and females. The average family unit is made up of about eleven animals, but a family can range in size from two to twenty-nine. The adult females are all related; they can be mother and daughter, grandmother and granddaughter, sisters, aunt and niece, or cousins. Females born into a family stay in the family for the rest of their lives; males, on the other hand, leave the family shortly after reaching sexual maturity.

Family units are tight-knit both socially and structurally. The group moves and functions in a cooperative and coordinated manner. Each family is led by the oldest female, known as the matriarch. The rest of the family take their cues from her and are guided by her. Activities in a family are usually synchronized and members reveal their strong bonds by frequent calling to one another, and touching and greeting each other. A family member is rarely more than 20 meters (about 65 feet) from another member and usually they are all within a few meters of each other. If two sections of the family get separated there is inevitably a highly emotional greeting ceremony when they are reunited. Sick and wounded family members are waited for and helped. Adult females and juvenile females cooperate in the care of calves.

When a baby elephant is born it immediately joins this rich and complex life of an elephant family. From the moment of its birth the calf is the center of attention, with its mother, other adult

▼ Play has a vital place in the development of young elephants; while engaging in simple enjoyable activity, they are simultaneously learning and refining essential physical skills for survival and the social skills necessary for communal living.

▲ (Top) The eyesight of an elephant is poor in the first days of its life, so it depends on the chemical and tactile information sensed by the trunk to identify objects and individuals. The calf's ever-watchful mother is always close-by to deliver assistance and protection.

▲ Infant elephants are cared for not only by their mothers. Aunts and older cousins and siblings similarly lavish attention on the herd's youngest and most vulnerable members, providing a reliable network of family support and security.

females and juvenile females all surrounding it. The newborn calf is completely dependent on its mother and other relatives for care and protection. It appears to be nearly blind and learns about the objects around it, including other elephants, by reaching and touching and smelling with its trunk.

Mature females who have their own calves will usually inspect the new baby and then go about their business, but juvenile females are irresistibly attracted to small calves and will crowd around the baby trying to touch it, pull it closer, or lift it. The mother may or may not tolerate their ministrations for the first few days. Often if there is too much frantic activity she'll chase away all but perhaps one of her older daughters. These juvenile female helpers are called allomothers (they are also called aunties), and they play an important role in the rearing of calves in elephant families.

Allomothers range in age from as young as two years old to about twelve years old. They help to take care of younger calves: following them, standing over them while they're sleeping, getting them up when the family moves on, helping them

if they get stuck in the mud or caught up in a bush, running to their aid if they make a distress call, and chasing after them and bringing them back if they wander. All these activities relieve the mother of time-consuming responsibilities and she is then able to spend more time feeding and resting which are important for lactation.

Studies have shown that in families with many allomothers, young calves have a better chance of surviving. Thus a calf born with an older sister or aunt or cousin is fortunate. One that is born into a family with numerous allomothers is even luckier. On the other hand, some families may have no allomothers, because they are exceptionally small or have only male juveniles, and in these cases the work load for the mother is much greater.

With or without allomothers, elephant calves are fussed over and fondled, and might even be considered spoiled by human standards. Their mothers are tolerant and indulgent. Calves suckle on demand and are very rarely denied access to the nipple. Usually a calf walks up to its mother, touches her as a signal that it wants to suckle, and the mother obliges by stopping, stretching one leg forward, and allowing the calf to suckle. If she keeps walking or doesn't stand in such a way that the calf can reach the nipple, the baby will scream and inevitably she'll give in.

During the first three months of life a calf is busy trying to conquer motor coordination and simply learning how to negotiate terrain. Just standing on the first day is difficult but eventually it gets its balance. After less than an hour it takes a few steps and before long it is walking along after its mother in a stiff-legged gait. In the first couple of weeks, some allowances are made for the new calf, but basically it has to follow its mother and family in their daily movements to find food. It has to learn how to cross muddy, slippery ground, climb over and among rocks and boulders, avoid the sharp thorns from acacia trees, and it even may be called upon to swim across a stream or lake.

Very early on the young calf starts to try to use its trunk. For a while the trunk looks like a wobbly, totally out of control rubber hose. The calf wiggles it up and down and around in circles, sticks it in its mouth and sucks on it, or trips over it while walking. But within a week the baby is trying to pick up and carry sticks; it is amazing how soon it is able to grasp with and maneuver its trunk. Between three and four months a calf will begin to try to feed itself. Small bits of grass are plucked up, sometimes only a single blade. It can take a calf several minutes to get hold of a blade of grass with its trunk, break it off and then carry it to its mouth. It usually drops it and then has to spend more time trying to pick it up. Often the calf seems to forget what it was doing and ends up with the piece of grass on top of its head. One shortcut often taken is simply bending down and biting the grass off with its mouth.

Christian Zuber/Bruce Coleman Ltd

The skill of drinking with the trunk is even more difficult to master. Adult elephants drink by sucking water up into their trunks, placing the tip in their mouths and letting the water run out and down their throats. Calves make a terrible mess of it, losing most of the water as they try to get their trunks to their mouths, or splashing it all over themselves, or getting mud, not water, in their trunks and having to blow it all out again. By the age of six months they can usually manage.

The trunk, of course, is not only an organ of communication with the physical world but also with the social world. By exploration and trial and error the calf begins to learn who's who in the elephant world. Its mother is always there for it; its allomothers are friendly and caring; the juvenile males in its family usually ignore it, but are not aggressive; adult males visit the family from time to time but show no interest in the calf.

The social circle does not end with family. Elephant society is complex and multi-tiered, involving other families, clans, and subpopulations. Eventually, an adult elephant will know every

Karl Ammann

▲ The baby elephant is filled with an insatiable curiosity about its surroundings, and it relies on its trunk as the principal organ of exploration. The youngster's zealous course of discovery is calmly tolerated, if not indulged, by the others in the group.

◄ Until it is about one year old, a calf can comfortably take refuge beneath the reassuring girth of its mother's underbelly. Here too, it need only reach for a breast between her front legs to find immediate nourishment.

Richard Packwood/Oxford Scientific Films

Clem Haagner/Ardea London Ltd

▲ Having been taught care-giving skills by the adult females, juvenile females begin to take on some of the responsibilities of looking after the babies of the herd. While lending the mother help in her time-consuming child-rearing tasks, these allomothers gain valuable practice for their future experience of motherhood.

▶ A herd taking refreshment at a waterhole in Etosha National Park, Namibia. Teaching by example, elephants impart to their young not only what to eat and drink, but how. Infants are eager learners, observing their elders closely and emulating their behavior as best they can.

elephant in its population and will know its relationship and position with regard to each. Slowly an elephant calf has to learn how it fits in: who might be aggressive towards it, whom it might dominate, and how it relates to others.

An elephant's place in the social system is determined by its sex. Once adults, male and female elephants lead completely different lives. Females experience intensely social lives, surrounded by close relatives and always in the company of other elephants, sometimes in herds of over 500. Males lead more or less solitary lives. They leave their natal families at an average age of fourteen years and, although they may spend time with other families and other independent males, they do not form close bonds. When they are older, bulls spend much of their time on their own or in a group of a few bulls and only visit families when searching for females in estrus.

The key to these differences is in the reproductive histories of males and females. An individual female might produce a calf every four years from the time she is thirteen until she is in her fifties. She might have as many as twelve calves in her lifetime. A bull's chances of having calves are more problematical. Bulls compete for access to estrous females, and the bigger and older the bulls the more successful they are at mating. The forty- and fifty-year-old bulls father most of the calves. An old bull might be the father of dozens of calves, while a bull who died at the age of thirty might not have had any calves.

It is a major goal of any individual to leave as many healthy offspring as possible. To succeed in this goal male and female elephants have different strategies. Calves flourish within a family that has access to good resources and contains members that will cooperate in the rearing of calves. Therefore, a female's family and her relationships with

Cynthia Moss

Konrad Wothe/Bruce Coleman Ltd

▲ (Top) As young elephants approach adolescence, the behavior of male calves and female calves becomes increasingly divergent. Mounting antics such as this are more characteristic of a male's behavior, as are sparring, head-on shoving, and trunk wrestling—all skills that he will likely resort to later in his competitive reproductive role as an adult bull.

▲ A baby Asian elephant sucks on its mother's nipple with its mouth, not its trunk. The milk of an elephant has a low fat content (0.63 percent–6.2 percent), but it is highly nutritious. By about age nine months, however, calves need to feed on vegetation as well for sufficient sustenance. Weaning usually occurs during their third year to make way for future siblings.

its members are all important. A bull, however, has to make it on his own and sort out his relationships with other bulls. It is crucial that he reach a size and age that make it possible for him to compete successfully for females.

One of the ways gender differences are reflected in early development is in play. Calf play takes the form of head-to-head sparring, chasing, mounting, climbing on an animal which is lying down, and pushing and shoving. From when they are as young as one month old, male calves are more likely to leave their mothers to play, and when they do they tend to engage in certain kinds of games. Males do more head-to-head sparring, and if one calf mounts another it is almost inevitably a male calf which does the mounting. Females tend to play running and chasing games and those that involve attacking imaginary enemies. Both are practicing skills they will need as adults: for the males, fighting and mating techniques; for the females, strategies for protecting their families.

While the behavioral differences are obvious from early on, the general developmental patterns of

the two sexes are similar in the first ten years of life. All calves are dependent on their mothers for milk for at least three years; and they are dependent on their mothers, allomothers, and other family members for protection and teaching. It is by watching the older animals that calves learn how and what to eat. By the age of nine months calves are spending 40 percent of their time feeding on vegetation as milk alone cannot sustain them.

The major event in a calf's early years is the birth of a younger sibling, which usually occurs when the calf is between four and five years old. The most dramatic and disturbing change is that its mother will no longer allow it to suckle and she may be aggressive in both her attempt to prevent suckling and in keeping the calf away from the new baby. Sometimes a mother will wean her offspring a few months before the calf is born but more often the older calf suckles right up until the baby is born. Needless to say, conflicts arise. If the older calf is extremely persistent or the mother is unusually tolerant, the calf might be allowed to suckle along with the baby, each on one breast. Usually the older calf stops demanding milk after a week or so. In a few rare cases when the calf persists, younger calves have been known to die because the mother does not have enough milk to nourish both calves. It is interesting that in most cases the calves most reluctant to be weaned are males, but that is not surprising considering that males grow faster than females and need more milk.

It is around the age of weaning that the sexual differences in appearance between calves become more pronounced. Aside from getting noticeably bigger than a female calf, the male's tusks, which begin to show beyond the lip at an earlier age (about two years old for males and two and a quarter for females) are distinctly thicker, particularly at the base. The male calf's head is already beginning to have a more rounded, less angular appearance at the forehead.

The behavioral differences also become more conspicuous upon weaning. After the initial shock and adjustment of having a new sister or brother, female juveniles four to five years old try to spend as much of their time as possible as close to the calf as they are allowed. If there is no older sister, then the juvenile female will become the major allomother to the new calf. In contrast a male juvenile will show no interest in the calf unless he is still trying to suckle. Once that conflict is resolved the young male gradually moves toward independence. The juvenile male will spend less time close to his mother, but he will still be very much part of the family for several years.

From five to ten years old, the lives of males and females continue to diverge. The female will remain closely tied to the family and will be strengthening and developing bonds within it. The relationships she forms with her age-mates and with the younger animals she takes care of will, in

Cynthia Moss

many cases, last a lifetime. The male juvenile, on the other hand, will gradually become more peripheral. He will tend to leave the family more readily to seek out play companions in nearby groups. If there are young males in his family they will often form a little subgroup which goes off together to feed, explore, or play.

Females can reach sexual maturity as early as nine years old, and come into estrus, mate and conceive. The experience of estrus and being pursued and mated by large adult males is bewildering for a young female. Fortunately, her mother and other adult females are usually with her to lend support and reassurance. Males reach sexual maturity a bit later, and usually leave the family to strike out on their own at around fourteen years old. However, males as young as nine have been known to become independent. The timing of a male's departure appears to depend on several factors: he might leave early if his mother has died, if he has no other males his own age in the family to interact with, if the adult females in the family are aggressive toward him,

or if he has an older brother who is leaving. The process can take several months or even years with the male getting more and more peripheral, spending a few days away, then a few weeks, until he is finally self-assured enough to leave for good.

Whatever his age the young independent male is setting off on a whole new life, which he has been practicing for since he was born. And the young female who reaches puberty will have a new perspective and new set of responsibilities when she gives birth to her first calf. She too has been practicing for her role. Both will continue to learn and develop. The female may eventually become a grand old matriarch full of knowledge, experience, and wisdom, leading and protecting her family. The male could become a magnificent bull with tusks weighing over 45 kilograms (100 pounds) each, the father of countless calves carrying his genes for success and survival.

Adapted from "The Young Ones", Cynthia Moss, *BBC Wildlife*, Vol. 8, No. 11, November 1990. Reproduced with permission.

▲ Trying to keep up with a youngster's seemingly boundless energy can be tiring work. This calf, urging her to continue in their play, seems to have all but exhausted its mother.

RAISING ORPHANED AFRICAN ELEPHANTS

DAPHNE SHELDRICK

▲ Playtime at Daphne Sheldrick's animal orphanage in Nairobi, Kenya. Here, a young elephant frolics about with his playmate, a rhino calf.

Of the many baby wild animals which I have been fortunate to raise, elephants are by far the most delicate and demanding, and therefore the most difficult. In the wild, baby elephants are seldom left alone; they are constantly touched and caressed, secure in the boundless love of a closely knit and caring family. They are also shielded from the elements by the bodies of their elders, sheltered at most times from the sun, the wind, and the rain. Initially a baby elephant suckles approximately once every ten minutes, using the mouth to suckle while the tender tip of the baby's trunk nestles against the comforting warmth of the mother's body, providing the sensation that is conducive to the suckling ritual. When hand-raising baby elephants, attention to such details is important to success— almost as important as is the formula of the artificial milk that will replace that of the mother. Infant elephants are intolerant of the fat in cows' milk, so the milk they are given has to be free of cows' milk fat. All the fat in the diet has to be vegetable in origin. Coconut oil is the nearest artificial equivalent to the fat of elephants' milk. Wyeth Laboratory's Infant Formula SMA Goldcap or S. 26 has been the breakthrough that has offered a chance for life to orphaned infant African elephants for the first time.

An elephant baby is milk dependent for the first full year of life, and partially so for two. No calf orphaned under the age of one can survive without milk, and those that survive in the wild when orphaned between the age of one and two are precious few. Extremely social and caring animals, elephants have a strong sense of family, a sense of death, and lifelong loves and friendships. They will display compassion for those in difficulty, particularly the babies.

A calf that has lost its mother will be protected by other family members and even by strangers. Some lactating cows will allow an orphan to suckle but others will not jeopardize the chances of survival of their own calf. This decision will be dependent on many factors—the cow's experience as a mother, whether she has lost a calf of her own, and, if not, the age of her last calf. If the calf is milk dependent, she would not have sufficient milk for two. In captivity, newborn elephants require at least 9 liters (just over 2 gallons) of milk over a 24-hour period, and at nine months the quantity will have increased to 27 liters (just over 7 gallons).

But, whilst the milk is an important element to success, it is by no means the only one. Baby elephants will only thrive if they are happy, and in order to be happy, they must have a family. Those who are entrusted with their care should replace, in every way, the elephant family they have lost. They can never be left alone, not even for a moment, for having lost a family once, they will be haunted by this memory for life. Yet it is equally important to guard against a calf becoming too devoted to any one person, for the absence of that person will cause renewed grieving and trauma. The keepers—and there should be enough of them to impart a sense of family—should constantly alternate, always dressed alike, so that the calf will associate anyone dressed thus as "family"—there to love and to care, to protect and provide, just as would its own elephant family.

Under the age of three months, a calf must be bottle-fed on demand, throughout the night as well as by day. The calf will gradually settle into a three-hourly round-the-clock feeding schedule that will apply until the age of one. Then the weaning process,

Daphne Sheldrick

▲ The keeper is virtually a surrogate parent to the orphaned calf, and a strong bond can develop between the two.

which will take another full year, can begin. As the calf grows, desiccated coconut and cereals are introduced. Initially they can be used to fortify the milk. They should replace the milk in the diet by the second birthday. They are mixed with water and still given through a feeding bottle and nipple. Suckling will be psychologically important until the calf reaches the age of five.

Each calf establishes its own feeding idiosyncrasy. In the absence of the cow, the tip of the trunk must rest against something that feels "right". Some like to rest the trunk against the canvas of a tent or tarpaulin, some need more intimate contact with the keeper—the armpit, nose, eye, mouth or ear. But until a suitable substitute for the cow has been found, there will be tantrums at feeding times. These must be handled with understanding and patience. The temperature of the feed is also important. Unless milk feeds are the correct temperature, they will be rejected.

Elephant calves must also be kept clean. They should be sponged down after each soiling, and the feces covered quickly with earth before being scooped up and buried. Yet the calves must not be kept so sterile that they will be intolerant of the normal bacteria encountered in day-to-day living. At a very early age they should have access to the fresh dung of other elephants; small quantities of this are ingested to establish the stomach microflora. Consistency and frequency of stools is not important, so long as the stool does not separate into "curds and whey", for this signifies deep trouble. Furthermore, oral medication, particularly antibiotics, should be avoided. Rice water, rehydration salts, and mineral injections should be administered during stomach upsets.

Baby elephants are susceptible to pneumonia. They must be kept dry and warm at all times, blanketed whenever there is a chill in the air, and protected by rainwear when necessary. Newborn elephants are also very prone to sunburn for the first six weeks of life, so their tender "pink" baby ears and back should be protected with sunblock and shade should be provided.

Like humans, baby elephants become easily bored, so interest may be stimulated by changing the surroundings. They like an earth pit to romp in, and, when it is very hot, a mudwallow is an essential. Mud not only cools the animal in the assumed absence of sweat glands, but also seals moisture in the skin, and protects against sun damage and biting insects. But, perhaps the most important requisite for elephants is space. In elephant terms, space is the freedom to roam far and wide by day with their human family, just as they would in the wild with their elephant family. Given this, they can be stabled at night, so long as their keepers are with them. To start with, the keeper should be in physical contact with the elephant. Later on, when the infant's grieving and nightmares have subsided, the keeper can enjoy a better night's sleep on a bunk slung from the roof of the stable, but still within trunk reach.

Raising wild animals provides a unique insight into the subtle complexities of animals: their thinking and their feelings, their explicit body language, and the hidden world of mysterious senses normally beyond human understanding. Elephants are richly endowed with all of these. Of all the animals, they are, perhaps, also one of the most human, sharing with us a parallel rate of growth and development and similar longevity.

ELEPHANT COMMUNICATION

KATHERINE B. PAYNE AND WILLIAM R. LANGBAUER, JR.

Elephants live in a society that is coordinated by layers and layers of communication. Short-range communication involving all sensory modalities—touch, taste, smell, vision, and hearing—provides continuous cohesion within small, close-knit groups, and enables individuals to identify and assess the condition of other elephants when traveling groups or individuals meet. Longer range communication integrates the behavior of widely spaced groups of cows and calves and enables males to find a female spontaneously during her brief window of estrus. The discussion which follows starts with communication at short range and works outward, considering the advantages and disadvantages of each sensory modality for the sorts of messages that elephants need to convey and the environments through which the messages must pass. Each part of the communication system is a valuable (but not an omnipotent) tool.

▶ Elephants use a combination of touch, smell, and taste to get to know one another. Contact generally involves mutual examination with the trunk tip, which is extended to various parts of the other's body: mainly, the mouth, ears, eyes, temporal glands, feet, tail, anus, and genitalia. Dung and urine also provide individual-specific chemical information. Touching around the mouth, as shown here, is a frequent greeting ceremony.

▼ The male elephant gently lays his trunk along the female's back just before copulation. The fertile period during the 4-month estrous cycle of the female lasts between 48 and 96 hours. A bull detects this crucial window for mating by sniffing the female's genitals, then placing his trunk in his mouth to test for chemicals signaling her sexual receptivity.

Our comments about the behavior of elephants are based largely on long-term studies of African elephants by Iain Douglas-Hamilton, Cynthia Moss, and Joyce Poole, and on our observations and field experiments. The few studies available on Asian elephants show them to be similar in most respects.

TACTILE COMMUNICATION

Elephants touch each other frequently, and at times the touching is obviously communicative. Adults and calves stroke each other with their trunks in greeting, or press on each other's heads in dominance assessment. Older elephants discipline younger ones by trunk-slapping, kicking, or shoving them. Elephants entwine trunks during greeting and in mild competition. Touch is involved in the play of elephants of all ages and both sexes, but particularly calves, which climb and slide over each other especially when they are slippery after mud-bathing. Some play among calves includes copulatory positions. Precopulatory behavior among adults includes touching of female genitals by searching males, and, once a mate is found, the male lays his trunk along the female's back before mounting. Similar behaviors are occasionally seen between adult males. Elephants of all ages and both sexes touch mouths, temporal glands, and genitals, especially during meetings or in response to excitement.

Tactile communication is particularly apparent in the family bonding and early "education" of calves. A cow with a newborn calf maintains contact with it most of the time, reaching down to it with her trunk or touching it with a foot when it walks beside her, or repeatedly tapping its back with her tail when it walks behind her. A calf solicits nursing by touching its mother's legs and breast and calling—eliciting either the desired response or a rejection accompanied by a call from the mother—and it may similarly communicate its desire to rest when a herd is on the move by pressing against the mother's front legs. When the herd stops to rest, a calf will often lie under the mother in the center of her legs, so that any motion can be easily detected by touch.

CHEMICAL COMMUNICATION

Elephants rely heavily on chemical cues. Often the first sign that two elephants have noticed each other is when they extend trunks toward each other. Tactile and chemical communication often occur simultaneously. Elephants frequently touch each other's genitals, mouths, temporal glands, dung, and urine with their trunks. All of these are sources of chemical cues. Elephants also often lift their trunks and rotate the open tips, testing the air. We can say with confidence that elephants use chemical communication for the transfer of short- and long-distance information.

Nigel Tucker/Planet Earth Pictures

Jonathan Scott/Seaphot Ltd. Planet Earth Pictures

Jonathan Scott/Planet Earth Pictures

Dieter and Mary Plage/Bruce Coleman Ltd

Frans Lanting/Minden Pictures

▲ (Top) While the visual acuity of elephants at close range is good, over greater distances they rely very little on vision to obtain information about their surroundings. Instead, they are able to use their trunks as olfactory "periscopes" to descry windborne scents, and possibly pick up advanced warning of the presence of other animals or humans in the vicinity.

▲ A baby Asian elephant seeking sustenance and reassurance. When a calf is hungry, it issues a suckle protest in the form of a tiny growl. Its mother responds with soft rumbles, followed by immediate gratification.

Much of the research on olfactory communication in elephants was initially done with Asian elephants in the Washington Park (now Oregon) Zoo in Portland. By smelling a female's urine or vulva, a male can tell whether she is in estrus (breeding condition): if she is, the male will lift his trunk to his mouth and flehmen—puffing a little air into a passage in the upper palate which sends it to the Jacobson's organ, where it can be tested for chemicals indicating the sexual condition of the female. This behavior is so predictable that some zoos use it as an assay of females' sexual condition.

By smelling an adult male's urine, females can tell if he is in musth (a condition of increased aggression and sexual activity). If he is, they respond even if the male himself is not present.

Elephants frequently put their trunk tips into each other's mouths, a behavior which increases when one of the animals is eating, and when previously separated individuals meet, suggesting that smelling and/or tasting is occurring.

The temporal glands, which lie midway between an elephant's eye and ear, are another obvious source of chemical information, and are frequently touched and sniffed by individuals of both sexes and all ages. The temporal glands of females drain in proportion to their level of excitement; in males these glands drain in extreme

excitement (during a serious fight or flight or mating); in addition, they drain prominently when the animal is in musth. Betsy Rasmussen and others found that this temporal fluid, or temporin, contains a higher concentration of testosterone during musth, and so provides a chemical cue as to an animal's condition. There is evidence that the chemical composition of temporin may differ between individuals, and elephants may use these differences as one of the ways in which they identify each other. Elephants sometimes rub their temporal glands against tree trunks, presumably leaving chemical evidence of their presence.

Dung is also sniffed. On one occasion a male, which had just defeated another in a three-hour contest, provided an anecdotal indication that dung and/or urine contain individual-specific information. The winner stopped to mud-bathe while the loser, fleeing, disappeared over the horizon. The winner then tracked the loser for over 1.6 kilometers (1 mile) with trunk to ground, following every turn of direction the other had taken and not diverging when the track intersected with dung, urine, and tracks of other elephants.

An elephant is continually attentive to windborne scents, sometimes raising its trunk, and directing and redirecting its trunk tip which presumably maximizes its ability to localize as well

as identify the source of a scent. Wind-borne scent usually provides elephants with their first clues to the proximity of any source of danger (that is, humans or lions in Africa; humans or tigers for Asian elephants): first one, then several trunks will be raised; group-alerting calls follow, then freezing (holding still) and listening or group flight.

From a combination of chemical signals, elephants apparently glean news about each other's presence, emotional and physiological states, and to some extent the trails over which they have passed. In comparison to tactile information, chemical cues are long lasting and can function over both short and long distances. Unlike visual information, chemical information can be received whether or not the receiver is facing the source. However, certain kinds of information about the origin of a scent, including its present location and the time of its origin, are imperfectly conveyed by the sense of smell and better perceived by other sensory systems, especially vision and hearing.

VISUAL COMMUNICATION

Elephants use visual displays to inform or influence each other over short distances. As we human beings well know, there is nothing like vision for rapid transmission of unambiguous information. Yet vision is a poor system to use over long

distances, for unless the perceiver is fairly close to and facing the signaler, with no obstacles between them, the message will not be received at all.

Visual displays are often used in adversarial contexts. Like many other animals, elephants attempt to appear larger during conflicts, and their classic threat display consists of the animal facing its foe head on, with the head raised and the ears spread wide. Other threatening movements involve shaking the head and sharply snapping the ears (which also produces a loud noise), and throwing dust and bushes into the air. These displays are often bluffs, and they may not escalate to further aggression. An elephant that is more aroused and likely to actually fight will often fold its ears into a V-shaped position. Ear folding and ear flapping also often proceed musth rumbles, distinctive calls made by bulls in musth. This is discussed in more detail under "Acoustic Communication". Bulls in musth often drape their trunks over their tusks, or fold their trunks back over their foreheads. However, both gestures occur in non-musth elephants as well; in the case of musth males these positions may relieve pressure on the temporal glands, which are swollen during musth.

There are many fine gradations of expressive movements and positions in elephants. Kuhme, who studied captive African elephants, described

▲ A family enjoying a midday bath suddenly takes flight, possibly after receiving a warning call from a distant herd alerting them to impending danger.

▲ (Top) An unusual encounter. As with other mammals, bull elephants will often avoid direct confrontations; these combatants seem to have found a suitable partition.

▲ An African elephant in Savuti, Botswana, with its trunk draped over a tusk. This gesture may be more common with musth bulls, where it may help to relieve pressure on the swollen temporal glands; however, it also occurs in non-musth elephants, possibly to relax trunk musculature or for reasons not entirely understood.

over twenty different combinations of head, ear, and trunk positions, each indicating various degrees of aggression and submission. In general, greater levels of excitement are accompanied by a higher head position, raised trunk and spread ears, while more submissive postures involve a lowered head, lowered trunk, and ears flat against the neck.

Not all ear movements are communicative in function. Elephant ears are also used as radiators to dissipate heat, and when it is very hot elephants flap their ears to increase the cooling effect.

On a larger scale, an elephant's location and movements within a group readily convey information about its role and condition as well. A female elephant which has just come into estrus will often advertise this fact by walking by herself at the outskirts of the group and running away from the young males that try to copulate with

her, although she is often caught and mounted anyway. Males in musth have a distinctive "musth walk", characterized by a head-high posture and enormous swaying strides, as opposed to the lower profile and slower walk when not in musth. The differences in posture and gait are distinct enough for a trained human observer to spot at a distance of over a kilometer (over half a mile). When a female is being guarded by a musth male she too has a recognizably altered gait; she leads him in large circles or figures of eight while looking slightly sideways to keep him in sight.

ACOUSTIC COMMUNICATION

Elephants have a large and varied repertoire of vocal behavior, ranging from their well-known trumpets to the infrasonic calls which are too low in pitch for humans to normally hear. All of these calls are presumably produced by the larynx, with some calls modified by the resonance of the trunk. Acoustic communication operates over both short and long distances in elephant society, with some infrasonic calls audible to other elephants several kilometers away. An advantage of acoustic communication for long-distance communication is that the source of the signal can be more sharply localized in time and space than chemical signals. And, unlike vision, an animal does not have to be facing the caller to receive the signal.

While much work still needs to be done to decipher the meanings of specific elephant calls (and even to determine how many different call types there are), there are a number of calls that are sufficiently distinctive, and given under circumstances that are sufficiently consistent, that we can guess their function.

Trumpets indicate a high state of arousal. They are given in aggressive situations (often accompanied by spread ears and a raised trunk), when in distress, and in exciting circumstances such as bond group greeting ceremonies. In these ceremonies, groups of elephants greet each other excitedly, trumpeting, screaming, bellowing, and rumbling, while urinating, defecating, exploring each other's temporal glands, vulvas, mouths, and other body parts with their trunks, and sometimes bumping into each other's bodies and clashing tusks. Every mode of communication is involved. Particular groups tend to greet each other in this way after periods of separation, and this behavior contrasts with the way they greet other groups, with apparent indifference, displacement, or avoidance. We suspect that groups that exhibit bond group greeting ceremonies are closely related to each other. Members of the same family also show this behavior after periods of separation.

Elephants that are involved in stationary activities such as eating, drinking, dusting, and mud-bathing, often move off together in unison after a member of their group emits a series of long, low-pitched, and (to human ears) soft calls,

S. Robinson/NHPA

known as "let's go" rumbles. Nearby elephants belonging to other groups do not respond.

Another call that functions over short distances is the suckle protest, given by calves attempting to suckle. This call usually elicits an instant rumbling response from the calf's mother. A recognizably different soft humming rumble is given by a mother with a new calf.

A number of calls are associated with musth. Males in musth make a pulsated, low-frequency call known as the "musth rumble". When alone, musth males will often stop and listen immediately before and/or after rumbling, holding perfectly still, with their heads erect and ears spread. It is thought that these calls may be, among other factors, a spacing mechanism, enabling aggressive musth males to avoid unexpected meetings. When these calls are made in the presence of a group of female elephants, the females sometimes answer with a set of low-frequency, overlapping calls. These may serve to advertise the presence of the musth male to other females in the group. Dominant musth males are the preferred sexual partner of estrous females; these animals tend to be the oldest and largest males in the population and presumably the most "fit".

Calls that function over longer distances include the "contact call" and "contact answer",

dissimilar but associated calls that seem to enable elephants in the same family group to maintain contact during times of separation.

We have evidence that elephants communicate over much longer distances, and that infrasonic calls play an important role in this communication. Infrasound is ideally suited to long-distance communication, since low-frequency sound propagates much more efficiently than high-pitched sound. High-pitched sounds, like the trumpeting calls of elephants, have short wavelengths, and are readily reflected by objects in the environment such as leaves of trees or stalks of grass. The longer waves of infrasound are essentially unimpeded by these obstructions. In addition, higher pitched sound vibrates the air at a greater rate than low-pitched sound, and with each vibration energy is lost in the form of heat. These heat and reflection losses can be substantial; in grassy savannas or woodlands trumpets may be audible to elephants over distances of several hundreds of meters, while infrasonic calls at the same sound pressure levels may be audible to elephants kilometers away. Some African and almost all Asian elephants spend most of their lives in dense forest; researchers have assumed that they derive a particularly great advantage from the use of infrasound.

▲ An African elephant in threat posture with head raised, facing the stimulus, and ears extended at right angles to the body. This impressive display, magnifying the animal's "largeness", is often also accompanied by exaggerated kicking of dirt and/or throwing dirt over the back with the trunk; the cloud of dust adds to the visual impact of the performance.

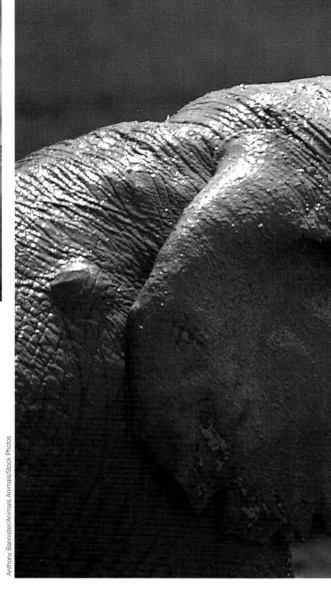

▲ Elephants at a waterhole in Savuti, Botswana, delicately caress one another in what appears to be a show of affection. Despite their ponderous bulk, elephants are extremely tactile, possibly capable of conveying tenderness and emotion.

The long-distance potential of elephants' acoustic communication system may have co-evolved with two unusual aspects of the life histories of elephants. The first is the efficiency with which males find a receptive female during her very brief period of estrus. It is rare for a female to go through her period of estrus without being impregnated. Since the interval between calves is usually about four years, and the fertile period of estrus only lasts two to four days, an estrous female is a scarce resource. This scarcity is compounded by the fact that mature males and females live and move for the most part independently from each other, often separated by a few kilometers. Yet mature bulls are able to find and mate with the receptive female during the brief time of her availability. A powerful repetitive low-frequency call which females give only during estrus provides one way in which the males and females can locate each other. Playback experiments have indicated that bulls can perceive these calls at least 4 kilometers (2 1/2 miles) from the sender. Chemical communication and other available cues probably combine with acoustic communication to support this mate-finding behavior.

Another behavior suggesting long-distance communication was documented by Rowan Martin during a radio-tracking project covering several years in Zimbabwe. He found that groups of elephants separated by several kilometers will often move along parallel or otherwise coordinated paths for days or weeks at a time, even when they are separated by substantial distances. This behavior continues during periods when wind conditions are inappropriate for the use of chemical cues, although chemical cues may well be utilized when available. The ability of elephants to keep in touch over several kilometers may allow them to spread out enough to exploit the limited resources during the dry season, while staying close enough to each other to protect their young from predators. Data from radio telemetry studies are now being analyzed to determine the role of infrasonic calls in this coordinated inter-group behavior.

It is important to note that the same call may function in both short- and long-distance contexts. The group pandemonium that occurs when a calf is caught by a lion or falls into a waterhole has the obvious short-distance function of mobilizing aid for the unlucky calf, but it also contains calls sufficiently powerful to be heard by other elephants several kilometers away. Although perhaps not the intended audience, these distant elephants are thus provided with information on the location and, presumably, identity of the calling group, information that can be of use if the elephant groups are attempting to keep in touch.

Let us now try to relate what we have learned of elephants' communicative abilities to some of the

other striking characteristics of these animals, and ponder over how these may have worked together over evolutionary time to produce elephants as we now know them.

Related to the enormous size and slow development of elephants are their twenty-two-month gestation period and four-year inter-calf interval. A calf lost to starvation, desiccation or predation is not readily replaced, and the early years in a calf's development are costly to the social group into which it is born. These factors have probably acted as selective pressures resulting in the evolution of a high level of sociality in elephants. Group living, however, confers a concomitant disadvantage on elephants since their daily food and water requirements are so great.

Nevertheless, elephants are found in areas which are seasonally so barren that it is hard to see how they survive and avoid exhausting the resources on which they depend. Two factors must be important in the exploitation of such areas by

elephants. The first is the combination of longevity (leading to accumulated experience), memory, and the matriarchal organization of families which confers leadership on older individuals. The second is the flexibility of elephant social groupings—the ability of large groups to subdivide for foraging yet quickly recombine for anti-predator solidarity.

The basis for this flexibility is long-distance communication, for which the olfactory and acoustic sensory systems of elephants are well suited. Long, maneuverable trunks enable them to continually sniff the ground in spite of their great heights, and thus easily track family members, mates, or rivals. Their enormous size undoubtedly has something to do with their ability to produce very low-frequency sounds at high-pressure levels. Elephants are unusually sensitive to low-frequency sound, and somehow manage to localize these sounds, a feat which is not fully understood but presumably enhanced by the wide separation between their ears.

▲ Two young bull elephants in Addo Elephant National Park, South Africa, intertwine trunks in a playful test of strength and status. With females, trunk-wrapping is more a family greeting ritual than it is an exercise in asserting dominance.

ECOLOGY AND BEHAVIOR

S. KEITH ELTRINGHAM

The elephant occupies an important place in the community of wild herbivores to which it belongs. Its sheer size indicates a demand for a vast amount of food to fuel its activities. Yet, relative to its weight, the proportion of food consumed by the elephant is much less than that of smaller mammals.

Although it is not easy to measure the actual weight of food taken by an elephant, estimates have recorded fluctuations of between 100 and 300 kilograms (220 and 660 pounds) each day for African elephants of both species and around 150 kilograms (330 pounds) for the Asian species. Female elephants eat less—about 80 percent, by weight, of the amount eaten by bulls.

As one would imagine, the large quantity of forage taken has a very significant effect on the vegetation, and the elephant is one of the few species that can fundamentally change its own environment. For this reason, the elephant is known as a megaherbivore (defined as a herbivore weighing more than 1,000 kilograms, 2,200 pounds). Other megaherbivores include the hippopotamus, four of the five species of rhinoceros, and the male giraffe.

Not only do elephants eat a large amount of the vegetation, they also have the ability to uproot trees, destroy bushes, and, by their weight, can compact the soil so that rain does not soak into the ground but runs off, causing erosion. Of the megaherbivores, it is without doubt the species with the greatest capacity for damage.

On the other hand, when elephants disappear from an environment, the change is marked and significant. Sadly, as a result of poaching, this has happened in many parts of Africa. One of the most striking changes can be seen in the Queen Elizabeth National Park in Uganda, where a flourishing population of some 4,000 elephants was reduced to a couple of hundred in the 1970s through poaching. Some regions which were once open grassland are now thick woodland and thickets have increased in size. This has also had a marked effect on the distribution of the other species of wildlife. Giant forest hogs, for example, are now seen in places many kilometers away from their usual haunts and grazing antelopes have been displaced from parts of their previous range.

In national park management, it is the destructive effect of its numbers on the vegetation that makes the elephant a problem animal and has led to culling programs to reduce the numbers to a level at which the damage is tolerable.

Despite their importance in modifying the vegetation, elephants remain near the base of the ecological pyramid along with other herbivores. All member species of an ecosystem occupy one or more of the trophic levels. At the base are the plants which support all other life in the system. The ecosystem can be considered as a pyramid because, as each trophic level is reached, the biomass (the weight of living matter) is reduced.

At the first level above the plants are the herbivores, or primary consumers, and it is to this trophic level or guild that the elephant belongs. Above them are the primary carnivores and at the top are the secondary carnivores, which eat primary carnivores as well as herbivores. Parasites also belong here. The omnivores may occur at several of the trophic levels.

Although the elephant is relatively free from predation, it nevertheless is in the same position as any small antelope in that it will eventually finish up in the stomach of a carnivore, possibly a scavenger's rather than a predator's.

The elephant appears not to fear other animals and, in fact, usually ignores them. Any possible interactions are rarely direct, unless, of course, another animal happens to get in the way. Usually a slight demonstration by the elephant is sufficient to persuade the other animal to move off but sometimes a cantankerous buffalo will hold its ground and it usually is the elephant that will defer.

Studies of aggressive interactions with other animals remain contradictory. For example, the elephant and the rhinoceros are traditionally supposed to be mortal enemies, but in fact, other studies show that the two species are usually mutually tolerant. One exception to this occurred several years ago, when a black rhinoceros was killed by a group of elephants at the Treetops Lodge in the Aberdare National Park in Kenya when it attacked a young calf.

Contests, when they occur, between the Asian elephant and rhinoceros are more even as the Indian rhinoceros is bigger and, unlike the African species, has sharp incisor tusks in the lower jaw, which are capable of inflicting severe wounds on elephants. Such confrontations are probably very rare in the wild but they have occurred with domestic elephants that have been ridden into the rhino's domain. If the elephant stands its ground, there is no attack, but should it turn and run, the rhinoceros may follow and slash it from behind.

African elephants are invariably hostile to lions, which they presumably see as a threat to their calves. There have been a few reports of

Peter Johnson/NHPA

encounters between tigers and Asian elephants although these may be tame elephants being clawed under the artificial conditions of a tiger hunt. Interactions with crocodiles have also been reported. For example, there are records of African elephants seizing crocodiles by the tail and killing them by flailing them against the ground.

For the most part, however, the activities of elephants and other species are relatively harmonious. The elephant's habit of knocking over trees, breaking off branches and pulling down lianas makes food available to smaller herbivores that they would not otherwise be able to reach. Other species contribute less in return, although the cropping of the grass by grazers ensures that it remains in a young, nutritious phase to the benefit of all.

Elephants also have a close association with several species of birds. Cattle egrets frequently ride on their backs, using them not so much as a means of transport, but as a lookout post from which to pounce on insects and small animals, such as frogs, disturbed by the passage of the elephant. Egrets also follow elephants on the ground for the same purpose. Birds like the piapiac generally feed on ticks or lice attached to the elephants. The piapiac is a sleek member of the crow family, which scuttles up and down the legs and body of the elephant, picking off ticks and other ectoparasites.

This is an example of mutualism in which one species benefits from the presence of the other. The elephant supplies the piapiac with a source of food and the bird clears it of irritating and potentially

▲ Because of their immense size, elephants need a great deal of living space. Sadly, the conflict between elephants and expanding human populations has forced these magnificent creatures into ever-smaller areas in Africa and Asia.

125

Michel Denis-Huot/Jacana/Auscape

▲ Browsing is usually a group activity led by a dominant female or matriarch. The vegetation on which elephants live is composed largely of cellulose, containing only small amounts of digestible protein and vital nutrients. As a result, they must spend at least 16 hours of each day just eating—up to 300 kilograms (660 pounds) of food per day for an adult bull.

pathogenic parasites. Only recently have there been reports of oxpeckers feeding on ectoparasites on elephants. It is usually the reaction of the host to the birds that determines whether or not they are allowed to feed. Some mammals, such as the impala, are very intolerant of tick birds and shake them off.

It is, incidentally, unlikely that the birds serve as a lookout, providing a warning service for the mammal, despite confident statements to the contrary in the literature. What may disturb a bird is usually of no consequence to the larger animal, which is unlikely to react to the alarm calls of other species. Egrets are bound to flutter off in noisy disarray when an elephant reacts to an approaching danger but this should not be interpreted as a warning signal.

Elephants, in destroying woody vegetation, can have a depressing effect on the survival of woodland species of birds. This was pointed out when the woodlands of the Murchison Falls National Park in Uganda were being threatened by the destructive effects of an overabundance of elephants. There are 410 bird species on the checklist of the park of which 41 were completely or mainly dependent on woodland and a further 35 for which woodland was a complete habitat. Another 127 species used the woodlands for some of the time. Hence the destruction of trees by elephants has a profound effect on the ecology of birds as well as on other species, such as monkeys, that occupy this habitat.

As with almost all animals, elephants suffer from a host of invertebrate parasites, including biting flies and bloodsucking mosquitoes. Twenty-one species of ixodid ticks have been recorded from the African elephant, of which two are rarely found on any other animal. Ticks are responsible for a number of viral diseases as well as depriving the host of blood. The latter might not seem

important in a beast as large as an elephant but its ticks are of proportionate size and a heavy infestation, particularly of a young animal, could cause a significant loss of blood. Other bloodsuckers include leeches, especially in the Asian jungles, which can extract even greater quantities of blood than ticks can. The only species of louse that attacks elephants is *Haematomyzus elephantis* which is found on both African and Asian elephants. This louse is of particular interest in that it is classified in a family of its own, quite different from all other types of lice. They usually concentrate around the underbelly and base of the tail and appear to cause intense itching, judging from the lengths to which the elephant will go to find a rock on which to scrape its skin. They are not known to transmit any diseases, however.

Both Asian and African elephants are often bothered by warble (or bot) flies, which lay their eggs on the surface of the skin. On hatching, the larvae burrow into the body, eventually making their way into the stomach, where they feed on the host's tissues before moving back to the skin and forming swellings. These swellings are known as warbles and appear on either side of the backbone. When mature, the maggots work their way out of the swelling and fall to the ground, where they pupate. Normally there are only a few larvae on each elephant, causing only minor annoyance, but sometimes very heavy infestations occur.

Elephants also play host to a variety of internal parasites. Liver flukes and tapeworms have been recorded as well as over thirty species of roundworms (ascarids), which include the potentially debilitating strongyloid nematodes (hookworms). Tiny nematodes (microfilaria), which cause serious illness in humans, are commonly found in the bloodstream of elephants. Despite the heavy load of parasites, elephants do not appear to suffer unduly from them although their presence might tip the balance if the host became sick or undernourished.

There are plenty of other little creatures living inside elephants but most are beneficial and, indeed, essential to the well-being of the host. These are the bacteria and protozoa that ferment the cellulose in the food and break it down into soluble carbohydrates (sugars) that the elephant can absorb into its system. All of the protozoa in the elephant are ciliates, one of the most advanced classes in the group. Cellulose is indigestible, as no mammal has an enzyme that can denature it, yet it is the principal component of the food of most herbivores. The micro-organisms that provide this service for the mammal are found in the rumen of those herbivores that chew the cud, but in others, including the elephant, the fermentation chamber is the greatly expanded cecum and colon, which lie further back in the gut.

Elephants spend much of their time feeding— as much as three-quarters of their lives, according to

Nigel Dennis/NHPA

one study carried out in Uganda. This appears to be typical of most elephants, whether African or Asian, although less is known about those in forests. Feeding is not continuous, however, for some time has to be spent in digestion.

The three principal feeding bouts occur in the morning, afternoon and night. There is usually a long resting period in the small hours, after the main night-time feed, and another, shorter period around midday, when the elephant retires under a tree, as much to avoid the heat of the sun as to rest. At night an elephant may lie down to sleep, whereas the midday sleep is more of a "snooze" than a sleep and is performed while it stands.

Although the teeth of the elephant suggest that it is a specialist grazer, a considerable quantity of the African elephant's food is in the form of browse (woody vegetation as opposed to grass). The proportion varies with the season with more being taken in the dry season, when the grass tends to be withered. In another study in Uganda, it was found that the proportion of browse in the diet ranged from 1 to 45 percent, depending on the availability of thickets as well as on the season. The amount of browse eaten increased once the monthly rainfall fell below 50 millimeters (2 inches). Elsewhere in Africa, it has been found

that elephants in open rangeland feed mostly on grass during the wet season and that they turn more to browse as the dry season approaches.

A recent study of the Asian elephant in grassland revealed a more equal selection of grass and browse, even in the wet season. During the dry season, the amount of browse taken exceeded grass by a factor of more than two on average. On the other hand, Asian elephants in forests still select grass preferentially.

The forest species of the African elephant feeds extensively on fruits and is hence important as a seed disperser. Thus, of the seventy-one tree species in the Tai Forest in the Ivory Coast, twenty-one (29.6 percent) are known to be dispersed by elephants. The number could well be higher as seeds from a total of thirty-seven tree species were identified in elephant droppings and of these only seven are known to be dispersed by other animals, such as monkeys or birds.

Interactions between plants and animals usually show a fine balance between destruction and construction. The elephant plays a pivotal role in the structure of its ecosystem; on the whole, its activities are beneficial. It is only under the somewhat artificial conditions of a national park that it becomes an instrument of destruction.

▲ In general, elephants coexist peaceably with other animals that share their domain. If threatened, however, the elephant can be a powerful and ferocious opponent. Although the rhino and the elephant have been traditionally regarded as foes, here they are seen drinking together from a drying waterhole.

EROSION BY ELEPHANTS

IAN M. REDMOND

Among the forces of nature that shape the surface of the land, there is one which has long been overlooked: elephant erosion. This process can be seen in action today only in Africa and southern Asia, but it may once have been much more widespread, when proboscideans were also found in Europe, northern Asia and the Americas. The key to understanding the phenomenon is salt appetite.

▲ The remarkable mining elephants of Mount Elgon, Kenya. All mammals need to maintain an internal salt balance against losses via various secreted body fluids. On the whole, carnivores are guaranteed a steady replacement supply through their animal diet, but herbivorous animals such as elephants are frequently stressed by this requirement, and often make up the deficit by licking or swallowing mineral salts directly from the ground. In the unique salt caves of Mount Elgon in East Africa, thousands of years of visits by elephants digging for salt underground have resulted in numerous substantial caves, each a cul-de-sac with scalloped walls covered in tusk-marks.

An elephant whose diet is deficient in essential salts will, like any other herbivore, seek out exposures of mineral-rich strata and eat the salty earth or rock. This behavior, known as *geophagy*, is quite commonplace in the animal world and is the reason farmers provide their cattle with salt-lick blocks. Unlike other herbivores, however, elephants don't just lick the salt (their tongues aren't long enough), they excavate it. Elephants are such large, powerful animals, and are so well equipped for digging, that their salt excavations can significantly alter the local landscape.

The long-term effect of this novel form of erosion varies according to the original topography. Where the minerals are found in fairly flat ground, a salt-hungry elephant will thrust its tusk into the earth, then pick up the loosened clods with its trunk-tip and loop them up into its mouth. Each elephant may ingest the equivalent of one or two buckets full of earth, and may visit the salt-lick every two or three days as the need dictates. Their digging also benefits other, smaller species of animal by exposing new deposits of salt. Over a period of time this process will create a deeper and deeper depression as more and more earth is carried away in elephants' stomachs. In the Dzanga-Sangha area of Central African Republic, for

example, forest elephants have dug holes in the ground so big that an elephant down in one is hidden from view.

Where the mineral-rich strata have been cut through by a stream or river, however, the most accessible source of salts may be in the cliffs or steep-sided walls of the river valley. In such locations, the elephants' tusking is usually directed laterally into the exposed salty layers, creating small caves and overhangs. This kind of excavation has been reported in elephant habitats ranging from the Ranun River in Sumatra to the outer slopes of Ngorongoro Crater in Tanzania. As these caves deepen, the soft, friable rock overhangs collapse. If salty, these rockfalls are also eaten. The effect over millennia is of a gradually receding cliff. Only in one known locality has this process resulted in deep caves, and that is on Mount Elgon, a huge extinct volcano on the Kenya–Uganda border.

On Elgon, the layers of volcanic ash which contain the most salts are those that lie beneath hardened flows of lava. When the lava cooled, it formed a layer of basalt-like rock which is impervious to the rainfall. Caves are usually found where forest streams slip over the lip of the lava, to cascade down the resulting cliff. Beneath this lava umbrella, elephants and other herbivores penetrate

C. & D. Bromhall/Genesis Films Ltd/Oxford Scientific Films

deep into the huge caverns, clambering over massive slabs of fallen roof and skirting deep crevasses, simply to satisfy their hunger for salt.

Why, though, are the herbivores of Mount Elgon salt-hungry? Heavy rainfall leaches the soluble salts from the surface soils and the underlying porous ash. Animals that feed on the plants that grow in these soils have a problem. They need salts—particularly sodium salts—to make up the deficit in their diet. The most abundant salt in the cave walls is sodium sulphate. Analysis shows that, weight for weight, rock from a cave wall contains 100 times the level of sodium ions present in samples of dried foodplants. This, then, explains the urge that drives elephants, hyraxes, buffaloes, antelopes, and even colobus monkeys into Elgon's unique subterranean salt-licks.

Some of the caves are immense, extending up to 200 paces more or less horizontally into the mountain, and widening in some instances to more than 100 paces across inside. The cave roof in most is about as high as an elephant can reach, but occasional rockfalls of salty rock occur, resulting in spectacular domed ceilings in some chambers—roost sites for thousands of bats.

Despite their size, most of Elgon's caves are well hidden in the forested valleys. The entrance

may be partially blocked by a rockfall and screened on either side of the waterfall by a curtain of crystal clear droplets and hanging plants. But the Elgon elephants know where to find the accessible caves. From their earliest days, tiny calves follow their mothers into the pitch black interior, and are guided to the mining bays deep underground. Baby elephants do not, normally, need extra salt. As long as they are suckled by their mothers, they get a balanced diet. But the mother *will* need extra salt, and so families of cows and calves are frequent visitors to the salt mines.

To the human witness, the sight of a long line of elephants disappearing slowly, one by one, trunk to tail, into a hole in the ground seems astonishing. But we must remember that to these particular elephants this is normal behavior.

Like humans, elephants learn from their mothers, and from the other elders in their family, how to behave in their society and how to survive in their local environment. The knowledge of where to find essentials, such as food, water, and mineral salts, at all times of the year, is passed on from generation to generation. In a very real sense, this is cultural knowledge. All over Africa, each clan of elephants is like a tribe in which the knowledge of generations—the tribal culture—is

▲ A visiting elephant surprised in Kitum Cave, Mount Elgon. Here, most elephants have their tusks extensively worn from frequent digging of the salt rock. Despite the complete darkness in some of the innermost chambers, these elephants are capable of negotiating their way through the cave's obstacle course, using their trunks like built-in white canes. Recent studies have revealed that beneath the bat roosts, the guano reacts with the rock to form an even more mineral-rich crust which the elephants seem to prefer.

▼ (Below) Side view and interior layout of Kitum Cave, Mount Elgon. Elephants, other herbivores, roosting bats, and nesting birds are among the cave's many visitors.

▼ (Bottom) This lick has been supplemented with extra salt (the white patch) to encourage elephants for tourists to watch.

vital for that tribe's survival in its own particular habitat. Without this knowledge, elephants could not live in the deserts of Namibia or Chad, they could not survive the droughts of Kenya's arid lands, nor could they live in forests where vegetation is low in salt.

For an elephant on Elgon, there is much to learn. Not only do they need to know the whereabouts of the best caves—and there are dozens, if not hundreds to choose from—they must also learn the interior layout and hidden dangers of each one. Dried carcasses of baby elephants, wedged in steep-sided crevasses, are testimony to the dangers of a careless footstep in these dark caverns.

For human observers, too, there is much to learn. We do not know how often an individual elephant visits a cave, nor whether each herd has its favorites. Do they simply utilize the nearest cave on their perambulations through the forest? We *do* know that 45 percent of elephant dung examined contained particles of rock, so cave visits may occur every few days. And we know that different groups of elephants may visit the same cave on consecutive nights. From observations underground, we can also estimate the rate of excavation, and conclude that a large cave might be created over a period of, say, 100,000 years, which, in the context of geological time, is but the blink of an eye. We can speculate that these caves might represent an unbroken line of instruction, from generation to generation of elephants, dating back to the first cliff-digging elephants that ventured onto the newly quiescent volcano 3 million years ago. But sadly, the chances of learning more about this amazing phenomenon are increasingly slim.

Like most tribes of elephants across Africa, the unique Elgon cave elephants have been badly hit by ivory poachers. Despite the fact that they live in a National Park and have worn-down, scratched and pitted tusks, the mid-1980s saw the slaughter of most of Elgon's elephants. From a 1970 estimate of 1,200, they were reduced to fewer than 400 by 1988. After the 1989 ban on ivory trading, poachers continued killing elephants and murdering park staff until 1991. But as the ivory trade dried up, elephant poaching on Elgon stopped for several years. Tragically, in July 1998, the bloodshed resumed. A gang of poachers killed an elephant, and then ambushed a park patrol, leaving one warden dead and four others wounded. Many concluded that the 1997 CITES decision to resume a limited ivory trade had rekindled the demand for illegal ivory.

How many are left? Dung surveys during the 1990s suggested that the population may still number in the low hundreds. Whether these few families survive to pass on the caving tradition to future generations, rests entirely on human attitudes to ivory. The Kenya government has enlarged the Mount Elgon National Park and teams of brave rangers daily risk their lives to protect it. But as long as ivory is worth a fortune the poaching will continue. It is up to the rest of the world to decide whether elephants will continue to roam there, both above and below ground.

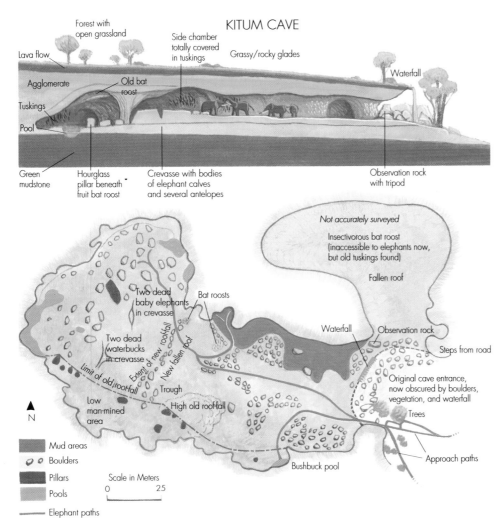

KITUM CAVE

Forest with open grassland
Lava flow
Agglomerate
Tuskings
Pool
Green mudstone
Hourglass pillar beneath fruit bat roost
Old bat roost
Side chamber totally covered in tuskings
Grassy/rocky glades
Waterfall
Crevasse with bodies of elephant calves and several antelopes
Observation rock with tripod

Not accurately surveyed
Insectivorous bat roost (inaccessible to elephants now, but old tuskings found)
Fallen roof
Two dead baby elephants in crevasse
Bat roosts
Waterfall
Observation rock
Steps from road
Two dead waterbucks in crevasse
Limit of old roof-fall
Extent of new roof-fall
New fallen roof
Trough
Low man-mined area
High old roof-fall
Original cave entrance, now obscured by boulders, vegetation, and waterfall
Trees
Approach paths
Bushbuck pool

N

Mud areas
Boulders
Pillars
Pools
Elephant paths

Scale in Meters
0   25

John Downer/Planet Earth Pictures

THE DESERT ELEPHANTS OF NAMIBIA

PHILIP J. VILJOEN

Few people would be able to forget the sight of a string of elephants, grotesquely distorted by mirages, walking in utter silence over an endless bare gravel plain. The harshness and desolation of the area make the elephants appear abstract, like a figment of the imagination. But the picture is real enough if you happen to be in the northern Namib Desert of Namibia. This is a land of beauty and harshness, where stark mountain ranges are intercepted by great sandy and endless gravel plains. Strange plants, which have adapted over millions of years to survive the inhospitable environment, are sparsely scattered over the region. Dry river courses, which create narrow oases with large, stately trees and hidden pools, form a network of lifelines throughout the area. This is part of the oldest desert in the world and it is unique in its vast spectrum of both plants and animals.

Situated in the northwestern corner of Namibia, the desert stretches from the Ugab River in the south to the Kunene River about 480 kilometers (300 miles) to the north. The desert is approximately 100 kilometers (60 miles) wide, encompassing an area of nearly 5 million hectares (12 million acres), which is larger than the whole of the Netherlands. Roads for modern vehicles are largely non-existent and vast tracts of land are inaccessible, even on foot. The rain is less than 150 millimeters (6 inches) per year, if it falls. The area is largely uninhabited: the only people who dare to venture here on a regular basis are the proud and elegant nomadic Ovahimbas and their

▼ In such an arid, inhospitable environment, elephants are able to survive because they can dig down with their tusks and trunk into dry river beds—as far as 2 meters (6 feet 6 inches) below the surface—to reach water. Once a deep seep-hole has been excavated, the elephant simply waits for it to fill with the precious liquid.

▲ Namibian poachers from the Himba Tribe in Kaokoland who "specialize" in killing the rare desert-dwelling elephant.

cattle who, to the present day, have withstood the onslaught of Western civilization.

This desert not only lies shrouded in the mystery of hidden treasures and ancient civilizations, but also boasts breathtaking scenery and an exceptional combination of flora, fauna, and topography. Its most striking aspect is the combination of desert and elephant together in a unique ecotype. The two blend to provide a constant source of wonder and amazement to traveler and scientist alike. The area is totally atypical of elephant habitat, and their adaptation, survival, and influence on the desert ecology make them one of the most intriguing and amazing elephant populations in the world. They appear to thrive in the desert and are equally at home on mountains, sand dunes, and rocky and gravel plains.

The influence of humans, however, has nearly deprived us of this unique population. Due to illegal hunting, an estimated population of about 300 desert-dwelling elephants in 1970 was steadily reduced to only 70 individuals in 1983, pushing this special breed to the brink of extinction. Fortunately, since 1982, illegal hunting has been eliminated to such a degree that the population has increased to more than 100 individuals.

While some of the questions about these elephants have been answered, there are still some mysteries. For example, why do these elephants live in the desert and how long have they been there? Reports of their occupation of this area date back to as early as 1793, but prior to that there is no record. Previously, it had been thought that the elephants only migrated to the desert seasonally until a study conducted between 1975 and 1983 established, beyond doubt, that they occupy the desert permanently. These elephants show a marked fidelity to their individual home ranges and, even during periods of extreme drought, they seem to show no inclination to move to the "greener pastures" in the east. Although confined to the desert, the elephants roam over large areas. The average home range size is 1,872 square kilometers (723 square miles) for family groups and 2,698 square kilometers (1,042 square miles) for bulls. This area is far larger than that recorded for other elephants and reflects the harsh environment in which they live.

Their permanent occupation of the desert has an interesting implication: that this special elephant group has been able to survive desert conditions and has learnt to adapt to them. This was actually illustrated during a recent five-year drought period when more than 80 percent of the other "desert" mammals like gemsbok and springbok died. As far as could be ascertained, not one of the desert-dwelling elephants died during this period.

The fact that elephants survived the other animals appears to be perplexing, but when examined more closely, the reasons are clear. Common to all elephants, including the desert dwellers, is that they feed at a higher level than most other browsers, thereby reducing competition for food. They are also unspecialized feeders, and so are able to utilize a variety of plant species, readily switching from grazing to browsing.

This group also has the ability to be extremely mobile, with movements of up to 195 kilometers (120 miles) per day in area recorded. Normally they travel 25 kilometers (16 miles) per day but can easily extend it to 70 kilometers (43 miles). Coupled with their seeming ability to go without water for up to four days, the elephants can utilize food resources as far as 80 kilometers (50 miles) away from the nearest source of water—a feat that can be equaled by few other animals. They are also able to utilize underground water by digging in the sandy riverbeds.

Probably the most important factor in their survival is their intimate knowledge of the resource distribution within their environment. A spectacular illustration of this was observed when the group set out to a waterhole, 60 kilometers (37 miles) away. Although they had not visited the site in months, they traveled there unfalteringly over the shortest and easiest route.

There has been some concern expressed at the impact of such a large animal on the fragile environment of the desert. Intensive studies, however, have shown that the present number of elephants poses no threat to the riverine vegetation in which they spend most of their time and that less than 8 percent of the woody vegetation outside river courses is being utilized. It is also interesting that the desert-dwelling elephants as a rule do not uproot trees as elsewhere in Africa. Whether this is a behavioral adaptation or a result of the different root system of the trees is unknown.

In fact, the presence of elephants in the desert appears to be to the advantage of the general ecology of the region. For instance, by digging for water in the dry riverbeds, they indirectly help numerous other animals to obtain water during droughts. The elephants also open up paths through thickets to water and choice food spots, enabling other animals to follow. They eat plants relatively unpalatable to other animals, thus preventing thicket formation at the cost of more palatable plants. Continuous browsing by elephants keeps most trees within reach of low-level feeders, and the low-growing trees and shrubs also provide a refuge for small animals and act as reservoirs of grass and herb seeds. The crude pruning effect of the feeding action by elephants, during which they break off branches and strip leaves, not only stimulates the sprouting of multiple stems which leads to an increase in browse production, but also reduces the transpiration surface of these plants, possibly then enabling them to survive on less water during the dry season.

Acacia seeds eaten by the elephants are softened by their digestive system and, in the process, water penetration for seed germination is facilitated. When the seeds are excreted, this results in a high germination success rate as opposed to uneaten seed pods which must weather for a long time before water can penetrate. Thus, the seeds in

elephant dung are immediately available for germination during the short rainy season of the desert. Also, the deep elephant tracks left in the mud during the first floods of the normally dry river courses act as seed traps that are subsequently filled up by silt and plant debris. During successive floods, this is an ideal environment for seedlings. In effect, the elephants plant their own trees. In addition, seeds in elephant dung, which otherwise remain in their hard pods, form an important food source for numerous birds.

Overall, the desert-dwelling elephants seem not only to be well adapted to the desert environment, but also to be an important facet of the desert ecology. Their rapid increase in the absence of illegal hunting also implies that they are a viable population and that, given a fair chance, they will thrive. The desert-dwelling elephants cannot be regarded as a separate subspecies, but they do represent an ecotype which illustrates the ultimate adaptational capacity of the African elephant. They also form a unique component of the ecological entity of the northern Namib Desert—a phenomenon which is not found anywhere else in the world at the present time. If we allow the desert-dwelling elephants to become extinct, a unique ecotype will be lost forever.

▼ The skeletal remains of an elephant gunned down by poachers, the stark beauty of its harsh Namibian home behind.

Mitch Reardon

INTELLIGENCE AND SURVIVAL

JEHESKEL SHOSHANI AND JOHN F. EISENBERG

Intelligence is often viewed as a human attribute, defined as the ability to exercise higher mental functions and the capacity to meet new and unforeseen situations by rapid and effective adjustment of behavior. In nature, intelligence is one of the factors linked to the survival prospects of a species.

▼ Playfulness and intelligence are often closely associated, especially in those long-lived animals, like the elephant, that have an extended childhood and adolescence. In this series a young African elephant playfully chases a baboon.

It is believed that the degree of intelligence can be correlated to the relative size of the brain to body size. In humans the brain is about one-fiftieth of body weight, whereas in elephants the brain is about one-five-hundredth of the body weight. The volume of the brain of an adult elephant is about 4,500–5,000 cubic centimeters (about 275–305 cubic inches); that of a human measures 1,400 cubic centimeters (85 cubic inches). The size of the brain of a newborn elephant is about 35 percent of an adult's brain; in many mammals this value is close to 90 percent, but in humans it is about 25 percent. Not only is the elephant brain large, weighing 4–6 kilograms (about 9–13 pounds) in adults, but it is highly convoluted in the cerebrum and cerebellum. The temporal lobes of the cerebrum are very large and bulge out from the sides of the brain. In humans the temporal lobes do not bulge. These lobes function in humans as the memory storage area.

Under captive conditions, the best method to estimate intelligence of an animal is to compare its

ability to that of some other animals, using "control" and comparable experimental situations. Such tests were conducted in the 1950s by Bernhard Rensch, and a few of these tests were repeated in 1990 by Charles W. Hyatt. Some of Rensch's experiments included visual and acoustic stimuli, for example, pairs of cards, one "positive" (food was given when an elephant chose it) and one "negative". Rensch's results show that the elephant appeared to perform better than equine species under similar conditions. It should be noted however, that these differences could be associated with the relative size of their brains; the larger the brain the better learning capacity an animal has.

Owners of elephants tell how intelligent their animals are and what excellent memories they have. They tell amazing stories of how elephants manage to solve particular problems. Bucky Steele, for example, reported that his bull, Buke, once undid himself from a chain which was fastened to a hook which was screwed to the floor of a

truck. To the surprise of an experienced elephant trainer like Bucky, Buke managed to turn the hook enough times to free himself. Tricks which elephants are taught for circus performances may take them a long time to learn, but once mastered, they may remember them until they die. Elephants can learn about 30–100 commands and can perform acts requiring a delicate sense of balance and complex neuromuscular coordination.

Measuring intelligence is close to impossible, but field observations provide us with a database which may be used to evaluate their ability to cope with changing environments. These observations need to be viewed in the perspective of the survival of a species, not individual animals. For example, elephants have been observed to exhibit altruistic behavior (an elephant will try to rescue another member of the herd even though the "rescuer" may be in danger). Some documented episodes with elephants show almost human attributes (for example, stories of elephants using leaves and grass

▶ Young elephants have been reported as playing with various objects in the wild. Here an African elephant frolics with an old car tire in Masai Mara Reserve, Kenya.

Edwin Sadd/Oxford Scientific Films

▼ "Pachyderm", the obsolete term for elephants, means "thick-skinned" but an elephant's skin is in fact quite sensitive. Here an elephant rubs his rump against a convenient tree. Elephants have also been seen to break off branches and use them as an aid to scratching places unreachable by their trunks.

Karl Ammann

branches from a tree and place them under his feet which were sinking into mud. He had been tied so that he could not reach dry ground. The branches supported him until his owner returned.

It has been said that humans are different from the rest of the primates and other animals because humans can produce and use tools, and more importantly they can pass on this information to the next generation. Elephants have also been known to make and use tools, and pass on their knowledge to younger generations.

The best example of elephants sharing useful information and passing their knowledge to the next generation relates to the accumulated experience a cow elephant uses as the best weapon to guard her family in time of stress and drought. She will guide them along the paths which are most easily traversed to places where forage may await behind a fold in the local topography, or far beyond the horizon where the eye cannot see. As the younger members of her family take their turn as leaders they too use these routes.

Another "secret" of survival is hidden deeper in the millions of body cells in the microscopic structures called genes. Like all animals and plants, elephants inherit certain characters from their parents. Living elephants possess mosaic (mixed) or generalized and specialized characters. It is those generalized or primitive features of elephants that enable them to adapt to the ever-changing environment and to the subsequent challenges, so making them true survivors; animals which are too specialized do not cope as well with changes. These features also enable them to migrate through

to cover dead elephants and humans; and of shattering tusks of dead elephants against trees or rocks; and the story, given in more detail later, of Chandrasekharan, the elephant who would not lower a pillar of wood into a hole containing a sleeping dog until the dog was chased away).

There have been numerous observations of elephants using a tree branch to scratch themselves in places where their trunk and tail would not reach, such as their back and legs. This behavior has been interpreted as tool using. On one occasion, an Asian elephant was observed to break

Joan Root/Survival Anglia

◀ The elephant's excellent memory no doubt proves useful in finding the places where water can be reached by digging during drought. These African elephants use their trunks to siphon water from a hole in a dry riverbed in Tsavo, Kenya. Elephants have even been seen to make plugs out of wads of chewed bark, which they seem to use to reduce evaporation.

▼ "Bottle baby performs 'feets' of agility." Much of the circus elephant's performance exploits its extraordinary sure-footedness and delicate sense of balance, as shown in this photograph of a young Asian elephant at the Bertram Mills Circus headquarters in England in the 1950s.

diverse habitats, across mountains, deserts, valleys, and through regions below sea level.

How intelligent are elephants? A partial reply to this question may be found in these three stories which are based on authenticated reports. Two of them are about captive elephants and the third is about a wild elephant.

The first took place in Myanmar (formerly Burma). J. H. Williams wrote in *Elephant Bill*:

Many young elephants develop the naughty habit of plugging up the wooden bell (kalouk) they wear hung round their necks with good stodgy mud or clay, so that the clappers cannot ring, in order to steal silently into a grove of cultivated bananas at night. There they will have a whale of a time, quietly stuffing, eating not only the bunches of bananas, but the leaves and, indeed, the whole tree as well, and they will do this just beside the hut occupied by the owner of the grove, without waking him or any of his family.

The second episode took place in India. The main figure in this story was a large bull named Chandrasekharan. The elephant was following a truck and, upon command, was pulling logs out of it to place in pre-dug holes in preparation for a ceremony. The elephant continued to follow his master's commands until they reached one hole where the elephant would not lower the log into the hole but held it in mid-air above the hole. When the mahout approached the hole to investigate, he found a dog sleeping at the bottom;

UPI/The Bettmann Archive

only after chasing the dog away would the elephant lower the post into the hole.

The third took place in South Africa. It was observed that an elephant, after digging a hole and drinking water, stripped bark from a nearby tree, chewed it into a large ball, plugged the hole, and covered it with sand. Later he removed the sand, unplugged the hole, and had water to drink.

The last story, in our opinion, illustrates a high degree of body and neural coordination and the elephant probably can be viewed not only as a tool user but also as a tool maker.

ELEPHANT MIGRATION

JEHESKEL SHOSHANI

The present-day zoogeographical distributions of the living species of the family Elephantidae which are separated by thousands of kilometers lead us to hypothesize that they or their ancestors must have had a shared habitat sometime in the distant past. Such a link is provided by the fossils found in different localities and the geological time frames assigned to these localities. Using this information, scientists were able to reconstruct possible ancient routes (see map, page 29) beginning around the shores of the Tethys Sea (at about 58 million years ago) and moving towards Africa, Eurasia and the New World. Fossil evidence indicates that proboscideans did not occupy Australia, Antarctica and some oceanic islands, but did inhabit the continents of Africa, Asia, Europe, North America, and South America.

▶ African elephants on the move usually travel in single file, led by the matriarch.

▼ An African elephant prepares to ford a river. Elephant migration implies that elephants wander with the seasons, tending to congregate in savannah regions during the wet season and in woodlands during the dry season.

Modern wild elephant populations are limited to local migratory patterns, which can be easily detected since individual elephants can be radio-collared and followed. Environmental terrains in which modern and extinct proboscidean remains have been found include extreme altitudes and latitudes, from 200 meters (about 655 feet) below sea level to snowlines at over 3,000 meters (about 9,850 feet) above sea level, and from desert to lush savannahs, forests, sea shores, and marshes.

During their wandering, elephants exploited many available niches including islands in the Mediterranean and Java Seas and the Channel Islands off the coast of California in the United States. As in many island populations, the result of isolation and lack of predators was the evolution of animals much smaller than contemporary elephants in other localities. One of the smallest pygmy elephants from the Mediterranean islands was smaller than a Shetland pony.

Migration also involves moving from familiar to unfamiliar places and subjecting the population to different sets of environmental stresses and unexpected dangers. The important point to remember is not the immediate but the ultimate results. Injuries and deaths during migration are perhaps part of a built-in mechanism of self-regulation in a population; the fittest will remain to pass on their genes to the next generation. Factors which contribute to the movement of elephants may not differ from those of other animals; they are geared towards one goal—survival.

STRUCTURE OF ELEPHANT SOCIETY: A PREREQUISITE TO UNDERSTANDING MIGRATION

A basic understanding of the family life of African and Asian elephants and their social structure is imperative to our understanding their daily and/or seasonal movements. Elephant societies are organized along matriarchal lines, with the family unit forming the basic building block of a herd. This unit is composed of a cow and 3 to 5 of her immediate offspring. Male elephants are usually driven away by older females when they reach puberty (between the ages of 8 and 13 years). These individuals either join or form bachelor herds, and may be seen to forage alone. The leader, or alpha female, is usually born and raised in that herd, and acquires her position after years of learning from older family members.

In some areas large concentrations of elephants are more prevalent during the dry than the wet seasons; they can be found in the vicinity of any type of wetland such as floodplains, lakes, swamps, marshes, bogs, and waterholes. At these times, all boundaries of home ranges (areas within which

Steve Turner/Oxford Scientific Films

▼ A herd of African elephants in Addo Elephant National Park, South Africa, as viewed from the air. There is no evidence that elephants are territorial. They do, however, move about within home ranges that may be anything up to 1,500 square kilometers in extent, and which often overlap with the home ranges of neighboring herds, a system that offers ample opportunity for mingling and interbreeding between herds.

Anthony Bannister/Animals Animals/Stock Photos

animals normally roam in the course of a season) are obliterated and members of different families and herds are intermingled, a process which allows for gene exchange to take place. At the onset of the wet season, perhaps with the fall of the first raindrops, or when the clouds may be darker than in the dry season, or when the wind may change direction and velocity, queues of elephants begin to form. From a bird's-eye view, it appears as though elephants within a basin several kilometers square coordinate their movements and walk away from the center in all compass directions. Their paths lead towards savannahs and grasslands where they will spend most of the wet season. Rains appear to be associated with two of the most important activities of elephant society—mating and parturition. It has been observed that frequency of elephant mating is greatest close to the middle of the rainy season. Since a successful pregnancy lasts up to 22 months (the longest of any living terrestrial mammal), birth would occur in the second wet season following conception. The best

time to raise young is when food is plentiful. A female can be seen with more than one offspring, either as a result of twinning (elephants are also known to give birth to triplets), or with siblings from more than one pregnancy; offspring average about five in the lifetime of one female. With extended families, elephants explore new niches within and outside their home ranges during the wet season. In doing so, they may have achieved two highly integrated goals known as "to and fro" and part of "one way" migration.

Movements within a home range constitute a loop or a circuit; these are also known as seasonal or "to and fro" migration. Home ranges of elephants vary in size from 15–50 square kilometers (6–19 square miles) to 500–1,500 square kilometers (190–580 square miles). The differences depend on the quantity and quality of the food and whether or not the area is occupied by bulls or by cows and their offspring. Home ranges of one family, clan, or herd, may overlap. Field studies show that there is no evidence for territoriality in

▲ The basic unit of elephant society consists of an experienced cow, the alpha-female, with a variable number of her young. The migrations of elephants are governed by the accumulated wisdom and experience of such a leader, dictating when to move, what direction to take, and when to stop.

▲ A phenomenon that is almost certainly gone forever: the sight of a vast herd of elephants on the move.

Peter Beard/VISIONS

elephants. Overlapping provides an opportunity for exchange between gene pools; in the long term this is a very important process for providing variability in the population and thus the ability to adapt to the ever-changing habitats. Sharing part of the home range also implies sharing the available resources and diseases.

Overlapping of home ranges and exploring new habitats may also be the beginning of a long-term "one way" migration because, should the newly explored niche prove to be worth further investigation, elephants would probably stay there longer than they usually would, and thus shift the area of the home range in the direction of the new habitat. In this way, successive new explorations can lead to an overall shift in the home range from one locale to the next which therefore translates into a "one way" migration.

Accumulated field observations lead us to conclude that there is a regularity in the pattern of elephant migration. But how long does it take them to reach their destination? A herd of elephants with large numbers of newborn calves is not likely to move as fast as one with fewer young. If we take an average of 5 kilometers per hour (about 3 miles per hour) for a family walking during the cooler part of a 24-hour period

through savannah, that would translate to about 30–60 kilometers (19–37 miles) per day. Sometimes elephants travel up to 100 kilometers (about 60 miles) to reach their "summer grounds"; they can trek this distance in a couple of days. A more distant destination would be traveled in accordance with the terrain and the distance to be covered. Theoretically speaking, if we assume that for about half the year an elephant may be moving toward a food source, simple calculation shows a herd can travel between 5,000–10,000 kilometers (3,100–6,200 miles) in one year to complete one cycle of seasonal migration.

FACTORS WHICH MAY CONTRIBUTE TO MIGRATION

Food and water intake of elephants has been the subject of numerous scientific articles on the ecology and behavior of these species and in turn the effect feeding has on their dispersion patterns. Salt and other minerals are important ingredients in elephants' diet; they are known to have traveled tens or sometimes hundreds of kilometers in search of these precious minerals (see also the section, "Erosion by elephants", by I. Redmond). With a body mass as large as 2,000–7,000 kilograms (4,410–15,430 pounds), the elephant requires

Dieter and Mary Plage/Bruce Coleman Limited

about 75–150 kilograms (165–330 pounds) of food, and about 80–160 liters (20–40 gallons) of water per day. It may feed on more than 80 different plant species, but preferences have been noted. African elephants, for example, consume leaves, bark, fruit, grass, and herbs. The diet of the Asian species contains more grass than that of the African. Their massive intake of food demands almost constant feeding or moving toward a food source; indeed it was observed that elephants spend about three-quarters of a 24-hour cycle in these activities. They usually stay for a few days in one area before moving to another.

Asian elephants have been observed to prefer ecotone zones over purely grassland or forest habitat. These zones include intermittent open grassy glades which contain transition areas with many species of plants between grass and forest. Such zones provide a rich variety of food types in open forest galleries not available in dense woodlands or a closed montane forest. These ecotone zones also provide a quick escape from the sun—the Asian elephant is believed to have a more sensitive skin than the African elephant. Some populations of the latter species have also been observed to feed in ecotonal areas, apparently for the availability of a greater variety of food.

LOCAL EXAMPLES OF "TO AND FRO" MIGRATION

Modern technology, coupled with recently discovered phenomena, enable us to investigate specific populations and individuals. The best examples are the radio-tracking of animals and detecting infrasonic sounds produced by elephants (see the section, "Elephant communication", by K. Payne and W. R. Langbauer). Some of the best known populations, in terms of their movements, are those of East Africa, southern Africa, and some isolated populations in West Africa. Within Asia, the fragmented populations are even more isolated than in Africa; those of Sri Lanka, Assam, and some populations in Indochina are best known.

The emerging pattern is that, during dry seasons, elephants across Africa and Asia congregate in and around waterholes, riverbeds, and other types of wetlands. The onset of rain apparently triggers movements toward drier savannahs, ecotone zones, and forested areas. As noted earlier, in these situations, the accumulated life experience of the lead elephants proves to be crucial to reaching their destinations. Field studies on the Asian and African elephant show that once a herd is reduced to a few individuals these survivors usually move into another herd.

▲ An Asian elephant on the seashore. Migration of any kind involves the movement of a population of animals in search of a more suitable living area, which necessarily implies the crossing of unsuitable areas. Perhaps the most important characteristic giving an animal the option of migration is the ability to cope with unsuitable or unfamiliar terrain.

▲ Worker elephants are bathed by their mahouts in the Ganges River, Bihar, India, as a new day begins.

ELEPHANTS

AND HUMANS

ELEPHANTS USED AS WAR MACHINES

KENNETH C. WYLIE

It may seem contradictory that the peoples of the Indus Valley and adjacent regions in the Indian subcontinent, who first tamed elephants and thereby created a mutually beneficial bond between human and animal, were also the first to train them for war. Sanskrit texts dating to about 1500 BC reveal an elephant lore already based on long experience. Probably it was inevitable that sooner or later these magnificent animals, used successfully in building, hauling, logging, and hundreds of other tasks since about 2000 BC, would be tested in battle. We know of at least one elephant killed in battle as early as 1100 BC.

Surely the very size of elephants was a major inspiration for soldiers, especially within a culture which emphasized show and form in the governmental process. The ritualistic aspect of war—with ranks of elephants in the vanguard—was all-important well before Alexander the Great descended on the Indus in 326 BC.

Certainly, previous to that date, the leader who had elephants deployed in his army possessed a psychological advantage over an enemy who did not. The impact of a serried rank of giants, armored and conspicuous, drawn up in line against footsoldiers, or cavalry, seems to have rendered their actual use superfluous in most instances. Long before Alexander's time the strength of an Indian prince was measured in part by the number of war elephants he could deploy in battle. This is probably why the use of elephants for paying tribute developed in the first place. This process was especially important to the Chinese since elephants were typically sent from lesser rulers to more powerful ones. In the exchanges of diplomacy and trade (including occasional wars) between the different Southeast Asian kingdoms and China, this was a vital factor, and tribute elephants played an important role.

Nevertheless, the training of elephants for war had its deadly side. Chronicles reveal the special armor forged to protect the animals' sides and heads. Obviously this varied in effectiveness. However, a highly trained, well-armored elephant (throughout Asia the elephants were, of course, of the species *Elephas maximus*) directed by an experienced mahout (trainer and rider), was a formidable weapon—the armored tank of the ancient world. In India swords were sometimes attached to the trunk, and if the elephant's tusks were large enough they were equipped with sharp points of brass or iron which were sometimes dipped in poison. The war elephant was trained to use tusks in close quarters against both man and horse, and to trample with the feet while employing the trunk. A typical technique was to train an elephant to pick up an enemy soldier and pass him up to the man (or men) riding on its

back, who would then effortlessly despatch the hapless fellow. (The *howdah* or basket affixed to the elephant's back was known by Alexander's time, though the Indians did not apparently use this device against Alexander.) Another method called for the elephant to hold an enemy down with the trunk and/or foreleg while impaling him.

All this was constrained by the natural inclinations of the elephant, which were well understood—as the Sanskrit text *Matanga-Lila of Nilakantha* indicates—throughout India. Elephants possess a high degree of natural intelligence (greater than the horse), which, despite their inherent courage, ironically limits their effectiveness amid the carnage. The literature reveals that only a highly trained mahout (or *oozie*) could control his war elephant and force it to act violently and with discipline against human or horse. Surely one of the reasons Alexander prevailed over King Porus at Hydaspes in 326 BC, despite the fact that the Indian king deployed at least eighty-five elephants against the Macedonians, was because Alexander (having already faced up to fifteen war elephants in his battle against the Persian King Darius at Guagamela five years before) knew exactly how to use his infantry to effectively harass and attack the mahouts themselves, who were apparently not armored in this battle. Furthermore, Alexander had trained his footsoldiers to use battle-axes and swords against the elephants' vulnerable trunks and legs, and in the end the elephants ran amok, indiscriminately trampling many Indian troops in panic. Clearly, when in pain and distress, elephants could not be held by any regime of training or discipline known to humans. In this respect, perhaps, the great pachyderms reacted with more sense than the typical soldier, who during the past 5,000 years has gone to death at the command of his sergeant or captain.

To the modern reader these episodes possess an air of unreality. One shrinks from the spectacle of these sensitive giants amid the mêlée, stuck like a cactus with arrows and spears, lifting soldiers high, crushing others beneath their feet, charging hither and yon and trampling friend and foe in

▼ Elephants have played various military roles from ancient times until very recently. Porus, emperor of India, used them to confront the armies of Alexander the Great at the Battle of Hydaspes in 326 BC (below), and they were also widely used as transport for heavy artillery, as shown by these elephants carrying field guns in Thailand, 1893 (bottom).

blind anguish. Unlike the peoples of earlier times we are unaccustomed to the slaughter of animals in our own ongoing human conflicts (and, when it does happen, and animals as well as humans fall prey to the fragmentation bomb and anti-personnel mine, we are rarely informed of the loss).

Nonetheless the use of elephants in war by no means ended with Alexander's distant victory. Indeed it is with that encounter that the common use of war elephants in the West begins. Ptolemy, one of Alexander's generals, who set himself up as ruler of Egypt after Alexander's death in 323 BC, acquired a corps of "Indian" elephants which he used to bolster his Pharaonic pretensions. However, as these Asian elephants aged and died, his son, Ptolemy II—solidifying the dynasty that would rule Egypt until Cleopatra—moved to assure a ready supply of elephants from closer to home by capturing animals from among the wild elephants (of the species *Loxondonta africana*) down in the Sudan, on both sides of the upper Nile, in what was then called Nubia.

Ptolemy and his trainers did not apparently share the modern (and false) prejudice that African elephants are untrainable. Within a generation or so the use of war elephants had spread across North Africa to Carthage, which ruled a vast expanse of North Africa at the time, as well as to much of the western Mediterranean. Far off in the

woodlands of Numidia (in what is now Algeria), were herds of a North African species (possibly *Loxodonta cyclotis*), and from these long-since exterminated elephants the Carthaginians built a special corps of war elephants which they used with varied success in their wars with Rome.

In the meantime the use of war elephants had spread even to the warring states of peninsular Greece. The ill-fated King Pyrrhus, when he took his army into Italy in 280 BC, gained his famous "Pyrrhic" victory over the Romans at Heraclea when in desperation he threw in his twenty elephants (these apparently of the Asian kind), thus causing the Roman horses to panic. Pyrrhus' army was, however, so decimated that he lost the war against Rome, and was forced to retreat. His elephants were not decisive after all.

Even the genius of Hannibal was not enough to prove the long-term effectiveness of war elephants. His invasion of Italy in 218 BC, the most daringly conceived and brilliantly executed invasion campaign in ancient times, is famous in part because he transported his corps of thirty-seven African elephants through Spain, southern Gaul (the south of France), and thence across the Alps, where he arrived in the lush Po Valley with all thirty-seven alive. Crossing the frozen Alpine passes with elephants was probably not as difficult as imagined, simply because elephants are notoriously

▼ The Roman general Scipio Africanus annihilated Hannibal's army at the Battle of Zama in 202 BC, finally bringing to an end several decades of epic struggle between Carthage and the Roman Empire. In this desperate last-ditch attempt to prevent the Roman legions from over-running his homeland, even Hannibal's awesome phalanx of trained war elephants could not prevail against Scipio's superior tactics.

Much later, following his retreat from Italy (after a campaign lasting fifteen years), Hannibal once more deployed elephants against Rome; this time it was at Zama in 202 BC, near Carthage itself, in a last-ditch attempt to defend his homeland. The Roman general, Scipio, successfully countered the eighty elephants by drawing up his legions in lines with large gaps running through them from front to rear, filling these gaps with a thin screen of lightly armed troops who ran quickly to both sides when the elephants charged. The effect of the elephants was nullified and Hannibal was defeated.

In retrospect it seems remarkable that war elephants were used for such a long time after their effectiveness was put in doubt. Presumably this was so because no other animal can compare with the elephant as a symbol of power and pageantry. The Romans, though they used some elephants for show in eastern border wars, preferred to use them in the arena, mostly pitted against humans, lions, and other animals. Thus, for centuries to come, the great beasts were reduced to the most bloody and senseless spectacle of all. Their occasional use in war continued throughout the Orient, and particularly in India, Southeast Asia, and China, right up to the era of firearms.

More recently, during the latter part of the Vietnam War, it was reported that American fighter-bombers were ordered to "interdict" elephants along the so-called Ho Chi Minh Trail because they were suspected of being used to transport military supplies. Let us hope this is the last recorded incident in a gory record which goes back at least three thousand years.

In the final analysis, elephants were decisive only when used against poorly disciplined troops, against inexperienced horse cavalry (untrained horses would panic when confronted with war elephants), or when other local conditions favored their use. They presented large and easy targets, and unlike horse cavalry, were difficult to control and maneuver in tightly orchestrated masses. The genius of Hannibal might make effective use of a few carefully deployed elephants for limited time, but the element of surprise was soon lost, and even Hannibal could not negate their one great disadvantage: namely that when confronted with repeated assault by arrows, javelins, or swords, and traumatized by the wounds repeatedly inflicted by such means, an elephant, as Juliet Clutton-Brock has put it, "will very sensibly turn around and go backward, thereby inflicting worse damage on its own army than on the enemy".

An ancient tradition, probably originating in India, but by no means confined to that land, claims that elephants possess certain spiritual qualities or that they symbolize a morally ordered universe. In medieval Europe they were believed to be special creatures of grace, knowing the difference between good and evil. Perhaps there is something in this legend after all.

▲ The Mogul emperor Akbar subjugated much of India during the sixteenth century. Contemporary accounts refer frequently to his favorite war elephant Hawai; this picture from an Akbarnameh manuscript, dated about 1590, illustrates an incident in which Hawai destroyed a boat bridge across the River Juma in 1561.

sure-footed, something Hannibal certainly understood. There is evidence that they aided in the crossing by removing rocky barriers and reassuring both man and horse with their careful progress. Perhaps elephants deserve at least some of the credit for the successful crossing.

Once in Italy, however, especially through the winter of 217 BC in the Apennines, Hannibal's elephants succumbed to disease and the vicissitudes of war in a hostile land. One elephant seems to have lived on for some time: and the poet sang of the "Getulian" beast upon which the one-eyed general rode (for Hannibal had lost the sight of one eye to infection), and the world never forgot.

ELEPHANTS AS BEASTS OF BURDEN

JEFFREY A. McNEELY

"Many people are bound to be surprised if told that there is available in Burma an extremely versatile, multi-purpose, self-regenerating heavy duty machine of great strength and the delicate sensitiveness of a ballet dancer, which is readily adaptable to all kinds of terrain and work conditions, including the capability of working in 4 feet [1.2 meters] of water, requires a minimum of maintenance, is able to work efficiently on all grades of a limitless fuel that grows on trees, and has a phenomenal built-in memory. And the beauty of it is that it does not cost us any foreign exchange."

(Burma *Daily News*, July 24, 1963)

The author was of course referring to the elephant, and has captured in detail the reasons the elephant is so widely appreciated as a beast of burden throughout its Asian range. About 13,000–16,500 elephants are now working in Asia, equivalent to at least 25 percent of the wild population (see table on page 177).

Elephants are employed to pull logs out of forests, carry tourists in national parks, haul loads in remote areas, pull wagons piled high with goods, lead religious ceremonies, capture wild elephants, and to assist in many other activities requiring strength and intelligence. The value of elephants lies in where they can go, not just how

▼ Elephants make highly skilled timber workers. At the command of their owners, elephants use their tremendous strength to carry and haul huge logs, balance and lift them on to trucks, and then nudge them securely into place. A tragic irony is that, in facilitating the process of forest clearance throughout Asia, elephants have unwittingly contributed to the destruction of their own natural habitat.

Luca Invernizzi Tettoni/Photobank

4 บาท
BAHT
POSTAGE

ประเทศไทย THAILAND

คล้องช้าง ROPING AN ELEPHANT

▲ A 1974 Thai postage stamp depicting the capture of a wild elephant: two catchers mounted on trained elephants (known as "koomkies") ride out in pursuit of their quarry, carrying lassoes of heavy rope. The target animal is usually between 10 and 20 years old, because at that age it can be trained relatively quickly and easily, as well as have a long working life ahead.

▶ With its weary mahout perched on top, an Asian elephant carries a load of firewood into a village. Ever since it was recognized that their great strength, intelligence and adaptability could be harnessed for the purposes of domestic work, elephants have been employed wherever possible to ease a variety of human labors.

much they can carry or pull. Visiting northeast Thailand in the rainy season, Henri Mouhot—the explorer who rediscovered Angkor Wat in 1860—learnt to admire his pack elephants: "The elephant must be seen on these roads, which I can only call devil's pathways, and are nothing but ravines, if you are to form any idea of his intelligence, docility, and strength, or how all those wonderful joints of his are adapted to their work. This colossus is no rough specimen of nature's handiwork, but a creature of special amiability and sagacity, designed for the service of man."

It is common for trained elephants to respond to over thirty commands. But they don't always wait to be told. Elephants working in sawmills will decide for themselves how to reposition huge logs so they can be cut in the most efficient manner, sometimes gently scolding their human overseers for not noticing problems themselves. Domestic elephants also use their intelligence for their own ends. In Myanmar (formerly Burma) domesticated elephants have been known to stuff mud into the bells around their necks to muffle them before going out stealing bananas. And an excited domestic bull elephant once destroyed the harness rack and all the gear belonging to other elephants, but left his own untouched.

As tractors and trucks have moved into many of the most remote areas of Asia, elephants have had to find employment elsewhere. In India, over six hundred elephants work in temples, and virtually all of the Nepalese elephants are used in the tourist trade. But in Myanmar, even World Bank forestry projects still depend on elephants because of their unmatched qualities: intelligence, flexibility, low maintenance costs, and minimal impact on the environment. Any credible human future in the hilly forested areas of tropical Asia will still have room for domestic elephants; indeed the most sustainable forms of development may well depend on elephants playing a major role.

THE ELEPHANT DOMESTICATION CENTRE OF AFRICA

KES HILLMAN SMITH

It is a widely held belief that African elephants *(Loxodonta africana)* cannot be domesticated and trained to work like their Asian cousins *(Elephas maximus).* Yet the Carthaginians fought the Romans with African elephants and Hannibal crossed the Alps with them. Even today, in the center of Africa, the Elephant Domestication Centre proves that African elephants can still be trained and worked.

Musée d'Afrique Noire, Tervuren

▲ Contrary to the belief that African elephants cannot be domesticated, this photograph, taken in the Belgian Congo in the late 1940s, shows a team of forest elephants specially trained to perform such tasks as ground clearing, tree felling, hauling and, in this instance, pulling a plow. Despite the success of the Centre since its opening in Gangala na Bodio in 1930, it is the only training station of its kind in Africa.

Elephant training in modern Africa was the brainchild of the Belgian king, Leopold II, whose kingdom included the vast area then called the Congo. In 1879 he had four Asian elephants, Sundergrund, Naderbux, Sosan Kalli, and Pulmalla, sent by ship to the coast of what is now Tanzania. There, to the amazement of the local people, the elephants were winched ashore. Under the command of a British ex-consul to Baghdad, a certain Mr Carter, a splendid expedition consisting of the elephants, thirteen mahouts, eight soldiers and seven hundred porters set off for the center of Africa. Sadly, the elephants began to die en route, until at Karema, on the shore of Lake Tanganyika, only Pulmalla was left alive. She became the popular "spoilt child" of the town, but when Carter left to return to the coast, taking her mahout, Pulmalla apparently refused food and died "of sadness". Carter's party, meanwhile, was attacked and massacred by a local chief.

In 1899, encouraged by the story of an African elephant tamed by missionaries, Leopold tried again. Commandant Jules Laplume was given the task of catching and training African elephants in the north of the Democratic Republic of the Congo and forming the "Service de Domestication des Elephants". He tried pit traps, but the

elephants were too clever to get caught at first. Eventually, when two youngsters fell into the pits they were rescued by the adult elephants. The third to be trapped died as Laplume and his soldiers worked to get her out. He tried the Asian *keddah* method, where the group is driven into an enclosure, but it proved difficult to deal with the strong adults or to separate the mothers from the youngsters. When they did separate them the young elephants died.

Towards the end of 1901 they finally succeeded in catching older juveniles at least 1 meter (3 feet 3 inches) high with a different technique. Basically the method was to grab a young elephant with bare hands and ropes after the mother had been shot. This often involved a hectic chase on foot and a wild grappling, until a rope could be looped round the youngster's leg and wound quickly round the nearest tree. With modifications, notably that in later years the mother was usually not killed, but merely chased off, this was the method used to catch all the juvenile elephants for the succeeding fifty-eight years at the Elephant Domestication Centre.

The capture period was limited to the dry and early wet season when the dense 2–3 meter (about 6–10 foot) high grass had been burnt off. In the heyday of the station the capture teams setting out would be an impressive group of men, usually of the local Azande tribe: two teams of sixteen hunters each, forty to fifty porters, and a group of trained adult elephants or *moniteurs* (experienced adults used for training), some of which pulled wagons of equipment, the whole commanded by one or two Belgian officers on horseback. The actual capture was done on foot with hand-made ropes. A line of men with the team leader and other armed hunters in the center advanced on the elephants. At a signal they fired in the air and in the resulting confusion the other hunters surrounded the chosen youngster. Once the young elephants had been caught the moniteurs were brought in and the youngsters were tied to them. Their presence quieted the young elephants and they could be walked back to the station. By the 1930s the elephants usually caught were of 1.5–1.8 meters (about 5–6 feet) shoulder height, aged about twelve to fifteen years. Younger than

Kes and Fraser Smith

this, they were more difficult to maintain in good health and took too long to be strong enough to work; older, they were too big to handle.

The early captures took place in the area of the Uele River and by 1904 the Elephant Domestication Centre was based at Api. By 1913 there were thirty-three elephants in captivity varying from 1.4 to 2 meters (4 feet 7 inches–6 feet 7 inches) in height. Due to financial difficulties the station was nearly forced to close after World War I, but the Belgian King Albert stepped in to support it. In 1920 seven Ceylonese mahouts were brought in to teach the local handlers (cornacs) a proper system of training the elephants.

Such intelligent and social animals as elephants respond well to training and usually form strong attachments to their cornacs as well as with each other. Each animal had its own cornac, who was helped by an assistant. The first stage of the training was to accustom the elephants to humans. In the early mornings and evenings each young elephant was surrounded by a few cornacs who chanted a rhythmic song, gently beating the elephant with branches and feeding it pieces of manioc or sweet potato. At a later stage they would get the elephants used to being sat upon. In the second or third month the elephants were taught

to lie down with long ropes attached to their legs. Simultaneously the ropes were pulled and the elephants given the order, "Lali, lali," and then rewarded. They were taught to retrieve objects from the ground. To learn to obey the orders to walk, stop, turn and reverse, the young elephant, ridden by a cornac, was attached to a trained adult elephant by a girth rope. Orders were verbal and accompanied by pressure from a hooked stick like those used in India. Kindness and rewards were the keynotes of the training.

When they were older the elephants were trained for transport and to work in agriculture and forestry. They pulled plows and carts, moved trees, and carried loads. Trained elephants could be hired or bought by agricultural stations. In 1927 a cost comparison between the labor needed to plow 100 hectares (about 250 acres) on a cotton station revealed that with a tractor it cost 704 Belgian francs, with oxen 156 francs, with 50 men 111 francs, and with elephants only 102 francs.

In 1927 the Elephant Domestication Centre began the move to Gangala na Bodio, an area where more elephants were available for capture. In 1938, the savannas north of Gangala, which abounded with wildlife, became the Garamba National Park. The station at Gangala na Bodio,

▲ Recent visitors to the Democratic Republic of the Congo on safari. Elephants provide tourists with a unique travel experience, ushering them sure-footedly into normally inaccessible areas of the countryside. Money raised from safari tours is reallocated into park projects and the development of agricultural programs to benefit local people.

▲ (Top) Modern darting techniques have contributed to the humane and safer capture of wild elephants for domestication. Compared to other animals, elephants are easy to approach, provided the darter keeps downwind and advances with care.

▲ A revitalizing drink and bath is the day's highlight for these working elephants. Kindness and care from their keepers ensure "happy" and healthy animals that are responsive and cooperative when called upon to work.

situated on the park border, was the center for control of the hunting reserves surrounding the park and was later one of the park headquarters.

By this time there were eighty-four elephants at Gangala. Although developments in agricultural machinery reduced their popularity, the capture, training, and work of the elephants continued until the country became independent in 1960. The cornacs continued to look after the elephants, and when the Simba rebellion swept the country in 1964, they and their families left with the elephants and hid in the bush until the danger had passed.

After 1960, despite a couple of unsuccessful attempts at capture, the decreased numbers of elephants were no longer used for agriculture. They gave occasional rides to visitors.

By the late 1970s and early 1980s the financial and logistical support for the conservation of the national park was so minimal that the wild elephant and rhino populations were devastated by the heavy poaching that was sweeping through Africa. In 1984, a conservation aid project, funded by the World Wide Fund for Nature, Frankfurt Zoological Society, and the United Nations Educational, Scientific, and Cultural Organization, started up to rescue the park from its deteriorated

state. The Elephant Domestication Centre was seen to have immense potential value in the development of tourism to help support the conservation effort of the park, and possibly in anti-poaching, and in the development of agricultural projects to benefit the local people.

By then only four trained elephants remained: Lwiru, Lukutu, Zombi, and Kiko. The first three had been caught between 1952 and 1957. Kiko had been born at Gangala in 1954. Saddles were built for them and they were accustomed to carrying tourists on safaris into the park.

In 1987 more young elephants were caught as the project's first stage in redeveloping the Elephant Domestication Centre. This time modern drug darting techniques were used and the young elephants were brought back to the station on a trailer shaded by a wet sacking tent, and revived in a wooden stable within a fenced paddock. The most suitable size for elephants was found to be the three to four year olds, which were weaned but small enough to be manageable. The age was estimated from tooth development and from the elephants' shoulder heights.

The young elephants were tamed quickly and could soon be herded free to feed all day. Each morning they had some training and were taught to be ridden and to obey basic commands. Kwanza, Rudi, and Ndima became a familiar sight around the station, delighting visitors, following the adult elephants on safaris, and giving children rides. Rudi, the little female, was very young when caught and she compensated for the loss of her mother by sucking Kwanza's ear for comfort. The elephants at Garamba are an intergrade between forest elephants (*Loxodonta cyclotis*) and bush elephants (*Loxodonta africana*). The *cyclotis* type have a reputation for being easier to train. Ndima was the only *africana* type. He always kept apart from the others and one day he ran away and could not be found. In 1989 more young elephants were caught. This time only females were kept and males were released as they become difficult to manage when adult.

One young female was easy to train, another was difficult, but the basic principle has been proved: young elephants can still be caught and domesticated; and adult elephants can earn valuable foreign currency for the support of the park. At 1992 prices, thirty-three people riding the elephants per year paid the equivalent of all the guards' salaries for the whole year. Now there is a chance of finding sufficient funds to redevelop the Elephant Domestication Centre properly. This unique attraction for visitors could enable the park to earn a large proportion of the funds needed to support long-term conservation, while the establishment of some agricultural programs that can benefit the local people should give them reason to value the conservation of tame and wild elephants and the ecosystems in which they live.

TRAINING ELEPHANTS

BUCKY STEELE

In domestic care of the elephant there are certain circumstances under which training an elephant is both essential and advantageous. A well-trained elephant is easy to handle and obeys commands—a condition which is imperative on occasions when zoo staff need to administer medication, trim its toenails, or perform any other daily routines which require physical contact.

Experience has demonstrated that trained elephants are more successful in breeding programs than untrained captive elephants. Further, for the purposes of living in a zoo environment, an untrained 5,000 kilogram (11,000 pound) beast, for example, would be a very dangerous inhabitant, regardless of its sex, not to mention if it was a mature male in musth (see sections on musth by P. S. Easa, J. Poole, and M. Schmidt). Cage or yard maintenance, for example, has proved to be much safer when the elephant has learned to be secured. Training also provides much needed exercise for many domesticated elephants.

For generations, there have been elephant trainers who have claimed that it is much easier to train Asian than African elephants. In my opinion,

both species can be trained to perform almost the same tasks. The differences lie in the fact that the African elephant is "high toned" and more sensitive than the Asian, and not as quick to learn as the Asian; it is always one step behind. As Hezy Shoshani has suggested, it appears that the cerebral motor coordination of the Asian elephant is more developed than that of the African species. In some instances, the African elephant performs better and learns tasks faster than the Asian; examples of this are learning to throw a ball and other simple tasks. In addition, I have noticed that the African elephant does not seem to be able to walk on its hind legs alone. All in all, one may compare the Asian elephant to a draft horse and the African to a thoroughbred horse.

▼ Tony the elephant gets a manicure at the Franklin Park Zoo, Boston, Massachusetts, USA. The care of animals in zoos involves many routine tasks—grooming, weighing and measuring, medical examinations, and the like—which require physical contact with the animal, and which are much easier, safer, and more efficient if the animal is trained. This is particularly true of elephants, where training has such added benefits as the relief of boredom and improved breeding success.

Rod Williams/Bruce Coleman Ltd

▲ A daily ritual: elephant-weighing at the London Zoo. Such routine activities and close human contact reinforce training and help in promoting the elephant's security and sense of well-being.

BASIC TRAINING

Techniques presented in this section are not intended as a manual for elephant training, but rather as an overview of the procedures that are used by professional trainers.

Training elephants is best achieved when the animal has been weaned and has reached at least two or three years of age, when it can digest solid foods such as grains and vegetable matter easily. For some elephants, this stage is achieved at about five years. Whenever possible, only one or two persons should perform the training and only one person, preferably the elephant keeper, should be trained with the elephant. Understandably, elephant keepers and handlers should be changed as infrequently as possible.

Teaching the simple ABCs and manners to an elephant can take as little as one month and as long as twelve months depending on the ability of the elephant to learn, the trainer to teach, and the environment. Environment is extremely important in training because the elephant must feel secure and relieved of stress so it can "concentrate on the lessons" and not on whether or not its safety is at risk. I do believe in giving rewards to an elephant which has performed its lesson correctly and the banana or carrot should be given at the right time. As an example, Zola, an Asian elephant, was one of the smartest animals I ever trained. It took her thirty days to learn all the basic routine commands, such as: (1) Lay down; (2) Stretch; (3) Pick up foot; (4) Trunk; (5) Sit; (6) Turn; (7) Waltz; (8) Stand up; (9) Come here; (10) Back; (11) Get over; and (12) Steady.

It must be remembered that basic training, or what we elephant trainers call "barn training", is only the first step in the training of a performing circus elephant. Following the barn training, the elephant must be acclimatized to traffic, the public, lighting, music, and all the stress associated with performing. This acclimatization process may take anywhere from one to two years.

STEPS IN TRAINING

Before you begin training a wild animal, you must be certain that you have all its necessities taken care of—everything for its survival, including food. Once this is done, the biggest problem at the beginning of the training process is gaining the elephant's confidence. If you are going to work together effectively, you must help the elephant to overcome its foremost instinctive drive which is for self-preservation, so that it learns to trust you and feel at ease. When you have achieved a rapport with your trainee and it appears to be content with its surroundings, training can then proceed.

During training most elephants become nervous and make a mess, so trainers should have some sawdust or sand handy, so that the floor does not get wet and slippery.

The next stage in the training process is the introduction of chaining, which should be practiced every day for an hour, perhaps during the time the elephant's quarters are being cleaned out. Start by using a 6 millimeter (¼ inch) or 38 millimeter (1½ inch) chain a few meters (several feet) long with a swivel to prevent twisting (this is particularly important for small elephants). To introduce the idea to your trainee, put one end of the chain loosely over it but leave the other end free. Initially, it will swing it around, but gradually it will learn to settle down. Then, if you haven't been hit with a flying chain, coax the animal to a suitable location for tying. Tie the chain around its front foot loosely, tie the other end off and leave it for three or four hours. Then feed and water it, and release it. Feed at the same time and place thereafter, always chaining it first. Eventually chaining will become familiar and the struggle will be over.

I feel that a rear chain should be used in the barn at night, and it also allows more sanitary conditions for feeding and easy clean up—it is commonly used in circuses for this reason. When chaining both front and rear legs, always connect the front leg first, then the rear, and continue to feed and water as usual afterward. The right front, left rear leg in combination should be used, alternating daily with left front, right rear leg.

The next step is to teach the animal to pick up the foot for the front chain and afterwards to back up for the rear chain. Teaching it to back up requires the use of the "hook". This tool is just like a bridle on a horse or collar on a dog—a controlling mechanism. The elephant respects the hook, if it is in the hands of a familiar person. In a sense, the hook is a sign of authority. However, I have seen normally docile elephants become dangerous and aggressive when a stranger picks up the hook. Chained or unchained, it will directly charge them and not even a pitchfork will stop it.

In such a situation, however, the person with whom the elephant usually works needs but to say a word and the elephant will freeze in its tracks. This person's presence alone may permit safe passage or approach by a stranger. The best rule here is to handle your elephant with respect and at all times: steer clear of the unfamiliar!

The hook is also used as a rapping instrument. At first, use it very lightly and be careful, because no matter which direction you choose to pull it, the elephant will invariably go in the opposite direction. In time, it learns which is the right way. Use the hook to teach the elephant to pick up its foot for the chain, and to back up. For backing up, hook it on the front side of the shoulder or leg, or the front of the rear leg. Use the desired command to coincide with the hook pressure.

Once the elephant has learnt to be chained, the trainer may then introduce some barn manners like "Get over", "Steady", "Pick up foot", and "Stand still". After the ABCs, I prefer to teach the task of lying down on command. This is difficult, because when an elephant does this, it is going against generations of learning. Innately, they know that it is unsafe to be in this position unless protected by their herd. The elephant is leaving itself wide open and lacks the defenses of running or fighting. As they gradually master this command, they learn to realize that they are safe. As I generally do not believe in their use, this is the *only* time I introduce rope or rigging of any sort. You may need to take some time to practice tying knots and splicing rope. Nevertheless, the main problem with the procedure is teaching the elephant to lie down—this requires much patience on the part of both the trainer and trainee.

THE EFFECT OF TRAINING ON BREEDING

Training also has a positive effect on the elephant's breeding habits. The zoos with the best records for breeding elephants are the ones which have elephants that were at one time circus performers. To the best of my knowledge, there have been no offspring from imported wild, or untrained elephants. The reason is simple: training involves a sort of mind conditioning—a way of assisting the animals to be at ease in their new environment.

I have been able to breed three elephant calves, all of which were born to performing parents. To my knowledge, Rex Williams and I are the only elephant owner/trainers with trained, traveling elephants who have had breeding success. I attribute this success to the fact we both have had trained males who could be taken on tour.

The success of the Washington Park (now Oregon) Zoo in breeding elephants is well known, but again the breeding animals were performers and had been taken on many tours. Similarly, successful breeding in Knoxville and at Busch Gardens in Tampa can be attributed to animals which had been touring with Ringling Brothers.

All these cases point to the importance of training. It is successful because it involves a socialization process whereby animals successfully adapt to a new environment which closely mimics patterns of elephant groups in the wild. It involves almost constant and complex interactions with other members of the group, a group which now includes humans. All these patterns ultimately lead to a sense of security which may be similar to that experienced in the wild.

This is not unlike the form of domestication which horses, dogs, and other animals have gone through with humans in the past. An important difference, however, is the occurrence of the musth cycle in male elephants. Musth interferes with training and breeding. It is a dangerous time for trainers, and, more importantly, it is dangerous for any members of the public who may come into contact with an elephant in musth.

If elephants are to be bred in captivity, training *per se* is very necessary for success. This involves an adaptation process much like that which a human immigrant goes through when entering a new country with a new culture, language, and customs.

Masahiro Iijima/Ardea London Ltd

◀ A group of young elephants learn their manners at a training camp in Thailand. Working Asian elephants and their handlers (mahouts) function as a team, and the early training focuses on forming a close mutual bond of trust and understanding between the animal and its mahout, a bond that often lasts a lifetime.

ELEPHANTS IN FOLKLORE, RELIGION, AND ART

JEFFREY A. McNEELY

As the largest animal on land, elephants have always been held in awe by the people who shared their habitat. The elephant is immense, strong, intelligent, and potentially devastating. In most years, more rural Asians are killed by elephants than by tigers, averaging 200–300 human deaths per year in India alone. It is difficult to ignore such a powerful presence, and elephants have long been prominent in the folklore of the forests and plains of tropical Asia and Africa. Even in the Western world where the elephant is not present, its influence has been felt in folklore and art.

Judging from Stone Age art, this relationship is an ancient one. Some of the earliest paintings and engravings in the caves of Europe depict mammoths and straight-tusked elephants, both of which are now extinct. One of the most interesting of these is the elephant of Pindal in Spain, which greatly exaggerates the size of the elephant's heart, perhaps in hopes of helping the hunters to conquer the animal.

Such beliefs continue to the present day among some of the hunting peoples of Africa. The Mbuti pygmies of the Ituri forest of the Democratic Republic of the Congo believe that elephants carry the souls of departed ancestors, and therefore surround any elephant hunt with complex rituals.

Agricultural peoples have a far more complex mythology than hunter-gatherers. In rural villages throughout Asia, elephants are considered cousins of the clouds, a reflection of their size, their smoky color, and their trumpeting like thunder. Indeed, some stories suggest that elephants once had wings and could fly (shades of Dumbo!), changing their shapes like the clouds. Alas, one day a small herd of flying elephants took refuge in a tree under which a group of students sat at the feet of a sage. Under the weight of the elephants, a branch broke and killed several students. The enraged sage cursed the elephants, causing them to lose their wings and their ability to change form at will. That is why, it is said, elephants are clouds sentenced to walk on earth. But whenever large groups of elephants gather, their cloud-cousins in the sky will come to visit and bathe them with showers.

So, in many parts of Asia, elephants are linked with the rains. In Sumatra, elephants are thought to cause lightning. In the Batak lands around Lake Toba, elephants are said to simply hurl the lightning from their trunks, while in Palembang thunderbolts are supposed to be caused by elephants sharpening their tusks.

The ancient Romans believed that the elephant was a religious animal which itself worshiped the sun and the stars. Elephants appeared regularly in Roman triumphs (parades celebrating their military victories and displaying the spoils of war). Medieval Europeans thought that elephants could not bend their knees, and so they had to sleep leaning against trees.

It is just a single elephant-step from folklore to basic religion. Alfred Foucher of the University of Paris has pointed out that long before organized

▲ For millennia the elephant has been a familiar icon in oriental art, as in this ornamental carving from Nalanda, India, which dates from the Buddhist Gupta Empire. Nalanda was an important destination for Buddhist pilgrims until India was overrun by the Muslims at the end of the twelfth century.

▶ Exotic animals are seldom prominent in classical Western art. Sir Peter Paul Rubens (1577–1646) was fond of incorporating animals into his vivid, swirling compositions: lions, tigers, peacocks, elephants and even hippos. *A Roman Triumph* now hangs in the National Gallery, London.

religion, villagers worshiped a stout, goblin-like elephant-god to prevent unreasonable attacks on crops, people, or dwellings by the real thing. The elephant-god met the needs of the villagers reasonably well for thousands of years, but the coming of state religions about three thousand years ago converted the crude jungle elephant-god into a miraculous creature who shared many of the same characteristics of the other, more anthropomorphic gods.

In Hinduism, Airavata was the founder of the elephant line, begetting all elephants who followed. He is the elephant mount of Lord Brahma, the creator of the universe. Airavata represents both the rainbow—which is regarded as a weapon of the gods—and a certain type of lightning, thereby linking the elephant with the luminous manifestations of thunderstorms (and maintaining the folklore link with storms still seen in some Sumatran villages).

In Myanmar (formerly Burma), Airavata is the source of the great river which provides life to the nation, and which takes a slightly different form of its name: Irrawaddy.

In Laos and Thailand, Airavata became the three-headed Erawan, whose three heads represent the three major gods in the Hindu pantheon—Brahma, Vishnu, and Siva—and statues, paintings, and decorations of the three-headed elephant are common throughout these countries. Erawan still reposes on the Laotian flag, years after the royal family has been deposed and a non-religious Communist regime has taken over, and many Thai temples are graced by statues, reliefs, and paintings of Erawan in a variety of poses.

Buddhism, which rejected the multiple gods of Hinduism and concentrated on the psychological well-being of the individual, was supported by a set of tales of earlier incarnations ("bodhisattvas") of the Buddha. The *Jataka Tales* adopted many of

▲ A pottery vase adorned with elephants.

C. M. Dixon

Mary Ann Owens

Luca Invernizzi Tettoni/Photobank

▲ (Top) Elephants adorn the important Buddhist shrine Ruvanvalisaya at Anuradhapura, Sri Lanka, built between 161–137 BC by King Dutthagamani.

▲ The design for this Mauritanian postage stamp, issued in 1975, is based on ancient rock carvings at Zemmour, Sahara.

▶ A statue of the elephant-headed god Ganesh in the Halebid Temple at Karnataka, India. Ganesh is the Hindu god of wisdom and good luck.

the earlier mythological characteristics of elephants. One of the most miraculous bodhisattvas was an elephant named Chadanta, who had a silvery trunk, six tusks of various heavenly colors, and who experienced a tragic demise. Living by the side of a lake, he was a king with eight hundred elephant subjects and two lovely elephant consorts. As might be expected, the ladies had a falling out and Chadanta wound up as the scape-pachyderm.

Imagining she had been gravely insulted, one of the elephant consorts became determined to teach Chadanta a lesson. With the aid of a holy man, she succeeded in marrying another king. She now had the power to take the revenge she lusted after, ordering the kingdom's most skillful hunter to track down the six-tusked elephant and bring back the ivory. After a long journey, the hunter reached Chadanta's palace, dug a pitfall, and captured the elephant-king. But the hunter's arrows were unable to kill the royal prey. The elephant-king gently asked his attacker why he was trying to kill him, and was told the story. Chadanta, being an incarnate Buddha, was not angry, having only compassion for the hunter and his former wife. He broke off his own tusks and handed them to the hunter to give them to the queen, dying in the process. When told of what had happened, the queen herself died of a broken heart.

A white elephant was the last incarnation of the Buddha before he was born again as a man to bring peace and contentment to the earth. The sacred white elephant is said to have appeared in a dream to Buddha's mother-to-be Queen Maya. The future Buddha, in his elephant form, held in his silvery trunk a white lotus flower, uttered a long, drawn-out cry, bowed three times, and touched his forehead to the floor. Then he gently struck Maya's right side, and entered her womb. Maya reported this extraordinary vision to the court astrologers, who divined that she would bring forth a great king or a great seer. Nine months later, Prince Gautama was born.

Since that miraculous birth some 2,500 years ago, white elephants have been closely linked with the Buddha and are still believed by some people to be reincarnated Buddhas. In Myanmar, such elephants have received amazing care. Some have been given regalia fashioned of pure gold and studded with rubies and emeralds, and fed only the greenest, most tender grass in vessels of silver and gold. White elephant calves have received even better treatment. According to U Toke Gale, Burma's leading expert on elephants, one baby white elephant in the 1850s was suckled by ladies who stood in a long row outside his palace, and the honor was eagerly sought after, for the creature was a national treasure. Troupes of palace dancers performed for his pleasure, and choruses of sweet-voiced singers lulled him to sleep.

White elephants—which are not really white but a light shade of gray or even pink—were

Bonhams, London/The Bridgeman Art Library

carefully scrutinized by the court astrologers for indications of what decisions should be made by the king. With their ancient symbolic link with the clouds, white elephants are considered excellent predictors of a monsoon's arrival; this is a matter of considerable concern to the rice farmers of Thailand, Cambodia, and Burma. They are also weather vanes for deciding on the merit of national strategies. One Thai ruler is reported to have quietly dropped plans to invade a neighbor after learning that one of his white elephants had broken a tusk while fighting another elephant in the royal stables.

Even today, such animals are treated with great respect; in Thailand, they become the property of the king, and the presentation of a white elephant is surrounded by age-old ceremonies. Since white elephants bring prosperity to the state, Thailand's once booming economy may be due, in part, to the fact that King Bhumibol has had eleven white elephants, as many as any previous Southeast Asian king has owned; the sleepy state of Myanmar has just two, and devastated Cambodia has none.

Luca Invernizzi Tettoni/Photobank

▲ *Toomai of the Elephants* by E. J. Detmold (1883–1957). Elephants have long been a symbol of power and majesty. They are sometimes depicted in paintings which have strong allegorical or symbolic overtones.

◄ An old Thai mural portrays a visit to earth by Indra, the Hindu god of thunder and of battle, astride the mythical three-headed elephant Erawan. In India, Indra's mount manifested itself as Airavata, the four-tusked elephant born of the sea and the ancestor of all elephants. Airavata was also honored by naming the Irrawaddy River in Myanmar after him; this was the area where remains of extinct stegodons were discovered.

▶ A painting of African elephants at a mud hole by Eric Forlee. Elephants became a favorite subject of Western wildlife artists of the late nineteenth and twentieth centuries.

▼ (Below) A batik of a royal procession in ancient India. To this day, richly caparisoned elephants remain the stars in oriental pageantry of all kinds.

▼ (Bottom) Elephants commonly appear as motifs in shrines and temples in both early Hindu and Buddhist civilizations. The approach is realistic rather than stylized, as illustrated by the friezes along the Elephant Terrace at Angkor, Cambodia, the Hindu capital of the Khmer Empire from the ninth to the fifteenth century.

Each of the current Thai white elephants has been received with due ceremony. The first female white elephant in Thai history was handed over to the king on a day in May 1976 that was considered by court astrologers to be particularly auspicious. On entering the palace grounds the elephant was showered with holy water and sand. The prime minister made the official presentation to the king, who lit sticks of incense and paid homage to a Buddha image while monks chanted

prayers. The king climbed a platform and anointed the elephant's head with holy water. The queen placed a garland of fragrant jasmine and colorful orchids around the animal's neck while the king fed the white elephant two pieces of sugarcane, one inscribed with a charm, the other with the holy pet's new royal name.

Not all of the religious manifestations of elephants are so noble. Around the fifth century AD, a new, more earthy elephant-god arrived on the scene as a son of Siva, the Hindu lord of creation and destruction. With the body of a rather portly human and the head of an elephant, the new god, named Ganesh, was very popular with the Hindu masses. Many entertaining stories are told about how Ganesh came to have the head of an elephant. In one story, Siva's wife Parvathi accused her husband of infidelity. Enraged and embarrassed because the accusation was true, Siva attacked his wife with a golden sword. Their handsome young son, Ganesh, intervened to save his mother and had his head chopped off. Siva and Parvathi were appalled, so Siva ordered his soldiers to cut off the head of the first creature they met to replace that of Ganesh. They soon found an innocent elephant ambling down the road, removed its head and took it to Siva, who placed it on the shoulders of his once-elegant son. Ganesh was restored to life, but forever after had the head of an elephant.

Adapted to the changing needs of the growing Indian civilization, Ganesh was a patron of writers (as literacy began to grow) and of merchants (who were beginning to trade as far afield as Indonesia).

Hervé Berthoule/Explorer

Michael Freeman/Photobank

Ganesh also bestows or withdraws success, removes or causes obstacles, and fulfills or ignores desires.

Ganesh quickly spread eastwards, carried by Indian merchants seeking the assistance of the benevolent deity on their risky trading missions to the villages of Myanmar, Thailand, Cambodia, Sumatra, and Java. The familiar elephant form was immediately popular in the new lands, and Ganesh is now an important figure throughout tropical Asia. Since Buddhism formally rejects all gods, Ganesh is never allowed in Buddhist temples in Thailand. He is confined to the temple courtyard where he is still very popular with the local villagers.

Small wonder, then, that elephants have earned such a large place in the hearts of people throughout the world. While few people will ever be fortunate enough to see elephants in the wild, everybody can enjoy them as paintings, sculptures, television or film images, and photographs. These images—whether they be as massive as the statues leading to the Ming tombs or as small as the postage stamps found on letters from Kenya—portray the elephant as the noble beast which has the power to dominate the land, but instead controls its baser impulses.

Elephants remain an omnipresent force in the lives of many villagers in Asia and Africa. And their attraction has spread throughout the world. Appreciating elephants may well help give people —at least temporarily—the qualities of strength, confidence, and fortitude which are timeless characteristics of our planet's largest land animal.

Luca Invernizzi Tettoni/Photobank

◀ White elephants parade across this old oriental wall-hanging. The sacred white elephant (in reality their color is not white but light gray) occupies a prominent place in the Buddhist religion: it appeared in a dream to Queen Maya before the birth of her son, Prince Gautama, the Buddha.

▼ *African Elephants*, by Charles Emile Tournemine (1812–1872). Such images are characteristic of a modern trend in Western art to portray wild animals in their natural settings. This way of seeing the natural world is indicated not only by the convincing grouping of these elephants, but also in the birds on the shoreline, identifiable as species that would naturally occur in such a setting.

Giraudon/The Bridgeman Art Library

THE ELEPHANT AS SYMBOL

MARY ANN OWENS

Elephants' importance to people cannot be judged only on their economic and practical value. They have long been important as symbols on stamps, coats of arms, and other decorative devices. They also feature in myth, legend, and literature.

When humans first appeared on earth, elephants and their relatives were already roaming its vast expanse. Humans learned early that elephants could be both beneficial and dangerous to their own longevity. To survive they learned to hunt the animals for their skins, meat, and tusks. Early humans left a legacy of their relationship with elephants in cave and rock drawings.

As ancient civilizations developed, elephants continued to emerge as a subject of significance. In the animistic religion, followers worshiped the things around them such as animals, trees, and forces of nature. As they did not understand these forces, they began to worship them out of respect and fear. Naturally, the size and strength of the elephants and their early relatives evoked awe. In tribal dances in areas where the elephants lived, only elite members of the ruling families could wear elephant masks.

In Asia, when the Hindu religion was developing, elephants became gods as well as "vehicles" for other gods. Many of those gods were adopted by Buddhism with a change of name. The best known elephant-headed god is Ganesha, known as Nakhanet to Buddhists. Ganesha, son of Lord Shiva of the Hindu Holy Trinity, wards off omens and has, therefore, become the god to worship when traveling, getting married, and taking a new job.

Buddha's mother was also supposed to have dreamt about a white elephant the night before he was born. As a result of this, most Buddhist celebrations have elephants, real or otherwise, included in festivities or decorations.

Much to the elephants' misfortune, their economic value has not diminished over the years. Following Marco Polo's return from Cathay, his glowing reports of the treasures of the Far East had most of Europe searching for sea routes to India and the Far East. Portugal partially financed their trips with African elephant ivory. They set up small "stepping stone" colonies along the coasts of Africa and harvested the ivory in the areas. Other countries followed suit.

Today the lust for ivory is still present. Fortunately, however, many countries are recognizing the danger of over-killing elephants and anti-poaching laws have been enacted and often enforced.

As a mark of esteem and recognition of its economic value, many of the countries and colonies inhabited by elephants have included this enigmatic animal in their coat of arms. The elephant is also included in stamp series depicting the countries' treasures.

In the late nineteenth century, the Belgians set out to try to exploit the African elephants' economic value by training them. While they proved it could be done, they also proved it was not financially feasible to continue at that time. The Asian elephant, on the other hand, has been relatively easy to tame and train, and has been used for everything from carrying people, goods, mail, and ceremonial trappings to being a palace pet.

Asian elephants can also be used as an economical way of getting logs from a forest to a factory. In teak forests, they learn early a single task from their mahout or oozie and over the years build up a special relationship with this human counterpart. The two usually

▶ Elephants have always held a great fascination for people, which is reflected in stamps issued in many parts of the world, even in countries quite remote from the animal's native homes. Clockwise, starting from top right: Nigeria (1965); Kenya–Uganda–Tanganyika (1967); Laos (1958); Upper Volta (presently named Burkina Faso) (1960); Nicaragua (1978); Denmark (1970); Sri Lanka (1983).

stay together until they become too old to work or until they die. Teak trees do not grow close together but are scattered throughout the forest so the elephants are more economical than machines. The first stamp to show any part of an elephant showed a trunk holding a teak log on the 1890 stamps of Bamra, a princely state of India.

Throughout history, elephants have been employed in wars because their size was useful to scare enemies. They served as excellent lookout posts and because of their strength could tote heavy loads. The most famous war elephants are the African elephants that Hannibal brought over the Alps into Italy in 217 BC. Elephants also carried the Trung sisters, queens of the Vietnam area, in war against China in AD 29–32, and King Naresuan of Siam rode an elephant to war in the 1600s, in other notable instances.

Modern humans have learned to recognize that elephants are excellent in building up tourism. In Africa and Asia, safaris are common and nowadays visitors more commonly shoot elephants with cameras than guns. Game reserves have also been introduced or enlarged and improved in many countries. As most people cannot conveniently get to Africa or to Asia, promoters have brought the elephants to the people via circuses, zoos, and safari parks.

Throughout commercial history humans have used the various attributes of the elephant in promotional concepts to sell their products. They have also used them as symbols and logos for objects other than commercial products. Both Siam (in the 1880s) and China (in the 1870s) considered elephants in designs for their first stamps but chose instead the ruler and a dragon respectively.

In three countries, prestigious accolades known as honorary orders have included the concept of the elephant, either in the name or in the design. The oldest known award is Denmark's Order of the Elephant, instituted by Christian I in about 1497. The Collar of the Order has elephants and towers alternately linked together plus a dangling gold elephant. King Mongkut of Siam in 1861 founded the Order of the White Elephant with gold elephants embossed in the collar and sunburst pendant. In 1877, Queen Victoria instituted the Most Eminent Order of the Indian Empire which featured a collar studded with four gold elephants.

Denmark's flagships have frequently been called *Elephanten*. At the Battle of Copenhagen, April 2, 1801, Denmark's ship *Elephanten* was grounded trying to halt Lord Nelson's ships, including one called *The Elephant*, from entering the harbor.

Humans have also imortalized their love of elephants in the arts, from the sixteenth century Mughal paintings to twentieth century children's art. Jules Verne mentioned elephants in at least three books: *Five Weeks in a Balloon, Around the World in 80 Days* and *The Steam House*. Some chess sets include the elephant. There is even an oriental rug pattern known as "Elephant Paw".

Elephants and humans have always been inextricably linked in varied and fascinating ways and as long as they both survive, this bond will not be broken.

COUNTRIES WHICH ISSUED STAMPS FEATURING ELEPHANTS

AFRICA: Angola, Belgian Congo, Botswana, Burundi, Cameroun, Chad, Eritrea, Ethiopia, French Congo, French Equatorial Africa, French Guinea, Gabon, Gambia, Ghana, Ivory Coast, Kenya, Liberia, Libya, Malawi, Mali, Mauritania, Middle Congo, Mozambique Company, Niger, Nigeria, Northern Rhodesia, Rhodesia, Rio Muni, Ruanda-Urundi, Rwanda, Saint Thomas and Prince Islands, Senegal, Sierra Leone, Somalia, South Africa, Southern Rhodesia, Southwest Africa, Spanish Guinea, Sudan, Swaziland, Tanzania, Togo, Ubangi-Shari, Uganda, Upper Volta, and Zambia.

AMERICAS: El Salvador, Nicaragua, and United States.

ASIA: Bangladesh, Bhutan, Burma, Cambodia, Ceylon, China, India, Indian Feudatory or Princely States (Bamra, Dhar, Duttia, Jaipur, & Sirmaur), Indo-China, Indonesia, Israel, Laos, Malaya (Pahang, Perak, Selangor, Federated States), Malaysia, Mongolia, Nepal, North Borneo, North Vietnam, South Vietnam, Sri Lanka, Thailand, and Timor.

EUROPE: Bulgaria, Czechoslovakia, Denmark, Germany (East), Germany (West), Great Britain, Hungary, Ireland, Monaco, Poland, Portugal (and Portuguese colonies), Romania, Sicily, and the Soviet Union.

FAMOUS ELEPHANTS

SANDRA LEE SHOSHANI

Over the hundreds of years of documented relationships between humans and elephants, both real and fictional elephants have risen to high stature. Surrounding each is a unique story. Glimpses into the histories of famous elephants in human culture can give us a sense of the nature of the elephant—those traits which evoke awe, fear, wonder, and love from humans. Below are thumbnail sketches giving information about some famous elephants.

OLD BET—A NOVELTY IN EARLY NORTH AMERICA

Imagine the novelty of such an unusually large animal as an elephant being walked from town to town for amusement and entertainment. Even a young female elephant would be as tall as a person and weigh three to four times as much. The first captive elephant to be exhibited in this way arrived in the United States in 1795 or 1796; no names other than "The Elephant" or perhaps "Rajah" have been recorded for this elephant. She was most likely only two years old on arrival from Bengal and she may have been shot in the state of Rhode Island about twelve years later.

Old Bet was the second elephant to be exhibited in North America. She was also a female Asian *(Elephas maximus)*, and was possibly about four years old when she arrived in 1804. For at least twelve years, and possibly as long as twenty-three, Old Bet was shown by Hachaliah Bailey of Somers, New York, and his partners.

Several historical reports indicate that Old Bet was shot either in Maine or western Connecticut. Shooting as the cause of death has been given for each of the first three elephants brought to North America. It is easy to imagine a farmer or townsman being startled and frightened by the sight of a single enormous animal moving along the roadway in early nineteenth century New England and firing a lethal shot at the beast. These recorded deaths also suggest the fear and awe that these creatures can excite in humans.

Today an unusual hotel built in 1825, bearing the name "Elephant Hotel", functions as the town hall for Somers, New York. In the square opposite the three-storey building stands a monument to Old Bet—a wooden statue on a granite pillar, a reminder of the "good old days" of traveling circuses.

COLUMBIA—THE FIRST MODERN ELEPHANT BORN IN NORTH AMERICA

On March 10, 1880, a female Asian elephant was born to two captive elephants in the Cooper & Bailey Circus in Philadelphia, Pennsylvania, USA. Although there were by this time numerous circuses with elephants in the menageries, the first birth of an elephant was a momentous event; *Harper's Weekly* boasted that this was the first authenticated birth in captivity. The Asian sire was a 23-year-old which came from Ceylon (now called Sri Lanka) with the dam, a 20-year-old that weighed 3,600 kilograms (8,000 pounds). The calf was almost 1 meter (3 feet) high, measured about 1.2 meters (3 feet 11 inches) around the body and weighed 96.7 kilograms (213 pounds).

James A. Bailey used the birth of the elephant in his advertising campaign for the circus, to the consternation of Phineas T. Barnum, the famous showman. Barnum tried to buy the young elephant from Bailey, thus feeding Bailey material for further advertising. Finally, it is said, Barnum entered an agreement to form a partnership with Bailey and thus began the Barnum & Bailey Circus which lasted until Bailey's death in 1906. Then the Ringling Brothers purchased the circus to form today's organization known as Ringling Bros. and Barnum & Bailey Circus. In this manner a baby elephant made circus history on two counts.

JUMBO—A SYMBOL FOR STUPENDOUS THINGS

The most famous captive elephant in recorded history was undoubtedly Jumbo. He was a male African elephant *(Loxodonta africana)*, captured as a calf in 1861, probably in the French Sudan, south of Lake Chad, and then transferred to the Jardin des Plantes in Paris, France. In 1865 he was exchanged for an Indian rhinoceros and was sent to the London Zoological Gardens, England, where he was named Jumbo. (The origin of the name "Jumbo" is not from a Swahili word meaning "Hello", as many people think, but most likely from the West African word *onjamba* meaning "an elephant".) For fifteen years his temperament was agreeable and he gave rides to many children in Regent's Park in London. At age twenty-one years, Jumbo began to attack the walls and doors of the Elephant House, breaking off his tusks and producing holes in the iron reinforcing plates of his stall. One man, Matthew Scott, worked with him reasonably well but there was much concern during the times when Scott was not present. Early in 1882 the London Zoological Society sold him to the American showman, P. T. Barnum, who had made an attractive cash offer. The public announcement aroused a strong reaction, since

Dieter and Mary Plage/Survival Anglia

Jumbo was regarded as a national figure. Neither Barnum nor the Society was discouraged however.

For three years Jumbo delighted Americans as he traveled in a special railway car with a companion elephant and Matthew Scott. Jumbo was the greatest and largest attraction shown in the Barnum & London Circus. He was heralded by Barnum as "the towering monarch of his race" Although Jumbo was large for his age, it was undoubtedly P. T. Barnum's showmanship which created the image that Jumbo was "bigger than life". That legend is perpetuated today when youngsters learn that the word "jumbo" is associated with large-sized things. When Jumbo left London he was probably about 3 meters (10 feet) tall, according to two estimates; he was twenty-two years old. Although not a record for African elephants, this size, plus his 5,900 kilograms (about 13,000 pounds) of weight, would have

been impressive since most elephants exhibited in North America were much smaller Asian females.

Jumbo's glorious career came to a tragic and sudden end on September 15, 1885, when he was struck by a freight locomotive at St Thomas, Ontario, Canada, where a monument was erected in 1985. His mounted skin was destroyed in a fire at Tufts College in Boston, Massachusetts, but his mounted skeleton is still at the American Museum of Natural History in New York (Catalogue No. AMNH 3287). Interest in Jumbo was not limited to children and adult lay people. From the scientific point of view, Jumbo was a type specimen used by Richard Lydekker, a British naturalist, in 1907 to describe a new subspecies *(Elephas africanus rothschildi)*, now believed to be the bush African elephant (**Loxodonta africana**). Jumbo will never be forgotten; his name lives on a synonym for all stupendous things.

▲ The nationally venerated Raja leads a street procession in the 1979 summer festival of Esala Perahera in Kandy, Sri Lanka. Escorted by other elephants similarly caparisoned in rich ceremonial garb, Raja bears on his back a golden casket wherein the reputed tooth of Buddha is safely encased.

JAP—AN ELEPHANT'S CONTRIBUTION TO RESEARCH

In the twentieth century elephants have achieved fame in biological research and conservation, rather than for entertainment and historical firsts. In 1935, Francis G. Benedict, Director of the Nutrition Laboratory, Carnegie Institution of Washington, Washington DC, found the right subject for a study on metabolism in an elephant, an opportunity for which he had waited twenty-five years. The elephant was Jap (short for Japilina); she had been brought from Europe by P. T. Barnum in 1902 when she was two or three years old. She was part of the herd when Barnum & Bailey Circus united with the Ringling Brothers and she had been with various other circuses from 1920 to 1948. In 1935 Jap was the sole elephant in the quarters of the Gorman Circus in New Jersey; this fact and her nonplussed attitude, as observed by Benedict on several occasions in 1934, made her "a fine specimen" for his physiological studies. His landmark study, conducted over a period of fifteen months, formed the basis for a book on the physiology of the elephant. Benedict used sixty-four additional trained elephants to confirm many of the observations made on Jap. But the extent of this study would have been impossible without one highly suitable female elephant.

IKI — AT THE CENTER OF "OPERATION IKI"

We of the Elephant Interest Group (now the Elephant Research Foundation) in Detroit, had long been preparing for the opportunity to dissect an elephant. We had asked institutions holding elephants to inform us if an elephant should die, and on July 8, 1980, the call came.

Iki was a female Asian elephant (*Elephas maximus maximus*) born in Sri Lanka in 1934, transported to West Germany at the age of two, and then to the United States at ten years of age. She was with the Ringling Brothers and Barnum & Bailey Circus until her death. Her carcass was transported by Hezy Shoshani and Mike Baccala from Florida, 1,500 kilometers (950 miles) to Detroit, Michigan, where she was dissected and parts were embalmed, a process which involved 137 people and lasted three days (see *Elephant*, 2(1):3-93). Many tissue samples and organs were preserved and have been studied by scientists worldwide. Most importantly, her trunk was embalmed and was examined extensively by L. Croner and S. Wainwright of Duke University (North Carolina) and by J. Shoshani, C. Gans, F. Hensen-Smith, C. S. Zajac, and K. G. Watson (from Michigan universities). In an effort to better understand how this marvelous organ works, the Michigan team derived a model with "about 150,000 muscle units" based on detailed counts and extrapolations made from Iki's trunk. Such studies are still in progress.

Presently, the trunk is displayed with Iki's skeleton and other items, in front of a life-size painting by C. A. Diehl and G. Marchant, as a unique permanent exhibit (dedicated April 18, 1988) in the Science and Engineering Library, Wayne State University, Detroit. While Iki entertained millions of children and adults in life, in death, her contribution to science has extended our knowledge of elephant anatomy immensely.

MOTTY—A UNIQUE BUNDLE

Theoretically, since the African and the Asian elephants are classified in two distinct genera, they would not be able to interbreed because that would violate the biological concepts of species and genus. The geographical distribution of these two genera is such that they are spread thousands of kilometers apart and therefore inbreeding in the wild is practically impossible. In captivity, however, conditions are artificial and inbreeding among species and genera may take place. An unusual cross-breeding occurred in Chester Zoo, England, in 1978, when a female Asian (Sheba) and a male African (Jumbolino) bred. The resultant hybrid (Motty) died ten days after birth. This is the only known case of interbreeding between *Loxodonta africana* and *Elephas maximus*. Immunological tests confirmed this identification.

Motty had an interesting mixture of external characteristics. His ears were large, with the shape of an African elephant's and the pointed lobes. His trunk was deeply wrinkled, like that of an African elephant, but it had one "finger" on the tip, like an Asian. His body was shaped overall like an African's but with a center hump, as in Asians, and a hump at the rear, as in Africans. His legs were long and slim, like an African's, but his forefeet bore five nails and his rear feet four, as in an Asian. The mounted skin is now housed at the British Museum (Natural History), London.

AHMED—A SYMBOL OF CONSERVATION

Very few wild elephants attain a legendary status when alive. Ahmed was one of them. Ahmed was a male African elephant *(Loxodonta africana)* born about 1919, possibly in the vicinity of Marsabit National Reserve, Kenya, East Africa. His name is of Arabic origin (pronounced Ah-med), and it means "praised". He had huge tusks for his size, which gently curved in a perfect symmetry and reached to the ground; they measured about 3 meters (10 feet) each and averaged about 68 kilograms (150 pounds) each. Undoubtedly, these tusks contributed to his legendary status in East Africa. They also brought his life into danger. In Ahmed's adult life, the average elephant tusk weighed about 32 kilograms (70 pounds). As the price of ivory on the world market rose following World War II, Ahmed's 136 kilograms (300 pounds) of ivory attracted hunters and, as a result, major concern for his safety developed among the general public and scientists. During 1972–73, a total of 5,000 letters and cards was delivered to the East African Wildlife Society which resulted in a Presidential Decree issued by the late President Mzee Jomo Kenyatta to protect Ahmed. In addition, a team of soldiers was assigned to watch his whereabouts.

On January 17, 1974, Ahmed died, probably of natural causes, and his carcass was found near Lake Paradise in the reserve. At his death, Ahmed was about fifty-five years old, was about 3 meters (10 feet) tall at the shoulder, and weighed approximately 5,000 kilograms (11,000 pounds). The skin could not be saved; a fiberglass replica of the skin was later made by the Zimmermann Limited taxidermist team. The skeleton was transported to Nairobi, where it was mounted by J. C. Hillman. Both the skeleton and the replica are now on display at the National Museum of Kenya in Nairobi. In 1977 Ahmed was chosen for the logo of the Elephant Interest Group (now the Elephant Research Foundation), Detroit, Michigan, USA.

Ahmed is Kenya's most celebrated elephant—he was, and still is, regarded as a national monument and remains a symbol of conservation.

RAJA—A NATIONAL TREASURE

From the 1930s to 1988, one captive male elephant led an annual procession in Kandy, Sri Lanka, to honor Buddha. Raja, deemed the country's "most venerated moving monument", carried the Tooth Relic of Buddha in a golden casket on his back, at the head of a ceremonial parade called the Perahera, each summer, with more than fifty decorated elephants in Sri Lanka's former capital. In 1985 the nation's president declared this elephant a national treasure. When Raja died in July 1988 at the age of eighty-one or eighty-two (according to various sources), Buddhist monks paid tribute to him, while thousands of mourners viewed his body. The national museums assisted the Buddhists in preserving the skin and creating a mounted version which was unveiled in December 1989. It stands in a museum at the side of the Temple of the Tooth Relic in Kandy. Raja was succeeded by Raja the Younger, a male aged forty-six.

Numerous other elephant personalities have stepped into the world's limelight from time to time; as well, the myriad of fictional characters such as Dumbo, Babar, and Kala Nag are mentioned here only in passing to acknowledge their roles in human culture. Elephants have been recognized in children's literature as favored creatures through which lessons may be conveyed and emotions may be evoked. From these stories and the now legendary characters of Jumbo and Ahmed, we can build a portrait of the nature of the elephant: an animal of giant structure whose characteristics include dignity and intelligence.

The Bettmann Archive

◀ The title page of the Book of Jumbo, featuring a woodcut (c. 1880) of the best known of the famous show elephants. Although Jumbo ceased to be used as a ride elephant once he left England at age twenty-two years, he was warmly embraced by the American public and was made a celebrity by the circus magnate, P. T. Barnum. Jumbo's name quickly made its way into colloquial parlance as a nickname for all elephants, as well as an adjective to describe anything "enormous".

Jeheskel Shoshani

◀ Welcoming visitors to Somers in New York, USA, stands the large wooden statue of Old Bet mounted on a tall granite pillar. Her many years of delighting an admiring public throughout North America were ended tragically by a lethal rifle shot.

Peter Davey/Bruce Coleman Ltd

◀ The fiberglass replica of Ahmed outside the National Museum in Nairobi, Kenya, suggests some of the majesty evoked by this great adult male elephant with the exquisitely curved symmetrical tusks of astounding length.

K. W. Green, Chester Zoo

◀ Motty, pictured with his mother. The only known hybrid elephant, Motty was born in Chester Zoo, England, with an interesting mixture of external characteristics of both the African and Asian species. Sadly, he survived only ten days.

▲ These zebras in Tsavo National Park keep their distance as an elephant ambles by; sitting beneath a tree is a baboon unabashedly surveying the scene.

CONSERVATION AI

ID MANAGEMENT

THE ASIAN ELEPHANT POPULATION TODAY

J. C. DANIEL

At the beginning of the 1990s, it was believed that the African elephant population was the more endangered of the species. Experts said it had been reduced in numbers over the past two decades from 1 million to 600,000. But by comparison, the Asian elephant with an estimated population in the wild of approximately 36,000–44,000 is truly endangered.

Experts would argue that the population decline of the Asian elephant has not been as catastrophic as that of the African species, but in fact the loss in

Elephant Specialist Group of the International Union for Conservation of Nature and Natural Resources (IUCN) estimates that the total wild

▲ Elephants and agriculture don't mix: destruction of their forest habitat and the difficulty of controlling the activities of elephants on croplands are two factors that seriously threaten the Asian elephant's precarious status. Here, Indonesian farmers chase a herd from a corn field near Lampung, Sumatra.

Asian populations has accelerated dramatically in the latter half of this century.

In the past the area of distribution of the Asian elephant was enormous, stretching as it did from the Tigris and Euphrates Valleys of present-day Syria and Iraq to southeast China up to the Yellow River in the east and Sumatra (Indonesia) in the south. Today the distribution is fragmented, and the Asian elephant only appears in parts of its former wide-ranging habitat including India, Sri Lanka, Nepal, Bhutan, Bangladesh, Myanmar (formerly Burma), China, Thailand, Laos, Cambodia, Vietnam, Malaysia, and Indonesia.

In keeping with the past, the present-day distribution of the Asian elephant reflects the continuing deterioration of the elephant's environment. In historic times there has been a progressive desiccation of west Asia. This deterioration is largely caused by humans—and the elephant has disappeared from areas where the forests have been cleared for human needs.

The Conservation Action Plan of the Asian

population of the Asian elephant is between 36,000 and 50,000. The country with the lowest population is Nepal with between 50 and 100, while India has the highest with between 23,000 and 28,000.

The problems that the elephant faces in India are broadly the same problems that it faces in other areas of its occurrence in Southeast Asia. The Indian population is discontinuously distributed in four major geographical zones: a south Indian population in the forests of the Western Ghat Hills in the states of Karnataka, Tamil Nadu and Kerala; a central Indian population in the forests of Bihar and Orissa; a northern population in the forests of Uttar Pradesh close to Nepal; and a northeastern population in the states of West Bengal, Assam,

Arunachal Pradesh, Nagaland, Manipur, Tripura, Mizoram, and Meghalaya.

Since 1860 an enormous area of prime elephant habitat has been lost to plantations of Indian coffee, tea, rubber, and teak, which were carved out of existing forests. After 1950, hydro-electric projects ravaged elephant habitats through the submerging of forests and unscrupulous exploitation of the remnant forests. In central India, the forests holding elephants cover the single largest deposit of iron ore in Asia and mining has been a continuous process since 1901.

The states of northeast India, which used to be the main stronghold of the elephant in India, are the areas where the main human–elephant conflict

▼ Asian elephants in Gal Oya National Park, Sri Lanka. This small nation still has more than 3,000 elephants, but extensive development leaves little room for the species outside national parks.

THE STATUS OF ELEPHANTS IN CHINA

YANG DEHUA

In ancient times, elephants *(Elephas maximus indicus)* could be found in China around the Yellow River, and throughout this region they were widely distributed. More recently, around three thousand years ago, in the Shang Dynasty (eleventh century BC), elephants populated the Henan province. In the late Ming Dynasty (1644 AD), Chinese elephants were found living in the Yunnan, Guangdong, Guangxi, and Hunan provinces.

Over the centuries, the domain of the elephants has continuously been reduced, due to human population explosions and the relentless development of agriculture. Today their existence is confined to China's southwest province of Yunnan.

RECENT DISTRIBUTION AND POPULATION

Recent studies show that within the Yunnan province the distribution of elephants is limited to the Xishuangbanna Prefecture. Within this area, elephants live in Mengyang and Jingnuo of the Jinghong County, the whole of Mengla County, in Banhong and Banlao of Cangyuan County within the Lincang District, and around the Niuluo River of the Jiangcheng County in the Simao District. Individual elephants have also been seen around the Mengwang village.

Depending on the region, the Chinese identify elephants by different names. Among the Dai Minority, elephants are known as *Zhang*, among the Aini as *Yama*, and in Wa Province as *Shan*.

BIOLOGICAL DATA

Although few formal studies of elephants have been undertaken in China, local zoologists have pieced together some brief facts on their biological make-up. After measuring the height of broken branches left on trees by roaming elephants, observers estimate that the tallest elephant in Mengla County, Xishuangbanna, is

◀ Issued in the 1870s, this postage stamp commemorates the elephant in China.

Mary Ann Owens

2.5 meters (8.2 feet). The greatest weight for a pair of elephant's tusks for this particular region, recorded at Mengla Preserve Station, is 52.5 kilograms (115.7 pounds).

The most popular area for elephants is the broad forest area around rivers where the elevation is under 1,300 meters (4,265 feet). Their main foods are palm *(Caryota urens)*, wild banana *(Musa acuminata)*, bamboo *(Cephalostachyum sp.)*, and reeds *(Phragmites australis)*. While the supply of palms is diminishing, the wild banana has become the elephants' most important food resource. The elephants seldom destroy rice fields.

STATUS

China's *State Roll of Wild Key Animal Conservation* was published in January 1989 by the Ministry of Forests and the Ministry of Agriculture and lists the elephant as a first-degree endangered species. Prior to this hunters were illegally killing the diminishing population of elephants at a devastating rate. During the Cultural Revolution (1965–68), more than thirty elephants were killed in the Cangyuan County and as many as fifty were killed in the period leading up to this upheaval.

Even as recently as the 1980s elephants were sometimes killed. Ten elephants in the Xishuangbanna Prefecture have been destroyed. Reports of the killing of two elephants were recorded in Cangyuan County in 1987; and there was a report of an elephant killing in Mengyang on November 14, 1990. By late November, the ivory extracted from this particular elephant was traced to the black market.

Since the declaration of the elephant's endangered status on the conservation roll, the level of preservation has improved.

PROBLEMS REGARDING THE ELEPHANT'S SURVIVAL

There are several issues affecting the survival of this endangered species that need to be addressed if they are to be preserved.

Elephant populations currently live in territories on the borders of Myanmar (formerly Burma) and Laos. If their habitats in China continue to be destroyed, these elephants will move into the surrounding countries and may be lost to China completely.

At present, elephant herds are distributed in isolated groups, especially in Cangyuan County, and if the status is not changed these groups will inevitably remain inbred.

Up until now, as there has been no special field study on wild elephants in China, a concrete measure for preserving them has not been found. To further encourage the conservation of elephants, the government needs to strengthen legislation against illegal hunting. In addition to the death of the two elephants in Cangyuan County in 1987, a group of twelve elephants has disappeared, indicating that a lenient attitude encourages further poaching.

In the late 1970s, as a result of deforestation, elephants disappeared from the area around the Nankang River of Ximeng County, the Simao District and from the Xima area in the Yinjang County, Dehong Prefecture. As this process continues, the habitats suitable for elephants are rapidly declining. Unless a serious attempt is soon made to conserve them, the elephants may be driven out of China forever.

POPULATIONS AND FOREST AREA			
Counties	Number of individuals	Forest area in square kilometers (square miles)	Forest area in square kilometers (square miles) per individual
Mengla	150–180	2,921 (1,128)	16.2–19.5 (6.3–7.5)
Jinghong	50–60	474 (183)	7.9–9.5 (3.1–3.7)
Cangyuan	14	79 (31)	5.7 (2.2)
Total	214–254	3,474 (1,342)	10.0–11.6 (3.9–4.5)

has developed. Exploding human populations have destroyed crucial elephant habitats for cultivation and plantations, extinguishing traditional migratory routes; slash-and-burn cultivation has devastated habitats, making the survival of the elephant in some of the states unlikely.

The status of the elephant in adjoining countries is equally bleak. Nepal, which has the lowest population for a country (50–100) has lost over 80 percent of its elephant habitat because of human settlements. Though Bhutan (100–300) still has substantial forest cover, its elephant population is influenced by conditions in adjoining India as the population is shared with that country. Bangladesh (200–350) is rapidly losing its elephant habitats to development programs and the population is likely to diminish rapidly.

The Myanmar population (4,000–5,000) has a reasonably undisturbed habitat and prospects of long-term survival. However, little is known of its present status. The elephant continues to be used in the extraction of Myanmar's timber wealth.

In Thailand, although the elephant has been protected since the eighteenth century, exploitation of the habitat and the pressure of human population have made the species vulnerable.

Cambodia (500–1,500), noted in the past for its abundant elephant population, has suffered disastrous environmental loss from the thirty years of war which ravaged the country and its forests. As in neighbouring countries of the Indo-Chinese peninsula namely Vietnam (100-200) and Laos (1,000–2,000), precise information on the status of the environment and of the wildlife, including the elephant, is not available.

The elephant population of China (200–300) is restricted to a small forested area in Yunnan province bordering between Myanmar and Laos.

Since the twelfth century, Sri Lanka (2,500–3,500) had upheld an ancient tradition of protection. However, during the colonial period they experienced a major loss in the population which continued until recently when the species regained protection. Presently large-scale development programs have destroyed the elephant's habitat and there is no future for the elephant except in a few protected areas.

The Malaysian elephant (800–1,000) has also become a victim of development programs and occurs in small groups, often pocketed in unsuitable habitats. There seems to be no hope for the elephants outside protected areas.

The elephants of Sumatra, Indonesia (2,000–4,000), and possibly the wild population of Kalimantan, Borneo (500–2,000), suffer from the same type of human population pressure which afflicts elephants throughout the range of the species and there seems to be little chance of survival outside limited protected areas.

Overall, it appears as though the Asian elephant is a victim of the overuse of the

environment by humans. Demands on natural resources for human needs and the needs of domestic stock are so great that there is little resource available for the large species of wildlife like the elephant, which require a tree canopy for survival. Loss of its habitat is the crux of the problem of the elephant's declining numbers, its endangered status, and threats to its survival.

The survival of the elephant in parts of the world most heavily populated with humans may be attributed to the fact that it is an integral part of the major religions of the Asian area, and because until recently most of the prime elephant habitats have been "protected" by diseases deadly to man.

Luca Invernizzi Tettoni/Photobank

▲ Street scene with elephant, Bombay, India. As elsewhere in Southeast Asia, elephants in India are intimately involved in the religious and cultural heritage of the nation.

ESTIMATED NUMBERS OF ELEPHANTS IN THE WILD AND IN CAPTIVITY IN ASIA

Country	In the Wild Data from IUCN/SSC estimates[1]	In Captivity Data from four main sources[2]	Total
Bangladesh	200–350	50	250–400
Bhutan	100–300	0	100–300
Cambodia	500–1,500	500–600	1,000–2,100
China	200–300	15	215–315
India	23,000–28,000	2,200–2,800	25,200–30,800
Indonesia	2,500–6,000	50–100	2,550–6,100
Japan	0	70	70
Laos	1,000–2,000	1,000–1,300	2,000–3,300
Malaysia	800–1,000	less than 50	850–1,050
Myanmar	4,000–5,000	5,400	9,400–10,400
Nepal	50–100[3]	60–80	110–180
Sri Lanka	2,500–3,500	400–500	2,900–4,000
Thailand	1,500–2,000[4]	3,500–5,000	5,000–7,000
Vietnam	100–200	100–600	200–800
Totals	36,450–50,250	13,395–16,565	49,845–66,815

1　Based mostly on figures of IUCN/SSC Asian Elephant Specialist Group Action Plan for Asian Elephant Conservation by R. Sukumar and C. Santiapillai, 1999.

2　Sources are C. Santiapillai (see note number 1), C. D. Tuttle, J. McNeely and R. Sukumar.

3　Numbers may change due to migration from India.

4　Numbers may change due to migration from Myanmar.

THE AFRICAN ELEPHANT POPULATION TODAY

IAIN DOUGLAS-HAMILTON

At the heart of the decision made by the Convention on International Trade in Endangered Species of Wild Fauna and Flora (CITES) in 1989 to ban the worldwide trade in ivory was the fear that the African elephant was endangered over most of its range, with poaching the major cause.

With the knowledge that well over half of Africa's elephants had been killed in the previous decade it was believed that no decision short of a total ban would halt the decline of the elephant. The facts presented to the CITES parties were the result of an impartial scientific consensus based on an African Elephant Database accumulated over fifteen years, and housed in a geographical information database

at the United Nations Environment Programme (UNEP) headquarters in Nairobi.

The African Elephant Database began with the Elephant Survey and Conservation Program of the International Union for the Conservation of Nature and Natural Resources (IUCN) in 1976. This program, supported by the World Wildlife Fund (WWF) and the New York Zoological Society (NYZS), made surveys of certain critical elephant populations, reviewed the scientific and historical literature, distributed questionnaires, and brought together many elephant experts with the aim of defining the range, status, and trend of the species. By 1979 these early studies arrived at a minimum estimate of 1,300,000 elephants in Africa. The

upper limit was left undefined although some experts thought it might be as high as three million.

Even in 1979 the ivory trade was recognized as a major threat to most elephant populations. Unfortunately, any decisive action to control the trade was paralyzed by the following paradox: that while the elephants were already undergoing a general continental decline, certain populations were locally overabundant and judged by national authorities to be in need of culling. Throughout the 1970s and 1980s this paradox served to perpetuate an ivory trade that steadily became more and more out of control.

Over the years the elephant database improved as more surveys were made, and information came

▼ African elephants at a riverside, at sunset. Although numbers of African elephants are increasing in some places, the continent as a whole has lost more than half of its elephants during the 1970s and 1980s mainly to ivory poachers. National parks and other reserves encompass only 1.5 percent of the species' total distribution range.

AFRICAN ELEPHANT NUMBERS: ESTIMATES BY COUNTRY

	Area Square kilometers	Area Square miles	Estimates Updated[1] 1995/1999 Minimum	Estimates Updated[1] 1995/1999 Maximum[2]
CENTRAL AFRICA				
Cameroon	253,000	98,000	1,100	17,213
Central African Republic	346,000	134,000	1,750	9,284
Chad	202,000	78,000	0	3,140
Congo	214,000	83,000	0	32,563
Democratic Republic of the Congo	1,420,000	548,000	4,470	83,618
Equatorial Guinea	23,000	9,000	0	407
Gabon	249,000	96,000	0	82,012
TOTAL	2,707,000	1,046,000	7,320	228,237
EAST AFRICA				
Eritrea	121,000	46,000	8	50
Ethiopia	1,133,000	437,000	847	2,407
Kenya	413,000	159,000	13,834	26,478
Rwanda	3,000	1,200	39	81
Somalia	56,000	22,000	0	250
Sudan	372,000	144,000	22,000	22,000
Tanzania	501,000	193,000	73,459	98,179
Uganda	16,000	6,000	1,318	1,848
TOTAL	2,615,000	1,008,200	111,505	151,293
SOUTHERN AFRICA				
Angola	458,000	177,000	0	8,170
Botswana	93,000	36,000	62,998	80,174
Malawi	19,000	7,000	1,111	2,337
Mozambique	246,000	95,000	825	14,900
Namibia	141,000	54,000	5,843	11,999
South Africa	23,000	9,000	9,990	10,010
Swaziland	17,000	6,000	20	20
Zambia	211,000	81,000	19,701	33,004
Zimbabwe	114,000	44,000	56,297	81,855
TOTAL	1,322,000	509,000	156,785	242,469
WEST AFRICA				
Benin	20,000	8,000	0	1,550
Burkina Faso	36,000	14,000	1,469	2,635
Ghana	22,000	8,000	245	2,531
Guinea	11,000	4,200	0	1,000
Guinea Bissau	400	150	0	35
Ivory Coast	51,000	20,000	551	2,196
Liberia	17,000	7,000	0	1,783
Mali	50,000	19,000	0	807
Mauritania	6,000	2,300	?	?
Niger	6,000	2,300	0	800
Nigeria	29,000	11,000	0	1,615
Senegal	10,000	3,900	0	40
Sierra Leone	3,000	1,200	380	380
Togo	7,000	2,700	0	228
TOTAL	268,400	103,750	2,645	15,600
GRAND TOTAL	6,912,400	2,666,950	278,255	637,599

Note: Numbers are rounded in columns two and three.
1 Data for the 1995/1999 estimates were compiled by J. Shoshani, after Said et al., 1995; data for Eritrea are from 1999. Except for this update, most of the text for this chapter was published in the 1992 edition of this book.
2 Minimum estimate for each country is the "definite" estimate of Said et al. (1995), and the maximum estimate for each country is the sum of "definite", "probable", "possible", and "speculative" estimates of Said et al. (1995).

in from a series of questionnaires distributed by the African Elephant and Rhino Specialist Group (AERSG) in 1981, 1984, and 1987. This body of scientists from different parts of Africa had been set up by the IUCN to coordinate their specialist knowledge of elephant populations and their advice was used to set the elephant policy of the IUCN, WWF, and other major conservation organizations.

From 1986 onwards all the elephant data were reviewed by AERSG, graded according to quality, and entered on the UNEP Geographical Information System (GIS) computer. A geographical analysis showed that of all the factors potentially affecting elephant numbers (such as human population, habitat, rainfall, and protected status) the degree of effective protection was by far the most important determinant of elephant density.

An important consensus was reached on elephant numbers and trends when AERSG met in 1987. By then the database had been refined over ten years and the elephant specialists concluded that only 760,000 elephants remained out of the original minimum of 1,300,000 estimated in 1979. For the first time the scientists all agreed that the ivory trade was the major cause of the elephant decline and that if the trends continued the elephant would become an endangered species in many parts of its range.

On the basis of the trends reviewed, David Cumming, Chairman of AERSG at that time, advised the CITES Conference of the Parties in Ottawa in June 1987: "The downwards trends for many countries are sufficiently large to predict extinction in the near future ... The situation is one of appalling conservation and mismanagement." He also pointed out that at low densities other factors would decrease the pressure, and the more likely scenario was reduction to low numbers, rather than outright extinction.

Despite recognition of the dangers posed by the ivory trade it continued to flourish under an ill-conceived ivory export quota system which encouraged African countries to declare an ivory quota under the CITES treaty. The idea was that only legitimate ivory that had been derived from legal culling or hunting would be traded. In fact massive illegal trade continued and elephant poaching reached new levels all over the continent. The database continued to log information as it came in and registered catastrophic reductions of elephants even in some of the most secure and famous national parks.

Leading up to the CITES conference of 1989 new data were acquired from many countries where censuses had never been made before. The European Economic Community supported WWF to make a new survey working with the Ivory Trade Review Group (ITRG)—biologists, population modelers, economists, lawyers, and journalists commissioned by AERSG to analyze the effects of the ivory trade on the African elephant.

Surveys were made in the forests of Gabon, Equatorial Guinea, Cameroon, Congo, the Central African Republic, and Democratic Republic of the Congo (DRC) under the leadership of Richard Barnes. Elephant population estimates for the rainforest were based on field data for the first time. These showed that even in the remotest parts of their range, in the depths of the equatorial forests, the elephants were no longer safe. Benin in West Africa was also recounted, and most of the parks and reserves in Kenya, Tanzania, and Uganda were surveyed. Holly Dublin visited five key countries in southern Africa to collect the latest and most reliable figures on elephant status from the acknowledged scientific authorities of the region. AERSG held regional meetings to cover West, Central, and East Africa, in which the elephant data were reviewed.

By 1989 the data suggested that some 609,000 elephants remained in Africa. The regional split was 277,000 in Central Africa, 110,000 in Eastern Africa, 204,000 in southern Africa, and 19,000 in West Africa. The estimate of 214,000 elephants within the rainforest was lower than expected, but not really surprising in the light of elephant poaching within the forest zone which had been prevalent for the previous 10 to 15 years. Only 1.5 percent of the elephants' total range of 5.8 million square kilometers (about 2.3 million square miles) lay within strictly protected and adequately financed areas.

Trend data for benchmark populations across Africa constituted the most convincing evidence of change in the last decade, and allowed a regional estimation of elephant trends. Unprecedented elephant declines were shown in the analysis for Kenya, Uganda, and Tanzania. The total loss of elephants in East Africa from 1977 to 1989 was 74 percent or 185,000. This included massive drops in large national parks such as Tsavo in Kenya, Murchison in Uganda, and Ruaha in Tanzania. The largest single drop was in the Selous Game Reserve which lost 80,000 elephants between 1976 and 1989. Negative trends since 1987 for the most part accelerated, as predicted by the modelers who simulated the effects of the ivory trade. More fragmentary data, including some good aerial surveys in the northern savannahs which stretch across Cameroon, Chad, the Central African Republic, DRC, Sudan, and Somalia, showed declines of even greater proportional magnitude, in the order of 80 percent and higher.

For the central African forests a new method of calculation suggests that forest elephants had been reduced by some 43 percent. in DRC's forests the calculated loss was about 58 percent. In southern Africa, the trends were mixed. In Zambia, Mozambique, and Angola, anecdotal reports of elephant declines, and a lack of conservation measures, were strongly suggestive of an elephant catastrophe similar to that of their northern

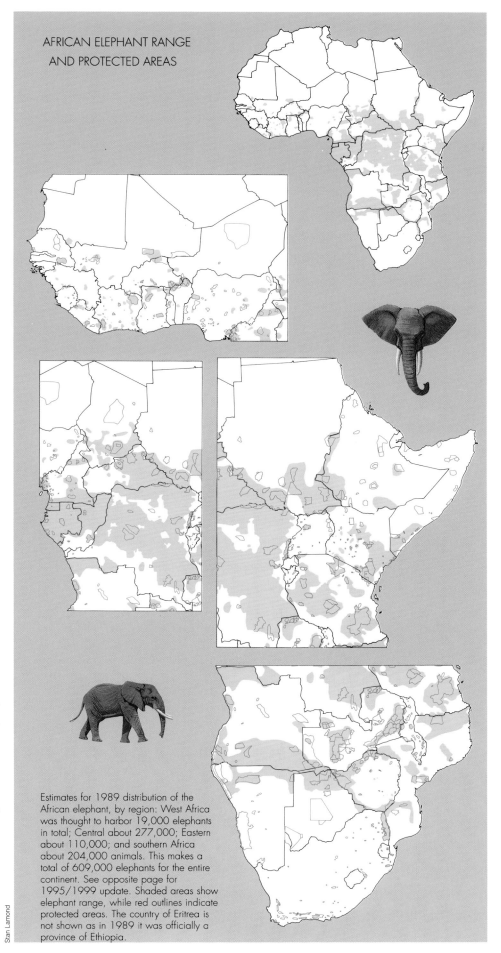

AFRICAN ELEPHANT RANGE AND PROTECTED AREAS

Estimates for 1989 distribution of the African elephant, by region: West Africa was thought to harbor 19,000 elephants in total; Central about 277,000; Eastern about 110,000; and southern Africa about 204,000 animals. This makes a total of 609,000 elephants for the entire continent. See opposite page for 1995/1999 update. Shaded areas show elephant range, while red outlines indicate protected areas. The country of Eritrea is not shown as in 1989 it was officially a province of Ethiopia.

Stan Lamond

▲ This young elephant was injured in a snare. Much public attention has been focused on ivory poaching in Africa, but it is also true that much poaching of large mammals also takes place, for meat for local consumption.

▼ A roadsign in Zimbabwe warns motorists of the presence of elephants.

neighbors, and this was supported by repeated aerial counts in the Luangwa Valley Census Zone, in which elephants had declined since 1972 by over 60 percent, in a supposedly protected area.

In Botswana and Zimbabwe, however, elephant increases were recorded on the basis of well-organized surveys. South Africa had a population which was stable, but which would expand at a rate of about 5 percent per annum if not held in check by culling. Namibia's elephant population was reported as stable, but increasingly in danger from ivory poaching. These countries, with their high standard of wildlife conservation, afforded a bright spot for elephants in an otherwise bleak continental picture, but doubts were felt that they would remain secure from the spread in ivory poaching witnessed elsewhere.

Although these southern African elephant populations were still intact the general trend of the previous fifteen years had shown that when stocks of elephants were exhausted in one locality, the killing moved to another. It was feared that if the ivory offtake continued, poaching would inevitably spread to the remaining untouched elephant populations of southern Africa. By then the elephant populations in the rest of Africa would have been largely eradicated.

All these factors were weighed by the parties who took the decision to ban the trade in 1989. On balance the increases in southern Africa, in particular in Botswana and Zimbabwe, were of the order of 50,000 animals, but the decreases for the whole continent, due overwhelmingly to the ivory trade, were of the order of 700,000.

Since the ivory trade ban the database has continued to be updated. In 1991 AERSG met again in Botswana and updated country estimates

(see the table on page 180). Several countries failed to present estimates, however, and at the time of writing there is no new overall elephant estimate for the continent.

The effect of the ivory trade ban has been an immediate drop in the ivory price in most of East and Central Africa. The fall off in poaching has been dramatic in the three East African countries, Kenya, Uganda, and Tanzania. Extensive aerial surveys in all three countries have spotted very few

fresh carcasses of elephants. In the Tsavo National Park, for example, a count in September 1991 found not one carcass of a recently poached elephant, compared to 160 in the 1988 count. This park, formerly one of the most heavily poached, is now typical of the region.

In southern Africa the effects of the ban are less clear and several countries would like to re-open ivory trading. While culling the locally abundant populations in parts of southern Africa cannot harm the continental population, trading in their products, especially ivory, would be disastrous and could open up all the rampant trading that was so destructive to the species in the past.

The elephants need a cease-fire to save them from near extinction in most of their range. To avoid local extinctions, they have to be shielded from the ivory trade. It is my belief that the only way to achieve this is a total worldwide ban which needs to be kept in force for many years.

▲ Elephants in the rain. The 1989 CITES decision to ban the worldwide trade in ivory seems to have had encouraging effects on the numbers of elephants in East and Central Africa, where the rate at which poached carcasses are found by ranger patrols has dropped significantly.

ELEPHANTS IN CAPTIVITY

C. DALE TUTTLE

Over the centuries, elephants have been used as instruments of war, as machines in forestry and the agricultural industry, and as objects of religious significance. Today, with their use in the logging industry declining and their numbers dropping sharply throughout their ranges due to a number of causes, the future of the elephant may depend on captive breeding programs.

Asian elephants were first brought into a captive environment over 4,000 years ago. The total number captured for work since then is staggering when compared to the remaining wild populations of today. In the last century alone, it is estimated that well over 100,000 Asian elephants have been captured for work and zoological exhibition.

The history of African elephants in captivity is not as well documented as that of the Asian

elephants, aside from the well-known account of Hannibal taking his African elephants over the Alps to attack Romans in 218 BC. Long before Hannibal's famous trek, the Romans captured African elephants from the Carthaginians to pit against other animals in the arena for their entertainment. Although not as widely used in the timber and agricultural industries as the Asian elephant, the African was used in the Belgian

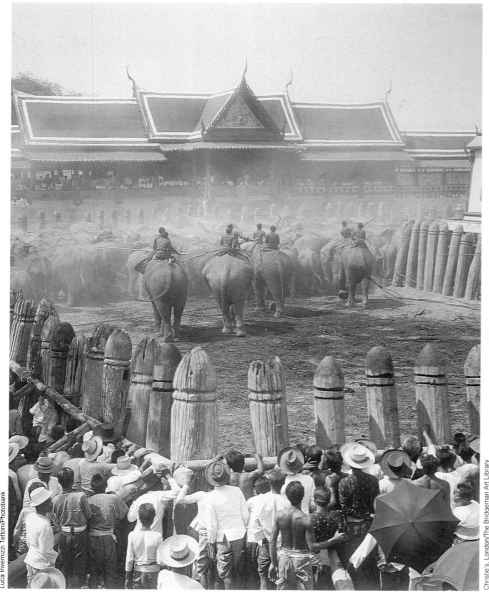

▼ Escorted by tame elephants, wild-captured animals are brought into a compound to begin their training. In India and Southeast Asia, there has historically been little emphasis on captive breeding.

Congo, where a domestication center was established shortly after the turn of this century. The center survives today but mainly uses the animals in tourist-oriented activities in the adjoining Garamba National Park. The original training of elephants in the Belgian Congo was done by Ceylonese mahouts brought in for this purpose. (See the section by K. Hillman Smith.)

Keeping track of captive elephants has proved to be no easier than documenting the numbers of wild elephants. Elephants in Asia are not registered and a permit system does not exist. According to the World Wildlife Fund Action Plan for Asian Elephants, there are an estimated 14,000–17,000 elephants used in the timber industry, for religious ceremonies, and in the tourist industry. Unfortunately, many of these animals are becoming increasingly unemployed. Thailand's estimated 3,500–5,000 captive elephants are primarily unemployed because very few forests remain; however, Myanmar's (formerly Burma)

estimated 5,400 working elephants are still busily working in timber extraction. Ironically, this very business is also destroying most of the remaining prime habitat for wild Asian elephants. Myanmar has traditionally replaced its annual losses with additional captured elephants; however, the wild populations can no longer sustain the annual removal of approximately 125 elephants.

Little has been done to breed working elephants because of the loss of work from pregnant females. After about a twenty-two-month gestation, a mother will nurse her baby for at least two years, causing a considerable loss of income to the mahout or owning company. Another reason breeding has been historically discouraged is that baby elephants become quite spoiled by the attention and hand-feeding by forestry hands and visitors that goes on in the camps, making them extremely difficult to train. It has been said that it is easier to train an elephant caught in the wild than it is to train one which is captive born.

▼ This typically Victorian painting, *At the Zoo*, by Guiseppe Barison, illustrates the contemporary preoccupation with elephants, lions, giraffes, gaudy parrots, and other exotic animals in zoos and circuses. During the late twentieth century, the emphasis has gradually shifted from exotic to indigenous species, and from mere display towards public education and the maintenance and management of viable captive breeding stocks of animals increasingly threatened by habitat destruction.

Ian Redmond

Mary Ann Owens

▲ (Top) An Asian elephant plays with a chunk of timber in its new enclosure at Cricket Saint Thomas, England. Unless the wholesale destruction of native habitat can be halted, maintenance of a healthy captive population may be the elephant's best hope of survival. But breeding success in Western zoos is so far not impressive (recorded births of Asian elephants total fewer than 200 and African births fewer than 20 in Europe and North America combined), placing a particular urgency on the development of improved facilities and management techniques.

▲ ▶ Contrary to widespread belief, the forest population of the African elephant, commemorated in the Belgian Congo (now Democratic Republic of the Congo) postage stamp (above) can be successfully domesticated, as has been demonstrated for almost a century at Garamba National Park. The magazine illustration (right), published in 1911, is an example of the accomplishment of such projects.

Mary Evans Picture Library

India is the only other country with a substantial number of captive elephants, with an estimated 2,200–2,800. In this country, captive elephants are primarily used in the timber industry and in temples. However, the capture of elephants has now been outlawed in India and this has encouraged captive breeding efforts. Even so captive numbers continue to decline and the role of the mahout is a dying profession.

In several Asian countries, either the elephant was never tamed or the art of training has been lost. Today, domestic elephants in China, Bhutan,

Kalimantan, and Sumatra either do not exist or are in insignificant numbers.

It is thought that the Indian Mughal, Jehangir possessed over 40,000 elephants in his kingdom in the early part of the sixteenth century. The numbers of elephants in captivity across Asia must have been phenomenal and certainly exceeded by severalfold the number of wild elephants today. Today's estimate of 14,000–17,000 captive Asian elephants in Asia seems insignificant when compared to the days of Jehangir. The number of captive elephants in Asia today is declining and will more than likely continue to do so because of lack of occupation as modernization occurs.

Following a major decline in captive elephants in Africa over the last thirty years, their number in the wild may actually be on the increase in some areas for the immediate future. Captive elephants used for domestic work in Africa are practically non-existent, although surprisingly, there is a renewed interest in the use of African elephants for safari work in the tourist industry. From 1901 to 1959, the elephant domestication project in the Belgian Congo flourished with numbers nearing a hundred at times. Since 1960, the numbers have fallen sharply and then, with the upheaval of independence, the domestication center has been reduced until today it has only eight adult elephants. It is worth noting that three of these were caught wild and one was born at the center.

Today, rebuilding the center is under consideration and methods of funding its operation are being studied. Recent correspondence indicates that the center is looking for elephants already in captivity and trained. The elephants would be used in the tourist industry to carry visitors into the park to view its wildlife, as the present four are. The elephants may also be used to monitor and guard a small surviving population of northern white rhinos as is done with the Indian rhino in Kaziranga National Park in Assam. The rhinos tolerate the elephants getting close to them and enable field biologists and game rangers to get much closer than they could on foot. (It is also far safer to be on an elephant's back than on foot.)

Elsewhere in Africa an elephant safari operation conducted in Botswana uses three African elephants imported from the United States. This type of safari activity stands a good chance of becoming immensely popular with wealthy tourists and will probably be on the increase in the near future.

Elephants used for zoological exhibition and captive breeding programs face quite a different set of problems. The earliest known zoos date back to domestication centers during the Mohenjo-Daro civilization of India about 4,500 years ago. Considerable effort was made to domesticate the Asian elephant during this period. Elephants were later kept as curiosity items in Egyptian, Greek, and Chinese menageries and still later in Roman zoos which often maintained animals for use in bloody arena events where animals were pitted against each other as well as against human opponents.

In modern times, the first elephant imported into the United States was a young Asian female which arrived aboard a sailing vessel on April 13, 1796. The first African, also a young female, followed in 1824. In 1862 the first African elephant since Roman times was imported into Europe. From this period, the elephant became a mainstay for zoological parks with the Asian far out-representing the African elephant. In the last decade, the number of African elephants in zoos has increased dramatically primarily due to the listing of the Asian elephant as an Endangered Species on Appendix I of the Convention on International Trade in Endangered Species of Wild Fauna and Flora (CITES) on July 1, 1975. Nevertheless, imports of the Asian elephant continued through most of the 1980s; however, by the end of that decade importations had been nearly brought to a halt. The African elephant on the other hand was still readily available and not protected by CITES until January 1990. During the mid-1980s culling operations in Zimbabwe created a surplus of African elephants in the United States because the adults were destroyed and the small calves were saved for export. The population of African elephants nearly doubled there in a very short time span.

Today an estimated 17,000 Asian elephants and 800 African elephants are held by the major zoological parks and private holding facilities (eg circuses) around the world. The general consensus is that the number of Asians is falling while Africans are on the increase.

North America holds a fair number of elephants with an estimated 327 Asian elephants and 268 Africans. Europe, including Great Britain, holds an estimated 509 Asians and 317 Africans. In the recently published Asian elephant studbook for Japan, 70 Asian elephants are listed and a recent census indicates there are 67 Africans in that country. The remaining areas of the world list considerably fewer elephants.

There are several reasons for the poor reproductive history of elephants in captivity in the last two hundred years. The main reason has been the inability of zoos to keep mature breeding-age bulls. During musth, bulls become quite dangerous and destructive to their holding facilities. From the mid-1800s to the mid-1900s, bulls were often destroyed before they had had an opportunity to reproduce because they had either killed someone or destroyed a considerable amount of property. Nonetheless those who endured the ravages of keeping bull elephants were generally successful in breeding. Research is being conducted now that will help us to understand better the process of musth and how we might control it in an effort to make the keeping of mature bulls safer. (See the section by Michael Schmidt.)

Photobank

Several zoos in India have managed to circumvent the problem of keeping bulls in their parks. They tether their females in the forest where known wild bulls range allowing the females to be impregnated—thereby avoiding the ravages of keeping the bull in their zoo. This type of uncontrolled breeding unfortunately does not allow us to keep track of the wild sires, and therefore accurate pedigrees cannot be maintained. This prevents us from determining the effects of inbreeding in future matings.

Another reason for failure in reproduction has been the lack of knowledge of the elephant's estrous cycle, which has only been clarified in recent years. Yet another problem has been our limited knowledge and ability to synthesize a diet for elephants in captivity.

▲ Domesticated elephants have a small but, in some situations at least, vital role to play in tourism. These tourists are preparing to set out in search of tigers at a national park in Nepal; the back of an elephant is one of the few safe ways of observing such potentially dangerous quarry at close quarters in the wild.

It is ironic that despite this long association of elephants with humans we have been so late in learning about the physiology, the behavior, and the nutritional needs of this, the largest of the living land mammals. In today's modern zoos, all of these problems are being actively addressed and all over the world considerable research in different institutions is taking place to overcome them.

The first recorded birth of an Asian elephant in a zoo or circus in modern times took place in winter quarters of the Cooper & Bailey Circus on March 10, 1880 in Philadelphia, Pennsylvania. The calf, named Columbia, was a female and stood 89 centimeters (35 inches) tall and weighed 96.7 kilograms (213 pounds). At the age of twenty-five, she was destroyed because she had reportedly become dangerous to her keepers. The first birth of an Asian in Europe was a stillborn recorded on August 31, 1902 at the London Zoo.

The first recorded birth of an African elephant in captivity occurred on April 11, 1943 at a zoo in Munich, Germany. On March 2, 1978 the first African birth in the United States occurred at the Knoxville Zoo in Knoxville, Tennessee. Because Africans have not been kept in large numbers and the fact that the current captive population is relatively young, there have not been many births. The domestication center adjoining Garamba National Park of Democratic Republic of the Congo has been successful in reproduction and actually exported several of the offspring produced there.

Despite these successes, the birth rate for captive elephants has not been impressive. North America, the largest holder of elephants, has recorded 103 Asian births since the first one in 1880. Following the birth of a male calf on April 29, 1918 to the Sells Floto Circus in Salt Lake City, Utah, there was a long absence of births in North America. The next birth did not occur until April 14, 1962 at the Washington Park (now Oregon) Zoo in Portland—a lapse of forty-five years. (Existing data indicate that the cause may lie in the absence of mature males in the captive population. The data also indicate very few, if any, imports throughout the 1920s and 1930s.)

The Bettmann Archive

▲ The elephant's generally amiable disposition, willingness to learn tricks, and extraordinarily delicate sense of balance earned it an enduring and universal popularity in the heyday of the traveling circus, as indicated in this advertising poster for the Ringling Brothers Circus.

▶ Considerable artistic license is shown in this nineteenth century woodcut illustrating an elephant steeplechase at Rangoon, Burma (now, Myanmar): an elephant at "full gallop" can reach nearly 30 kilometers per hour (about 18 miles per hour) for short distances, but it cannot jump.

▶ (Opposite) The elephant's large size and ponderous dignity have made it an integral part of pageantry and ceremonial occasions in the East for millennia. These elephants in full regalia parade with Thai royal guards in traditional costume at the annual elephant fair at Surin, Thailand.

The Bettmann Archive

A NUTRITIOUS DIET FOR A CAPTIVE ELEPHANT

JOHN LEHNHARDT

This information is based on diets for the elephants at the Calgary Zoo, Botanical Garden and Prehistoric Park, Calgary, Alberta, Canada, and at the National Zoological Parks, Washington, DC, USA. The components of the basic formula are obtainable almost anywhere in the world, with regional variations. The following daily diet is suggested for an elephant weighing 2,900 kilograms (about 6,400 pounds). It should be adjusted proportionally for elephants of different weights. It is suitable for elephants of either species.

The commercial preparations, Dairy Crumble (a supplement for calcium and phosphorus missing in oats), and Zoo Premix (a supplement for vitamin and trace mineral missing in hay) are both commonly used by the Calgary Zoo to offset deficiencies. They are sprinkled on the oats in a powdered form. Herbivore pellets, which are a combination of cereal grains, meal, vitamin, and mineral supplements, are made specifically for the National Zoo to make up for deficiencies in hay.

The need for, or level of, dietary supplementation of protein, vitamins such as vitamin E, and trace minerals such as selenium depends upon the contents of the hay fed. The easiest method of supplementation is through a pelleted ration that is made to specifications by a local feed company in the US. Vitamin supplements or medications can be given orally by cutting the top off an apple, hollowing it out, placing the item in the hollow, putting the top back on, and feeding the apple whole to the elephant. It has been observed that some elephants have been aware that such apples have been "tampered" with and effectively remove the "contents" and then consume the apples only.

The amount of protein in this diet is 3.8220 kilograms (7.8623 percent of total diet), fat 0.5957 kilograms (1.2254 percent), calcium 0.1301 kilograms (0.2676 percent), phosphorus 0.1708 kilograms (0.3514 percent), and fiber 11.1970 kilograms (23.0335 percent). The vitamin content of this diet (in milligrams per day) is for vitamin A 676,921; for vitamin E 556.404; and for vitamin D 24,550.

Caloric calculations for a 2,900 kilogram (6,400 pound) elephant indicate that 55,325.6512 calories per day are needed. The total of this list supplies that many calories, taking into account the fact that an elephant does not digest all of its food intake but only 44 percent of it.

SUGGESTED DAILY DIET FOR A MATURE CAPTIVE ELEPHANT	
Description	**Amount**
Mixed hay	30 kilograms
Lettuce	5 kilograms
Carrots	5 kilograms
Apples	4 fruits
Herbivore pellets	3 kilograms
Oats	4.5 kilograms
Dairy Crumble	500 grams
Zoo Premix	10 grams
Vitamin E powder	0.25 teaspoon

Special instructions: 3 kilograms of browse may be offered when available.

▲ Bottle-feeding a 12-hour-old baby elephant; calves need up to 11 liters of milk per day.

Imports began to increase in the 1940s, primarily by circuses, and it was naturally advantageous to the circus to have only females. In 1947 a male was imported from Cambodia. This male became the next successful breeder in North America at the zoo in Portland, Oregon, in 1962. As of September 1999 there have been 103 Asian elephants born in North America.

In Europe, a more consistent record has been maintained. Since the first birth of an Asian in 1902 a total of 103 births (30 males, 63 females, and 10 unknown) had been recorded by 1992. The Europeans have consistently maintained males with a reasonable amount of success.

The breeding record for African elephants is even less impressive and not as well documented as that of the Asian. There have been only 17 births (excluding stillbirths) in the United States since the first birth of an African elephant in 1978 and in Europe there have been ten births (four males and six females) since the first in 1943.

Some of these births, both Asian and African, have resulted in stillborns or short-lived babies. The problems may have ranged from dietary deficiencies to a relatively inexperienced captive population of elephants. These elephants have not had the socialization and exposure to birthing and rearing of young that they would get in the wild environment. Consequently, the rate of rejection of calves by the mother is high. We are gaining in our knowledge of nutrition and with every new birth our elephants become more familiar with the birthing process. The result will certainly be more successful births and rearings.

In recent years, captive breeding programs have taken on a more intense nature. It is no longer just an effort to get animals to breed, but an all-out attempt to guarantee the genetic survival of the species. Not only do we have to achieve controlled and scheduled breeding, we must also carefully consider the genetic combinations being produced. Genetic viability is necessary in order to maintain a healthy, evolving population of any species. If reintroduction into a former habitat is a prime concern, then viability is of absolute importance.

In an effort to meet these needs and to assist with the conservation of species, many national zoological park and aquarium organizations have established intense genetic management programs. These programs have various titles and acronyms, such as the Australasian Species Management Program (SMP), the British Joint Management of Species Group (JMSG), the European Europaisches Erhaltungszucht Programme (EEP), the Japanese Species Survival Committee (SSC), and the Species Survival Program of the American Assocation of Zoological Parks and Aquariums (referred to as the SSP or the SSP of the AAZPA). The primary purpose of these programs is to provide long-term, self-sustaining captive populations to reinforce survival of the species in natural habitats. In short, it is an

insurance policy in case the species fails in the wild or needs bolstering with additional viable stock.

The SSP for Asian elephants in North America is the oldest program in existence for the species, having begun in September, 1985. The initial planning and data collection is being performed to institute a species survival program for the African elephant. The basic objective of the Asian program is to preserve 90 percent of the available genetic diversity for the next two hundred years. A master plan document has been produced to accomplish this. In order to produce this document, a detailed studbook had to be developed delineating the known history of the current North American Asian elephant population. From this, we can trace the input of countries of origin and lineages. With the studbook in place the master plan analyzes the existing North American population, establishing its

Jenny Mills

▲ The capture and training of elephants for use in logging and lumber operations has been practiced throughout Asia for hundreds of years. But as Asia's forest areas continue to diminish, lack of occupation in the timber trade has meant that many captive elephants have been redeployed into the tourist industry. This freshly bathed elephant in the lush northern hill region in Thailand demonstrates its suitability for use as a vehicle for people.

Andi Cole

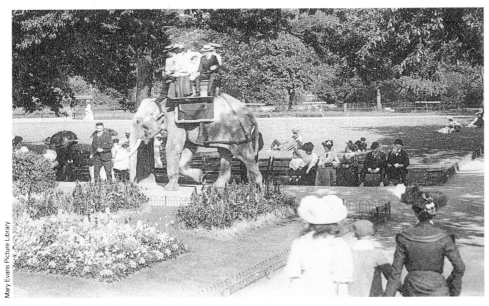

Mary Evans Picture Library

founder status and developing a demographic profile to determine the fitness of the population. (A founder is generally considered to be an animal from a wild population.) After the analysis of this data, recommendations can be made concerning the need for additional founder stock, sex ratio to aspire to, size of stabilized population, and annual production needed to sustain a viable population. The North American SSP recommends an ideal population of 250 elephants to obtain the goal of preserving 90 percent of the available genetic diversity for the next two hundred years.

In order to accomplish these goals, zoos must attain a better and more dependable breeding record than ever before. Since the main reproduction problem in the past has been our inability to house bulls as well as a lack of desire to do so, we have much to do in the way of changing methodologies and upgrading facilities to accommodate the destructive behavior of males in musth. It may be noted that the North American births indicate a 58 percent male birth rate, thus further compounding the problem of housing bull elephants. It is also interesting to compare this to the much lower male birth rate of 29 percent in Europe.

In order for national breeding programs to succeed, there will have to be a great deal of cooperation among institutions. In order to maintain the necessary genetic variation, those institutions holding mature males must be prepared to house females from other zoos for breeding. These efforts may take several years before a successful first-time breeding. After the animal is bred, it can be returned to the owning institution to make room for another female at the zoo holding the bull. To accomplish this type of maneuverability, the elephants will have to be carefully managed so they can be easily and safely loaded and transported to the breeding facility and back again. It is crucial that a cow be reasonably comfortable riding in a vehicle so that she does not abort during the return trip.

This program is further complicated by space requirements necessary for such a long-lived creature. The space problem will arise as the young males and females are held until they are ready to make their genetic contribution to the captive population which could take fourteen or fifteen years. Another potential problem is what to do with elephants that have made their contribution and are no longer needed in the breeding program but still have fifteen or so years of life remaining. As our knowledge of how to keep elephants healthy grows, so will their lifespan. A captive breeding program must be carefully thought out.

Much research is being conducted as a result of these programs, some of which may be beneficial to elephants in the wild. Some of the current research is on musth, which has inhibited us in the past from keeping adult bulls. It is our hope to find a way to control musth. This would have several

ESTIMATES OF CAPTIVE ELEPHANTS WORLDWIDE
Data compiled by Sandra Lee Shoshani as of 1999

Continent	Asian Elephants	African Elephants	Total numbers
Africa	7-10	?20–30	?27–40
Antarctica	0	0	0
Asia	13,395–16,565	122–172	13,517–16,737
Australia and New Zealand	7	6	13
Europe, including Russia and Israel	509	317	826
North America	327	268	595
Central and South America	15	14	29
Totals	14,260-17,433	747–807	15,007–18,240

Anthony Bannister/NHPA

benefits, such as making the animal safer to confine, making it safer for the keepers, and reducing the likelihood of the bull injuring himself.

Control of the estrous cycle in females is another desirable goal. There is some possible evidence that animals which continually cycle without conceiving develop a considerable amount of scar tissue in the ovaries which may render them sterile. Regulating the estrous cycle via hormone implants could be very useful in controlling the growth rate of wild herds and thus eliminating the need for culling.

Artificial insemination (AI) is another very active area being researched at the Washington Park (now Oregon) Zoo in Portland, AI could possibly eliminate the need to transport female elephants to bull-holding facilities. It could also allow the transport of semen from wild bulls without having to move the animal.

Prenatal sex determination is also being studied as a means of controlling the number of males born. This could be performed via amniocentesis, allowing the abortion of unwanted sexes early in the pregnancy.

We still have much to learn about the nutrition of elephants, and there is research being done to determine the various daily needs of this huge herbivore. We know that vitamin E plays a big part in a healthy pregnancy, but we are not sure how much should be present in the blood and how to maintain its desired level.

The status of elephants in captivity is one of decline even though there have been some gains, as with the African elephant in recent years. The major decline in the captive Asian population in its traditional range has been due to lack of occupation for elephants previously used in the forest industry. Asian elephants in zoological parks and circuses are also on the decline due to the Appendix I listing of CITES which makes it difficult to import new animals. With the African elephant recently listed on Appendix I of CITES it is logical to expect a slowdown of imports of this species and hence a gradual decline in the number in captivity. It is imperative that breeding programs become effective and timely so that the genetic viability of both species of elephants can be protected for the future.

▲ In some areas, such as Kruger National Park in South Africa, the numbers of elephants locally exceed the carrying capacity of the land available for them, and culling them becomes an unpleasant reality that should be confronted. One of the more constructive possibilities available for young animals is to export them to zoos overseas to enrich the genetic diversity of captive populations. Here, a youngster is crated for transport.

◀ (Opposite, top) Zoos have come a long way from the cramped, metal cages of old. Being completely unable to leap, elephants can be confined just as easily by means of a concrete ditch as by massive iron bars, but with a much improved rapport between the viewer and the viewed. Here, a young Asian elephant extends an exploratory trunk at Taronga Zoo, Sydney, Australia.

◀ (Opposite, bottom) The elephant ride at London Zoo, Regents Park (c. 1905). Elephants have always been among the most popular of zoo inhabitants, but modern zoo practice has tended to discourage such contact with the public because of the tendency of people to feed the animals. Maintenance of a controlled diet in long-lived creatures such as elephants is of vital importance.

THE QUESTION OF CULLING

ANTHONY J. HALL-MARTIN

There are about 860 species of mammals on the continent of Africa. Of these, only one (if we exclude humans), the African elephant, has the capacity to utterly change, even destroy, its habitat. Because of its great size, prodigious strength, and its requirement for enormous quantities of food and water, the elephant has a visible and ecologically meaningful impact on the environment. But it is not only by their demands for food that elephants can have such a devastating effect on their environment. Adult elephants, especially bulls, can tear sufficient bark off trees and shrubs to kill them; they can also break branches and uproot trees, even when this material is not needed for food. The destructive capacity of elephants is such that savanna, or woodland with mature trees, can be reduced to scrub or open grasslands in the space of a few years; elephants can literally eat themselves out of house and home.

If the habitat changes wrought by elephants are accepted by park authorities as part of a natural ecological cycle, there is no perceived management problem. It can be argued that when the food supply is exhausted the elephants will die. Their death will allow a slow recovery of the vegetation and ultimately an increase in the elephant population once again. So, it is argued, the cycle has been since modern African elephants (*Loxodonta africana*) appeared in the early Pleistocene epoch over a million years ago; at times with elephants dominant, at other times the woodlands dominate. The culling of elephants, it is argued, will disrupt this ancient ecological cycle with consequences that cannot be predicted. Exactly where the truth of the matter lies has been a topic for stiff debate over the past few decades.

THE "ELEPHANT PROBLEM"

At present the only "elephant problem" thought of in the Western world is the decline in numbers of the African elephant population. An assessment of the controversial issue of elephant culling must take a step back into recent African history so as to gain a clearer perspective.

Humans and elephants are two species that are, in a biological sense, in direct competition. Both show a preference for areas of fertile soils and high rainfall. This competition has been a feature of the interaction between the two species ever since humans became cultivators. Recent studies of this phenomenon going back to the fifteenth century show that where human societies developed dense populations, it was usually at the expense of elephant range. At times, due to disease and war, humans have retreated from such areas and elephants have then been able to reoccupy them. During the present century, the evidence of this competition is particularly strong from East Africa, where in Kenya, Uganda, and Tanzania, the first formal wildlife management agencies were created solely for controlling crop-raiding elephants—in effect for culling elephants. Over a longer time scale the same phenomenon operated in southern Africa. In South Africa the competition was so strong that by 1900 elephants numbered only about 120 in the entire country. It was only when humans were prevented from competing with elephants, in areas such as national parks and game reserves, that elephant numbers increased.

Throughout much of colonial sub-Saharan Africa, and certainly in the areas of fertile, well-watered country with large human populations, the competition between humans and elephants was most intense, mediated only by the areas set aside for elephants. Outside these areas thousands of elephants were shot or culled every year throughout Africa, and the ivory derived from this

▶ Elephant carcasses being transported to Skukuza camp in Kruger National Park. Culling, however repugnant, enables elephants to survive within the limited areas available to them, while providing economic benefits to local people. Almost every part of the animal is put to profitable use: the skins are turned into shoes, belts, and bags; the meat is processed for consumption; and the sale of ivory earns the country substantial foreign exchange.

▶ (Opposite page) Kenya's Tsavo National Park, 20,700 square kilometers (8,000 square miles) of open woodland designated as an elephant sanctuary in the 1950s, was reduced to a virtual wasteland by the uncontrolled over-population of elephants. As a consequence, many species of animals dependent on the ravaged vegetation, including elephants and black rhinos, died of malnutrition over a decade later. Much of the vegetation has since recovered due to culling.

Anthony Bannister/NHPA

Joseph van Wormer/Bruce Coleman Ltd

▲ In keeping with their awesome size and bulk, elephants have a colossal appetite. They can destroy areas of woodland faster than nature can regenerate them, hence, their capacity for devastating relatively small, confined habitats.

"elephant control" sustained a thriving trade throughout the present century. This continued until the post-colonial period when illegal poaching of elephants for their ivory on a large scale in many countries first became noticeable.

In the general debate about culling, the elephant control practices of colonial and post-colonial governments have not been regarded as "culling". Insofar as it was, and still is, in many areas aimed at controlling elephant numbers to avert a perceived undesirable effect—in this case competition with agriculturalists—it differs little in principle from elephant control or culling practiced in national parks or other protected areas. Perhaps because the benefits to humans of this kind of culling were so obvious it never excited the debate and controversy caused by elephant culling carried out by park authorities. This latter culling—the killing of elephants within those areas set aside for their protection—because it seems to be at cross-purposes with the ideal of conserving elephants, is the real subject of the elephant-culling debate.

In the early 1960s researchers in East Africa were increasingly drawing attention to "elephant problems" in the major national parks of Uganda and Kenya. A little later, by the mid-1960s, the same phenomenon was seen in the national parks of South Africa, Zambia, and Zimbabwe.

The general outlines of the problem were very similar. Elephant populations had been steadily increasing inside national parks. The increase resulted in the large-scale destruction of trees and woody plants and the conversion of woodland and savanna to shrubbery and grassland. In some cases the increase in elephant populations appeared to have been augmented by the concentration of elephants from surrounding areas of land into the parks. The causes of this squeeze on elephant range were the growing human population, the

expansion of settlements, cultivated and ranched areas, and other human influences.

In the 1960s this compression effect was not clearly understood. Subsequent detailed research on human demographic patterns has, however, clearly substantiated the phenomenon. In the Bunyoro district of Uganda, for example, and in some parts of Zimbabwe, the increase of people in areas surrounding parks has been precisely matched by declining elephant populations outside the parks and increases inside the parks.

In South Africa's Kruger National Park the elephant population was virtually eliminated by 1900, with only a remnant of twelve animals left. Once protected, however, this nucleus increased and was augmented from across the international boundary by the movement of immigrant elephants out of hunted and settled areas in Mozambique into the park. The sanctuary afforded, as well as the provision of year-round waterholes in a largely semi-arid area by the sinking of boreholes and building of dams, made the park an attractive range for a growing elephant population.

ELEPHANT POPULATION INCREASE

Under natural conditions—free of human influence—elephants can maintain a theoretical maximum rate of population increase of just under 7 percent per annum. For various reasons, such as the effect of drought on food sources and resultant loss of condition in adult females, few populations reach the maximum rate of increase. Most populations, however, can manage 4–5 percent per annum comfortably. Natural mortality in elephants is low as predation is rare. Like most other mammals, elephants are susceptible to diseases and parasites, but these seldom slow population growth. Many calves survive to maturity. So, despite their long gestation period, long inter-calving period, and advanced age at sexual maturity, and the fact that elephants rarely have twins, their numbers can grow steadily. At 5 percent per annum, the population doubling time is about fifteen years.

FOOD AND FEEDING

Various field studies carried out in Africa have documented the wide range of plants and plant parts eaten by elephants. Elephants are bulk feeders with a fairly inefficient digestive system, unlike the ruminants such as buffalo or antelopes. They require a large volume of food that passes relatively rapidly through the gut. Elephants, consequently, devote a great deal of their time and energy to gathering food. For this task they are uniquely equipped with a trunk which is a highly specialized organ. In the African elephant, the trunk tip ends in two sensitive lobes or "fingers" which can pluck individual leaves, flowers, or fruits from plants. The trunk can also be used to strip bunches of leaves from branches, to pull up grass (roots and

Frans Lanting/Minden Pictures

Mitch Reardon

all), and to pick up fallen fruit from the ground. The tusks are also used for gouging loose strips or pieces of bark which are then stripped off the tree by the trunk. Elephants also use the tusks to break branches and uproot plants. In addition to using trunk and tusks for food gathering, they can dig up roots, bulbs, and tubers with the sharp-edged toenails of their forefeet.

The elephant then is a formidable feeding machine. An adult bush African elephant may require as much as 150–300 kilograms (330–660 pounds) fresh weight of food material per day. This is harvested from virtually all types of plants— from grasses, herbs, shrubs, and creepers, to trees. In some areas they have been found to feed on 100–200 different species of plants. They take leaves, twigs, shoots, branches, succulent plants, bark, flowers, fruit, pods, seeds, roots, tubers, and bulbs; they even on occasion chew wood. Elephants quite often feed on a shrub or tree for long periods and can then totally demolish a plant. Apart from the plant parts that they detach, they can also break large branches off trees, smash tree trunks, and uproot or push over trees. They are very wasteful as they often only take a small part of the trees they destroy. In some areas, apart from the vegetation and habitat changes which elephants have brought about, they have also endangered the survival of various species of plants.

HABITAT CHANGE

The "damage" of which some scientists and park managers speak is a subjective judgement of the result of the wasteful feeding strategy of elephants. It is "wasteful" only in human terms because elephants often destroy more than they utilize of a plant. In a strict ecological sense this process may not be "wasteful" at all. It could merely be a process of change, from one state to another— elephants have many other, poorly understood, ecological effects which benefit an ecosystem. This process can, however, under heavy elephant pressure, result in areas of woodland or forest with dense tree cover being converted to savanna and later, with the added influence of fire, to grassland. This process is akin to ecological changes brought about by human cultivation.

In the African ecosystem, however, the loss of trees is only one factor in a complex set of interactions. In general, where trees are killed off or pushed over, there is a more luxuriant growth of grasses. These, when the dry season has sapped the moisture from them, provide ideal incendiary material. The grass fires in turn kill other trees, especially vulnerable seedlings, and ensure that grass has a further advantage in the competition for life-sustaining moisture after the rains. Elephant damage to trees can, therefore, set in motion an entire cycle of events which can totally change the

▲ The waterhole is often a meeting place for a host of animals. This young African elephant quenching its thirst is joined by some giraffes and Egyptian geese.

Ian Redmond

▲ An elephant scouring the rubbish tip of the Vitshumbi fishing community in the Democratic Republic of the Congo. Displaced by the encroachment of human settlements, elephants will often visit them in search of food, at times raiding crop plantations and ransacking entire villages.

ecological scene over extensive areas. This is particularly so in the relatively confined elephant ranges in many African national parks—where most of the problems exist.

The changes set in motion by elephants damaging trees not only affects the fire regime, but also changes the amount of browse available to elephants. The loss of woody plants can have a negative impact on other browsing species of mammals. Many birds, especially the larger birds of prey that build their nests on the very tops of tall trees from where they can easily launch into flight, find themselves with fewer nesting sites. Other forms of life, including the insects that pollinate woody plants, birds that feed on the fruits of woody plants, and small primates such as bushbabies and night apes, all find the habitat changes difficult or impossible to adapt to.

ECOLOGICAL UNITS AND BIOLOGICAL DIVERSITY

Many protected areas in Africa, though large by standards of such areas in Western Europe, are ecologically very small. So, if elephants are allowed to change the nature of the habitat, the result may be local extinction of some specialized plant species. If the parks were large enough to allow recolonization in an ongoing process, then elephant culling would not be necessary. Few, if any, protected areas in Africa are large enough to cope with the ecological consequences of vegetation changes due to "overcrowded" habitats.

One of the objectives of most national parks is to ensure maximum biological diversity—in effect to minimize the chances of extinction of any forms of life. The overpopulation of elephants, because it can lead to such enormous changes that species can become locally extinct, is therefore regarded as being counter to biological diversity.

Julie Bartlett/Ardea London Ltd

PARK DIVERSITY

Elephant overpopulation is, and has been, a problem only in national parks and game reserves where law enforcement maintains security. This was the case in Uganda before the rise of the Idi Amin regime, and in Kenya and Tanzania before the post-independence wave of ivory poaching gathered momentum. It was also the case in Zambia's Luangwa Valley, the parks and game reserves of Zimbabwe, and the Kruger National Park in South Africa; where elephants enjoyed

security, numbers increased dramatically and the process of vegetation change was set in motion.

As soon as park security declined, as it did in virtually all African countries following independence, poaching was sufficient to control, and bring down, the numbers of elephants. Idi Amin's army, for example, reduced the elephant population of the Murchison Falls National Park from 14,000 to 2,000 within two years. Subsequent poaching has kept the population small. This was, in practice, an illegal, but highly effective

culling of the elephant population. Within years the vegetation changes brought about by the elephants had been reversed and the forest and woodland were recolonizing large areas that had previously been opened up by elephants.

Today it is only in the southern African countries and a few localized areas elsewhere that there are overpopulations of elephants. In these areas vegetation change of a kind generally regarded as undesirable by park managers will take place, unless elephants are culled.

▲ An elephant browsing on acacia flowers in Namibia. The trunk is a highly sensory and versatile feeding organ. Lacking bones and equipped with thousands of muscle units, the trunk can be folded, bent or curved in any direction and is capable of plucking a single leaf from a plant, as well as tearing whole trees apart. When there is an over-abundance of elephants within a given space, however, this ability to raze vegetation can have a serious impact on the area's ecology.

ALTERNATIVES TO CULLING

IAN M. REDMOND

The great paradox of elephant conservation in Africa is that while the total number of elephants is falling, there are a few areas where local overpopulation occurs. In well-protected areas this can result from natural population growth, the immigration of "refugee" elephants, or the concentration of activity around unnatural permanent waterholes. Whatever the cause, the effect is the same: elephant feeding destroys trees at a rate that exceeds regeneration, and woodland may be converted to open grassland.

In some areas this process is seen as beneficial. For example, an increase in savannah-dwelling species improves wildlife-based tourism, and where scrub encroachment threatens ranching, farmers may also benefit from improved pasture. If, however, a change to savannah is seen as an impoverishment of woodland fauna and flora, steps may be taken to control the elephant population. In southern Africa, culling is considered to be the best method, but there are strong arguments against it, and a range of seldom-discussed alternatives do exist.

IS CULLING HUMANE?

Culling is portrayed as the humane, almost clinical, removal of a proportion of the population. Whole families of elephants are surrounded and killed in order to avoid leaving stressed individuals or groups which have lost their close relatives. This reasoning ignores the higher social organization of elephant clans, their ability to communicate over several kilometers by means of infrasonic distress calls, and their acute sense of smell. Calves which are kept to be sold into captivity undergo severe trauma.

CAN CULLING PAY FOR CONSERVATION?

It is often claimed that sales of elephant products from culls can help to pay for conservation work. And yet culling elephants is an expensive business. In 1989 Zimbabwe published the cost of a cull at $436 per elephant. This includes recovering the carcass, but not the cost of staff salaries. At these prices Zimbabwe's proposed 1992–1995 cull of 35,000 elephants would cost its Wildlife Department more than $15 million. But in Zimbabwe at that time, revenues from the sale of culled ivory and skins accrued to the central treasury, not to the conservation projects.

CULLING AND IVORY

Culling whole families does not yield many large tusks, but a range of tusks from calves to matriarchs. The most profitable way to harvest ivory is to allow each elephant to die of old age, or to humanely kill very old individuals so that every tusk has reached its maximum size. Another suggestion—removing tusks from live elephants, both to harvest the ivory and to deter poachers—is sometimes heard. Although technically possible, it would be impractical, expensive, and risky to both humans and elephants.

CULLING AND TOURISM

Revenues from tourism may suffer in two ways from culls. First, tourists who oppose culling are likely to visit other countries with more benign attitudes to elephants. Second, as long as elephants perceive humans and vehicles as harbingers of death, high-profit, close-quarters observation by tourists will be impossible.

NATURAL POPULATION REGULATION

Many scientists are of the opinion that elephant populations will find their own level, but that this may fluctuate in cycles. In times of stress or food shortages, elephant reproduction is slowed: the onset of puberty is delayed in young cows; the interbirth interval increases in breeding cows; and bull elephants delay coming into musth. In addition, calf mortality is likely to increase, and old or sick members of the population may die.

The population is thus reduced, but those that remain are the ones best able to survive the extremes—in genetic terms, the survival of the fittest. Culling, on the other hand, does not improve the gene pool; instead it reduces the genetic and cultural diversity of the population.

INCREASE ELEPHANT RANGE

There are two ways to reduce elephant densities: the number of elephants can be decreased or the area available to them can be increased. As profits from ecotourism grow, private wildlife reserves are seen as an alternative, more sustainable form of land use to agriculture. And when the local community benefits from tourist revenues, wildlife suddenly becomes popular; land which had been closed off to elephants once again becomes available, negating the need to cull to lower elephant densities.

RELOCATION OF ELEPHANTS

In Asia, elephants whose habitat is being converted to agriculture, or whose crop-raiding behavior becomes a problem, are moved. Individuals, particularly bulls, are tranquilized and transported on trucks or barges, and herds are driven—even over considerable distances—to safe protected areas. In Africa, a method of darting and moving whole family herds in specially adapted trucks was developed in Zimbabwe in 1993. Since then, hundreds of elephants have been relocated instead of being shot.

BIRTH CONTROL

Potentially the best alternative to culling, where human intervention is deemed essential, is the remote injection of a long-lasting contraceptive. Research began in South Africa in 1996 into two methods of fertility regulation in elephants. One involves darting a female, checking she is not pregnant, and injecting some slow-release hormone implants under the skin behind her ear. These have the same effect as the taking of a daily contraceptive pill, and prevent pregnancy. The second is called immuno-contraception and involves a vaccine that "tricks" the female's immune system into reacting against sperm, and so preventing conception. Each method has certain drawbacks but the hope is that, after a few years of refinement, one or both methods will find a practical application.

CONCLUSION

Culling is not the only solution to the problem of local over-population of elephants. The alternatives presented here could, by capitalizing on ecotourism, be more profitable than culling, and would be more compatible with the mood of the public worldwide. They also have the advantage of saving, rather than destroying, the lives of elephants.

LAISSEZ-FAIRE POLICIES

The problems perceived in the 1960s have all been solved, or no longer exist. In South Africa, Zimbabwe, and Namibia elephant numbers have been controlled by culling. In some areas, like the Serengeti National Park of Tanzania, only limited culling of bull elephants which were damaging scenic acacia trees was deemed sufficient to contain the problem. In Uganda and Zambia culling was done by poachers. It was only in Tsavo National Park of Kenya that the consequences of not culling elephants have been demonstrated, and then only for a short period of time. When subsistence hunting of the Watta tribesmen, who had kept the elephant population of Tsavo in check, was stopped by the authorities in the early 1950s, there were two consequences. The first was the end of the Watta culture and way of life, the second was an increase in elephant numbers which brought about dramatic vegetation changes as elephants ate up or broke down the woodlands. These changes were aggravated by fire which accelerated the process of vegetation change from woodland to grassland.

During a drought in the area in 1960 the food shortage brought about by vegetation changes resulted in the deaths of many black rhinoceros and elephants. The warnings, however, were ignored by the park authorities and no attempt was made to limit the elephant population to a level that the habitat could support during droughts, which is conventional wisdom in wildlife management. During 1970–71 another drought caused major mortalities when 6,000–9,000 elephants and about 5,000 black rhinoceros—more than exist in all of Africa today—died of starvation. Other browsing species such as lesser kudu, gemsbok, dik dik, and giraffe also declined, but grazing species increased. Bird diversity was reduced as the habitat was modified.

Worse perhaps than the die-off was the response of local people and former residents of the park to the fact that thousands of tusks and rhino horns were lying around for the taking. When they could no longer pick up tusks they found it easy to shoot elephants in the opened up habitat of the post-crash Tsavo. Another 20,000 elephants were killed over the next few years.

The decision of the park authorities not to control elephant numbers, therefore, had led to the death of about 30,000 elephants and 5,000 black rhinoceros, and dramatic changes in the vegetation and fauna of Tsavo. Now the vegetation is recovering, but the changed circumstances have also resulted in incursions of settlers and livestock into the "empty" park; the competition between elephants and humans begins again.

Active steps have recently been taken to re-establish firm control over Tsavo, but it may be too late. The unforeseen political consequences of not culling the Tsavo elephants may eventually prove far more damaging than those which were predicted.

▲ A family group feeding in Amboseli National Park, Kenya. With Kenya's rapidly burgeoning human population, elephants can only thrive under strict protection and if their numbers in restricted areas are controlled by culling.

◄ Hides of culled African elephants being auctioned to raise funds for wildlife management.

THE NECESSITY OF CULLING

Culling may be an integral part of husbanding wildlife throughout the world. Examples as diverse as vicuna in Peru, elk in North America, capybaras in Venezuela, polar bears in Greenland, and many species of wildlife in Africa illustrate the point. In all cases the populations of these animals exceed some human-made criterion of abundance, or inflict some undesirable effect on the habitat.

As elephant populations expand in protected areas there is, in modern Africa, another imperative for culling. With rapidly growing human populations facing land shortages, land degradation, and famine, the option of allowing any species to increase to a level where they destroy their habitat and die in large numbers will no longer be politically feasible. An elephant die-off, which is an inevitable consequence of elephant protection in the absence of culling, will have to be weighed against the rational and sustainable utilization of elephant populations for the benefits it can provide to their chief competitors—the human community. With culling, revenues from elephant byproducts may be used for conservation efforts. For this reason alone, if not for reasons of maintaining biological diversity, elephant culling appears to be an absolute necessity in Africa.

THE RISE AND FALL OF THE IVORY MARKET

ESMOND BRADLEY MARTIN

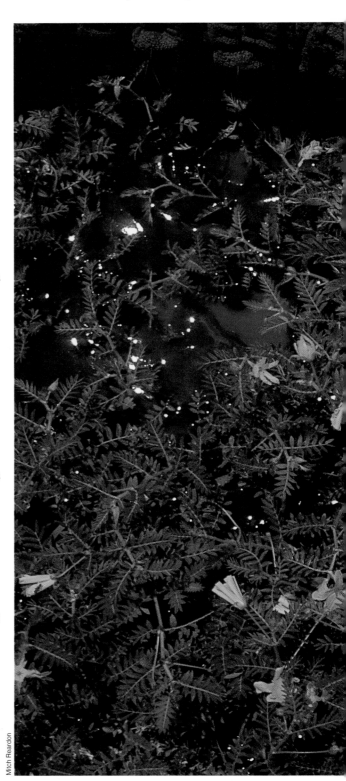

In 1980 more than 1 million elephants roamed Africa, but by 1990 poachers, catering to soaring demands for ivory, had cut that number in half. Responding to this crisis, in June 1989, the United States banned ivory imports. Soon the restrictions were extended into North America, western Europe and Japan.

▲ Carved elephant tusks in Thailand. Though the use of ivory for carving is unsustainable from various points of view, it is also undeniable that ivory has provided the raw material for some of the finest examples of the craftsman's art, with an unbroken heritage extending back—in China, at least—for several millennia.

By October 1989, four months after the United States ban, the Convention on International Trade in Endangered Species of Wild Fauna and Flora (CITES) approved an international ban on ivory. The ban came into effect on January 18, 1990.

Out of approximately a hundred CITES members, six countries (China, Zambia, Zimbabwe, Malawi, Botswana, and South Africa) took reservations which allowed them to continue legal trade in ivory. To date, however, none of these countries has imported or exported significant quantities of ivory.

At the time, economists and conservationists debated whether the bans would drive the trade underground, forcing up the price of ivory and thus giving incentives to poachers and middlemen. This, of course, would further endanger the African elephant. Alternatively it was thought that the bans might lower the demand for ivory by persuading Americans and Europeans not to buy it, which would thus reduce the price of tusks. The debate was a major concern of the October 1989 meeting of CITES members.

Between January and May of 1990, I traveled to ten Asian countries on behalf of the World Wildlife Fund (WWF), examining various aspects of the trade in endangered species. After the CITES ban went into effect, traders, conservationists, governments and others involved in the trade wanted to know what had happened to the world's major ivory-carving centers since June 1989. Had the price of raw ivory declined sharply, as some proponents of the ban predicted? Had the bans succeeded in their goal of stopping elephant poaching? I set out to find the answers.

Prior to the CITES ban, a minimum of three-quarters of the world's raw ivory was carved in Asian workshops and factories. Of the world's total amount of worked ivory, the Japanese were buying about 38 percent, Europeans 25 percent, and Americans 16 percent.

JAPAN
While generally the production and sale of carved ivory has plummeted, a major exception is Japan, which produces pieces primarily for local consumption. Items produced include signature seals, jewelry, sculptures, netsukes (toggles for kimonos), and parts of traditional musical

instruments. From 1980 to 1986, Japan used more ivory than any other country—38 percent of the world's total of 800 tonnes (1.8 million pounds) on average per year.

By the mid- to late 1980s the Japanese were carving about 100 tonnes (220,500 pounds) of raw ivory per year and importing large quantities of worked ivory from Asian countries where labor is cheap. In early 1990, the retail price of musical instruments which contain ivory rose 100 percent;

and seals, for which more than half the ivory is used, also increased in value. While some manufacturers have replaced ivory seals with ones made of gold, titanium, and silver, they have not found total acceptance in the marketplace.

Anticipating a shortage, Japanese traders increased the wholesale price from US$300 per kilogram ($136 per pound) in May 1989 to $700 per kilogram ($318 per pound) in early 1990. But they did not take into account the possibility that

▼ The demand for ivory still continues, but with greater impact on existing, much reduced, wild populations of elephants. Here, blood drains from the trunk of an elephant, shot for its ivory tusks.

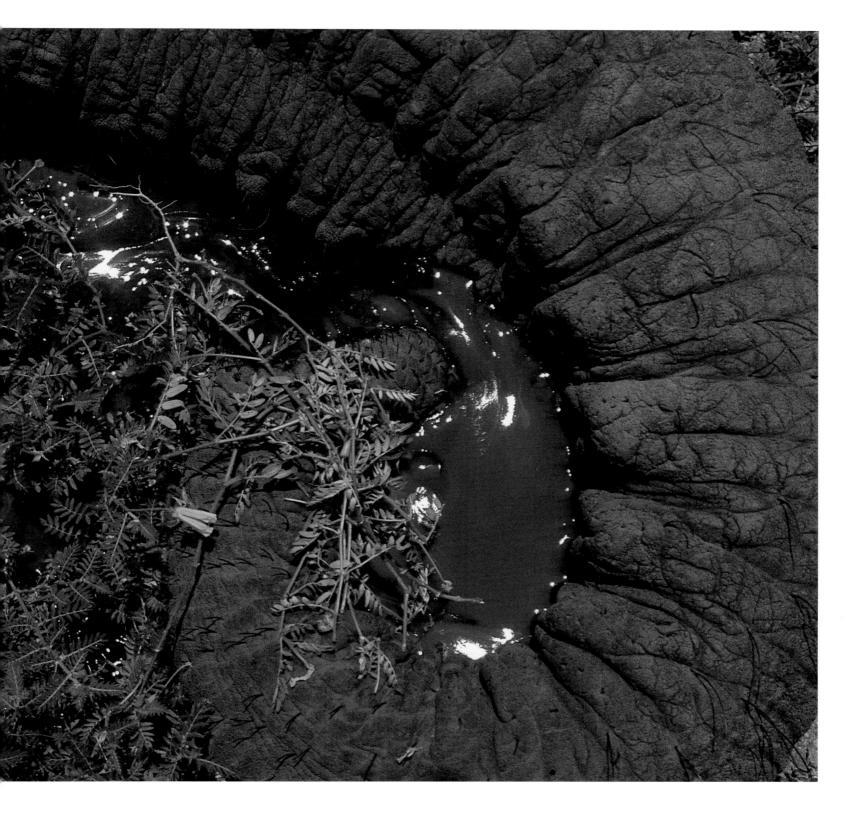

Ian Redmond

P. Morris/Ardea London Ltd

▲ (Top) The increasing difficulty of finding reliable sources of ivory at stable prices has prompted many craftsmen to experiment with other possible materials, as illustrated by these carved hippopotamus teeth on display in a souvenir shop in Goma, Democratic Republic of the Congo.

▲ (Above) Exploitation of animals for paraphernalia is not limited to the use of ivory. During the nineteenth century, animal artifacts, such as this drink cabinet fashioned from the foot of a rhinoceros, were fashionable.

demand for ivory items might decrease. When jewelry prices subsequently rose, retailers found that the public refused to buy. At the same time, conservationists in Japan for the first time began to discourage the desire for ivory jewelry. By June 1990, the price of raw ivory had fallen to about $400 per kilogram ($182 per pound). Ivory items began to disappear from shop windows, while a growing number of ivory craftsmen stopped working in the trade.

Japanese businessmen in the industry were aware, at the time of the first bans, that a substitute for elephant ivory was necessary. During 1989, 1.2 tonnes (2,645 pounds) of hippo teeth were imported from Tanzania, South Africa and Malawi. Although hippo teeth are small, relatively difficult to carve due to their hardness, and unsuitable for statues or musical instrument parts, their low price (about $60 per kilogram [$27 per pound] in 1989) provided good incentives. With skilled labor they could be made to look like elephant ivory. Hippopotami are poached mostly for their meat and the demand for their teeth; so far this trade is too small to have an impact on wild populations.

During 1989 Japanese traders also imported 2 tonnes (4,410 pounds) of mammoth tusks from the USSR, Greenland, Canada, and the United States at prices of $180–340 per kilogram ($82–155 per pound). The tusks of mammoths have been harvested from the tundras of Siberia and in other countries for more than a hundred years. In early 1990, a group of Japanese businessmen visiting the USSR were shown 2.8 tonnes (6,173 pounds) of mammoth tusks, almost a third of which was scrap and waste—absolutely useless. The rest, in awkward shapes, had a bad smell and was too soft for making quality signature seals. When they were told the price was $890 per kilogram ($404 per pound) for that which could be used, the businessmen left in disgust. Similar mammoth tusks had been sold for $25 per kilogram ($11 per pound) in 1985. Had the price been more reasonable, the Japanese would have purchased some for making netsukes and other items.

The recent imports of mammoth ivory are related to the unavailability of legal imports of elephant tusks, and the high price of elephant tusks in Japan. By the end of the June 1989 to June 1990 period, the price for raw elephant ivory had gone up by approximately 30 percent.

CHINA

The situation is far different in China, which has probably suffered the most economically. The Chinese carved ivory trade is largely export and tourist oriented and generally out of reach for the local population who are too poor to afford it.

As a result of the decline in demand in the Western world for worked ivory items, the Beijing Ivory Carving Factory, formerly the world's largest single employer of ivory craftsmen, cut its staff by

a drastic 98 percent. In May 1989, the company had 300 ivory craftsmen working for it but by April 1990 only 6 of them remained.

Most of the craftsmen had been asked to stay at home because there was no work for them. They were being paid 75 percent of their basic salaries through a bank loan which the factory had obtained. Hitherto their total income was often twice as high as their basic salary because of bonuses they received. Earning almost no income, the factory's prospects were dim. In an attempt to keep the skills of senior carvers, some were retained to work on cow bones.

In the last year of full production (1988), the factory consumed 9 tonnes (19,840 pounds) of raw ivory, converting it into $1,892,000 worth of ivory products wholesale. In the following year, only 4 tonnes (8,820 pounds) were carved, valued at $1,081,000. From January to April 1990 no raw ivory had been carved at all, and no ivory items had been sold. The factory had last bought raw ivory in the spring of 1989, paying $400–500 per kilogram ($182–230 per pound) for 20 kilogram (44 pound) tusks, between $250 and $300 per kilogram ($113–136 per pound) for 10 kilogram (22 pound) tusks, and $200 per kilogram ($91 per pound) for 5 kilogram (11 pound) tusks. The manager claimed that because of the ivory bans it had already lost $3,200,000. In addition, 2 tonnes (4,410 pounds) of raw ivory were unused, tying up $500,000 of potential income.

Established in 1954 in Guangzhou, the Daxin Ivory Carving Factory, which was until recently the second largest ivory factory in China, had suffered just as badly. Its production had gradually increased in value to a peak in 1988, when 10 tonnes (22,000 pounds) of ivory were made into $2,405,000 (wholesale) worth of goods. The following year, production fell to 6 tonnes (13,225 pounds), made into $1,486,000 worth of goods. From January to May 1990, the factory had sold only $63,158 worth of ivory items.

Like the Beijing Ivory Carving Factory, drastic staff cuts were enforced so that by May 1989, only 1 of 370 craftsmen remained to make ear-picks from small slices of ivory. Two-thirds of the former ivory workers were staying at home and were being supported by factory bank loans. Most of the remaining craftsmen had switched from ivory to plastic carving but no market could be found for the figurines they produced. Stocks of carved ivory worth $5 million had been accumulated and the factory discounted some pieces by up to 70 percent in an attempt to encourage sales. Even so there were hardly any buyers.

The Chinese have begun trying to establish a new market for ivory in South Korea (a non-CITES member) but because of political complications and other problems, they have so far been unsuccessful in their efforts. In fact, none of the Asian countries that process ivory has been able to locate a new market. It is noted, however, that managers of the ivory factories and of import/export firms are unwilling to sell their raw ivory cheaply, because they believe that after the next CITES meeting in 1992 some of their old markets will be reopened.

HONG KONG

The island of Hong Kong has a relatively short history as a major ivory-carving center. The industry only became important after the Communists took power in China in 1949. By the late 1950s it had become the largest raw ivory importer in the world, as well as the largest ivory manufacturer. Since June 1989, the sale of worked ivory has declined by at least 70 percent, despite the fact that prices have been reduced by 33–50 percent. The remaining buyers are Europeans, Americans, and Taiwanese, who generally know that it is illegal to import ivory into their countries, but who are prepared to take the risk, buying small items which they conceal in their luggage. Most tourists will not buy ivory, because either they feel it is morally wrong, or they do not want to take the risk of getting caught.

More than two-thirds of ivory craftsmen in Hong Kong have moved out of their profession. Unlike India and China, Hong Kong has no unemployment problem, and ivory workers have been able to obtain other jobs quite easily. The government has offered to retrain them and support them financially in the process, but oddly, few have taken up this proposal and are instead earning their livelihoods as taxi drivers, construction workers, restaurant waiters, or in other such service occupations.

Low demand for ivory in Hong Kong has forced the industry to adapt in different ways. Certain retail shops, for example, have begun specializing in other merchandise, in particular gem stones and porcelain from China. Others have reduced their prices by as much as 50 percent to attract customers, and a few have gone out of the ivory business. To try to ease the situation, the British government took a limited legal reservation for Hong Kong to allow the shop owners and traders to sell stocks of raw and worked ivory until July 1990, but not allowing any new imports.

From October 18, 1989 to January 17, 1990, only 5.3 tonnes (11,685 pounds) of raw ivory and 4.8 tonnes (10,580 pounds) of worked ivory were exported from a total stock of 474 tonnes (1,044,975 pounds). The stock is made up of 217 tonnes (478,395 pounds) of cut pieces and scrap, 150 tonnes (330,690 pounds) of worked ivory and 107 tonnes (235,890 pounds) of tusks. Even by early April 1990, traders had not been able to sell much of their huge stockpile simply because they could not find a market for it. Official statistics show that from January 18 to May 18 of 1990, only 3.3 tonnes (7,275 pounds) of raw ivory were

sold to China and 272 kilograms (600 pounds) of worked ivory were exported, out of a total stock of 474 tonnes (1,044,975 pounds).

Some merchants have been trying to sell their ivory to South Korea which is not a CITES member and has few restrictions on ivory. From 1984 to 1988, South Korea imported an average of 958 kilograms (2,112 pounds) of ivory a year, but in 1989, about 800 kilograms (1,760 pounds) of raw ivory and 28.8 tonnes (63,500 pounds) of worked ivory came in although South Korea has had no domestic ivory market this century. More traders, not necessarily just those in Hong Kong, may be moving ivory into South Korea to try to create a market or to hold stocks temporarily.

INDIA

In 1988 it was believed that India had the highest number of ivory craftsmen in the world, approximately 2,000 workers, but by the time of my visit in 1990, the industry had largely collapsed.

According to the CITES Management Authority, in 1989 traders imported 6.76 tonnes (14,909 pounds) of raw ivory but legally exported only 590 kilograms (1,300 pounds) of finished products. By the end of that year, the export business had declined further with traders struggling to look for wholesale markets abroad for their ivory. Just before the CITES ivory ban came into effect in January 1990, one trader managed to find markets in Andorra and Aruba.

With sales plummeting by 85 percent, almost two-thirds of the Indian carvers went out of business. Tourists, who were the mainstay of the industry, had declined in their buying. The North Americans had almost completely stopped shopping, while Europeans and Japanese still continued to purchase a few usually small items,

▼ (Bottom) An ivory carver in a street in Bangalore, India. Much ivory is still marketed in India for religious and esthetic purposes. Such articles may be traded legally in India, but cannot be exported.

▼ (Below) The use of ivory for ornamentation has been rivalled only by gold in many cultures and many ages. It is mentioned in biblical accounts and was used freely by the Romans; it is recorded that Caligula's horse, for example, had a stall and manger of ivory. This carved ivory bracelet is from Benin (formerly Dahomey) in western Africa.

British Museum/The Bridgeman Art Library

Lucy Vigne

▲ A boy displays culled elephant mandibles in Zimbabwe. Elephants are actively culled in southern Africa. This and similar management techniques may become necessary in east Africa as well, inflaming the long controversy over whether it is better to sell the resulting ivory to offset management costs or to outlaw the ivory trade entirely, regardless of source. CITES approved such a ban internationally on January 18, 1990, but the controversy has not entirely subsided.

especially jewelry and paintings on ivory which can easily be hidden in a suitcase.

Bangles are still being bought, very cheaply, partially because the Nepalese have been smuggling them into India since 1987. They sell them by weight for as little as $14 a kilogram ($6.35 per pound). Indians are also continuing to buy carved ivory for religious, esthetic and investment purposes. As long as they keep the items within India, such sales are legal. Retail prices for ivory pieces have generally not been reduced in India; and the prices carvers must pay suppliers for raw ivory have only dropped an average of 15 percent (about $200 per kilogram [$91 per pound]).

Traders believe that the fear of getting caught smuggling, not the price, is deterring tourists from buying. That is their justification, perhaps, for not lowering their prices; they seem determined to wait as long as it takes to recoup their investment. The fact that there is little raw ivory on the Indian market adds weight to their argument. When the new government was formed at the end of 1989, the big traders urged officials to file for a reservation to the CITES ban, but by the time action was taken it was too late to beat the January 18, 1990 deadline.

Indians who have had close contact with ivory worry that if some international markets do not reopen after the 1992 CITES meeting, the cultural tradition of carving and painting ivory, which goes back thousands of years, will be irrevocably lost.

The industry's future is also dependent upon the Indian government's policy on internal sales of worked ivory. If the government decides to outlaw domestic sales or makes it difficult to obtain raw ivory, then the industry will die.

LAOS

Analysis of the available data on worldwide retail sales of worked ivory shows a decline of at least 70 percent between June 1989 and June 1990, but the prices for raw ivory in Asia have not fallen as dramatically. In fact, prices have increased in two markets not hitherto studied. In Laos, the cost of raw ivory has risen steadily since 1988, from $100 per kilogram (about $45 per pound) to $200 per kilogram ($91 per pound) at the time of my February 1990 visit. After the Communist takeover in 1975, the Laotian ivory industry practically collapsed, but in 1989, the government began allowing thousands of Thai businessmen and tourists into the country.

The demand for locally carved ivory pendants, rings, and bracelets flourished, with nearly all the ivory coming from Laotian elephants. I found ivory products for sale in at least eight shops in the capital city of Vientiane and twelve in Luang Prabang. The industry remains small, with only about ten carvers in Vientiane and a few in Luang Prabang who work in wood as well as ivory. The increase in demand has led to poaching.

In January 1990, twelve men were caught shooting elephants in the southern province of Attapeu. Poachers may threaten the country's wild elephant population of about 2,000 elephants, and 1,000–1,300 domesticated elephants.

VIETNAM

Raw ivory prices in Vietnam have similarly doubled during the same period and, as in Laos, the authorities have made it easier for tourists to visit and to purchase carved tusks and ivory lamp stands, figurines, seals, chopsticks, and jewelry. Salaries in Laos and Vietnam average less than $15 per month, and thus few local people can afford such luxuries. Most of the ivory comes from elephants poached in neighboring Laos and a small quantity from Vietnam's 200 wild and 100–600 domesticated elephants. Although Laotian and Vietnamese industries are tiny, they could threaten the Asian elephant populations within their boundaries. Unlike most countries, Laotian and Vietnamese traders are increasing their prices for raw ivory. Prices now are similar to those in India, about $200 per kilogram ($91 per pound).

UNITED ARAB EMIRATES

From 1987 to mid-1989, ivory factories flourished in the Jebel Ali Free Trade Zone near Dubai, in Dubai itself, and in Ajman (although not simultaneously). Some of the factories were owned and managed by the Hong Kong Chinese who were unable to import their dubious raw ivory stocks into Hong Kong or Macao, and who were taking advantage of the United Arab Emirates' (UAE) few import and export restrictions. Large quantities of ivory, generally lacking proper CITES documents (because they originated mostly from poached elephants), were being made into signature seals for Japan and jewelry for the Hong Kong market.

During mid-1989, the situation changed drastically and raw ivory imports were prohibited in all of the Sheikdoms. Furthermore, the government closed down the existing factories and refused to allow the establishment of any new ones. No ivory factories were operating in January 1990, when I visited the UAE. The Dubai authorities strictly enforced their new laws and had, in fact, confiscated large amounts of raw and worked ivory. In one raid, the Dubai municipality authorities seized 10 cartons of roughly carved signature seals and 47 other items worth in total about $110,000. In another seizure, $550,000 worth of raw ivory was impounded from a shop owned by a local Arab who had two Indian partners.

Demand for ivory had gone down in late 1989, and so some shopkeepers had reduced their prices by 20 percent. Worked ivory can theoretically still be legally sold in the UAE, but not much is being openly offered in Dubai because the shopkeepers fear possible government confiscation.

In January 1990, in Abu Dhabi, not a major shopping city, I saw only small amounts of worked ivory, such as Indian and Chinese jewelry in the luxury hotels. The biggest quantity of worked ivory that I saw for sale in the UAE was in the main market in Sharjah. Indian shopkeepers were selling Indian-made items, including bangles, paintings, and figurines, to European customers.

WHAT WILL THE FUTURE BRING?

To date, the ban has been more effectively upheld than expected. Although CITES cannot impose penalties on member states, the individual governments have practically eliminated ivory imports and exports by legislating against them and introducing stiff fines and even imprisonment for citizens who contravene the laws. On the consumer front, not only have retail sales fallen dramatically, but Europeans, Americans, and Africans would rather not admit they once purchased ivory items. Almost everywhere it has become socially unacceptable to wear ivory jewelry, and many people also believe it is morally unacceptable to buy it.

Probably the most difficult, yet most important, question is whether the implementation of the ivory trade ban and the campaign to stop people from buying ivory items has resulted in a significant decline in the poaching of African elephants. It is not possible yet to reply to this question.

We do not even know how many elephants have been killed illicitly since 1989. The countries with the most severe problems include DRC, Tanzania, Zambia, Mozambique, Somalia, Sudan, and the Central African Republic. Authorities in Tanzania believe that poaching has declined in their country since June 1989, and they have certainly made strides combating it in the huge Selous Game Reserve, which has more elephants than anywhere else in Tanzania. In Kenya, the situation was better than the above-mentioned countries. On average, three elephants a day were lost in 1988, and in 1990 the figure was less than one a day. It is believed that middlemen in Kenya who buy from poachers are better informed about the closure of international markets than their counterparts in other African countries, and that is why poachers are being paid relatively little for the tusks they supply. If this trend is correct then proponents of the ban and the campaigns have achieved their goal in East Africa. Kenya, on the other hand, has greatly improved its wildlife management during the past year, putting more resources into the fight against poaching. Yet it is impossible to assess how much of the success is due to these measures. For whatever reason, in 1992 the director of the Kenya Wildlife Service, Richard Leakey, did have evidence that the price of raw ivory in his country had dropped from $50 per kilogram ($23 per pound) in early 1989 to $3.00 per kilogram ($1.36 per pound) in 1990, and that elephant poaching had dropped significantly in Kenya.

Detailed information on the price of raw ivory elsewhere in Africa is difficult to obtain. Countries that took out legal reservations against the CITES ban have not had ivory auctions since the ban went into effect. These countries, like private traders, are hoping that Asian markets will reopen. For that reason they are reluctant to lower their prices, and as a result they cannot sell. The World Wildlife Fund in the United States claims that the price of elephant tusks has declined by 65–75 percent in the Central African Republic and parts of DRC, even so there are few buyers. Reports from the West African nation of Liberia tell that the price of raw ivory increased in 1990 to about $132 per kilogram ($60 per pound) wholesale for large tusks and $94 per kilogram ($43 per pound) for smaller ones. It was suggested that difficulties in importing raw supplies and no reduction in demand for worked ivory were responsible.

The legal ban and consumer campaign appear to be at least helping in the efforts to save the elephant in some parts of Africa. Two factors, however, mitigate against an immediate, significant decrease in Africa's elephant poaching. Few poachers have other ways of earning as much money as they do killing elephants, even if the price of ivory drops by half. Secondly, ivory traders hoped and believed that after the 1992 CITES meeting more legal international ivory markets would open up. These beliefs provide incentives to buy ivory, which in turn perpetuates poaching. Only the future will tell how this network of events will affect long-term prospects for the survival of the elephants. I personally think that the ivory ban has been more effectively upheld than expected.

From articles by Esmond Bradley Martin, in *BBC Wildlife* (September 1990) and *Wildlife Conservation* (November and December 1990). Reproduced with permission.

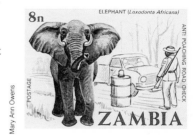

▲ A ranger (top) displays a large elephant tusk, surrounded by various other wildlife artifacts seized from poachers in Nairobi, Kenya. Most are slated for destruction: on July 18, 1989, for example, Kenyan government agents burned a total of 12 tonnes of confiscated ivory. Neighboring Zambia has also mounted vigorous anti-poaching campaigns, as symbolized in this postage stamp (bottom) issued in 1978.

THE 1989 CITES MEETING IN LAUSANNE, SWITZERLAND, AND ITS AFTERMATH

RONALD ORENSTEIN

The most important, and controversial, event in the history of elephant conservation occurred on October 16 and 17, 1989, when the African elephant was transferred from Appendix II to Appendix I of the Convention on International Trade in Endangered Species of Wild Fauna and Flora (CITES), effective January 18, 1990. As species on Appendix I, and their parts and products, cannot be imported or exported for primarily commercial purposes, this action amounted to a ban on the international ivory trade.

The parties to CITES, the chief international instrument for the control of the wildlife trade, had been concerned about ivory poaching since at least 1981. The Asian elephant had been placed on Appendix I in 1973. The more numerous African elephant was retained on Appendix II, which allows commercial trade accompanied by export permits. Legal trade had its tenacious supporters. Some countries, particularly those in southern Africa, claimed to be deriving revenue used for conservation and wildlife management from legal ivory sales.

All attempts to control poaching through CITES while permitting legal trade to continue proved futile. A variety of schemes was tried, culminating in a complex quota system put into place in 1985. Despite this, dealers in smuggled ivory became expert at disguising shipments, forging permits, and using other means of avoiding CITES restrictions.

African elephant populations were in free fall across much of the continent. There was disagreement among scientists as to whether this was the result of poaching, as Iain Douglas-Hamilton and others believed, or of habitat loss, as Ian Parker insisted. But in 1989, a massive study by the specially convened Ivory Trade Review Group proved that the primary cause was poaching pressure. Some 200 elephants were being slaughtered every day. Since 1979, half of Africa's elephants had been killed, and populations in East Africa had declined by 80 percent or more. An exponential rise in ivory prices coupled with a huge inflow of weapons into the continent provided poachers with the motive and means to slaughter the herds. The failure of customs officials to distinguish the small amounts of legal ivory from the poached merchandise that amounted to some 80 percent of world supply provided the opportunity.

In May 1989, the East Africans, whose herds were in desperate straits and whose wildlife-related tourism (the chief source of income for Kenya at least) was in serious jeopardy, called for transfer to Appendix I. The proposal was sponsored by a record seven countries: Kenya, Tanzania, Somalia, Gambia, Hungary, the United States, and Austria. Conservation and animal protection groups worldwide began intensive lobbying for an end to the ivory trade. In June the Worldwide Fund for Nature (WWF) and IUCN—the World Conservation Union—came out in favor of a ban. Within days, unilateral import bans were instituted by the United States, Canada, the European Economic Community, and others to prevent a mass slaughter during the ninety-day waiting period before a CITES listing, once passed, could take effect.

By now the issue had become a cause célèbre. The supposedly impartial CITES Secretariat, which received money from ivory traders to fund its control efforts, lobbied heavily for continued trade. Richard Leakey, then newly appointed as director of Kenya's wildlife

department, launched a vigorous public campaign in favor of a ban. In July Kenya attracted world attention by publicly burning 12,000 kilograms (26,500 pounds) of confiscated ivory worth some $3 million. Meanwhile, international diplomatic efforts were underway to try to forge an agreement between the East African countries and the southern states, vehemently led by Zimbabwe, that opposed an Appendix I listing for their populations. Despite these efforts, a compromise worked out in July at a meeting in Botswana had collapsed by the time the CITES parties met in October.

The Seventh Meeting of the Conference of the Parties to CITES opened in Lausanne, Switzerland, on October 9, 1989, attended by delegates from 91 countries and a host of observers. Authorities on the African elephant, including Iain and Oria Douglas-Hamilton, Cynthia Moss, Joyce Poole, and David Western, attended to argue the case for Appendix I. The meeting became the focus of world media attention.

But the two sides were still far apart. IUCN and WWF proposed a compromise which would have left the elephants of Zimbabwe, Botswana, and South Africa on Appendix II, but would have instituted a two-year moratorium on trade. This was rejected by the southern Africans, who demanded that the other parties in their customs union, including Mozambique (which was in a state of civil war) and Angola (which was not a CITES party), be included. Zimbabwe insisted that the parties accept a marketing scheme that it proposed to set up with its neighbors, and its position became even more intransigent as the meeting progressed.

Meanwhile, some Central African states, such as Gabon, announced that if southern African states were to receive special treatment merely because of their proximity to Zimbabwe, they would seek an exemption for themselves as well. Other countries feared that the CITES rules would make it impossible to return the elephant to Appendix II even if populations recovered. By the end of the first week, there seemed little chance that the proposal would receive the two-thirds majority necessary for passage.

At this point Ruth Mace, Mark Stanley Price, and I suggested a new compromise: transfer the African elephant to Appendix I, but institute specific criteria under which any African country could apply to have its population downlisted to Appendix II. A panel of experts, with strong African representation, would then survey that country's elephant populations, its anti-poaching controls and the degree to which it could control ivory smuggling through its territories. If the country received a satisfactory assessment from the panel, the CITES parties may vote to downlist its population, allowing it to begin trading in ivory once more. Our suggestion was taken up by the proposal's sponsors, and was formally introduced by Somalia as an amendment.

In spite of attempts by the Secretariat to prevent the Somali amendment from coming to the floor, it was the amended proposal that was overwhelmingly adopted by the parties, by a vote of 76 to 11, with four abstentions. During the remainder of the meeting a working group, chaired by Perez Olindo, met to develop the details under which the new rules would operate.

Immediately after the vote, Botswana, Zimbabwe, Mozambique, Malawi, and Burundi announced that they would enter a reservation

▶ Anti-ivory protesters demonstrate outside the Palais de Beaulieu, Lausanne, during the 1989 CITES meeting in Switzerland. Events like this helped raise social awareness of the danger the ivory trade posed for the African elephant. Public support, including a refusal to buy ivory, was crucial for both the passage and the subsequent successful operation of the CITES ivory ban.

against the listing, a procedure by which parties can refuse, within 90 days of a final vote, to recognize an amendment to the CITES Appendices. Mozambique and Burundi did not, in fact, file reservations, but after the meeting the other states were joined by Zambia (which withdrew its reservation in 1997), Namibia (upon its accession to CITES in 1990), China, and the United Kingdom, which entered a six-month reservation on behalf of Hong Kong to permit it to sell off its stocks of largely poached ivory.

Ivory prices had begun to fall even before Lausanne, following the various unilateral bans. After the meeting the ivory market went into rapid collapse. Prices in Africa fell as low as $2 per kilogram (90 cents per pound). Ivory, particularly in Western countries, became practically unsellable. Hong Kong was unable to dispose of more than a fraction of its stocks, and China, its carving industry nearly bankrupt, withdrew its reservation early in 1991. Poaching declined in some countries by as much as 90 percent. The trade ban seemed an overwhelming success.

A number of countries, though, continued to resist. In September 1991 Zimbabwe, Namibia, Botswana, and South Africa applied for the Somali amendment procedure. Speculation that the trade would soon be legal again led to a renewed upsurge of ivory smuggling. At the March 1992 CITES meeting in Kyoto, Japan, many African countries, including some that opposed Appendix I in 1989, strongly objected to any downlisting. In the face of this united opposition, the proponents withdrew all their proposals.

At the 1994 CITES meeting, in Fort Lauderdale, Florida, both South Africa and Sudan proposed downlisting their populations. The Sudanese proposal was poorly justified and failed to win support. The South African proposal, though restricted to sales of meat and hides, made it clear that ivory would be on the table at the next meeting. Once again, there were minor upsurges of poaching, particularly in Zambia. South Africa withdrew its proposal after a private meeting with other African delegations, who made it clear that they would not support any listing change.

At a highly politicized CITES meeting in 1997, in Harare, Zimbabwe, Botswana, Namibia, and Zimbabwe lobbied heavily—in some cases, with direct intervention by Zimbabwean President Robert Mugabe—for a downlisting of their populations, with trade in ivory restricted to a one-time controlled sale of material in government stockpiles directly to Japan. They promised to drop their reservations and offer other guarantees if they succeeded. The parties finally agreed, but imposed conditions that had to be complied with before the sale could proceed. Though some argued that not all the conditions were fulfilled, the sale and shipment took place in 1999.

South Africa has submitted a new proposal to downlist its own population for the April 2000 CITES meeting in Nairobi. Botswana, Namibia, and Zimbabwe have asked for further ivory sales. However, a proposal from Kenya and India would reverse the 1997 decision and return all populations to Appendix I. A number of African countries have already expressed support for the Kenya/ India proposal, voicing concerns that the 1997 downlisting and subsequent sale may have contributed to a new poaching initiative. Whether the ivory ban will be reimposed, or whether a renewed ivory trade will expand still further, remains to be seen.

Ian Redmond

WHO VOTED FOR APPENDIX I?
The final vote tally for the proposal to put the African elephant on Appendix I, as amended by Somalia

For: Afghanistan, Australia, Austria, Bangladesh, Belgium, Belize, Benin, Bolivia, Brazil, Canada, Central African Republic, Chad, Chile, Colombia, Costa Rica, Denmark, Dominican Republic, Ecuador, Ethiopia, Finland, France, Gambia, Federal Republic of Germany, Ghana, Guatemala, Guinea, Honduras, Hungary, India, Indonesia, Iran, Israel, Italy, Jordan, Kenya, Liberia, Luxembourg, Madagascar, Malaysia, Malta, Mauritius, Morocco, Nepal, Netherlands, New Zealand, Nicaragua, Niger, Norway, Pakistan, Papua New Guinea, Peru, Philippines, Portugal, Rwanda, St Lucia, St Vincent, Senegal, Singapore, Somalia, Spain, Sri Lanka, Sudan, Suriname, Sweden, Switzerland, Tanzania, Thailand, Togo, Trinidad and Tobago, Tunisia, Soviet Union, United Kingdom, United States, Vanuatu, Venezuela, Zaïre.

Against: Argentina, Botswana, Burundi, Cameroon, China, Congo, Gabon, Mozambique, South Africa, Zambia, Zimbabwe.

Abstaining: Japan, Panama, Paraguay, Uruguay.
TOTAL: 76 for, 11 against, 4 abstentions.

Not present or voting: Algeria, Bahamas, Cyprus, Egypt, El Salvador, German Democratic Republic, Guyana, Lichtenstein, Malawi, Monaco, Nigeria, Seychelles.

(Data provided by the Environmental Investigation Agency.)

UNITED STATES POLITICS AND ELEPHANT CONSERVATION

ANTHONY C. BEILENSON

On June 4, 1989, the President of the United States, George Bush, acting under authority created by the African Elephant Conservation Act (AECA) of 1988, ordered an immediate ban on all imports of African elephant ivory into the United States. Hailed around the world as the first significant action by an ivory-importing nation to halt the decimation of the elephant, the President's order would later be regarded as the beginning of a major international campaign to save this majestic species from extinction. Following the US example, the European Economic Community, within days, and Japan, within three months, copied the ban, creating a momentum which led to the October 1989 decision by the 103 member nations of the Convention on International Trade in Endangered Species (CITES) to end all trade in African elephant ivory.

But to those of us who had been advancing the cause of the elephant in the United States for nearly two decades, the US ivory ban marked a hard-won victory in a battle to protect the elephant before it was too late. Our consolation for this delay in enacting legislation in the US was a crucial, but unexpected, bonus: in addition to eliminating the US as a consumer of ivory, the AECA served as a timely catalyst just as conservationists around the world were desperately calling for action.

The plight of the African elephant was brought to my attention in the early 1970s when, as a Senator in the California State Legislature, I was drafting that state's first endangered species law. I was convinced that the bill should contain a ban on ivory imports into California, and wrote the prohibition into the law as it was enacted. That initial victory for the elephant was later overturned by a US federal court, based on the constitutional prohibition against state regulation of interstate commerce. As it turned out, the California law was both the easiest and the last victory for the elephants for fifteen years.

When I was elected to the United States Congress in 1976, federal protection for the African elephant became one of my highest priorities. The species then numbered in the neighborhood of 1.5 million, and experts were becoming increasingly alarmed by reports of rapidly rising ivory prices, rampant poaching, and the helplessness of African governments to protect their wildlife. The situation was on the verge of crisis and, in 1977, I first introduced the Elephant Protection Act (HR 10083), a bill to ban all imports of ivory into the US. Unfortunately, the task of winning Congressional approval for the bill proved far more difficult than I had expected.

By far the biggest obstacle I faced in achieving passage of the elephant bill was not opposition to a ban on ivory imports but, more frustrating still, a lack of interest on the part of the House and Senate

committees with jurisdiction over the issue. The problem simply did not seem critical enough to attract Congress's attention. In addition, because of limited time and resources, the committees maintained a strict policy of considering no legislation designed to address a particular species, focusing instead on measures to solve some of the larger threats to wildlife habitats and ecosystems. Nevertheless, in 1979, with the help of a small group of dedicated wildlife protection organizations, and after intensive lobbying, the House Committee on Merchant Marine and Fisheries approved the bill (renumbered as HR 4685), and the House of Representatives passed it soon after. The momentum was ended when the Senate failed to consider the measure.

And so, for the next eight years, along with devoted members of the wildlife protection community, I patiently maintained a fruitless pursuit of protection for the African elephant, all the while growing increasingly concerned about its chances for survival.

By the mid-1980s, the situation was so dire that experts were estimating that the elephant population was close to reaching the point of no return. The mean weight of elephant tusks being traded on the world market had dropped since 1979 from 35 pounds to just 13 pounds, evidence that in some places entire generations of older elephants had been wiped out, leaving only the younger ones to be killed. Conservationists in the US and elsewhere were calling for international action, and in 1985 the parties to CITES voted to limit the international ivory trade. But the CITES restrictions proved unenforceable and ineffective. It was clear that decisive action was required.

▶ (Overleaf) In an internationally televised ceremony on July 18, 1989, Kenya's President Daniel arap Moi set ablaze the tusks of more than 1,200 poached elephants, as an unequivocal smoke signal to the world of his country's commitment to ending the illegal ivory trade. In destroying the tusks, Kenya sacrificed an estimated $3 million in ivory sales.

▼ A tusk hacked from the jaws of an elephant shot to death by poachers. Before the African Elephant Conservation Act (AECA) of 1988 and the historic CITES meeting the following year, about 2,000 elephants were being killed across Africa every week to supply a booming illegal trade in ivory.

Mauri Rautkari/World Wildlife Fund

▲ Carved ivory curios for sale in Douala Town, Cameroon, Africa.

▼▲ The bumper sticker (above) and this poster from the African Wildlife Foundation highlight the bloody reality and tragedy underlying the ivory trade. By aiming to spur public conscience, publicity material such as this may somehow help curtail the market demand for ivory that poachers strive to satisfy.

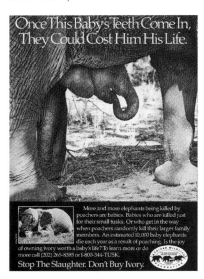

Once This Baby's Teeth Come In, They Could Cost Him His Life.

More and more elephants being killed by poachers are babies. Babies who are killed just for their small tusks. Or who get in the way when poachers randomly kill their larger family members. An estimated 10,000 baby elephants die each year as a result of poaching. Is the joy of owning ivory worth a baby's life? To learn more or do more call (202) 265-8393 or 1-800-344-TUSK.

Stop The Slaughter. Don't Buy Ivory.

It was at this time that Congressman Gerry Studds, a longtime friend and colleague of mine who was sympathetic to the plight of the elephant, became chairman of the House Subcommittee on Fisheries and Wildlife Conservation and the Environment, giving us a fresh opportunity to push for action in Congress. And so in July 1987, when I re-introduced the Elephant Protection Act, mounting concern at the international level about the elephant's survival and a more supportive Congressional chairman combined to put protection for this endangered animal within reach.

As our goal was becoming attainable, and I was finally given the chance to put elephant protection on the Congressional agenda, it became apparent that the issue's higher profile had aroused considerable controversy over how best to address it. The urgency of the crisis meant we could no longer settle for a purely symbolic action which would have little actual impact on the world demand for ivory; we had to set a standard for international action as well.

Thus, our preliminary task was to answer two questions: how large a role was the US playing in the international market, and how could we manipulate that role to have the greatest possible impact on world demand for ivory? In answer to the first, we discovered that the US was a minor actor—importing only an estimated 10 percent of the ivory exported from Africa. Most of that 10 percent was carved in Hong Kong and then re-exported to the US. That fact led to a split within the wildlife conservation community in the US over the best answer to the second question.

World Wildlife Fund, one of the conservation groups studying the problem, believed any US action would be meaningless unless it provided a long-term "African solution". Such a solution meant recognizing that Africa's elephants are a unique and valuable resource—valuable for the ivory they produce and the tourism dollars they generate. Eliminating the ivory trade, they argued, would diminish that value and eliminate any incentive for local governments to provide elephants with adequate protection from poachers. Ivory would continue to be sold on the illegal black market, and the elephant would be driven to extinction even faster.

Other groups strenuously disputed that argument, insisting that without an immediate halt to the ivory trade the elephant would be extinct within a decade. No time remained for a long-term strategy, they argued.

Both sides were right. Immediate action was necessary. As experts Iain Douglas-Hamilton and David Western testified at a June 1988 hearing, the elephant's status was urgent. But it was true, they also agreed, that survival of the elephant would ultimately depend on the ability and willingness of African countries to value and manage the species. The compromise we eventually reached reflected both of these facts.

Approved in the summer of 1988 by both the House of Representatives and the Senate, and signed into law by President Ronald Reagan on October 7, the African Elephant Conservation Act called for an immediate country-by-country evaluation of the effectiveness of the elephant conservation programs of all ivory-producing countries. The US would institute a ban against ivory imports from any country which could not, or would not, protect its elephants from poaching. Also banned were imports from ivory-carving countries, like Hong Kong, unless they too agreed not to import ivory from those African countries which did not meet our criteria. Finally, and perhaps most important, to assist in the long-term effort, the AECA established a federal grant program of up to $5 million a year for projects to help stop poaching in Africa.

By early 1989, African leadership, having despaired of ever winning the war against poachers so long as a legitimate ivory trade persisted, turned world opinion in favor of at least a temporary halt to the trade. With the AECA in place, the US was at long last prepared to respond to their call—and to lead the rest of the world to follow suit.

Steve Turner/Oxford Scientific Films

A WILDLIFE DIRECTOR'S PERSPECTIVE

RICHARD E. LEAKEY

During the late 1970s and the 1980s, gangs of poachers were very active in our parks and elsewhere in Kenya, slaughtering elephants to obtain ivory from their tusks to sell. Few poachers were effectively prosecuted and reports of corruption added to the total atmosphere of gloom and doom.

We saw a continual, rapid increase in the number of elephants being killed and a total inability or unwillingness of the agencies concerned with protecting these animals to take action. The roads used by anti-poaching forces were almost gone due to erosion and lack of maintenance. The vehicles provided had ceased to function. The men were demoralized, ill-equipped, ill-clothed, and under-paid. We had incidents where tourists were robbed, threatened, and even killed.

In this state of affairs, you can understand how surprised I was when, in April 1989, I was unexpectedly asked by the President of Kenya, Daniel arap Moi, to take over the directorship of Kenya's wildlife program. I felt it was highly doubtful that the elephants could be saved in the time we had left. I thought a number of populations could not sustain themselves on a viable basis for more than a few years.

Wildlife, especially the elephant, is the foundation of Kenya's number one industry, tourism. The president made it absolutely clear that the poaching of elephants and other animals had to stop. Further, the threats to tourists must be eliminated, and the parks had to be put in working order, and quickly. I was given all the authority that was needed to do the job.

This, of course, was a critical factor, and emergency assistance from various elephant and conservation groups in North America as well as in Europe and Kenya has enabled us to begin to put right the wrong. I believe that it is fair and correct to say that the parks of Kenya are safer now than they probably have been for the last ten or fifteen years. We have aerial surveillance, and foot and ground patrols, and we are reopening areas that had long ceased to function as viewing areas since the roads had disintegrated.

Poaching has dropped off dramatically. From losing three elephants a day in our national parks over a period of years, elephant loss is now sporadic and infrequent. In Kenya and Tanzania, stockpiles of ivory have been found abandoned as the poachers have fled the parks and the country. This turnabout has happened simply because the market for ivory has, in large measure, dried up. Raw ivory prices have dropped by at least 50 percent. It is now social anathema to buy ivory

Okapia

in Europe and North America. This new attitude is due mainly to the support of the various elephant and wildlife-oriented groups, education campaigns, petitions, and financial support.

Many rural people in Africa struggle daily to make a living, social welfare programs do not exist, salaries are low, and opportunities for children to go to school or college are few. So, if there is a commodity such as ivory that has high value, even though we destroy one gang of poachers, another will take its place. The only way to permanently stop poaching is to destroy the ivory market.

This is why Kenya officially burned about US$3 million worth of ivory in July 1989—over 12 tonnes (26,500 pounds)—that came from approximately 2,000 elephants. To destroy the market we had first to get the attention of the consumers who are accustomed to being influenced by advertising campaigns and who have the money to buy souvenirs and trinkets. We were determined to demonstrate our commitment. We felt it hypocritical to say "Don't buy ivory" to the world while we were selling it. So ... we burned ivory and the world noticed!

▼ Anti-poaching squads scored a rare success in this particular raid in the early 1980s, when rangers were constantly outgunned and outmanned, and thwarted in their efforts by corruption at various levels of government. This situation turned around abruptly in 1989, when Kenya's President Daniel arap Moi committed his government to stamping out the ivory trade, and appointed Richard Leakey to the directorship of Kenya's wildlife program.

▲ This elephant (top) was poached for its tusks and left to rot. Such sights were common in the 1970s and 1980s, when Kenya lost an average of three elephants per day to ivory poachers. Later on as anti-poaching efforts increased in effectiveness, so too did the hauls of confiscated ivory (bottom).

The Convention on International Trade in Endangered Species (CITES) introduced policies and bans that reinforced our actions, and ivory prices have fallen. Enough pressure is off the elephant so that we can confidently predict that the elephant population of about 20,000 in Kenya will remain steady or even increase slightly. And, because the price of ivory has fallen, we no longer fight daily battles against poachers. Now we can devote our efforts to painting houses and repairing roofs, and fixing roads and bridges. There is very little poaching activity in the field at the moment. I think this is true in Tanzania, Uganda, Somalia, and Ethiopia, and certainly true in central Africa. Although the price of ivory does vary, it is generally way, way down and there are great stocks of ivory that cannot be sold.

Not only have we made progress in dealing with the poachers, but we are reorganizing those institutions that manage wildlife. The government of Kenya saw fit to change the legislation and to provide an opportunity for wildlife to be managed under a parastatal, rather than as a government, department minus the inevitable bureaucracies that government departments carry. The Kenya Wildlife Service is owned by government, with a board of directors that is appointed by the minister. The organization is run as a corporation; men and women are paid salaries for the jobs they do. If we make wildlife management self-sufficient and independent of government subsidy, then some of the money saved can be diverted to other important causes, such as schools, hospitals, clinics, veterinary services, roads, ports, and highways. But this is not the time to become complacent. Although poaching is now negligible in Kenya and probably the rest of Africa, the tide could still go the other way. We've won a battle, but not the war, and more effort is required. The elephant will be secure only if the ivory ban is continued.

It is essential to disassociate elephant management from ivory management. While Kenya would agree that the management of elephants is a sovereign issue, the management of ivory is a matter that affects the whole of Africa. The issue is not whether a country should or should not cull its elephants, but what it should or should not do with the ivory that results from the cull. When analyzed closely, the southern African argument for trading in ivory becomes absurd, particularly when juxtaposed with the relatively meager profits that could be made by southern African nations from a sustainable offtake of ivory.

If we assume a sustainable offtake of 3 percent of elephant populations per year, the 1986 ivory price of $80 per kilogram ($36 per pound) at an average weight of 10 kilograms (22 pounds) per elephant, South Africa would make some $200,000 per year, Zimbabwe $1.3 million, and Botswana some $1.6 million. These profits are insignificant relative to the cost of effective anti-poaching campaigns which would be incurred as a direct result of the existence of the ivory trade.

We also still need the elephant books, and the elephant organizations, and the campaigns for and about elephants. And we need all the conservationists—the "soft" ones who want to protect "all those loving creatures," and the "hard-nosed" ones who accept the principle that under some circumstances culling may be necessary. Both sorts of people are necessary in this struggle.

In closing, I think we will one day have more elephants in certain places than these places can support. But I believe we can deal with that openly and constructively in time. Further, I believe that the worst of the poaching is now behind us.

From speeches delivered in 1990–91.

Karl and Karen Ammann

AN ADDENDUM: 1999[1]

Though Kenya's protected area network covers 8 percent of the country, much of our wildlife lives outside or migrates between wildlife areas. This means that wildlife is under pressure in all the areas outside the protected area network because of our growing human populations. Conflict between animals and humans is escalating and often the losers are the wildlife. Elephants are perhaps under greater threat now than ten years ago when they were largely confined to the protected areas where they sought refuge from the poachers. Safety has allowed them to return to their previous ranges where they encounter farms and homesteads. Most farmers are too poor to be able to afford to tolerate these pachyderms. The Kenya Wildlife Service (KWS) has been able to partially alleviate the problem by promoting the establishment of private or community-managed wildlife sanctuaries, some specifically for elephants. These areas are converting to ecotourism as an alternative to cultivation or pastoralism, and elephants are safer in sanctuaries like Namunyak and Mwaluganje than in many Parks. Local communities benefit from the security created from tourism revenue.

The KWS initiated an experimental Wildlife User Program that allowed the controlled cropping of some species of wildlife in those areas that have serious conflict with the wildlife. Land owners were allowed to cull a small percentage of the wildlife herd, and sell the meat and skins locally. In the year 2000, nine years of this experiment will be evaluated to determine whether it has been financially worthwhile, and beneficial to biodiversity conservation at the same time.

The Kenya government still maintains a total ban on wildlife hunting with the exception of game birds. This law is unlikely to change in the future. Kenyans believe that the partial lifting of the ban on trade in ivory was premature. The split listing of elephants with some on Appendix II and some on Appendix I is a dangerous trend that could result in its use as a loophole for trade in ivory. Elephants do not respect political boundaries. Across Africa elephants continue to be threatened by the illegal ivory trade. They should be afforded the highest level of protection available—Appendix 1.

[1] By Paula Kahumbu, KWS (approved by the current Director of KWS, Nehemiah K. arap Rotich).

▲ Kenya's dedicated stand against the ivory trade is largely in recognition of the fact that tourism is that country's primary earner of foreign exchange: in Kenya, elephants are worth more alive than dead.

MEMORIES OF AFRICAN ELEPHANTS

SYLVIA K. SIKES

Between 1950 and 1970 was a special period in Africa's history when gusty winds of change radically altered not only the continent's politics but also the totality of its population and environmental dynamics. It was inevitably to become a watershed in the status of its elephants.

It was the period when European colonial governments handed over national management to new indigenous politicians and civil servants, who were assisted by a variety of expatriate "experts" and large sums of competitive overseas financial "aid". Briefly this period saw, in large areas of Africa, the disappearance of traditional elephant hunting. Primarily hunting had been undertaken as a village social event; it was also seen as a way of protecting crops. It yielded, per kill, about 3,000 kilograms (6,600 pounds) of edible elephant meat and salable byproducts (ivory, hairs, and leather). But then elephant hunting became restricted to license holders with modern firearms. Also sanctuaries, game reserves, and national parks were demarcated, where game—including elephants—both immigrated and multiplied.

Elsewhere a steady environmental change proceeded due to human and domestic animal population explosions, incursions by roads, and the commercial exploitation of forests and savanna woodland. These included the clearance of some thousands of square kilometers of bush in ill-conceived tsetse fly eradication schemes. In the course of such schemes, innumerable game animals, including elephants, were displaced.

During this period elephants had not been readily "visible" to many people because they tended to live in places mainly inaccessible by car. Only indigenous villagers, hunters, and nomads encountered them. Others who wished to see them had to mount great foot safaris with up to fifty or more porters. Behind the scenes, the "invisible" elephants of the forests and savanna were rapidly being eliminated (with the exception of those in some equatorial and montane rainforests) while the "visible" elephants of the protected areas were suddenly becoming available to tourists.

I had the rare privilege of coming into this era by way of the folklore and teaching of indigenous hunters. My first job (in Central Africa) required language study, which frequently took me to remote villages. I was armed with the essentials—a bicycle, a second-hand camera, an old army rifle, a first degree in zoology, and my Bible. But I was well equipped, as it is to my parents that I owe my early childhood training in the careful and accurate use of cameras and firearms. From them I also learned the thrill of "safari" on foot or mule back

Karl Ammann

into remote places beyond the limits of the then sparse vehicle roads and tracks.

Eccentric as it may seem, I have usually hunted in the company of only one, or maybe two, senior traditional indigenous hunters, and very rarely with expatriate companions. For this reason my best memories of elephants in the wild comprise the whole scene from the tracking and stalking of the elephant, to the actual encounter, as well as its relationship to the local people and its place in the environment.

In most of the west and some Central African countries, flintlock and shotguns were continuously available to indigenous hunters right through this period, while only the few wealthier residents, including some emirs or chiefs, could afford high-velocity rifles. Village hunters would also employ the technique of trapping. For example, a typical trap consisted of a woven ring of sharp thorns, dosed with cortisone from the *Strophanthus* vine, and weighted with a heavy drag log. Others used foot-wounding. This was a very cruel method of

▼ A family of elephants enjoying their afternoon refreshment—the kind of delightful scene so familiar to and so fondly remembered by the author in her many years of research into African elephants.

immobilizing an elephant so that the hunter with a less reliable type of firearm could move closer to it and kill it at close range with a single bullet or arrowhead fired by a 12-bore, or a flintlock gun.

Licensed hunting was allowed for a nominal sum (£10 for an elephant in Nigeria in the 1950s and 1960s); however, if one was serving on elephant "control", one was allowed to go out and kill elephants raiding farms. Unabused, this arrangement could perhaps have continued to keep the elephant populations in balance and, most important, to keep villages adequately supplied with a steady supply of dried protein.

In 1962 I was in Nigeria, lecturing in zoology, and building up a basic teaching museum. At the time, few students or townspeople would ever have seen an elephant or any part of it. So, hearing of serious raids by elephants on village farms in the rocky hills north of Abuja, I arranged to take on the so-called "control". Accompanied by Mohammadu Shehu, a Nigerian traditional hunter with whom I had hunted and collected specimens for teaching museums and a local zoo for several years, I set off by Land Rover for a village at the end of a very wild track. There we were joined by a local guide, and soon reached a sizable river, where we left the car. Carrying our basic equipment, including rifles, we waded shoulder deep across the muddy torrent and then mounted bicycles which had been brought for our use. The tires were tubeless, filled instead with sand, and beautifully bound round with palm twine. We rode these, suffering unique torture, along some 11 kilometers (7 miles) of narrow twisting paths until we came to hills. Here we abandoned the bicycles. Some miles later we arrived at a compact, unspoiled "Stone Age" village with round, dried-mud, thatched huts and grain bins, and a scatter of clay pots, pestles and mortars, grindstones, scrawny chickens, and the odd dog and goat. I was welcomed, given a hut to stay in and food to eat. Some villagers were suprised that a white woman had come to deal with their elephants.

Late that night the hunters returned from a search for the elephants. The village was noisy with their talk as they ate and related exploits for Mohammadu's benefit. Before dawn I ate a good picnic breakfast and prepared for a longish day. Soon Mohammadu called me and we set out, clambering up onto the nearby plateau, which was studded with rounded inselbergs (huge isolated rocky humps rising out of the plateau) so characteristic of this area. Some of these had a scatter of great boulders around them. The valleys between were cool but airless and contained riverine forests, with streams and animal paths through them. There was plenty of fresh antelope, buffalo, and baboon spoor. It was not until the afternoon, hot and tired, that we first found fresh elephant tracks and droppings. We paused and rested, drinking from the clear-water seepages that emerged from under the boulders.

Up … over another huge inselberg … and then we saw egrets, heard vervet monkeys in the trees, and saw a mixed herd of elephants (of all ages and both sexes) slowly moving up the valley in the general direction of the village, feeding on the trees and undergrowth as they went. We slithered down the boulder-strewn slope of the inselberg, following elephant paths, and were amused at the slides they had made by slipping down on their buttocks. We arrived alongside the herd in the valley bottom and crept into cover between three big boulders, settling down to watch. The shallow river here was flowing fast over its rocky bed, and some of the youngsters were playing with the water, squirting it about, rolling, and kneeling in it. Our local guide told me we should be able to follow the elephants "to the fields they may raid tonight", kill "one or two", and thus drive the rest away!

To me, it did not seem to be a very convincing plan. My two rifles were loaded, Mohammadu holding one for me on my left. Our guide seemed nervous; I suspected he might prove unreliable. The wind was also very uncertain.

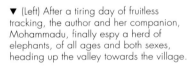

▼ (Left) After a tiring day of fruitless tracking, the author and her companion, Mohammadu, finally espy a herd of elephants, of all ages and both sexes, heading up the valley towards the village.

▼ (Right) Tourists in motor cars were beginning to catch sight of those elephants in protected park areas that were previously encountered only by remote villagers, nomads and hunters, or "visible" only by way of organized foot safaris.

Jonathan Scott/Planet Earth Pictures

◄ "They always came in a hurry to the salt as if they could not wait, throwing themselves into the gray, slippery pools, stabbing down with their tusks to loosen the salt, even kneeling in the mud." Just like the elephants of Kinangop Mountain in Kenya that Sikes would watch on cold, moonlit nights, this threesome revel in the feeling of mud on their skin and the taste of salt in their mouths.

We watched as the elephants swished and pushed the vegetation, muttering, popping, and gurgling. Suddenly everything changed. Two merry little calves, about two years old, rushed through the water to our side of the river, flapping their ears, tails up, and trunks waving hilariously ... and almost ran into our hide-out. They stopped in their tracks as they spotted us, paused, shook their heads and fled back to their mothers. A sharp warning hoot from the leader called the herd to attention and they set off in a deliberate, but unpanicked, manner. We still waited.

As they went we heard others below us, following them. Then an adult passed right beside us and must have caught our scent. She turned, saw us, and swung in between two of our boulders. The ears were spread, and her eyes—the same size as our own—engaged mine and focused. I had already raised the rifle and held it aimed. I waited. It was neither my purpose nor my wish to kill out here away from the fields. All three of us had frozen, but how long could I trust our guide to keep still? The elephant was too close and too dominant to risk the gimmicks suggested by some hunters, like shouting, throwing one's hat at it, falling flat on one's face, or even singing Gilbert and Sullivan. I decided that if it took one more step in our direction, I must then shoot. The scent of the elephant was strong and there was a swish-swish sound of other elephants passing below us in the valley. Our elephant began to "dance", that restless weaving of the head and shoulders suggesting uncertainty. Her trunk reached down forward: stiff, tense. Then, decisively, she lowered her head and thrust forward. I fired, her eyes only

about 4 meters (over 12 feet) from my own. We leapt aside as she crashed on to her brisket, dead exactly where we had been crouching.

Dusk was falling. The herd had panicked and disappeared, and our guide left to go to the plateau edge to alert the villagers. We heard him in the darkness, calling with a long-distance yodeling sort of sound. Then he came back to rejoin us. We were hungry, and it rained during the night. We huddled around a fire beside the carcass, and heard the night sounds: crickets, an owl, and a leopard.

As dawn broke, the sound of celebration songs and the ululation of women joined the other morning sounds around the kill. A joyous procession of men, women, and children was approaching. They brought a congratulatory meal for Mahommadu and me at the kill site—a custom now possibly lost forever. The villagers immediately set to work stripping all edible meat, special parts as charms and medicines, and the ears for leather, from the carcass. I kept the tail (my seal of ownership) and the skull and tusks (for the zoology museum in Zaria).

I spent the next twenty-four hours in that friendly village, watching as the strips of meat were spread on wooden frames over smoky fires in the sunshine to be dried and later stored as bundles slung high in the smoke-filled, fly-free darkness of the thatched roofs of the huts. To me, this hunt and its conclusion will always stand out as the epitome of what village life used to be, and the way a hunted elephant was rightly used. It was an exciting, very memorable event.

I was able to revisit the area several times during the next ten years as State Wildlife

Consultant, and sadly saw the elephants dwindle steadily as forests were clear-felled, and agricultural land use took their place. On that day in 1962, there must have been about seventy to eighty elephants in the one herd, moving up the valley. Where are they now? Where are those unsophisticated little villages? Today Nigeria's new capital city adorns that place, with all its ancillary features surrounding it. The people are caught up in it; the elephants are no more.

My best memories of elephants relate to herds living in genuinely wild, natural habitats still following their ancient migration routes both annually and during nature's cycles of climatic stress. The elephants of Kinangop Mountain in Kenya still had this privilege in the 1960s, and by this time my association with them had already covered some thirty years. A favorite place to watch them was on a salt lick just west of the forest edge, facing Mount Longonot. On a moonlit night, I would settle downwind, although it could get very cold there. First came the buffalo in huge herds, and it was safest to keep out of their way until they left. Then came the elephants. They always came in a hurry to the salt as if they could not wait, throwing themselves into the gray, slippery pools, stabbing down with their tusks to loosen the salt, even kneeling in the mud.

They were very vocal indeed, but if one made a false move and disturbed them, instant silence would fall until the leader gave either the "all-clear" or the "run-for-it" signal. When their visits were over, they hurried back up into the forests. These were extremely healthy, active elephants, known then to migrate far over the mountain northeast to the forests of Mount Kenya and northwestward to the Thomsons Falls area in glorious uninterrupted freedom. They were

however prone to encounters with European settler–ranchers along the lower forest edges. One of the ranchers set up an electric fence which was successful until the elephants discovered that their tusks were non-conductors and they were able to push the fence down.

One day my tracker Mutarimbo, a local Ndorobo hunter, and I were searching for elephants high above the salt lick on Kinangop Mountain, at the interface between the rain-forest and the great bamboo forest, where the bamboos frequently attained a diameter around 15 centimeters (6 inches). We were hoping to find herds and do structure analyses. Elephants rarely deliberately *hunt* an intruder, but prefer to give warnings—intimidation or a mock charge are common. We had located a mixed herd (all ages and both sexes) peacefully feeding. There was a complex mass of tree branches and broken bamboo stems among the undergrowth, and only dappled light was shafting through the canopy. The red soil was wet and slippery, with deep pits where the elephants had trodden.

We crept toward the herd, the wind uncertain, and tried to reach the bole of a giant vine-draped tree. We did not see the herd bull at first, but now suddenly spotted him as he stood motionless, alone, in the shadows, facing us, only his eyes and trunk tip moving. Ominously his ears were closed against his body—he was too close for safety. Carefully we reversed, one very slow step at a time toward another giant tree. He saw us, and appeared to be angry. He started to move restlessly back and forth, always half-facing and hunting us, his ears never fully extending. He was trying to get close to us but was prevented by the sharp broken bamboo stems which can pierce elephants' sensitive soles. Reaching our tree we squeezed behind it, and kept absolutely still. It was very eerie. Every now and then he stopped, shook his head, and started off again. Then he began clearing out a path towards us with his trunk and tusks. There was no easy escape route behind us. We held still for about twenty-five minutes, and by this time our self-discipline was at its limit. Just then, the matriarch ordered her family to move off. The bull was slow to respond, and made a final sally toward our tree before swinging away to follow the herd.

People who hunted elephants in the past often referred to *rogue* elephants, but in fact true rogues are rare and are usually vicious only because of wounding or other abuse by humans. All my memories of such elephants are sad—the killer of a farmer in Nigeria which turned out to have multiple, festering foot wounds; the bull on a dune island in Lake Chad with a large arrowhead in his skull just above the brain; the young bull in Uganda with half his trunk snared off so that he could neither eat nor drink with it, and only survived by standing in lake waters and sucking nutrients with his mouth like elephant calves.

▼ A bull elephant, peacefully snoozing during the midday heat and oblivious to his two observers, was rudely awoken by a small, low-flying plane deliberately circling the animal. Seconds later Sikes and her partner, Erika von Bernuth, were running for their lives. As von Bernuth leapt for cover, she accidentally pushed the camera release, and thus captured on film the elephant towering above them.

Erika von Bernuth

Even in the 1960s there were those who still thought there was an extra-small species, the "pygmy" elephant, living in the equatorial forests of the Congo basin and the West Coast rainforests. The round-eared forest elephant (*Loxodonta cyclotis*) did indeed live in these forests and the average stature in adulthood is a bit less than that of *L. africana*. The ears are more rounded that in the savanna (*L. africana*) species. Otherwise, one sees little difference between them when observing them wild within thick forest. My personal experience of the forest species was primarily in Ghana and, at the interface where the two species overlapped, around the Ruwenzori Mountains.

Deeply memorable was a visit in 1953 into the Ituri Forest in the Belgian Congo, later DRC. At this time modern roads had not scarified the Ituri as they have today. Then they were just narrow motor tracks of damp forest soil winding through the forest with, at intervals, heart-stopping bridges of squared-off tree trunks dragged across the swirling rivers. Irregular gaps between these logs taxed the motorist's mettle to the full. It was particularly exciting to see a steaming heap of fresh elephant dung and rows of well-molded footprints leading along the track ahead, with a scattering of characteristic fibrous "twizzles" dropped from the elephants' mouths as they fed.

I never witnessed an elephant hunt by the pygmies of the Ituri Forest in DRC. I did, however, have the wonderful experience of arriving in a pygmy encampment, after a long and memorable walk along animal paths through the unspoiled jungle. This was just after the pygmies had captured (in a pitfall) and killed (with short stabbing spears) a forest elephant (*L. cyclotis*).

There had been an abrupt break from the dappled forest shade as we came into the blinding sunlight of the clearing. I could see the circular encampment of tiny round shelters, busy with forest people cutting strips of elephant meat for sun and smoke drying, tending the fires, working the ear leather, and honing their knives and spearheads. The average height of these marvelous people was about 1.5 meters (about 5 feet), they were pale in color, clad only in a little bark-cloth apron hanging from a waist thong which was itself also festooned with charms, leather snuff box, and medicine phials made from duiker horn. The women also wore a few bright little glass beads, and a leather necklace. The men showed me their short, strong elephant-stabbing spears and the double-edged, sheathed dagger bound on the upper arm. They were hospitable, bringing me an open gourd containing roasted fresh elephant meat, garnished with large, fat chafer (beetle) larvae, and greenish, wild spinach gravy—delicious!

Although at that time they traded useful parts of the elephant, as well as dried meat, with their non-pygmy neighbors who lived on the forest

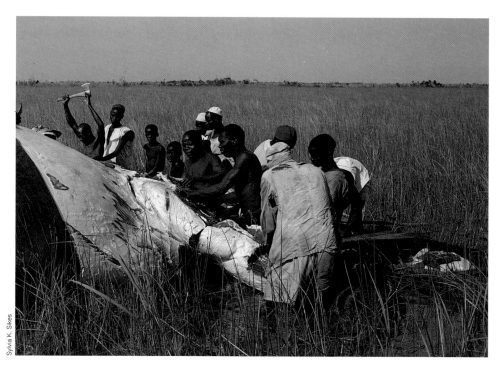

Sylvia K. Sikes

fringes for other items like forged spearheads and arrowheads, they hunted elephants only when they needed a good supply of biltong. This could be carried with them as they moved about in the forest, changing their encampment every week or two. The elephants were not overhunted or wasted, the environment was not damaged and camp sites quickly regenerated. But all that is just a memory. Returning some years later, I found that education, intermarriage with non-pygmy tribes, the roads, and the opening up of the forest for forestry and agriculture, had changed everything almost beyond recognition, and the elephants were rarely seen.

It was gratifying in the mid-1960s, during research on elephants for the Zoological Society of London, to work for a time with other research workers in national parks and protected areas, as the larger species were already increasingly abundant and new data were being obtained. Generally, however, I conducted my own work with a hand-picked team of African assistants. I had the advantage of fluency, or at least capability, in four local languages. In late 1963, I traveled into northern Uganda to work in the "Elephant Sanctuary". It was Christmas Eve and I had culled a bull and a cow elephant just beside the railway track from Pakwach—the rail terminal on the River Nile. My team and I were looking forward to a Christmas break. Camp had been struck, both necropsies were complete, and tusks, jaws, samples, and data were all stowed in the trucks. Sadly, however, all the edible meat was going to be abandoned because there were no villages in the sanctuary, until, at that moment, we heard the train chuffing up the line from Pakwach. We waved to the driver and the train slowed to a halt beside us. "Is the meat for us?" "Yes, it's good—

▲ This elephant was legally shot in the fringe swamps of Lake Chad in the southern Sahara in 1969. The meat was stripped and then transported by canoe to be sold fresh in the local village market on the lake shore. Such traditional use of a hunted elephant stood out for the author as the epitome of what village life used to be like.

► Keeping up with the pace of this huge, well-tusked bull elephant in musth proved to be an arduous task for the author, her tracker, and a local guide, although she recalls a sense of exhilaration in having stalked him so closely. In the years of research that followed this episode, Sikes found that this was the largest elephant she would ever see, given the dramatic changes to the habitat resulting from modern developmental pressures.

Sylvia K. Sikes

take it." Instantly all the passengers poured down onto the track, knives in hand, and, before it seemed possible, every scrap of edible flesh had been transferred to the train. With a merry hoot, and "Happy Christmas" all round, the train puffed away to bring a rare and welcome Christmas dinner to many town and village families who could not readily obtain so ample a supply of meat.

Tsavo in Kenya, known to me in childhood as a wilderness of strong savanna woodland and "wait-a-bit" thorn scrub (or "nyika"), was by the 1960s a severely degraded habitat overflowing with elephants. While arguments raged as to whether or not to cull them, the degradation of the habitat continued. Fire wreaked havoc, and drought wrecked much vegetation that could have been sustained with fewer elephants.

One day Mutarimbo and I were out on foot studying a large herd (of mixed ages and both sexes) outside the park boundary in open savanna with poor vegetation and numerous termite hills. We had arrived in the pre-dawn period, had heard and smelt the elephants, and had been able to move into and all around the downwind aspect of the herd, making notes and trying to assess ages and relationships. Two very large bulls had been mating with cows. The scent was very powerful both from their bodies and from the damp sticky penile exudations on the ground suggesting that the bulls were in musth. (The word "musth" is a Hindi word not used much in Africa until recent times. The condition, however, was always known to, and recognized by, indigenous Africans who hunted elephants traditionally.) The rest of the herd was very peaceful, mostly just resting or toying with dead branches. We had been with the herd for about two and a half hours, when a light plane flew toward the herd and, unbelievably, "buzzed" it. With warning screams, the cows called up the

youngsters, bunched, and fled. It was a thoroughly traumatic experience both for the infants and for us. Indeed, if we had not been in the lee of a termite hill we might ourselves have been flattened. Airplanes, helicopters, and hot air balloons are quite extensively used nowadays in wildlife work and sadly sometimes cause considerable losses.

The elephants (*L. africana*) of Lake Chad in the southern Sahara were great favorites of mine, for their habitat was as yet unspoiled and they were still numerous. The exploitation of their ivory for the trans-Saharan market had been going on for centuries, possibly since the time of King Solomon, but without exceeding the renewable capacity of the herds. Moreover, their uninterrupted migrations still followed established routes up to 200 kilometers (125 miles) west, south, and east of the lake. They were large, tall, lively, and very healthy animals. The bulls were well tusked, although it is doubtful if the tusk sizes attained those of East or Central Africa.

As with all African tribes, those of Lake Chad itself and the surrounding areas (Kanuri, Yedina, Shuwa, Hausa, and Fulani) have a specific word in their language for elephant, as well as a wealth of hunting tales and even dances about the animal. One tribe calls the species "Kumaan". They say the elephant is humankind's direct ancestor—an attractive belief for those who love the elephant.

Lake Chad is an interesting and unusual lake. It is like a huge fluctuating puddle with no outlet, lying in the southern edge of the Sahara Desert, varying in area between about 22,000 square kilometers (about 8,500 square miles) and 10,000 square kilometers (about 3,900 square miles). During the cooler dry season months (September–March) the lake water level rises to its annual maximum depth of between 1 and 4 meters (about 3 and 13 feet).

Swamp vegetation, dominated by *Papyrus* and *Phragmites*, both fringes the shoreline and also comprises thousands of vagrant and fixed floating islands, so it was always a marvelous habitat for elephants. They could be approached in the lake by canoe, or on foot in the dry season in the swamps and open woodland on shore. In the rainy season they were more difficult to locate as they traveled widely and did not need to use specific waterholes.

One December in the early 1950s, I was on the southwestern part of the lake shore, and, hearing that there were "many elephants" in the area, set off with my tracker, Mohammadu, and a local guide to find them. We hired horses and later walked along the spoor of a large herd. We caught up with the rearguard in the shape of an enormous bull, majestically ambling along and leaving a heavily scented trail from a dangling, very long male organ. As we were downwind, and directly behind him, he seemed unaware of our very close presence. There is a sense of exhilaration following an elephant so closely, especially when you are about 10 meters (about 33 feet) or less behind it. This one moved leisurely and very silently apart from the occasional ear slap — but, oh! The speed! A racing walk (running would thump the ground too much) is needed to keep up. The sun burns your back, flies settle on your sweaty shirt and neck, and the kilometers slip by.

This bull's tusks were thick and well set, and I thought the weight of each was about 35 kilograms (75 pounds). The main herd had now veered off to our right—its position clearly indicated by the mass of attendant egrets. We left the bull as he stopped to sniff a foaming urine pool left by a passing female—he seemed to be fully in musth—and cut across to the thicker trees. I climbed up into an acacia tree with Mohammadu to watch and count. The herd seemed to total around 150, but we may have underestimated the calves as so many were very young and hidden among the legs of the adults. Many adults seemed very tall, and some younger bulls were playing energetically, tussling their tusks together. Mostly they fed peacefully, gradually moving on toward the lake, conversing in their sociable pop-pop-popping and gurgling sort of family language.

Eventually we slid down from our tree. Our guide had long since vanished. Just at that moment, a tall, wizened and wrinkled old cow, with longish, slender tusks and a toothless-looking mouth, headed straight into our patch under the tree. We stepped smartly aside and she came forward, her thin, sensitive trunk reaching ahead, touching the path and bushes. She was completely blind. Through my subsequent studies of elephant ageing, I now know that she must almost have reached nature's absolute limit of elephant survival, when all the molars have gone.

My research over the years and in various African countries has convinced me that longevity is greater in this type of habitat than in less rich and perhaps more restricted protected habitats where many workers think elephants only attain a fifty- to sixty-year age limit. In older, richer habitats, longevity may well attain seventy years, a view supported by accurate information on the Asian elephant. This particular cow would probably survive a while longer yet, as she could obtain soft grasses and vines in the swamps. I also know now that the huge bull we followed was the largest I personally would ever see. In my subsequent research on Lake Chad I was also to take vertical (non-contour) shoulder measurements of other bulls, some over 3.6 meters (11 feet 10 inches), confirming that these elephants, up to at least 1970, included some of Africa's tallest. (Contour measurements, measured by laying a loose curving tape along the skin, give an exaggerated measurement. Non-contour measurements are measured the way a standing horse is measured, by taking the measurement of a rigid pole from the ground, or side of the sole, to a bar across the

Mitch Reardon

shoulders.) Sadly, however, developmental pressures around Lake Chad have changed the habitat and herd status is today in jeopardy.

My memories of African elephants are told here as individual events, for I want to recapture the feel, scent, sound, and action, as well as the surrounding scene. I believe they reflect the experiences of past hunters and observers during and before the two decades that became the modern watershed in the history both of Africa's elephants and of those African communities for whom the relationship with elephants was important and practical. I hope too that they reflect something of the exhilaration, surprise, and frequent exhaustion felt by those who followed these strong, yet generally gentle, giants. Such encounters will become more rare as elephant habits and lifestyle become ultimately restricted to those havens (the protected areas) so essential now for the species to survive at all.

▲ The Tsavo known during Sikes' childhood in Kenya was one of thriving savannah woodland; but by the 1960s the woodland was clearly succumbing to the pressures of an elephant population explosion, and eventually disappeared, along with those animals dependent on it. Fire and drought added to the devastation.

WHY SAVE ELEPHANTS?

JEHESKEL SHOSHANI

We have just begun to understand elephant behavior and its role in the ecosystem, and we have just begun to understand why we must do our utmost to save elephants specifically.

Field observations during the past few decades have enriched our knowledge and brought us to realize that elephants are not just *a* species in a savannah or a forest ecosystem, but, in some places, they are *the* species. The pivotal role which elephants play in their respective Asian or African ecosystems cannot be overstressed.

A simple list of elephants' attributes and their contributions, and their role in their environment, may read: dispersing seeds (for example, of acacia trees) via their dung, which promotes rapid germination; distributing and recycling nutrients in their feces; converting savannah/woodlands to grasslands and thereby creating new habitats for other species; providing water for other species by digging waterholes (also, elephants' paths to waterholes act as fire breaks and as channels for runoff of rainwater); enlarging waterholes as they plaster mud on their bodies when bathing and wallowing; "excavating" and/or enlarging existing caves (for example, on Mount Elgon, Kenya) where other species also benefit, as they use the caves for salts and shelter; providing food for birds when walking in high grass by disturbing insects and small reptiles or amphibians; and providing protection for other species, as their warnings to the members of their own group also alert the smaller animals to approaching predators.

For these reasons alone, it may be noted that elephants are an inseparable component of their environment and are a significant part of wildlife heritage for future generations. But there is much more implied in these attributes and contributions.

An interpretation of this list yields a description of a species which is capable of shaping the environment in which it lives. The key phrase is "capable of shaping the environment". The transformation of savannahs into grasslands (by clearing large areas of young trees and underbrush), and the creation of "oases" in time of drought (by digging waterholes which other animals also use) are two examples of the crucial role elephants play in creating habitats (even though temporary) for dozens, or perhaps

Gunter Ziesler/Bruce Coleman Limited

▶ With a retinue of cattle egrets, African elephants graze peacefully at Amboseli, Kenya. Cattle egrets habitually accompany elephants and other large African herbivores, feeding on the insects startled into flight by the movements of the larger animals in the grass.

▼ This simplified diagram shows how a large area suitable for elephants also provides a good habitat for other smaller species. The rectangular areas represent habitats sufficient for (A) a pair of rock hyraxes; (B) a pair of bushbucks and 7 pairs of rock hyraxes; and (C) a pair of elephants, 4 pairs of bushbucks, and 19 pairs of rock hyraxes.

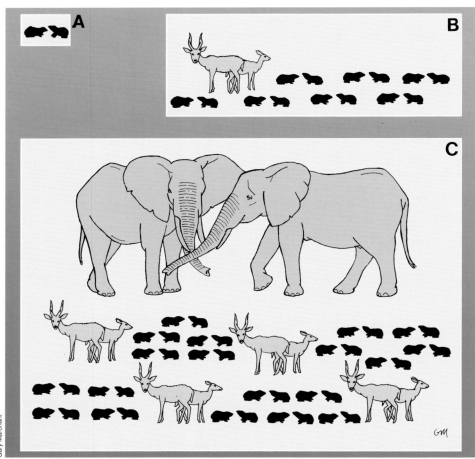

Gary Marchant

hundreds, of species. By ecological definition, an animal which has the capacity to shape or modify its habitat is called a *keystone* species.

The best example of elephants as a keystone species modifying their habitat and benefiting other species is the "excavation" of caves by elephants on Mount Elgon, Kenya. Here ungulates, hyraxes, monkeys, bats, and birds use the caves either for mineral salts to supplement their diets or as shelters. Other animals and insects also use the caves. Based on the available information, elephants are the only living mammals capable of habitat transformation on such a large scale. Kitum Cave, for example, is approximately 160 meters (525 feet) long and, in places, over 100 meters (330 feet) wide. No other living animal has been observed to create such large underground habitats for so many species.

An integral part of the elephant's role as a keystone species is its size; no other living terrestrial animal is heavier than an elephant. A fully grown male African elephant may weigh 7,000 kilograms (about 15,430 pounds); the next heaviest land animal is the white rhinoceros, which may weigh 5,000 kilograms (about 11,000 pounds).

The amount of food consumed by an animal is directly proportional to its size; the larger species require larger quantities which in turn require larger home ranges than smaller species. It follows,

ELEPHANTS: THE SUPER-KEYSTONE SPECIES
Ecological relationships between the elephant and its ecosystem

then, that an area large enough for sustaining an elephant can automatically support other species as long as they are not directly competing for the same food source.

Understanding this principle (habitat size, and the type and number of species it can support) is crucial for understanding how to preserve certain ecosystems and perhaps even to restore those which have been lost. Protecting elephants may prove to be a very costly operation. Yet it is essential to the protection of other wildlife in the environment because, by preserving a large area for elephants to roam freely, one also provides a suitable habitat for many other animal and plant species of the same ecosystem; the reverse (preserving many small areas) is not true.

Earlier in this book Richard M. Laws (in the Foreword) summarized some of the ecological similarities between elephants and early humans. Here are some further considerations. Since elephants and humans have some of the longest life spans among mammals (over seventy years), and their body plan exhibits certain common features, they share ecological similarities such as unspecialized food requirements; wide range of habitat occupancy (in terms of climate and vegetation type); ability to modify their habitat; social organization of family units; extended families and bachelor herds; similar walking and

running speed; effective absence of predators of adults (excluding humans as the only predators of elephants; tigers and lions are known to attack young elephants); deferred sexual maturity; post-reproductive phase; relatively naked skin; natural mortality pattern and birth interval; cardiovascular diseases and arthritis; longevity; long childhood associated with learning; and tool use and manufacture. These observed parallels may allow researchers to extend their knowledge of long-lived mammals (such as humans) by studying elephants.

Following this outline of the elephant's contribution to our understanding of long-lived mammals, and its fundamental role as a keystone species in a number of different habitats, it may be understood why the elephant can be considered a *super-keystone* species.

According to legend when a person observes elephants in the wild, that particular day, week, month or year is not counted in the person's allotted life span. Adding in all the days that I have observed wild elephants in Africa and Asia, I have therefore extended my life span by about six months. I hope that this book will encourage further elephant conservation; if not for the sake of the elephants, then for the sake of those individuals who want to live longer by seeing elephants in the wild! Only the future will tell how much can be accomplished in our lifetime.

▲ This diagram shows the ways elephants interact with their ecosystem.
1. Elephants often convert woodland into grassland, providing new habitats for other species. An animal which modifies its habitat is called a keystone species.
2. Carcasses of elephants are food for vultures, jackals, hyenas, and insects; decomposition helps recycle nutrients in the soil.
3. Seeds which pass through the elephant's digestive system are said to have a better chance to germinate.
4. Dung beetles and other invertebrates eat undigested nutrients and lay eggs in dung.
5. Monkeys also find tasty items in elephant dung since only 44 percent of the elephant's food is digested.
6. In times of drought, elephants dig waterholes in dry riverbeds; this benefits hoofed mammals, monkeys, and birds.
7. Excavation of caves by elephants on Mount Elgon, Kenya, is the best example of elephants modifying their habitat, where ungulates, hyraxes, monkeys, bats, birds, and other animals use the caves either for salts to supplement their diet or as shelters.
8. When elephants walk through grass they disturb small animals, such as frogs, and insects which are fed upon by egrets, piapiacs, and other birds.
9, 10. Lions and crocodiles are at the top of the ecological pyramid; they feed on small herbivores as well as on young elephants, the sick, and the dead.

EPITOME

JEHESKEL SHOSHANI

"You do not appreciate the value of something until you lose it," one old Masai saying states. We have come close to losing *it*—the elephant.

The capacity for loving elephants, or any wildlife, does not come with our birth certificate, or with the animal's purchase documents. Loving animals and appreciating the need to conserve them are aspects we learn at home, in school, or read about in newspapers and books. There is a natural tendency to love and subsequently want to save those animals which a person knows the most. Getting to know elephants and developing caring are primary to this book.

These thoughts could not have been better summarized than in the words of a Senegalese writer Baba Dioum, who said:

In the end, we will conserve only what we love.
We will love only what we understand.
We will understand only what we have been taught.

I began to love elephants in earnest when I was twenty-five years old after reading a book called *Burma Boy* by Willis Lindquist. At that time I worked and lived in Tel-Aviv Zoo, Israel. It is a book for a young audience, written in a suspense style; I "consumed" it in one sitting and I had tears in my eyes when I finished.

The second phase of my "engagement" to elephants took place in 1972, on the splendid island of Sri Lanka (then Ceylon), where I spent about six months collecting blood samples as part of the research for my PhD. My friend G. P. B. Karunaratne gave me R. Carrington's classic book, *Elephants*, which became my constant companion. It was particularly enchanting and effective to read this book in a country where wild elephants were plentiful and where people held elephants in their backyards as an American would hold a Cadillac or a Chevrolet.

The final phase in the evolution of my "marriage" to elephants came during my stay in Kenya for almost one year in 1973. During that time, I had two close encounters with elephants. One was in Amboseli Game Reserve, where a female elephant attacked me and three other tourists who were with me when we came too close to the carcass of an elephant. The second incident was a very close and memorable encounter with a bull elephant named Ahmed in Marsabit Game Reserve. A brief account of Ahmed is given by my wife Sandra in the section, "Famous Elephants"; here I wish to close this Epitome with a few personal observations.

Having heard many stories and legends about Ahmed, naturally I wanted to see the "King of all Elephants" in his home, some 300 kilometers (about 185 miles) north of Nairobi, at Lake Paradise, in the Marsabit Game Reserve of Kenya. This is a land of forests, mountains, hills, and valleys, rising like an island-oasis in the middle of the desert. It was a pleasant day in July 1973, when I first saw his huge tusks and ears between branches and leaves. There was something special about those huge tusks, which were about 3 meters (almost 10 feet) long and each weighed about 68 kilograms (150 pounds). It was their curvature and symmetry. When still, his tusks rested on the ground, and to walk he had to raise and lower his head so as to coordinate his gait—it was like watching a giant extra-terrestrial beast ambulating in a primeval forest! Seeing him alive was a spiritual experience, a turning point in my life. Sweat ran down my spine, my heart pounded fast and I grasped my friend's wrist and squeezed it so hard that I startled him. That moment was forever engraved in my memory. I believe that I then decided I must devote my life to the study of elephants.

Ahmed died on January 17, 1974. I often wonder whether Ahmed's statue (now standing in the grounds of the National Museum of Kenya in Nairobi) represents the last of his noble line. Should the decimation of elephants continue, it would be impossible to predict what will happen to the elephant. Perhaps it will adapt. In some places, elephants are already changing their habits; they are becoming crepuscular—active mostly during twilight and at night when they are safe. A vision I sometimes see has haunted me: instead of an Ahmed with ears spread wide, huge tusks, and a trunk raised to trumpet, a different kind of elephant may develop: a stealthy, tuskless animal, which will communicate in a way that humans cannot hear, never announcing its presence. Perhaps it will be smaller, and not require as much food, or perhaps it will move to remote areas, away from dead elephants and their dry bones, and be wary of its only natural enemy: humans.

This vision of an apparently gloomy future can be forestalled. The current success of the ivory ban, a product of international cooperation, is a milestone in the history of wildlife conservation. Let us hope that the momentum will not cease and that future generations will be able to observe other Ahmeds, for losing elephants inevitably means losing entire ecosystems.

▶ Young African elephants, Etosha National Park, Namibia. The future of wild elephants will depend greatly on our own understanding of them and their natural habitat, and the actions we take now to safeguard their ongoing survival.

▼ Ahmed, king of all elephants. Dignity and power in every line, this magnificent old bull became the stuff of legend long before he died in northern Kenya in January 1974. His statue now graces the grounds of the National Museum, Nairobi.

Jeheskel Shoshani

FREQUENTLY ASKED QUESTIONS

Q. How many muscles are in an elephant's body?
A. Approximately 394 skeletal muscles.

Q. How many bones are in an elephant's body?
A. The total number of bones varies among individuals and species; it is somewhere between 324 and 347.

Q. How many chromosomes do elephants have?
A. Both living species of elephants have a diploid number of 56 chromosomes in the somatic (body) cells. The haploid number (28) in gamete cells (sperm cell or ovum) consists of 27 autosomes plus a single sex chromosome, either X or Y.

Q. How many muscles are in an elephant's trunk?
A. There are eight major muscles on each side of the trunk (16 total, because, like most organs in the body, the trunk is bilateral), and a total of about 150,000 fascicles (portions of muscles) for the entire trunk.

Q. How long is an elephant's trunk?
A. In a small adult, in relaxed state, a trunk is 1.8 meters (about 6 feet); in a larger elephant it can be 2 or more meters (about $6^1/_2$ feet or longer).

Q. Does an elephant use its trunk for smelling?
A. In most cases an elephant uses its trunk to smell, but sometimes it will use the combination of trunk and upper palate, which contains a chemo-sensory devise called the Jacobson's organ or vomero-nasal organ.

Q. How does an elephant pick up food?
A. Asian elephants usually pick up objects with their trunks by the "grasp" and "pinch" methods, and Africans by the "pinch" method. Under captive situations when both species of elephant are together, African elephants learn that the grasp method enables them to collect food faster, and they employ that method as well.

Q. What are the functions of the trunk?
A. Functions attributed to the trunk include help with: breathing, feeding, drinking, bathing, sprinkling (dust and grass on body), smelling, detecting (e.g., when a female is in estrus), offense, defense, sound production, courtship, calf assurance (a mother elephant frequently reassures her calf by touching it all over its body with her trunk, especially during nursing), and a variety of behavioral signals and displays.

Q. Can an elephant survive without the trunk?
A. In captivity, probably yes. In the wild, it would depend on how much of the trunk is missing and the degree of infection from the wound.

Q. Do elephants drink through their noses?
A. Elephants do not drink through their noses. They use their trunks to bring water to their mouths. A trunk is a combination of nose and upper lip. Since the elephant's neck is so short, it would be difficult and awkward for it to kneel down to reach the water with its mouth.

Q. Do elephants use their trunks, tusks, and feet as weapons?
A. In desperate situations, they will use any organ or part of their body as weapons. Under normal circumstances, however, tusks are the most frequenty used weapon of offense.

Q. Do elephants have brown eyes?
A. Elephants' eyes are yellow, brown, hazel, gray, blue, and pink-like.

Q. Between an elephant and a giraffe, which can reach higher vegetation, and by how much?
A. An elephant can reach higher than a giraffe by about 3.2 meters ($10^1/_2$ feet). The height an elephant can reach with the tip of its trunk while standing on its hind legs is 9.5 meters (31 feet). A giraffe, stretching its 50.8-cm (20-inch) tongue, can reach a height of 6.3 meters (20 feet 8 inches).

Q. How big is an elephant heart?
A. The heart of an elephant may weigh between 12 and 21 kilograms (about 26 to 46 pounds) depending on its size, age, and possibly sex. The length of an elephant heart varies from 44 to 57 centimeters (about 18–22 inches); the width varies from 32 to 48 centimeters (about 13–19 inches).

Q. Do African elephants flap their ears?
A. Yes, both African and Asian elephants flap their ears.

Q. How often does an elephant bathe?
A. Depending on circumstances, 3–4 times per week in the wild and 3–10 times per week in captivity.

Q. Why do elephants have tusks?
A. Tusks are incisor teeth ("front teeth") which are a part of the set of teeth that most mammals (humans included) have developed during millions of years. Tusks are used for defense, offense, display, digging in the ground, lifting objects, food gathering, and for stripping bark from trees to eat.

Q. How thick is the skin of an elephant, and how many cell layers thick is the epidermis?
A. Data taken from the skin of Iki indicate that thickness of skin (dermis and epidermis) varies from 1.8 mm ($^1/_{10}$ inch) on the medial side of the ear to 32 mm ($1^1/_4$ inches) on the rump and parts of the head. There are 50–100 cell layers in the epidermis and it can be up to 10 mm ($^1/_2$ inch) thick.

Q. Why are elephants so heavy?
Size is hereditary and could also be influenced by environmental factors. Bigger animals have fewer enemies than smaller ones. Relative to the size of their bodies, heavier animals eat less food than smaller and lighter animals. This means that relative to smaller mammals, elephants invest less energy in searching for and digesting food.

Q. How much water and how much food does a grown elephant need to consume per day?
A. An elephant drinks between 100 and 200 liters (26–52 US gallons)

per day. The trunk of an adult elephant can hold 8.5 liters ($2\,^1/_4$ gallons) of water. An elephant eats between 100 and 400 kg (220–880 pounds) of food per day. Only about 44 percent of the food is digested. Elephants may consume anywhere from 100 to 500 plant species.

Q. Do elephants eat coniferous trees (e.g., pine and/or spruce)?
A. According to Sheree Walters of Ivory Haven in Michigan, her female 17-year-old African elephant Laura always eats pine trees when they go for walks through the woods. "She will eat needles and smaller branches. We always recycle the Christmas trees by letting Laura and Buster (male 18-year-old African elephant) eat them. The turpentine in the sap has me worried but then on the other hand many healing liniments have essences from trees like these, I think, though you would not generally eat them. I have found that elephants seem to be quite adept at knowing what is poisonous and not good for them to eat."

Q. How good is an elephant's sense of smell?
A. Elephants have a keen sense of smell, manifested by seven turbinals (scrolls of bones with sensitive tissue sensitized for olfaction); dogs have five such turbinals.

Q. Of all five senses, which is most developed in elephants?
A. Acuteness and ability to detect external stimuli vary with age, but compared to other mammals, and generally speaking: sense of sight—poor, but good in dull light; hearing—excellent; smell—acute; touch—very good; taste—seems to be selective.

Q. How much heat or cold can elephants tolerate?
A. It is better to avoid extreme environmental conditions. In the wild, elephants live in desert conditions and on the fringes of snow-capped mountains. They are free and capable of moving to more suitable conditions when the situation becomes intolerable.

Q. Do elephants have four knees?
A. No, all mammals have two knees and elephants are no exception. The so-called "knees" in the front legs are the wrist joints, but because the elephant is large, their wrist joints are elevated above the ground, and appear to some people as "knees". Knees (the joints between the femura and the tibiae and fibulae) are found only in the hind legs.

Q. Is it true that the structure of an elephant's foot aids circulation?
A. Pads at the posterior side of elephant feet are composed of elastic tissue, fat, connective tissue, blood and lymph vessels, and nerves. As in other parts of the body, muscles in the feet and legs, when contracting, act as "vascular pumps"; they squeeze blood vessels and aid in circulation. When walking, an elephant squeezes blood vessels in the vicinity of its foot pads, and thus may accelerate blood flow. Another function attributed to foot pads is "shock absorbers". The pads also enable an elephant to walk in soft soil and thus reduce the risk of getting mired down.

Q. How long is the estrous cycle in elephants and how often are they in estrus?
A. The estrous cycle lasts for about four months, which is the period between ovulation; ovulation which occurs during estrus lasts about four days. If a successful pregnancy occurs, and the calf nurses healthily (suckling strongly to stimulate continuation of milk production, and thereby suppressing hormones which stimulate the ovarian cycle), the mother will not enter into the estrous cycle until weaning, which is about two years. Taking about two years for gestation plus two years for nursing adds up to a four-year calving interval, but it may last for 10 years.

Q. Do elephants sweat?
A. Many investigators have searched for sweat glands, and found none. Nonetheless, it has been reported that when a saddle is removed from an elephant, moisture is noticed.

Q. If an elephant were blind, would it still be able to live and survive in the wild?
A. Chances of survival would be greater if the elephant were to live in a herd.

Q. Who was Jumbo, where was he born, how was he found, where did he live, and for how long, and how tall was he?
A. Jumbo, an African elephant (*Loxodonta africana*), was the most famous elephant that ever lived. He was born in the French Sudan in about 1861 and transported to the Jardin des Plantes in Paris, France. He lived there until June 26, 1865, when he was exchanged for an Indian rhinoceros by the London Zoo, where he lived until 1882 when he was sold to P. T. Barnum. Jumbo died on September 15, 1885, in a train accident in St. Thomas, Ontario, Canada (a statue of Jumbo stands there now). Jumbo's height was 3.25 meters (11 feet) tall when he left London Zoo and he undoubtedly grew some few inches afterwards; some figures run as high as 4 meters ($13\,^1/_2$ feet). His weight was said to be as much as seven tons. The skeleton of Jumbo is in storage at the American Museum of Natural History, New York.

Q. How long does an elephant live? Who is or was the oldest?
A. The elephant's life span is approximately equal to that of humans. The oldest documented age of a captive Asian elephant was that of Jessie in the Taronga Zoological Park, Sydney, Australia; her estimated age at time of death was 69 or 77 years. Raja (the Holy Elephant of Sri Lanka), however, was reportedly 81 or 82 years old when he died.

Q. What is musth?
A. Musth is a physiological condition found in male elephants when testosterone levels in the blood are high. The elephant is often uncontrollable and may kill even its own mahout when in musth. Both male and female elephants have temporal glands from which temporin is excreted, but only males enter into musth.

Q. Can you explain the erratic behavior and attacks by elephants in captivity on people as we have seen on TV?
A. Four aspects of elephant behavior need to be taken into consideration simultaneously: (1) Idiosyncrasies of elephants and people who work with them; (2) Dominance; (3) Musth; (4) Encephalization quotient. Idiosyncrasies require familiarity with the animals. Dominance implies that certain elephants seem to behave as if they, and not the keepers, are the dominant animals. Encephalization Quotient (EQ) is the relative size of the brain compared to the body size; elephants have large EQ value (about 2, similar to some higher primates). It is possible that a combination of "bad" temper, being in musth, "not willing" to be dominated, and a relatively high EQ result in an elephant attacking even its own mahout/trainer.

Q. What is the correct term for an elephant's breast, a teat or a nipple?
A. An elephant's breast (or mammary gland), like most mammals, terminates in a cone-shaped process containing milk or lactiferous duct(s). A nipple is such a process with two or more ducts, whereas a teat (found only in derived artiodactylans, e.g., cow, sheep) has only one lactiferous duct. In some elephants there are about 10–12 lactiferous ducts.

Q. Do female Asian elephants have tusks?
A. The majority of female Asian elephants do not have tusks. Some do have small tusks, which some authorities call "tushes".

Q. Do elephants sleep both lying down and standing up?
A. They sleep lying down on their sides; they do not sleep (but doze) when standing.

Q. Can an elephant stand on its head? Are there any other animals which can?
A. Yes, trained elephants can. So can humans, trained dogs and bears.

Q. Is it true that it is easier to train Asian than African elephants?
A. Assuming that all training methods are equal, and that the elephants are of comparable ages, some trainers/handlers believe that Asian elephants are more intelligent than the African elephants. Certain "tricks" that Asian elephants perform in circuses (e.g., carrying a person by the knee or the head and swirling around) are not commonly performed by African elephants. On the differences between the two elephants' training ability, Bucky Steele noted that: the African elephant is ". . . not as quick to learn as the Asian; it is always one step behind." He added that ". . . the African elephant does not seem to be able to walk on its hind legs alone. All in all, one may compare the Asian elephant to a draft horse and the African to a thoroughbred horse."

Q. How old can or should an elephant be before it is put to work?
A. About 10 years or older.

Q. Do scientists plan to clone or produce a mammoth, and how?
A. Yes, there have been reports that certain scientists plan to clone or grow mammoths. According to Dr. Adrian M. Lister (University College London, England) in order to have a successful cloning it is necessary to have intact DNA from a mammoth (male or female). All conditions must be absolutely correct. First, scientists must remove an ovum from an Asian elephant and extract the nucleus from it. Next, the DNA from the mammoth is inserted in its place. This man-made "zygote" is implanted in the uterus of an Asian elephant. Theoretically, if a successful pregnancy ensues, the offspring is a mammoth. Another method to "produce" a mammoth is to fertilize an elephant egg with a mammoth sperm. This would produce a hybrid which could then be repeatedly back-crossed with mammoth to produce an offspring increasingly like a mammoth.

Q. If elephant legs were too long for the trunk to reach the ground, would they develop longer trunks over evolutionary time?
A. Different body parts evolve in concert, that is, they complement each other for the greatest efficiency in terms of energy conservation. For example, when the neck is short, the trunk is long, and when the trunk is short the mandible may be longer, or a combination thereof. In other words, if the legs were not so long, instead of the trunk being longer, the mandible might lengthen. But if the mandible were too long, it would upset the center of gravity in the head. Thus, a balance among different body parts would be Mother Nature's solution.

Q. How are the sea-cow (manatee) and hyrax related to the elephant?
A. Relationships are based on morphological (e.g., bones) and molecular (e.g., blood proteins) data. An example of a unique morphological character shared by an elephant, a manatee, and a hyrax is the arrangement of wrist bones in a straight line (serially), one on top of another, like tiles on a floor. The wrist bones of a cat or a human, for example, are arranged alternatively (staggered, the primitive condition), one on top of two, like bricks in a wall.

Q. Is it possible for countries in Africa that have an excess of elephants to move them to countries where elephants have been depleted?
A. Physically possible, yes. Realistically, it is difficult, laborious, and expensive. It has been done on a small scale, from Zimbabwe to South Africa.

Q. To stop culling and killing or poaching elephants, would it be possible to cut the tusks of wild elephants and, secondly, would it be possible to make false ivory to satisfy the demand?
A. A tusk is an incisor tooth, live tissue containing pulp cavity with blood and lymph vessels and nerves. It is not possible to tell how far the pulp extends from the base, thus cutting the tusk may cause infection and pain. It is extremely costly and requires professional personnel to tranquilize elephants; they often die. According to Dr. Kay Mehren of the Toronto Zoo, it takes about three hours to remove a tusk from an adult elephant, using a steam winch, and would require daily post-operative care for about two months. Substitute ivory does not satisfy ivory collectors, just as false diamonds would not satisfy diamond collectors. There are ivory substitutes, from artificial resins to mammoth and mastodon ivory, compressed bone, hippo teeth (a growing item in trade) and "vegetable ivory", the endosperm of the seed from the tagua, a South American palm. All of these have been used commercially (as have false diamonds) and can replace demand for ivory for certain purposes (e.g. piano keys).

Q. Is it still legal to hunt elephants in Africa?
A. Some countries, mostly in eastern and southern Africa, permit the hunting of elephants with registered guides. There is supposedly strict regulation as to the number of elephants that can be killed, though abuses have occurred.

Q. Can sterilization be used to avoid elephant overpopulation?
A. Yes it can be, but it has its own complications. It is costly and requires professional personnel to tranquilize elephants that often die in the process.

Q. What can I do to help save the elephant?
A. Tell your friends and family members that elephants are important members of the ecosystem in which they live—they have been called "Keystone Species" and "Super Keystone Species" (a Keystone Species is one which modifies the habitat in which it lives, and other animals benefit from the modifications). Become a member of an organization that strives to save elephants.

BIBLIOGRAPHY

Aldhous, P. 1991. "African Rift in Kyoto". *Nature* 354:175.

Beard, P.H. 1988. *The End of the Game.* Chronicle Books, San Francisco.

Benedict, F. G. 1936. *The Physiology of the Elephant.* Carnegie Institute, Washington, DC.

Bosman, P., and Hall-Martin, A. 1986. *Elephants of Africa.* C. Struik (Pty) Ltd, Cape Town.

Buss, I. O. 1990. *Elephant Life: Fifteen Years of High Population Density.* Iowa State University Press, Ames.

Carrington, R. 1958. *Elephants.* Chatto & Windus, London.

Coppens, Y., Maglio, V. J., Madden, C. T., and Bedden, M. 1978. "Proboscidea". Pp. 336–67 *in* Maglio, V. J., and Cooke, H. B. S. (eds). *Evolution of African Mammals.* Harvard University Press, Cambridge, Massachusetts.

Cuvier, G. 1849. *Anatomie Comparée Recueil des Planches de Myologie.* Published under the auspices of C. Laurillard and Mercier, Paris.

Deraniyagala, P. E. P. 1955. *Some Extinct Elephants, Their Relatives and the Two Living Species.* Ceylon National Museums Administration, Colombo.

DiSilvestro, R. L. 1991. *The African Elephant: Twilight in Eden.* John Wiley & Sons, Inc., New York.

Douglas-Hamilton, I., and Douglas-Hamilton, O. 1975. *Among the Elephants.* Viking Press, New York.

Douglas-Hamilton, I., and Douglas-Hamilton, O. 1992. *Battle for the Elephants.* Doubleday, London.

Eisenberg, J. F. 1980. "Ecology and Behavior of the Asian Elephant". *Elephant* 1(supplement): 36–56.

Eisenberg, J. F., McKay, G. M., and Jainudeen, M. R. 1971. "Reproductive Behavior of the Asiatic Elephant *(Elephas maximus maximus* L.)". *Behavior* 38:193–225.

Eltringham, S. K. 1982. *Elephants.* Blandford Press, Poole, Dorset.

Eltringham, S. K., and Ward, D. (consult. eds). 1991. *The Illustrated Encyclopedia of Elephants.* Salamander Books Limited, London.

Freeman, D. 1981. *Elephants: The Vanishing Giants.* G. P. Putnam's Sons, New York.

Gould, E., and McKay, G. (consult. eds), Kirshner, D. (illustrator). 1990. *Encyclopedia of Animals: Mammals.* Gallery Books, New York.

Guthrie, R. D. 1990. *Frozen Fauna of the Mammoth Steppe: The Story of Blue Babe.* University of Chicago Press, Chicago.

Hanks, J. 1979. *The Struggle for Survival: The Elephant Problem.* Mayflower Books, New York.

Haynes, G. 1991. *Mammoths, Mastodons, and Elephants: Biology, Behavior, and the Fossil Record.* Cambridge University Press, Cambridge.

Hess, D. L., Schmidt, A. M., and Schmidt, M. J. 1983. "Reproductive Cycle of the Asian Elephant *(Elephas maximus)* in Captivity". *Biology of Reproduction* 28:767–73.

Howard, A. L. 1979. "'Motty'—Birth of an African/Asian Elephant at Chester Zoo". *Elephant* 1(3): 36–41.

Huxley, J. 1961. *The Conservation of Wild Life and Natural Habitats in Central and East Africa.* UNESCO, Paris.

Jackson, P. 1990. *Endangered Species: Elephants.* Chartwell Books, Inc., Secaucus, New Jersey.

Laursen, L., and Bekoff, M. 1978. *"Loxodonta africana".* *Mammalian Species* (92): 1–8.

Laws, R. M. 1966. "Age Criteria for the African Elephant, *Loxodonta a. africana".* *East African Wildlife Journal* 4:1–37.

Laws, R. M. 1978. "Déjà Vu ...". *Swara* 1(3): 126–8.

Laws, R. M., Parker, I. S. C., and Johnson, R. C. B. 1975. *Elephants and Habitats in North Bunyoro, Uganda.* Oxford University Press, Oxford.

Lewis, G. S., and Fish, B. 1978. *I Love Rogues: The Life of an Elephant Tramp.* Superior Publishing Co., Seattle.

Macfie, D. F. 1916. "A Case of Triplet in an Elephant". *Journal of the Natural History Society of Siam* 1:53.

Maglio, V. J. 1973. "Origin and Evolution of the Elephantidae". *Transactions of the American Philosophical Society* 63(3): 1–149.

Mariappa, D. 1986. *Anatomy and Histology of the Indian Elephant.* Indira Publishing House, Oak Park, Michigan.

Martin, E. B. 1990. "Ivory Billiard Balls". *BBC Wildlife* 8(9): 622–3.

Martin, P. S., and Klein, R. G. (eds.). 1984. *Quaternary Extinctions: A Prehistoric Revolution.* The University of Arizona Press, Tucson.

Matthiessen, P. 1991. *African Silences.* Random House, New York.

Moss, C. 1988. *Elephant Memories.* William Morrow & Company, Inc., New York.

Moss, C. 1990. "The Young Ones". *BBC Wildlife* 8(11): 738–44.

Nott, J. F. 1886. *Wild Animals Photographed and Described.* S. Low, Marston, Searle, & Rivington, London.

Olivier, R. C. D. 1978. "Present Status of the Asian Elephant *(Elephas maximus* Linnaeus, 1758)". *Elephant* 1(2): 15–17.

Orenstein, R. (ed.). 1991. *Elephants: The Deciding Decade.* Key Porter Books Limited, Toronto.

Osborn, H. F. 1936. *Proboscidea.* Volume I. The American Museum of Natural History, New York.

Osborn, H. F. 1942. *Proboscidea.* Volume II. The American Museum of Natural History, New York.

Parker, I., and Amin, M. 1983. *Ivory Crisis.* Chatto & Windus, Ltd., London.

Payne, K. 1989. "Elephant Talk". *National Geographic* 176(2): 264–77.

Pfeffer, P. 1989. *Vie et Mort d'un Geant: L'elephant d'Afrique.* Flammarion, Paris.

Poole, J. H. 1987. "Elephants in Musth, Lust". *Natural History* 96(11): 47–55.

Poole, J. H., and Moss, C. J. 1981. "Musth in the African Elephant *(Loxodonta africana)".* *Nature* 292(5826): 830–1.

Racine, R. N. 1980. "Behavior Associated with Feeding in Captive African and Asian Elephants". *Elephant* 1(supplement): 57–71.

Rasmussen, L. E., Schmidt, M. J., Henneous, R., Groves, D., and Daves, G. D. Jr. 1982. "Asian Bull Elephants: Flehmen-like Responses to Extractable Components in Female Elephant Estrous Urine". *Science* 217:159–62.

Redmond, I. 1982. "Saltmining Elephants of Mount Elgon". *Swara* 5(4): 28–31.

Redmond, I. M., and Shoshani, J. 1987. "Mount Elgon's Elephants Are in Peril". *Elephant* 2(3): 46–66.

Redmond, I. 1990. *The Elephant Book.* Walker Books Ltd., London.

Romer, A. S. 1966. *Vertebrate Paleontology* (3rd ed.). University of Chicago Press, Chicago.

Schmidt, M. J. 1989. "The Fine Art of Elephant Breeding". *Animal Kingdom* 92(5): 44–51.

Sheldrick, D. 1979. *My Four-footed Family.* J. M. Dent & Sons Ltd, London.

Sheldrick, D. 1980. *An Elephant Called Eleanor.* J. M. Dent & Sons Ltd, London.

Shoshani, J., and Eisenberg, J. F. 1982. *"Elephas maximus".* *Mammalian Species* (182): 1–8.

Shoshani, J., et al. (76 coauthors). 1982. "On the Dissection of a Female Asian Elephant *(Elephas maximus maximus* Linnaeus, 1758) and Data From Other Elephants". *Elephant* 2(1): 3–93.

Sikes, S. K. 1971. *The Natural History of the African Elephant.* Weidenfeld & Nicolson, London.

Sukumar, R. 1989. *The Asian Elephant: Ecology and Management.* Cambridge University Press, Cambridge.

Tassy, P., and Shoshani, J. 1988. "The Tethytheria: Elephants and Their Relatives". Pp 283–315 in Benton, M. (ed.). *The Phylogeny and Classification of the Tetrapods. Volume 2: Mammals.* Clarendon Press, Oxford.

Thornton, A., and Currey, D. 1991. *To Save an Elephant: The Undercover Investigation into the Illegal Ivory Trade.* Doubleday, London

Vereshchagin, N. K., and Mikhelson, V. M. (eds.). 1981. *The Magadan Baby Mammoth* Mammuthus primigenius (*Blumenbach*). Nauka, Leningrad.

Western, D. 1986. "An African Odyssey to Save the Elephant". *Discover 7* (10): 56–8, 60, 62, 64, 68–70.

Williams, H. 1989. *Sacred Elephant.* Jonathan Cape, London.

Williams, J. H. 1950. *Elephant Bill.* Doubleday & Company, Inc., New York.

Williams, J. H. 1954. *Bandoola.* Doubleday & Company, Inc., New York.

Wylie, K. C. 1980. "Ivory, Elephants and Man". *Elephant 1* (supplement): 3–18.

ACKNOWLEDGMENTS

The publishers and the consulting editor would like to particularly thank the following people: Susan K. Bell, Greg Campbell, Estelle R. Davidson, Raphael Geron, Jann S. Grimes, Roger L. Henneous, M. Philip Kahl, Michael N. Keele, David J. Lowrie, Susan Mainka, Gary H. Marchant, Donald S. Marcks, Charles A. Marks, Eleanor C. Marsac, Malcolm C. McKenna, George W. Overbeck, Jules L. Pierce, Lois E. Rasmussen, V. Louise Roth, Anne M. Schmidt, Sandra L. Shoshani, Raman Sukumar, and Susan M. Wolak. Ana Maria Boza, Emmanuel Gheebrant, Colin P. Groves, Ronald I. Orenstein, Ian M. Redmond, and Celia Westwood helped update this book from the original 1992 edition.

The Frequently Asked Questions on pp. 232–234 have been reproduced with permission from *Elephant*, Vol. 2, no. 4, © 2000 Elephant Research Foundation.

ILLUSTRATIONS

A simplified evolutionary tree of the Proboscidea (pp. 26-27) Research by J. Shoshani and P. Tassy; reference artwork by G. H. Marchant and J. S. Grimes.

A simplified migratory map of the Proboscidea (p. 29) Research by J. Shoshani; reference artwork by G. H. Marchant and J. S. Grimes.

Past and present distribution of the African and the Asian elephant (pp. 30-31) Modified after various sources, especially *National Geographic Magazine*, May 1991, Vol. 179, no. 5, pp. 14–15.

Major differences between the African and the Asian elephant (p.39) Reference artwork by G. H. Marchant.

Family tree of the extinct woolly mammoth and American mastodon (p. 53) Data supplied by J. M. Lowenstein and J. Shoshani.

The mammoth "death trap" (p. 55) Reference: *Mammoth graveyard: a treasure trove of clues to the past.* © Northern Arizona University, p. 3.

Skeletons and teeth of the mammoth and the American mastodon (p. 57) Slightly modified after H. F. Osborn, 1936 and 1942.

Map of mammoth sites in Siberia (p. 58) Data supplied by V. M. Mikhelson.

A hypothetical scheme for cloning a mammoth (p. 59) Reference artwork by V. M. Mikhelson.

Simplified section of skin and associated structures (p. 68); skeleton (p. 69); muscles (p. 74) Research by J. Shoshani (based on studies of N. B. Eales, 1925, 1926, 1928, 1929; G. Cuvier, 1849; D. Mariappa, 1986; and personal observations); reference artwork by G. H. Marchant (except that of the skin which was by J. Shoshani).

Sequence of tooth eruption (p. 70) Modified after R. M. Laws, 1966.

Cross-section of trunk (p. 75) Artwork by Atako Kikutani (as it appeared in *Natural History Magazine* Vol. 106, no. 10, November 1997), based on research by J. Shoshani.

Internal organs (p. 78) Partly after W. C. O. Hill, 1953, and J. S. Perry, 1964 (see Bibliography in S. K. Sikes, 1971). Data from J. Shoshani; reference artwork by G. H. Marchant.

Reproductive organs (p. 80) Slightly modified after J. Hanks, 1979.

Musth gland (p. 80) Slightly modified after M. Haron, 1975.

Family trees, Washington Park Zoo (p. 94) Reconstructed by J. S. Grimes and J. Shoshani based on information provided by M. J. Schmidt and R. L. Henneous, Washington Park Zoo, February 25, 1992.

Picture of elephant enclosure (p. 95) Courtesy Washington Park Zoo.

Hormone cycle of the female elephant and male urine test behavior (p. 97) Observations by M. J. Schmidt and colleagues (see D. L. Hess *et al.*,1983).

Age criteria for the African elephant (pp. 100-101) After R. M. Laws, 1966, and J. Hanks, 1979.

Kitum Cave (p. 130) Modified after I. M. Redmond.

African elephant range and protected areas (p. 181) Map reference and data supplied by I. Douglas-Hamilton and F. Michelmore, European Economic Community (EEC) African Elephant Survey and Conservation Programme; artwork by S. Lamond.

Poster and bumper sticker (p. 212) Courtesy of the African Wildlife Foundation.

Diagram (p. 228) Concept by J. Shoshani; artwork by G. H. Marchant.

Elephants: the super-keystone species (p. 229) Composite drawing modified after I. M. Redmond, J. Shoshani, and G. H. Marchant.

Mary Evans Picture Library

INDEX

Mary Evans Picture Library